Psyche of Asian Society

About the Editors

Aradhana Shukla is Professor and Head of Psychology at Kumaun University, SSJ Campus, Almora and Dean (Arts) Kumaun University, Nainital. She is serving in this university for the last 35 years and before joining this university she was UGC fellow at DDU Gorakhpur University, Gorakhpur and Assistant Research Officer at Department of paediatrics, IMS, BHU. She has guided 52 Ph.D students completed 4 major research projects from UGC and ICSSR. She has written and edited 15 books and developed 15 psychological tests. More than 150 papers written by her have been published in the journal and books of national and International repute. She has co-edited a four volume series on Mental Health: Psycho-Social Perspectives, Volume one 'Issues and Intervention' (2015), Volume two 'Multigroup Analysis' (2015), Volume three 'Strength of Human Resources' (2017) and Volume four 'Therapeutic Applications' (2017). Her major areas of interest are cross-cultural psychology, health psychology and psychological intervention

Anubhuti Dubey is Professor of Psychology and has been teaching for the past 20 years at Department of Psychology, DDU Gorakhpur University, Gorakhpur (U.P.). Apart from publishing more than 40 articles in journals of national and international repute and 30 chapters in different edited volumes, she has written book entitled 'Psychological Perspectives on Chronic Illness' (2012) and also co-edited a four volume series on Mental Health: Psycho-Social Perspectives, Volume one 'Issues and Intervention' (2015), Volume two 'Multigroup Analysis' (2015), Volume three 'Strength of Human Resources' (2017) and Volume four 'Therapeutic Applications' (2017). Her research interest includes Health Psychology, Applied Social Psychology, Gender issues and Counselling. She has also carried out ICSSR research project on 'Psychological Dynamics of Health and Illness in Women of Eastern Uttar Pradesh'. She has guided 11 Ph.D. scholars so for. She is also a Master Trainer and Supportive Supervisor for Training HIV/AIDS counsellors under GFATM-Round 7 programme.

Narendra Singh Thagunna was awarded his Ph.D. in Cross Cultural Psychology from Kumaun University, India. He has been teaching Psychology for the last 5 years at Department of Psychology, Tri Chandra Campus, T.U, Nepal. Before this, he served as a Principal in Khatyadi HSS (+2 level), Doti, Nepal for 5 years. He was involved in emergency Mental health Psychosocial Support in refugee setting for four years as psychosocial trainer. He also designed and facilitated more than fifteen modular trainings which are useful for emergency setting and community mental health.

PSYCHE OF ASIAN SOCIETY

Edited by
Aradhana Shukla
Anubhuti Dubey
Narendra Singh Thagunna

CONCEPT PUBLISHING COMPANY PVT. LTD.
NEW DELHI-110059

ISBN-13: 978-93-86682-82-6

First Published 2019

Published and Printed by:

Concept Since 1974

Concept Publishing Company Pvt. Ltd.
A/15-16, Commercial Block, Mohan Garden,
New Delhi-110059 (INDIA)
T: +91 11 25351460, +91 11 25351794
E: publishing@conceptpub.com, *W*: www.conceptpub.com

Cataloging in Publication Data--Courtesy: D.K. Agencies (P) Ltd. <docinfo@dkagencies.com>

Psyche of Asian society / edited by Aradhana Shukla, Anubhuti Dubey, Narendra Singh Thagunna.

pages cm
Contributed articles.
Includes bibliographical references and index.
ISBN 9789386682826

1. Asians—Psychology. 2. Ethnopsychology—Asia. 3. Mentally ill—Asia Psychology. I. Shukla, Aradhana, editor. II. Dubey, Anubhuti, editor. III. Thagunna, Narendra Singh, editor.

LCC GN270.P79 2019 | DDC 155.8095 23

Acknowledgements

In our regular course of life we believe in our observations and dealing with different society we see that every culture has its own values and, of course, they are different in every walk of life with more or less magnitude. We can see a lot of variation in two cultures in regard to their way of thought, way of behaviour parameters and so many other things.

Keeping these views in consideration, this piece of work is planned and it deals with culture and psyche of Asian society. We have taken ample support and co-operation from many people. We are thankful to them and want to place our gratitude on records.

We are also grateful to the contributors who supported us by giving their articles and waited patiently to get it in shape. We are thankful to Mr. Abhishek for doing the tedious job of the systemization of the articles.

We place our thanks and regards on record to Mr. Ashok K. Mittal, Concept Publishing Company Pvt. Ltd., New Delhi to shape this book.

Sharad Poornima
24-Oct-2018

Aradhana Shukla
Anubhuti Dubey
Narendra Singh Thagunna

Acknowledgement

[illegible]

Contents

Section V
Psychological Hazards of Mental Health in Asia

Section VI
Parenting Behaviour

Section VII
Work Life Balance

List of Contributors

A.K.M. Rezea Karem is Professor, Department of Psychology, University of Dhaka, Bangladesh. He did his post doctoral in Neuroscience and neuro rehabilitation from Envision Research Institute USA; The Smith-Kettlewell Eye Research Institute USA; University of San Francisco, USA. **Email:** *rezaul76@yahoo.com*

A.R. Prasetyo is Faculty of Psychology, Diponegoro University, Tembalang, Semarang, Indonesia.

Resdasari, A.R. is Faculty of Psychology, Diponegoro University, Tembalang, Semarang, Indonesia.

Akbar Hussain is Professor and Coordinator, UGC, SAP (DRS-I) at the Department of Psychology, Faculty of Social Sciences, Aligarh Muslim University, Aligarh (U.P.), India. He was awarded the D.Litt. degree in Psychology in 2015 for his work on Explorations and Applications of Spirituality in Psychology. His current areas of research includes Islamic Psychology, Clinical Psychology, Health Psychology, Counselling Psychology, and Positive Psychology. **Email:** *profakbar6@gmail.com*

Anubhuti Dubey is Professor of Psychology and has been teaching for the past 20 years at Department of Psychology, DDU Gorakhpur University, Gorakhpur (U.P.), India. Her research interest includes Health Psychology, Applied Social Psychology, Gender issues and Counselling. She has also carried out ICSSR research project on 'Psychological Dynamics of Health and Illness in Women of Eastern Uttar Pradesh'. **Email:** *anubhutiddu@rediff.com*

Aradhana Shukla is Professor of Psychology and Dean Faculty of Arts, Almora Campus, SSJ Kumaun University, Almora (Uttarakhand).She received award of distinguished Psychologists by Harprasad Institute of Behavioural Science, Agra. Recently, she has again awarded as Prof. L B Tripathi Memorial Award for best Social Psychologist in India by Harprasad Institute of Behavioural Science, Agra. Her research interest includes Developmental Psychology, Personality, Cultural Psychology and Mental Health Care.**Email:** *aradhana.shukla5@gmail.com*

Bhagyashree Joshi is research scholar in the Department of Psychology, Kumaun University, SSJ Campus, Almora and currently serving as counsellor at Army School Kashipur, Uttarakhand. Her major area of interest includes culture and cognition. **Email:** *joshisweety09@gmail.com*

Christopher D. Tori is Professor in the Psychology Department at Alliant International University, San Francisco, CA, USA. His research interest is in Psychotherapy process and outcome; Buddhist perspectives on cognitive psychology; psychometrics and statistics; international and multicultural research; psycho diagnostic assessment; institutional studies; psycholinguistics.

Dhananjay Kumar is Professor of Psychology and has been teaching for the past 20 years at Department of Psychology, DDU Gorakhpur University, Gorakhpur (U.P.), India. His research interest includes social cognition and intergroup relation, health and counselling psychology. **Email:** *dk_ddugu@yahoo.co.in*

Diane C. Zelman is Professor, Hong Kong Clinical Psychology Program at California School of Professional Psychology (CSPP), Alliant International University, Hong Kong. Her research interest is in Clinical health psychology, Addiction psychology, and behavioural medicine. **Email:** *dzelman@alliant.edu*

Dinie Ratri Desiningrum is Faculty of Psychology, Diponegoro University, Tembalang, Semarang, Indonesia. Her research intrest includes gerontology children with special need positive psychology.
Email: *dn.psiundip@gmail.com*.

E.R. Kustanti is Faculty of Psychology, Diponegoro University, Tembalang, Semarang, Indonesia.

Garima Singh is Research Scholar at Department of Psychology, DDU Gorakhpur University, Gorakhpur (U.P.), India and submitted her Ph.D. thesis entitled 'Mental health and well being of caregivers of chronically ill patients: Role of Psychological Resources'.
Email: *garimakeepintouch@rediffmail.com*

Kamal Khurana is social psychologist and his basic aim is to prevail positivity and harmony in society. He is an International mentor.
Email: *kamalkhurana76@gmail.com*

Kuhu is Research Scholar at Department of Psychology, Banaras Hindu University, Varanasi (U.P.), India **Email:** *kuhoo.sb@gmail.com*

Laxmi Vajpeyi is Assistant Professor at Department of Humanities, B.B.D.National Institute of Technology and Management, Faizabad Road, Lucknow (U.P.), India. Her area of interest is Clinical and Counselling Psychology. She had published two books on 'Manovigyan men Prayaog' and 'Industrial Psychology'. **Email:** *vajpeyi.laxmi@gmail.com*

Narendra Singh Thagunna is Lecturer, Tri Chandra Campus, Tribhuwan University, Kathmandu, Nepal; CEO, President Psychdesk Foundation, The School of Psychology, Nepal. He is extensively working in the field of Cross-cultural psychology, Suicide prevention, Parenting, Internet Addiction and growth of psychology in Nepal.
Email: *thagunnanarendra81@gmail.com*

N. Fauziah is Faculty of Psychology, Diponegoro University, Tembalang, Semarang, Indonesia.

Naima Nigar is Lecturer, Department of Psychology, University of Dhaka, Bangladesh. She is interested in Biological Psychology.
Email: *naima.nigar@du.ac.bd*

Parul Batra is Executive Director at Vision First, London, Greater London, United Kingdom. She completed her education from Alliant International University, Los Angeles, USA.

Priyanka Pathak is Research Scholar at Department of Psychology, Banaras Hindu University, Varanasi (U.P.), India.
Email: *priyankapathak456@gmail.com*

Purnima Awasthi is Associate Professor of Psychology at Banaras Hindu University, Varanasi, India. Her research interest includes Health Psychology, Clinical Psychology, Rehabilitation Psychology, and Adolescence Psychology. She had carried out Indian Council of Social Science Research project entitled 'Understanding and Management of Some Critical Health Problems in an Underdeveloped Kharwar Community'. Also published book on 'Leadership' (2009) from PHI, New Delhi. **Email:** *awasthip9@gmail.com*

Radha Maddhesia is Research Scholar at Department of Psychology, DDU Gorakhpur University, Gorakhpur (U.P.), India. She has submitted her Ph.D. thesis entitled 'Mental Health and Distress: A Cross-cultural Study'.
Email: *radha.maddesia@gmail.com*

Ramesh C. Mishra is Professor Emeritus of Psychology at Banaras Hindu University, Varanasi, India. He has been a post Doctoral Research Fellow and Shastri Research Fellow at Queen's University, Canada, and a visiting Professor at the Universities of Konstanz (Germany) and Geneva (Switzerland). He has also been a Fellow-in-Residence of the Netherlands Institute of Advanced Study, Wassenaar (The Netherlands) and a Fulbright Scholar-in-Residence at Wittenberg University, Springfield (USA). His research is focused on understanding ecological and cultural influences on human development. He is the co-author of Ecology, Acculturation and Psychological Adaptation: A Study of Adivasis in Bihar (Sage) and Development of Geocentric Spatial Language and Cognition: An Ecocultural Perspective and co-editor of Psychology in Human and Social Development: Lessons from Diverse Cultures (Sage).
Email: *rcmishra_2000@yahoo.com*

Ram Kalap Tiwari is Associate Professor, Department of Psychology, K.S. Saket P.G. College Ayodhya, Faizabad (U.P.) India. He has published 30 Research articles and 4 books and completed 2 Minor research projects funded by UGC and 1 Major Research project funded by NCERT, New Delhi. He has supervised 25 Ph.D. research scholars.
Email: *tiwarirk111@gmail.com*

Prativa Sanchary is MS Student, Department of Psychology, University of Dhaka, Bangladesh.

Shobhna Joshi is Professor of Psychology at Banaras Hindu University, Varanasi, India. Her research interest is in areas of Developmental Psychology and Sports Psychology. She completed research project entitled 'A study of some psychological barriers to educational development of Kharwar children of the Naugarh region'.
Email: *getshobhna@yahoo.com*

Jyoti Verma is a retired Professor of Psychology, Patna University, Patna, Bihar, India. She got Post Doctoral Fulbright Fellowship USA. She visited Paris under the India French Social Scientist' Exchange Program on the fellowship of the French Ministry of Research and Higher Education. Her expertise includes cross-cultural psychology and teaching Organizational Behaviour in the MBA Program. She has completed two research projects with the support of Indian Council of Social Science Research entitled 'Bihari Migrants in Mumbai' (2011) and 'Bihari Identity: An Uncharted Question' (2015). She was associated with Emic Labs.c.Ul. Grochowska, Warszawa, Poland. She has been Consulting Editor of Asian Journal of Social Psychology, and member of the Editorial Board of the Journal of Culture and Psychology.
Email: *vermaj46@gmail.com*

Yubraj Adhikari is MSc, Mental Health Psychology, University of Liverpool, England. Presently, he is Ph.D. Researcher on "Psychological Distress and Professional Quality of Life of Medical Doctors" at University of Nicosia, International Committee of the Red Cross-ICRC.
Email: *yadhikari@gmail.com*

SECTION I
Introducton of Asian Psychology

1
Asian Psychology: Contribution can never be Counted

Aradhana Shukla, Anubhuti Dubey and *Narendra Singh Thagunna*

Psychology is the science of behaviour and it is based on the innate tendencies and external surroundings. In addition, it is also based on cultural context in which the human behaviour and situations occur. This cultural orientation has highly highlighted in Asian studies related to human behaviour. In Indian wisdom, human reality is purely based on existing socio-cultural milieu and standards and the psychology of human behaviour can better be understood on the basis of *desh* (place), *kal* (time), *patra* (individual) and *vatavaran* (environment and pushing forces). This orientation can be considered as the capsule of cross-cultural psychology.

It reveals the fact that Asia is the continent of cultural diversity. This continent can be considered as highly culturally rich and variant. This continent provides unlimited diversity and heterogeneity in relation with geographical, religious, demographic and socio-cultural characteristics. These diversities, not only vary in different continuum, but they are visible in our country also. It needs a careful observation to explore the diversities within a country and across the continent.

Asia due to their heterogeneity open up immense possibilities for cross-cultural research. It is, therefore, not surprising that at the turn of the century the first observations on the influence of culture on psychological processes like perception, memory, susceptibility to certain types of geometrical optical illusions were made among the Asian people by W.H.R. Rivers (1901), the founding father of cross-cultural psychology. The studies conducted display varying levels of scientific sophistication.

At one end there are studies where the main thrust has been to obtain differences on certain psychological characteristics by comparing cultural groups that are easily available. No rationale is provided for making the comparison or to examine the relevance of the characteristics in question or appropriateness of the measure used. On the other hand, there are studies —and their number is fortunately growing—that emanate from a distinct theoretical model, generate specific hypotheses after taking into account the cultural features of the groups, and instead of using "borrowed" tests they suitably modify or develop appropriate tests, and interpret the findings in the light of ecological and cultural characteristics of the groups. Careful ethnographic analysis often precedes the designing of such studies. Studies of Triandis and his Asian colleagues (Hui, Triandis and Yee, 1991) on individualism, collectivism, and of DeRidder, Tripathi and their associates (1992) ecocultural model is highly studied by Sinha (Sinha, 1979, 1980; Sinha and Bharat, 1985) are the ultimate examples of investigation in Asia.

Need of the volume: As it is apparent that Asian psychology reveals the cultural studies under one roof, therefore, it was thought to invite such studies from different parts of Asia and put them in one volume that is "Psychology of Asian People". The aim of this volume was to present different cultural features of Asian countries and tag them into a volume so that it will be comfortable to know the cultural diversities of Asia comprehensively. We, simply thought that this volume may be useful for researchers, teachers, professionals and book lovers. Moreover, it will be sufficient to open new walks of researches in psychology and provide new vision to the researchers.

There are twenty three chapters in this volume and we have classified them according to the themes of the papers. They are:

I. Introduction of Asian psychology
II. Grassroots of religions and religious practices in Asia
III. Hindu culture and acculturation
IV. Psychological facilitators of mental health in Asia
V. Psychological hazards of mental health in Asia
VI. Parenting behaviour, and
VII. Work life balance

In the introductory part there are two chapters. In the introducing chapter "Asian Psychology: Contribution can never be counted" **Aradhana Shukla, Anubhuti Dubey** and **Narendra Singh Thagunna** have shed light on the socio-psychological parameters and behavioural pattern of Asia. The next chapter "Asian Psychology: What does it tell about human cognition" **Ramesh Chandra Mishra** has deeply analysed the cognitive framework of Asians.

The second theme is based on grassroots of religions and religious practices in Asia. There are two articles regarding this theme. The chapter "Sufism and Sufi Practices" by **Akbar Hussian** deals with the ground work of Sufism and related behaviour. **Ram Kalap Tiwari** in his chapter "Ram Janma Bhumi V/s Babri Maszid: A faith based dispute" has described the very long but faith related dispute of Ayodhya's Ramjanma Bhumi mandir and Babri Maszid.

The third theme is based on the studies revealing Hindu's culture and acculturation and there are six chapters in this section. **Anubhuti Dubey** and **Laxmi Vajpeyi** in their chapter "Triyoga and Triguna in Bhagavad Gita: An Empirical Validation" have presented a deep analysis of *Srimad Bhagavad Gita* with special reference to its *triyoga* and *triguna* concepts. Astrology is a wide and universally accepted measure of future predication and past explanation. Although, it is widely accepted and followed but its grassroots are emerged in India. These views are very clearly narrated in the chapter "Role of Astropsychology in Personality Making: An Empirical Observation" by **Bhagyashree Joshi and Aradhana Shukla. Anubhuti Dubey** and **Radha Maddhesia** in their chapter "Acculturative Strategies in Nepali Immigrants: Impact of Social Factors" have narrated the acculturative devices followed by Nepali immigrants. **Aradhana Shukla** in "Culture, Family and Cognitive Behaviour" presented an empirical analysis of the Kumaouni families and their cognitive behaviour. This trend is also visible in the chapter written by **Diane's C. Zelman, Cecile Valantin** and **Michele Bland.** This chapter's title is "Asian Female Foreign Domestic Workers as Immigrants in Hong Kong" and the authors have staked the psychology of Asian foreign female domestic workers very well. A study namely "Social Identity and Acculturation Attitudes Among Different Tribal Groups of Jharkhand, India" was presented by **Dhananjay Kumar** in which he has studied the various tribal groups in Jharkhand, India.

The next theme deals with psychological facilitators of mental health in Asia and there are seven articles pertaining to this theme. The first article "Sources of Happiness: A Qualitative Analysis" is presented by **Anubhuti Dubey** and **Garima Singh.** The authors have explained the concept of happiness following qualitative approach. The notion of happiness is again studied by **Anggun Resdasari Prasetyo, Erin Ratna Kustanti** and **Dinie Ratri Desiningrum.** They in their chapter "What

Does Happiness Measure: An Indigenous Psychological Analysis on Colleges Students' Sources of Happiness in Semarang Central Java, Indonesia" have very beautifully sketched the profile of happiness. **Priyanka Pathak** and **Shobhana Joshi** have stated the influence of self-compassion on procrastination in their chapter "Influence of self-compassion of procrastination". The next chapter of **Anggun Resdasari Prasetyo, Erin Ratna Kustanti** and **Dinie Ratri Desiningrum** has shed light on "Letting go Method as Self-Help Alternative Solution to Increase Resilience Ability on People with Lupus". **Narendra Singh Thagunna** in his chapter entitled "Empowerment on resilience and coping skills of frontline workers of earthquake affected area of Nepal" has shed light on the resilience of the residents of Nepal even suffered from earthquake. In this sequence **Kamal Khurana** and **Aradhana Shukla** have also tried their best to integrate self in theoretical and therapeutically perspective. The title of their chapter is "Integrating Inner Self: Theoretical and Therapeutic Perspective". **Yubaraj Adhikari** in his chapter entitled "Review on the dielectric behaviour therapy (DBT) with mindfulness technique for the prevention of the suicide and its applicability in Nepali context" has reviewed mindfulness for the prevention of the suicide and its applicability in Nepal.

The next theme of the volume deals with the psychological hazards of mental health. There are three chapters in this section. The first chapter namely "Psychological heath of informal caregivers of cancer patients: the population at risk" is written by **Purnima Awasthi** and **Kuhu.** In this chapter they have studied the mental health of the caregivers of cancer patients. The chapter of **Parul Batra Sabey, Diane C. Zelman** and **Christopher D. Tori** deals with the pattern of childhood anxiety in Hong Kong under the title of "Evaluation of the FRIENDS intervention for childhood anxiety in Hong Kong". In this sequence **Dinie Ratri Dosiningrum, N. Fauziah, Erin Ratna Kustanti** and **Anggun Resdasari Prasetyo** have studied depression among elderly under the roof of "The Structural equation, Modelling approach: future time perspective unintegrated personality and depression of elderly people in nursing home".

Some very interesting chapters are covered in the next section which focus on parenting behaviour. There are two chapters in this section. In the chapter "Parenting style of the working and non-working mothers: implications for cognitive emotional functioning in offspring". **Prativa Sanchary, Naima Nigar** and **A.K.M. Rezeal Karem** have shed light on the difference between the parenting style of working and non-working mothers. **Dinie Ratri Desiningrum, Narendra Singh Thagunna** and **Anggun Redasari Presetyo** have discussed the importance of breast feeding in motor development. They reflected it in their chapter "Exclusive breast feeding and motor development of children under five: comparative shades in toddlers in the region of control JAVA Indonesia".

The last section is based on the theme of work life balance and covers only two chapters. **Jyoti Verma** in her chapter "Some representations from work life: A narrative based study of Indian immigrants in Paris" has shed light as the Indian immigrants of Paris in relation to their balance in work and life. **Purnima Awasthi** in her chapter "Justice towards Women' Empowerment: Some Reality based Issues", reported some issues related to Justice towards Women' Empowerment.

We have tried our best to provide a cognitive capsule of Asia to the readers. We hope that the researchers will be inspired from the studies done in abroad. They can contact the authors of their choice of papers because we have given their e-mail address. We think that this volume will motivate the researchers to get a complete profile of Asia and invent something new. Thus, this volume will enrich the cognition along with the fresh breeze of new notions to do something more. We will be grateful by your valuable comments and your feedback will always be appreciated.

References

DeRidder, R. and Tripathi, R.C. (Eds.)(1992). *Norm Violation and Intergroup Relations*. London: Clarendon Press.

Hui, C.H.; Triandis, H.C. and Yee, C. (1991). Cultural differences in reward allocation: Is collectivism the explanation? *British Journal of Psychology*, 19, 159-172.

Rivers, W.H.R. (1901). Introduction and vision. In A.C. Haddon (Ed.), *Reports of the Cambridge and Anthropological Expedition to the Toores Straits:* Vol. 2, Part 1, Cambridge: Cambridge University Press.

Sinha, D. (1979). Perceptual style among nomadic and transitional agroculturist Birhors. In L. Eckensberger, W. Lonner, and Y.H. Poortinga (Eds.), *Cross-cultural Contributions to Psychology*. Lisse: Swets and Zeitlinger.

Sinha, D. (1980). Sex differences in psychological differentiation among different cultural groups. *International Journal of Behavioural Development, 3*, 455-466.

Sinha, D. and Bharat, S. (1985). Three types of family structures and psychological differentiation: A study among the Jaunsar-Bhawar Society. *International Journal of Psychology, 20*, 693-708.

2

Asian Psychology: What Does It Tell Us About Human Cognition?

R.C. Mishra

Introduction

Psychology in recent years is moving through a period of transition. Today it is studied, taught and practiced almost in all parts of the world. However, the discipline remains largely bound to the Euro-American culture (Berry, Poortinga, Segall, & Dasen, 1992; Henrich, Heine, & Norenzayan, 2010) where it first originated and developed as a scientific enterprise. Theories, models and principles of behaviour, which are contained in the textbooks of psychology and taught to students world-wide, have been developed in the West drawing upon data obtained from the Euro-American university students. Psychology textbooks written in other countries (e.g., India) contain the same contents as do the American textbooks.

In addition to being 'culture bound', psychology is also 'culture blind'. It is largely insensitive to the differing cultural realities of human populations living in different parts of the world. Knowing that humans are embedded in a complex cultural context, which plays an important role in the development and display of their behaviour, there is a general disregard for these factors in research. In fact, many psychologists consider culture as "noise" in psychological research and try to keep it away as much as possible. By engaging in such "cultureless" studies, researchers believe that they would achieve a universal or "global" psychology (Berry, 2013).

In Asian countries (e.g., China, India), the Euro-American brand of psychology is a relatively recent phenomenon. Being associated with the origin of the most ancient civilizations of the world, these countries carry a rich heritage of knowledge, both in their ancient writings and in folk traditions. Grounded in these knowledge systems are several concepts and theoretical formulations related to social and psychological phenomena, which are unknown to the Western psychologists. Due to colonial domination and the British impact on education, it is unfortunate that the traditional psychological knowledge of Asian countries could not flourish on their respective soil. Transportation of psychology from the West on a wholesale basis particularly prevented integration of traditional Asian knowledge with the Western knowledge. As Sinha and Kao (1997) indicate, despite having a long history of existence, the traditional psychological knowledge was suppressed, denigrated and replaced by modern scientific psychology. Thus, the psychology that eventually developed, and got into teaching ana practice in many Asian countries, was a Western Euro-American brand of psychology.

Reactions to Euro-American Psychology and Alternatives

The pervasive influence of the modern psychology, however, could not completely demolish the indigenous traditions in countries like China and India. As Mohiddin (1993) points out, one can still find in these countries the existence of two parallel systems of psychology with almost no evidence of interaction between them. While the indigenous traditions constitute the contents of disciplines like philosophy and religion, psychology includes the same topics that are contained in standard British or American textbooks. Rarely can one find in these textbooks a topic that deals with cultural concepts derived from indigenous knowledge traditions that have psychological moorings.

As a result of this kind of development, psychology today largely misses the insights of psychological knowledge from the largest, most complex and, in many ways, the earliest developed societies of the world (Berry, 2013). These early societies can now be viewed as the "recipients" of psychological knowledge, whereas the Western world is the "donor". In fact, psychology today is "made in" America" and "marketed to" the whole world. The evidence for this state of affairs is presented by many researchers (e.g., Adair, Coelho, and Luna, 2002; Allwood & Berry, 2006; Cole, 2006). Colonial domination seems to be evident in the academic world as well.

During the last few decades, some psychologists working in Asian countries have shown their discontentment with this state of affairs. As early as 1965, Sinha had argued that, in order to be relevant and useful, development of a science in any country had to be in tune with the socio-cultural realities of life of its people. Because these realities differ sharply in the Eastern and Western societies, Sinha (1965) pointed out that, by closely adhering to the Western theories and models of behaviour in their research, Indian psychologists have not been able to present a vigorous scientific psychology rooted in their own cultural tradition; instead, they have developed a pale and insipid edition of American or British psychology. In later writings, Sinha (1980, 1994, 1997) urged upon Indian psychologists to outgrow the alien framework in research, evolve perspectives that represent the realities of their own culture and life, and do psychology in culturally appropriate ways.

Similar voices have been heard in many other parts of the world. Even in Europe, in spite of the apparent similarities between the European and American models of behaviour, there have been calls for establishing a separate identity of European Psychology (e.g., Faucheux, 1976; Ingleby, 1974; Moscovici, 1971). Within the United States, there have been attacks on the relevance of a large body of psychological research for its people. Assertions that the American psychology suffers from 'insularity' (Kennedy, Schierer, and Rogers, 1984), or it needs to develop a 'world view'(Russell, 1984), or it needs to get away from 'isolationism' (Sexton & Misiak, 1984) reflect on limitations of the American psychology.

The relevance of Euro-American psychology has also been questioned in Canada, where the society is multicultural, and the national policy is in support of multiculturalism. These features of the Canadian society make it distinct from the US society. Hence, researchers (e.g., Berry, 1974; Berry & Wilde, 1972) have argued in favour of a psychology in Canada that uses theoretical and empirical perspectives different from those prevalent in the US. The concern is still alive in the form of support to certain fundamental principles of peaceful living together, which are subscribed by people in many societies where multiculturalism is accepted, respected and encouraged (Berry, 2017).

Calls for incorporating traditional systems of thought and ideologies in the analysis of human behaviour have been made from many other corners of the world (Ho, 1988; Kao & Sinha, 1997; Serpell, 1984). Local relevance of Western psychological knowledge is often questioned. In general, Western psychology is considered inappropriate and inadequate to address the cultural and behavioural diversity that exists in human populations around the world (Berry, 2013).

Development of Asian Psychology

Asian psychology has grown out of concerns similar to those mentioned above. As a large geographical continent Asia includes countries some of which (e.g., China, India) represent the oldest civilizations of the world. The philosophical traditions of these countries bear many similarities, which get reflected in their behaviour in almost all domains of life.

The lack of sensitivity about cultural diversity and its role in behaviour on the part of many psychologists in the West is not surprising. What is difficult to understand is the prevalence of cultural myopia among Asian psychologists. Ho (1988) has observed that Asian psychologists, by virtue of their Western education and training, are generally well informed about Western psychology, but they hardly have any knowledge of psychology rooted in their own cultural traditions. That they are ignorant about Asian psychology is a matter of concern; that they "... seem not to be aware of or concerned with their ignorance" (Ho, 1988: 66) is a more serious matter of concern. Many Asian psychologists consider the traditional psychological knowledge as unscientific, useless, and not worth pursuing in research or practice. In a country like India, effort towards the analysis or explanation of a psychological phenomenon by using traditional concepts or systems of thought is often labelled as 'ethnocentric' and taken as challenge to, or attack on, the 'secular' status of education.

In spite of these difficulties, several psychologies (e.g., Chinese, Indian, Filipino, Japanese, and Korean etc.) are now visible in Asia. It may be noted that societies in Asia till very recently were agrarian societies. Industrial growth and development of urban centres in these societies is a relatively recent phenomenon. These societies share many common features (e.g., family structure, social norms, values, and orientations), which are based on Confucian, Taoist, or Buddhist philosophies. They lay emphasis on harmony with others by putting family and group needs ahead of individual needs, and fulfilling expected familial and societal roles. These shared common features have been used not only as basis for carving out an overarching Asian psychology, but also for facilitating development of Asian societies (Sinha & Kao, 1988).

Whether the Asian psychology we know about today is a particular brand of psychology, or it is just a different perspective on human experience and behaviour, is a matter of discussion. In essence, the term 'Asian psychology' suggests that it is a psychology rooted in culture and life of Asian people. In the Wikipedia, Asian psychology is defined as a branch of cultural psychology that studies psychological concepts as they relate to Asian culture. It is also indicated that psychologists studying these concepts are often aligned with cross-cultural psychology. If this characterization is accepted, then Asian psychology looks like one particular cultural perspective that is used, or can be further used, for understanding and explaining experience and behaviour of people living in the geographical regions of Asia.

The Asian perspective, which was initially provided by psychologists like Quicheng Jing (China), Hiroshi Azuma (Japan), Ku-Shu Yang (Taiwan), and Durganand Sinha (India), has grown stronger over the years. So much so, that it has led to the formation of an Asian Psychological Association some ten years ago with the mission of advancing psychology and the application of its scientific findings throughout Asia. Now, there are many researchers in Asia, or of Asian origins in the West, whose work is acclaimed by the international community of psychologists. Some of these researchers reflect their strength in the development and use of modern technology (e.g., imaging techniques), but a majority of them examine psychological processes as they develop and are displayed in the Asian cultural context.

Changing ethnic composition of societies in different parts of the world in recent years has brought issues related to culture and ethnicity in the forefront of research both in the basic and applied fields of psychology. It is now widely realized that culture's practices and meanings have significant influences on how people think and behave. Because these practices and meanings vary considerably across Asian and Western nations, many Asian psychologists, independently or in collaboration with Western psychologists, have examined the ways in which Asians and Westerners perceive and think about objects and events of their environment.

The importance of studying human behaviour in cultural context has been emphasized in cultural and cross-cultural psychologies during the last decades. Both have influenced contemporary psychology so much so that Asia has become a major site of research for those who want to see if psychological phenomenon, which were earlier believed to be universal, are culturally mediated and cross-culturally variable. For example, Markus and Kitayama (1990) have pointed out that North Americans hold the idea of the self as independent, whereas for Asians, it is natural to think of the self as interdependent. Morris and Peng (1994) have shown that the fundamental attribution error, which was believed to be universal, does not occur in Asia. Individualism and collectivism, which were considered as opposites, stay in a state of coexistence among Indians (Mishra, 1994; Sinha & Tripathi,1994).

Psychological research in Asia during the last two decades has greatly contributed to theory and empirical database of psychology. The most fundamental contributions are the research ideas that are informed by the unique philosophical, epistemological, and ontological perspectives of Asian thought. The application of behavioural technologies along with fine experimentation techniques (e.g., the fMRI) has made these ideas more forceful and persuasive in recent years than in earlier decades.

Some Classical Examples of Research with Asian Samples

Why do Asians behave the way they do? This question has often been asked in cultural and cross-cultural psychological research. Two probable answers can be given in this respect. One is that the physical conditions of living in Asia have led to certain ways of thinking among people, which enhance the probability of their cultural and psychological adaptation with the world. Another answer is that the ancient philosophical and religious traditions, which are still widely shared and observed in daily lives by the Asian people, provide them with ways of perceiving, organizing, and interpreting their physical and social worlds in ways that are different from those of the people of other subcontinents. Both of these possibilities have been examined in research, and the evidence is generally in support of them.

In the following sections we will look at some selective studies carried out with Asian groups to demonstrate how their behaviours are patterned differently from those of other cultural groups. While many aspects of behaviour have been examined in research (e.g., cognition, emotion, health, self-concept etc.), the focus of this chapter is on cognitive behaviours. In particular, we will focus on their thinking styles, reasoning processes, attention, and spatial cognitive processes in a comparative perspective.

Thinking Styles

Cultural philosophers for a long time have argued that Asians and Westerners think differently. This is explicit in the contrasting views they have had about the concept of "truth" and the way it works. This viewpoint goes back to the cradles of ancient Greek and Chinese civilizations. The Greeks followed the "law of the excluded middle", which states that, if two people are debating on an issue, then one of them must be right and the other one wrong. On the contrary, the Chinese followed the "doctrine of mean", which states that, if two people are debating on an issue, then both are partly right and partly wrong.

The "doctrine of mean" is taken as the highest ideal in Confucianism even today (Ji, Lee, and Guo, 2010). Accordingly, the Chinese culture encourages people to argue for both sides in a debate (i.e., both arguments are partly correct). This is in contrast with the "law of the excluded middle" emphasized in Western philosophies, according to which the conflict can be resolved by selecting only one of the ideas.

Evidence for the existence of these ancient viewpoints can be found in relatively recent psychological research. Peng and Nisbett (1999) gave Chinese and American college students a range of scenarios that described conflicts between people, and asked for advice about how to resolve them. The responses of Chinese students (72%) were oriented to seeing truth and fault in both parties, whereas the responses of American students (74%) were oriented to seeing fault on one side only.

Nisbett (2003) has offered an explanation of the difference between Eastern and Western thoughts in terms of the demands of their respective ecologies. The ecology of China, primarily consisting of fertile plains, low mountains, and navigable rivers, has favoured agriculture. This economic activity requires sharing, coordination, and harmony with others. These qualities are more importantly needed in the case of rice farming, and are facilitated by centralized control on resources and people. Thus, an ordinary Chinese negotiates life in a complex social world.

Contrary to this, the ecology of Greece, mostly consisting of mountains, has favoured economic activities like hunting, herding, fishing, and trade, which require less sharing, cooperation, and harmony with others. Agriculture, which came to Greece much later than to China, quickly became commercialized. To make better deals, the Greeks got into the habit of arguing with one another in the marketplace (and later in political assembly). In the competitive market life, harmony with fellow members was sidetracked for maximizing personal gains. That is how the Greek's emphasis on the individual and argument, and the Chinese's emphasis on the collective and harmony can be understood.

Using simple quasi-experimental procedures Nisbett and colleagues (Nisbett, 2003; Nisbett, Peng, Choi and Norenzayan, 2001) have studied the cognitive functioning of Westerners and East Asians. They have found that Westerners engage in "analytic thinking", whereas the Easterners engage in "holistic thinking". The former is characterized by focus on objects and their attributes; in this case, the objects are perceived as existing independently from their context. The latter is characterized by an orientation to the context as a whole; in this case, the objects are perceived in relation to each other and the surrounding context. As a result, when Westerners perceive the world, they focus on objects and their attributes, whereas Asians focus on the field in which the object is located. Also, the Westerners use formal logic, whereas Asians use a dialectical approach for comprehending objects and events in their world. Analytic thinking in general is more common in Western cultures than it is elsewhere (e.g., China, Japan, Korea), whereas holistic thinking is more common in East Asian and other cultures than in Western cultures.

It may be noted that ecological factors underlying the development of different patterns of cognitive functioning were reported in research on perceptual and cognitive styles much before the Nisbett's studies (see Berry, 1966, 1976; Berry, *et al.*, 1986; Mishra, Sinha, and Berry, 1996). In some recent work carried out in China, the origins of these thinking styles have been attributed to different socialization experiences of people in their respective societies. Wang and Conway (2004) have indicated that people in collectivistic societies are socialized to be interdependent and to have their attention directed at relational concerns. In contrast, people in individualistic societies are socialized to be independent and to have their attention focused on specific objects.

While Nisbett's work is quite attractive, there are some difficulties associated with his way of characterizing cognitive processes. For example, Nisbett perceives a clear opposition between Western and Asian thought and denies that everyone has the same basic cognitive processes, or that all rely on the same tools for perception, memory, causal analysis, categorization and inference. Summarizing the findings of his studies Nisbett (2003) concludes: "The research shows that there are indeed dramatic differences in the nature of Asian and European thought processes" (p. xviii). Nisbett also claimed that "Most of the time, in fact, Easterners and Westerners were found to behave in ways that were qualitatively distinct" (Nisbett, 2003: 191).

Berry, *et al.* (2011) ask whether these differences in performance between Easterners and Westernersare really qualitative or only quantitative variations in performance on a common underlying cognitive process. For Nisbett (2003: 191-193), the East-West differences refer to qualitative differences in the cognitive performances of participants. Two difficulties are encountered in accepting this claim (Mishra and Berry, 2017). First, the evidence of qualitative differences in performance is not convincing. The fact that all participants could perform the tasks to some degrees indicates that the cognitive process was present in both the cultural groups. Second, even if the claim about qualitative differences in performance is accepted, this would not permit an easy conclusion that there are differences in the underlying cognitive processes. The inference required to go back from performance to process is a complex one, which Nisbett and his colleagues seem not to examine.

We can draw two conclusions from this programme of research on Asian *vs.* Western thought. First, the performance differences presented by the two cultural groups are largely a matter of stylistic differences, rather than a reflection of qualitative differences in the cognitive life of populations in the East and West. Dasen and Mishra (2010, 2013a) have drawn a similar conclusion from examining their research on the development of spatial language and cognition carried out in India, Indonesia, Nepal and Switzerland. Second, there are important links between this body of work and the Berry's (1976) ecocultural approach to understanding the basis for human cognitive diversity, but using rather novel quasi-experimental cognitive tasks. As Mishra and Berry (2017) argue, the findings related to Asian and Western thought support the view that individuals in cultures develop ways of perceiving and cognizing the world that allow them to best adapt to the demands that they confront in their daily lives. In other words, they use different cognitive styles to deal with situations (Dasen & Mishra, 2013).

Some recent research suggests that holistic thinking is spread throughout the world, whereas analytic thinking is largely restricted to people who have been in contact with the Western society or education system (Varnum, Grossman, Kitayama, & Nisbett, 2010). For example, in one study Arabs were found to show as much evidence of holistic thinking as Chinese (Norenzayan, Choi and Peng, 2007). Russians have been found to be more holistic in their thinking than Americans (Grossman & Varnum, 2011), as are Turkish farmers and fishermen than herders (Uskul, Kitayama and Nisbett, 2008). Even within cultures, there are parallel differences: working class Americans and Russians are more holistic than their middle class counterparts (Grossman & Varnum, 2011). These studies indicate that there are factors within Eastern and Western cultural context, which might lead to differences in the development of analytic or holistic thinking.

Attention

One of the most fundamental psychological processes is attention. Broadly speaking, it is concerned with where one's cognitive activity is directed and/or focused at a given point of time. Analytical thinkers, who tend to perceive the world as consisting of discrete objects, are more likely to focus their attention on separate parts of a scene. In contrast, holistic thinkers, who tend to perceive the world as consisting of interrelated objects, are more likely to direct their attention across the entire scene.

Difference in attention to stimuli between Asians and Westerners were brought out long time ago in the analysis of their responses to the Rorschach ink blots (Abel & Hsu, 1949). It was observed that responses of the Chinese Americans were largely based on the entire image, whereas Americans tended to describe the image based on a single aspect or a particular part of the Rorschach card. In a relatively recent study, Ji, Peng and Nisbett (2000) compared Chinese and American participants for judgement of "the likelihood of appearance" of objects that were paired with coins by using different presentation probabilities. It was noted that Americans focused more on the individual objects than on the object-coin relationships.

In an interesting study Masuda and Nisbett (2001) showed American and Japanese participants some animated computer images of an underwater scene, which contained a swimming fish, waving seaward, and floating bubbles. The participants were asked to describe what they saw. The Japanese participants made about 60 per cent more reference to background objects than the Americans, who tended to talk more about the fish. Presentation of the fish in a novel background did not influence recognition of the American participants, but it did for the Japanese participants. The Japanese recognized the fish more often when it was shown with the original background than when it was presented in a novel background, indicating a kind of "context-driven" cognitive functioning of the Japanese.

The difference in how Asians and Americans attend to parts of scenes, as noted in the above-mentioned study, has been found to be present not only at the behavioural level, but also at the neural level. Gutchess, *et al.* (2006) did fMRI scans of the East Asian and American participants while they saw pictures of either an individual object (e.g., an elephant alone), or empty background scenes (e.g., savannah scene, with no animals), or an embedded scene (e.g., an elephant in a savannah) presented to them. Compared with the East Asians, the American subjects showed more activation of "object processing regions" in the brain, whereas no cultural difference was found in activation of "context processing regions". These studies and many others (Park & Huang, 2010) indicate that Asians and

Americans seemingly rely on different brain regions for processing object-related information available in scenes. There is also the evidence to show that cultural differences in object processing are more pronounced between the elderly Asians and Westerners than between the younger Asians and Westerners (Goh, *et al.*, 2007). It appears that, in the course of development, neural functions continue to be shaped by normative cultural attention patterns to reach consolidation in the elderly people across cultures.

These findings about East-West differences raise an important question: Do people from different cultures really see things differently, or do they process the same information differently? In other words, does the difference lie at the level of information processing, or at the level of cognition? Studies, which use eye tracker, partly answer this question. In a study Masuda, *et al.* (2008) showed Japanese and American participants some animated scenes on a computer screen. In one scene, the participants saw a "target" person in the foreground surrounded by other people in the background, each showing an emotional facial expression. The background faces showed expressions that were sometimes consistent and sometimes inconsistent with the "target" person's emotion. The participants had to identify the emotion of the target person.

The analysis revealed that, in the case of Japanese participants, judgements of the "target" person's emotional expression were influenced by the expressions of the people present in the background. In the case of American participants, the expressions of persons present in the background had no impact on the judgement of the "target" person's emotional expression. Eye tracking records indicated that in the first 1,000 milliseconds, there was little cultural difference: both the Japanese and Americans spent about 90 per cent of the time on the central figure. In the next 1,000 millisecond intervals, participants in both cultures started looking more at the background than the foreground figure, but the Japanese did it more than the Americans. This finding indicates a slightly greater tendency for Westerners than Asians to attend to focal objects, suggesting that cultural difference lies in the processing of information than at the level of cognition.

Reasoning Process

Some research has brought out a difference in the Asian and American ways of reasoning. A distinction is made between "rule-based reasoning" and "associative reasoning". The former is evident when people use a set of abstract rules and laws in trying to make sense of a situation. The latter is in evidence when people try to make sense of a situation by considering the relationship between objects and events. Norenzayan, Smith, Kim, and Nisbett (2002) presented East Asian and American participants with a set of pictures of flowers for judgement of their similarity with the target stimulus figure. The decision involved a conflict between the application of reasoning based on rule and relationship. It was found that the judgement of Americans was largely based on the application of "rule", whereas the judgement of East Asians was largely based on the perceived resemblance of stimuli (i.e., relationship).

This study clearly shows that East Asians are more likely to use holistic reasoning in a situation when there is conflict between an analytic and a holistic solution of the problem. What will happen in situations when there is no conflict? Will the East Asians engage in similar reasoning in such situations also? The answer is that they may switch from holistic to analytical reasoning. Supportive evidence for the use of analytical reasoning on the part of Asians is provided by studies of self-description (Dhawan, Roseman, Naidu, Rettek, and Thapa, 1995; Triandis, McCusker, & Hui, 1990). The indication is that Asians wheel in an analytical mental module when they are encouraged to think about their uniqueness. In a study based on fMRI scan, Ma, *et al.* (2012) reported no difference between the brain activation pattern of Danish and Chinese participants when they considered their personal characteristics, but a significant difference when they described their social roles.

Another support for the use of analytical reasoning can be obtained from Asians' performance in math and science, which require analytical thinking for solution of problems. There is strong evidence to show that, in solving these problems, Asians efficiently employ analytical reasoning strategies and perform better than Westerners (Stevenson & Stigler, 1992). These studies provide us with convincing evidence for the presence of both holistic and analytical reasoning strategies among Asians. Depending on the demand of the task or situation, they can employ each one of them with almost equal effectiveness.

Spatial Language and Cognition

Studies of spatial language and cognition present us with another good example of East-West difference in the development and display of psychological processes. In tracing the development of spatial concepts, Piaget (Piaget and Inhelder, 1956) had proposed that children develop spatial understanding first by using topological references (also called object-centred, such as "the ball is near the chair"); these are later on dominated by the use of projective references (also called relative or egocentric, such as "the ball is to the left of me"). The last to appear in the sequence are the Euclidean references to space (also called environment-centred or geocentric references, such as "the ball is to the east"). In the mainstream developmental psychology, this sequence of spatial cognitive development is taken as "universal".

A similar sequence of development has been discovered in the case of spatial language. It has been shown (Bowerman and Levinson, 2001) that children start with the deictic (e.g., saying "this way-that way" often accompanied by gestures). Later on they move on to the use of relative language (also called egocentric, such as the use of left, right, front, back), and finally they acquire and use the absolute language (also called geocentric, such as the use of north, south, east, west). This pattern of language development is generally considered as "universal".

The "linguistic universalism" described above met challenge from some work, which demonstrated that, in some cultures, there was clear preference for the use of 'absolute' frame of reference (FoR) in language even though other spatial language frames (e.g., intrinsic, relative) were potentially available (see Levinson, 2003). In the case of Tamil language (Pederson, 1993), it has been shown that Tamil speakers in rural settings predominantly use an absolute FoR, whereas Tamil speakers in the urban settings predominantly use a relative FoR. Similar preference is also reflected in spatial encoding of the objects. This strong form of "linguistic relativism" (that language determines cognition) holds that people engage in encoding of spatial displays depending on which spatial language is emphasized in their cultural context.

Dasen and Mishra (2010) carried out a series of co-ordinated studies in India, Indonesia, Nepal and Switzerland with 4-14 year children to examine the development of spatial FoR in language and cognition, and their relationship in the course of development. They systematically documented the languages children used when they described a variety of tasks and situations (called language elicitation tasks). They also used a variety of tasks and procedures to examine the ways in which children non-linguistically encoded spatial displays in quasi-experimental situations (called encoding tasks).

The results indicated that children did not always use the same spatial FoR in language and cognition. More interesting was the fact that in Switzerland (a Western culture), children moved from the use of deictic to the use of egocentric FoR, but they hardly ever used, either in language or encoding, a geocentric FoR, which was available and also used by people while driving on roads. In Asian cultures (e.g., in Varanasi, India and Bali, Indonesia), children largely used a geocentric FoR right from the early age, which in the course of development became stronger. At each of these locations, there were clear variations in the use of spatial FoR according to children's ecological and cultural conditions. For example, in India, children, who lived in a village or attended a Sanskrit-medium school in the city, mainly used the geocentric FoR, whereas children, who lived in the city and attended a Hindi-medium school, mainly used the egocentric FoR. In Nepal (another Asian country), children of the mountainous region mainly used a geocentric FoR, whereas those living in the city of Kathmandu and attending English-medium schools largely used the egocentric FoR. Similar differences in the use of spatial FoR were noted in Bali (Indonesia) between rural and urban children, and between children attending schools in the traditional Balinese and standard Indonesian languages.

These studies and many others (Dasen & Mishra, 2013; Mishra & Dasen, 2013a, 2013b; Mishra, Niraula, and Dasen, 2003; Niraula, Mishra, and Dasen, 2004) indicate that, while the basic psychological processes, both in language and cognition, are potentially available with individuals everywhere, ecological and cultural contexts create variations in the development and display of these processes. Despite the underlying common psychological processes, people often develop competencies in different ways, depending on which kind of competence is relatively more salient and emphasized in daily life of individuals in their respective cultural contexts. People also display their underlying competencies when the appropriate contexts call for them, as we have seen earlier in the case of Asian and Western participants. "Task dependency" in cognitive performance has often been demonstrated in research (Dasen & Mishra, 2010). My own work, spanning over the last four decades with a variety of populations, has led to the belief that, depending on the demands of ecological and cultural settings, people develop a cognitive style (i.e., a preferred way of dealing with tasks and situations), which is adaptive to their respective settings. Since each cognitive style carries functional value, evaluative judgements (e.g., good or bad, superior or inferior) about any one of them will be ethnocentric.

Conclusion

Cross-cultural research during the last decades has quite often included

Asians as participants for the comparative study of several psychological phenomena. Although Chinese samples are more often represented in studies than samples from other cultures, researchers seem largely convinced that the findings will apply to other Asian cultural groups. Looking at the studies related to cognitive domain, it is difficult to claim that there is a distinct kind of Asian psychology of cognition. Perspectives derived from the studies discussed above do provide us with alternative ways of examining and explaining psychological phenomena as they operate in the case of Asian people. Studies indicate that the Asians approach tasks and situations in ways, which are considerably different from those of the people of Euro-American cultural background.

Nevertheless, research so far has not identified any psychological process that is present among Asians, but not among members of other cultures. Differences between the Asians and Westerners pointed out in studies are more a matter of preference for engaging with tasks and situations in one particular way over many other possible ways. In studies of cognition particularly, that we have examined in this chapter, innovations displayed by researchers with respect to designing tasks and experimental situations are highly appreciable. On the other hand, there is no evidence in support of the existence of any cognitive phenomenon, which may be labelled exclusively as 'Asian', and not found in other cultural groups. This is indeed true about much of the cross-cultural research on cognition and cognitive development carried out world-wide (Mishra, 1997, 2001).

Some decades ago, the interest of cross-cultural psychological research was on the search for differences between cultural groups and the behaviour of their individual members. In recent years, the interest has shifted to the understanding of what is similar among them. Although these interests apparently seem to be in conflict with each other, in essence they are not. As Berry (2013) argues, the "...search for what is common to human behaviour around the world requires the examination of behavioural diversity" (p. 56). In other words, similarity in human behaviour can be discovered and understood only against the background of differences. In studies examined in this chapter, the focus seems to be more on the search for differences than similarity between Asian and Western thought processes. We may hope that psychological studies in the upcoming years would also try to focus on the similarities displayed in cognitive behaviour of these cultural groups. There is also the need for examining similarities and differences in cognitive functioning across diverse cultural groups represented within the Asian region. Such studies are important because they can inform us about the variables that play out differently within and across cultures to generate variations in human behaviour.

Culture in the form of cumulative learning is unique to human beings. Language and other processes (e.g., imitative learning, theory of mind) contribute significantly to this uniqueness. The effects of enculturation, socialization and acculturation processes on individuals' functioning can be observed in all domains of their life. By ignoring culture in the pursuit of a 'universal' science, psychological studies have provided us with a sketchy and incomplete picture of the complex human behaviour. Societies, which are inherently characterized by cultural diversity, need to pay greater attention to culture in the study of human behaviour. Asian societies present us with ample opportunities for engaging in comparative psychological research with groups characterized by ecological, cultural, ethnic, religious and linguistic diversities. Active research collaborations among Asian psychologists can open up possibilities for enriching their database before claiming that there is an Asian psychology, which is distinctly different from the Western psychology that we currently study, teach and practice in Asia.

References

Abel, T.M., and Hsu, F.I. (1949). Some aspects of personality of Chinese as revealed by the Rorschach Test. *Journal of Projective Techniques, 13*(3), 285-301.

Adair, J., Coelho, A., and Luna, J. (2002). How international is international psychology? *International Journal of Psychology, 37* (3), 160-170.

Allwood, C.M., and Berry, J.W. (2006). Origins and development of indigenous psychologies: An international analysis. *International Journal of Psychology, 41* (4), 243-268.

Berry, J.W. (1966). Temin and Eskimo perceptual skills. *International Journal of Psychology, 1* (3), 207-229.

Berry, J.W. (1974). Canadian social psychology: Some social and applied emphases. *Canadian Psychologist*, 15 (2) 132-139.

Berry, J.W. (1976). *Human Ecology and Cognitive Style: Comparative studies in Cultural and Psychological adaptation.* New York: Sage/Halsted.

Berry, J.W. (2013). Achieving a global psychology. *Canadian Psychology, 54* (1), 55-61.

Berry, J.W. (2017). *Mutual Intercultural Relations.* New York: Cambridge University Press.

Berry, J.W., *Poortinga,* Y.H., Breugelmans, S.M., Chasiotis A., and Sam D.L. (2011). *Cross-cultural Psychology: Research and Applications.* Cambridge: Cambridge University Press.

Berry, J.W., Poortinga, Y.H., Segall, M.H., and Dasen, P.R. (1992/2002). *Cross-cultural Psychology: Research and Applications*. New York: Cambridge University Press.

Berry, J.W., Van de Koppel, J.M.H., Senechal, C., Annis, R.C., Bahuchet, S., Cavalli-Sforza, L.L., and Witkin, H.A. (1986). *On the Edge of the Forest: Cultural Adaptation and Cognitive Development in Central Africa*. Lisse: Swets and Zeitlinger.

Berry, J.W., and Wilde, G.J.S. (1972). *Social Psychology: The Canadian Context*. Toronto: McClelland and Stewart.

Bowerman, M., Levinson, S.C. (2001). *Language Acquisition and Conceptual Development*. Cambridge: Cambridge University Press.

Cole, M. (2006). Internationalism in Psychology: We need it now more than ever. *American Psychologist, 61* (8): 904-917.

Dasen, P.R., and Mishra, R.C. (2010). *The Development of Geocentric Spatial Language and Cognition: An Eco-cultural Perspective.* Oxford: Oxford University Press.

Dasen, P.R. and Mishra, R.C. (2013). Cultural differences in cognitive styles. In B.R. Kar (Ed)., *Cognition and Brain Development: Converging Evidences from various Methodologies* (pp. 231-249). Washington DC: American Psychological Association.

Dhawan, N., Roseman, I.J., Naidu, R.K., Rettek, S.I., and Thapa, K. (1995). Self-concepts across Two cultures: India and the United States. *Journal of Cross-Cultural Psychology, 26*(6): 606-621.

Faucheux, C. (1976). Cross-cultural research in European social psychology. *European Journal of Social Psychology*, 6 (3): 269-322.

Goh, J.O., Chee, M. W., Tan, J.C., Venkatraman, V., Hebrank, A. (2007). Age and culture modulates object processing and object-scene binding in the ventral visual area. *Cognitive, Affective and Behavioural Neuroscience, 7* (1), 44-52.

Grossman, I., and Varnum, M.E.W. (2011). Social class, culture, and cogntion. *Social Psychological and Personality Science*, 2(1), 81-89.

Gutchess, A.H., Welsh, R.C., Boduroglu, A., and Park, D.C. (2006). Cultural differences in neural functions associated with object processing. *Cognitive, Affective and Behavioural Neuroscience, 6*(2): 102-109.

Henrich, J., Heine, S., and Norenzayan, A. (2010). The weirdest people in the world. *Behavioural and Brain Sciences*, 33 (2-3): 61-83.

Ho, D.Y.F. (1988). Asian psychology. A dialogue in indigenization and beyond In A.C. Paranjpe, D.Y.F. Ho, and R.W. Reiber (Eds.), *Asian Contributions to Psychology* (pp. 55-77). New York: Praeger.

Ingleby, D. (1974). *The job psychologists do.* In N. Armistead (Ed.), *Reconstructing Social Psychology* (pp. 314-328). Harmondsworth: Penguin.

Ji, L., Lee, A., and Guo, T. (2010). *The thinking styles of Chinese people*. In M.H. Bond (Ed.), *The Oxford Handbook of Chinese Psychology* (pp. 155-168). New York: Oxford University Press.

Ji, L.J., Peng, K., and Nisbett, R.E. (2000). Culture, control and perception of relationships in the environment. *Journal of Personality and Social Psychology, 78* (5): 943-955.

Kao, H.S.R., and Sinha, D. (1997). *Asian Perspectives on Psychology.* New Delhi: Sage Publications.

Kennedy, S., Schierer, J., and Rogers, A. (1984). The price of success: Our monocultural science. *American Psychologist*, 39(9): 996-997.

Levinson, S.C. (2003). *Space in Language and Cognition.* Cambridge: Cambridge University Press.

Ma, Y., Bang, D., Wang, C., Allen, M., Frith, C., Roepstorff, A., and Hans, S. (2012). Socio-cultural patterning of neural activity during self-reflection. *Social, Cognitive and Affective Neuroscience, 9* (1): 73-80.

Markus, H., and Kitayama, S. (1990). Culture and the self: Implications for cognition, emotion, and motivation. *Psychological Review, 98* (2): 224-253.

Masuda, T., Ellsworth, P.C., Mesquita, B., Leu, J., Tanida, S., and van de Veerdonk, E. (2008). Placing the face in context: Cultural differences in the perception of facial emotion. *Journal of Personality and Social Psychology, 94* (3): 365-381.

Masuda, T., and Nisbett, R.E. (2001). Attending holistically *vs.* analytically: Comparing the context sensitivity of Japanese and Americans. *Journal of Personality and Social Psychology, 81* (5): 922-934.

Mishra, R.C. (1994). Individualist-collectivist orientations across generations. In U. Kim, H.C. Triandis, C. Kagitcibasi, S. Choi, and G. Yoon (Eds.), *Individualism and Collectivism: Theory, Method, and Practice* (pp. 225-238). Thousand Oaks: Sage Publications.

Mishra, R.C. (1997). Cognition and cognitive development. In J.W. Berry, P.R. Dasen, and T.S. Saraswathi (Eds.), *Handbook of Cross-cultural Psychology* (Vol. 2, pp. 147-179). Boston: Allyn and Bacon.

Mishra, R.C. (2001). Cognition across cultures. In D. Matsumoto (Ed.), *The Handbook of Culture and Psychology* (pp. 119-135). New York: Oxford Press.

Mishra, R.C., and Berry, J.W. (2017). *Ecology, Culture and Human Development: Lessons for Adivasi Education.* New Delhi: Sage Publications.

Mishra, R.C., and Dasen, P.R. (2013a). Culture and cognitive development: The development of geocentric language and cognition. In B.R. Kar (Ed.), *Cognition and Brain Development: Converging Evidences from various Methodologies* (pp. 211-230). Washington DC: American Psychological Association.

Mishra, R.C., and Dasen, P.R. (2013b). Development of spatial language and cognition in Hindi and Sanskrit medium schools. *Psychological Studies, 58* (4): 446-455.

Mishra, R.C., Dasen, P., and Niraula, S. (2003). Ecology, language and performance on spatial cognitive tasks. *International Journal of Psychology*, 38 (6): 366-383.

Mishra, R.C., Sinha, D., and Berry, J.W. (1996). *Ecology, Acculturation and Psychological Adaptation: A Study of Adivasis in Bihar*. New Delhi: Sage Publications.

Moghaddam, F.M. (1993). Traditional and Modern Psychologies in competing Cultural systems. In U. Kim, and J.W. Berry (Eds.), *Indigenous Psychologies* (pp. 118-132). Newbury Park, CA: Sage Publications.

Morris, M., and Peng, K. (1994). Culture and cause: American and Chinese attribution for social and physical events. *Journal of Personality and Social Psychology, 67* (6): 949-973.

Moscovici, S. (1971). Society and Theory in Social Psychology. In J. Israel, and H. Tajfel (Eds.), *The Context of Social Psychology* (pp. 17-68). London: Academic Press.

Niraula, S., Mishra, R.C., and Dasen, P. (2004). Linguistic relativity and spatial concept development in Nepal. *Psychology and Developing Societies, 17* (1): 99-124.

Nisbett, R.E. (2003). *The Geography of Thought*. New York: Free Press.

Nisbett, R.E., Peng, K., Choi, I., and Norenzayan, A. (2001). Culture and systems of thought: Holistic *vs*. analytic cognition. *Psychological Review, 108* (2): 291-310.

Norenzayan, A., Choi, I., and Peng, K. (2007). Cognition and perception. In S. Kitayama and D. Cohen (Eds.), *Handbook of Cultural Psychology* (pp. 569-594). New York: Guilford Press.

Norenzayan, A., Smith, E.E., Kim, B.J., and Nisbett, R.E. (2002). Cultural preference for formal *vs*. intuitive reasoning. *Cognitive Science, 26* (5): 653-684.

Park, D.C., and Huang, C.M. (2010). Culture wires the brain: A cognitive neuroscience perspective. *Perspective in Psychological Science, 5* (4): 391-400.

Pederson, E. (1993). Geographic and manipulable space in two Tamil linguistic systems. In A.U. Frank, and I. Campari (Eds.), *Spatial Information Theory* (pp. 294-311). Berlin: Springer.

Peng, K., and Nisbett, R.E. (1999). Culture, dialectics, and reasoning about contradiction. *American Psychologist, 54* (9): 741-754.

Piaget, J., and Inheder, B. (1956). *The Child's Conception of Space*. London: Routledge & Keagan Paul.

Serpell, R. (1984). Commentary on the impact of psychology on Third World development. *International Journal of Psychology, 19* (1-4), 179-192.

Sexton, V.S., and Misiak, A. (1984). American psychologist and psychology abroad. *American Psychologist, 39* (9): 1026-1031.

Sinha, D. (1965). Integration of modern psychology with Indian thought. *Journal of Humanistic Psychology*, Spring, pp. 6-21.

Sinha, D. (1980). Non-Western perspectives in psychology: Why, what and whither? *Journal of Indian Psychology*, 3 (1): 1-9.

Sinha, D. (1994). Origin and development of psychology in India: Outgrowing the alien framework. *International Journal of Psychology, 29* (6): 695 706.

Sinha, D. (1997). Indigenizing psychology. In J.W. Berry, Y.H. Poortinga, and J. Pandey (Eds.), *Handbook of Cross-cultural Psychology* (Vol. 1, pp. 310-371). Boston, MA: Allyn & Bacon.

Sinha, D., and Kao, H.S.R. (1988). *Social Values and Development: Asian Perspectives.* New Delhi: Sage Publications.

Sinha, D., and Kao, H.S.R. (1997). The journey to the East: An introduction. In H.S.R. Kao, & D. Sinha (Eds.), *Asian Perspectives on Psychology* (pp. 9-22). New Delhi: Sage Publications.

Sinha, D., and Tripathi, R.C. (1994). Individualism in a collectivist culture: A case of coexistence of opposites. In U. Kim, H.C. Triandis, C. Kagitçibasi, S. Choi, and G. Yoon (Eds.), *Individualism and Collectivism: Theory, Method and Applications* (pp. 123-136). Thousand Oaks: Sage Publications.

Traindis, H.C., McCusker, C., and Hui, C.H. (1990). Multimethod probe of individualism and collectivism. *Journal of Personality and Social Psychology, 59* (5): 1006-1020.

Uskul, A.K., Kitayama, S., and Nisbett, R.E. (2008). *Eco-cultural basis of cognition: Farmers and fishermen are more holistic than herders.* Proceedings of the National Academy of Sciences of the United States of America, *105* (25): 8552-8556.

Varnum, M.E.W., Grossman, I., Kitayama, S., and Nisbett, R.E. (2010). The origin of cultural differences in cognition: The social orientation hypothesis. *Current Directions in Psychological Science, 19*(1): 9-13.

Wang, Q., and Conway, M.A. (2004). The stories we keep: Autobiographical memory in American and Chinese middle-aged adults. *Journal of Personality, 72* (5): 911-938.

SECTION II
Grassroots of Religions and Religious Practices in Asia

3
Sufism and Sufi Practices

Akbar Hussain

Introduction

Sufi practices are the right path of understanding and manifesting true love, leading to healing and transformation, and harness harmony and peace among people. Sufis cultivate the right thinking and perception among people which can remove discrimination, intolerance, aggression and violence. Cultivation of openness, non-discrimination and compassion protect the lives of people. Sufis gave the message of true love and happiness.

Sufism is a path of experiences in which the very inner substance of the individual is totally changed. Moreover, through experiences we can tell others how love is created within the heart, how this divine love is experienced as yearning. The slow process of experiences down the ego until the disciple surrenders totally to the Beloved.

There are multiple ways of practices in Sufism which are based on the schools of thought. Sufism is based on the high ideals of philosophy and is linked with State of Annihilation in God, *Urafa*, Faithfulness, Inclusive love, Sound and Silence, and Mystical Experience. Practically, it involves ritualistic worship, constant remembrance of God and yearning of a higher order through love.

State of Annihilation in God (*Fan-Fi-Allah*)

A *Sufi* is one who annihilates, after passing though the different stages of spiritual journey, an *Arif* or *Sufi* reaches at the 'station' of annihilation in

God "*fana-fillah*". This is one of the most difficult spiritual discussion. State of Annihilation in God (*Fana-Fi-Allah*) has been interpreted in three ways: annihilation of will, annihilation of attributes and self-annihilation in God. A Group of Gnostics, who have laid emphasis on the aspects of ethical and practical Sufism, interpret *fana* as extinction of attribute, especially annihilation of the Will of man before the 'Will' of God. Theosophists and those who stress on aspects of theoretical Sufism especially Monists, interpret *fauna* as extinction of the carnal attributes so that the Divine is manifested. They believe that the higher stage is 'self-annihilation'. Thus, following are three meanings of *fana*:

(1) ***Annihilation of Will***: In a very simple meaning of the annihilation of will is that a will of a person may become completely subservient to will of God. This annihilation is the highest sort of worship, when a devotee completely surrenders to God. This interpretation is accepted even by non-Sufis.
The author of the book, *al-Ta'arruf* says: "Annihilation means extinction of carnal desires and sensual so that and the matter of *Zikr* and worship of God might be his guardian." He says: Annihilated person reaches to a stage, where all the pleasures of the world are neutral and equal for him, there remains no difference between woman and wall."
Another famous explanation is the *Tawhid-i-Af'ali* of Sufis. Author of the book, *al-luma*, it is realization of *Tawhid-i-Af'ali* that a person should know that only 'will' is that of 'God' all else is illusion. Extinction of self-attributes and entering into the sphere of divine qualities means to come out from his self-desires and submit to the Divine Will. This stage is one of the stages of *Tawhid*. But Saharwardi has presented a very profound explanation regarding annihilation of the Will: he says: "External annihilation is that God manifests and illuminates his devotee's heart. He reaches to the stage when he has no 'will' but the 'Will' of God."

(2) ***Annihilation of Attributes:*** Second meaning and dimension of *fana* is annihilation of attributes (*Fana-i Sifat*). In simple meaning, it is extinction of all carnal desires and attributes, so that man's character becomes a fade reflection of the Divine Attributes. Another description of annihilation of attributes is that the devotees acknowledge that all the excellent qualities belong only to God who is source of all perfections.

(3) ***Annihilation of Self:*** Last stage of Sufi's spiritual journey is vision of God and extinction of 'self' in Divine. Self-annihilation is depicted on the basis of particular mystical ontology. As mentioned above, on the basis of mystical monism (*Wahadatal Wujud 'Irfani*) there is only one reality that is the Absolute Existence of God, and all other existences are imaginary conditioning and imposition of distinctive identities. To annihilate these identities, is to discover the ultimate Truth and be dissolved in that. The *Urafa* says *'fana'* does not mean that we had a real 'existence' which is annihilated, but it is the stage of realization that there is only His existence, here knowledge results in becoming.

But attainment of Reality means that the devotees get separation from imaginary and limited existence, which is due to differentiation of the creatures from God: realizes and becomes one. Again the poet said: *Wisal* (reaching to God) is just getting rid of imaginative assumptions. Once, 'I' has disappeared, there is none but 'He'.

Along with the discussion of annihilation of God (*Fana-Fi-Allah*), Gnostics also have spoken about Eternity with God (*Baqa-bi-Allah*). When the finite dissolves in infinite, it becomes eternal.

'Urafa

'Urafa believe in intense and profound spiritual experiences which cannot be described. After passing through three stages and stations of annihilation, *'Arif* or *Sufi* reaches to the stage of realization and vision of ultimate realities. These realizations and visions about the infinite cannot be described by a language that has been formed to express affairs of the finite. These realizations cannot be communicated because it is beyond the capacity of the human language.

Despite this, Gnostics try to explain their mystical experiments. These definitions of Sufis are a sort of rational interpretation of what they have come to know. It is possible that an *'Arif* (Gnostic) might have realized higher realities, but in the stage of explanation and interpretation, he could commit mistake. This is one of the causes of the differences between Gnostics (*'Urafa*) in every stage of description (*tabir*).

However, it is also possible that in matter of the vision, there may be difference among '*urafa*. This difference is due to different grades of these masters. Besides this, Sufis have themselves explained that it is possible that some of the perceptions may be the devil's inspiration; while others may be God gifted. '*Urafa* have described the ways for recognition of the divine inspiration as differing with devil's inspiration.

Faithfulness

The followers of Sufism are loyal to their beliefs and practices regardless of what happens. From Sufism perspective, faithfulness is a part of eternal existence. Life is transient and death is a reality. For the Enlightened One, spiritual life is eternal. Faithfulness connects to your eternal nature; prove to the world how special and unique you are. Sufi practices lead you towards peace connects to God and destroy your ego. You can attain 'Self-realization' through faithful beliefs, and practices.

Inclusive love

Sufism teaches the lesson of inclusive love. To quote Rabindranath Tagore, "The world needs a mystic's universal and inclusive love, not the exclusive love of a faithful." Nothing is more important than love to maintain peace and attain happiness. This world is also a home of God, so spread love in all directions. Through finite love one can behold the infinite love. The whole world is surviving because of love.

Farishat boodam munhir zaat, insaan ferazat aseet. "Strive to become angels and spread love like fragrance" wrote Rumi in *Masnavi.*

To the followers of Sufism anything given with love is uplifting. They express love to other human beings in terms of relationship at various levels of social interaction. It is their basic nature to love. Love is pure energy. Remember, God's attachment and inclusive love surrounds you.

Sound and Silence

The following discourse is an introduction to the realities of Sound and Silence according to the spiritual teachings of the Naqshbandi-Haqqani School of Thought. Grand Shaykh Muhammad Nazim Adil al Haqqani (QS) is the worldwide Leader of the Naqshbandi-Haqqani Sufi Order.

We usually think of sound and silence as two opposite concepts. In fact, they are not really opposites of each other. Both sound and silence represent two forms of sounds: sound as we know it represents audible sound. It is the sound of the Known. On the other hand, silence represents non-audible sound. It is the sound of the Unknown.

The Unknown is referred to as "HU" in Islamic Spirituality. "Hu" is both a sound and a Holy Name of God. The sound "Hu" is the most basic vibration in the universe. It is the smallest sound, or the smallest vibration, that is produced whenever an object moves in the universe. Since nothing in creation is in perfect state of rest (electrons are constantly moving around the nucleus), it is safe to say that there is no place in creation where that sound "Hu" is not produced.

Therefore, the real meaning of Silence, which is perfect absence of sound, does not exist in the universe. In this world, when we seek to immerse ourselves in Silence, we are not trying to shut our ability to hear sounds. On the contrary, we are trying to increase our ability to hear a very specific sound: the vibrating sound of the Universe, which is the sound of our inner Soul. That sound is the eternal vibration of "Huuuuuu".

Importance of Sound

A sound represents a Message. When a sound is emitted, some information is moved from the person emitting the sound to the person hearing it. At the very first stage of spiritual development, that Message is the Calling towards Islam, which means submission to the Lord. That initial stage of spiritual development is very critical because it is at that stage that the child in us (the child represents the pure human soul) hears for the first time the sound of his parents' calling toward a righteous and spiritual life. This is why whenever a baby is born; his parents whisper at his ears *Adhan* Islamic Prayer. Through the sound of the *adhan*, the baby can hear before he can see. The sounds are reminders for the child. Indeed, they remind that child of his true Origin in the Presence of the Lord.

Mystical Experience

Sufism is the force which creates and sustains all manifestations of humankind. One may access to mystical experience through deep meditation and able to attain bliss. Those who go into deep meditation discover the mystical experiences. Sufis had mystical experiences in deep meditation. The mystical experiences of the Sufis have beautiful expressions in shrines.

Mystical experiences can be enjoyed by the common people only after transcending the mind, intellect and heart. In spiritual terms, everyone has infinite possibilities of mystical experiences. Sometimes, we call mystical experiences as miracles. If we believe or have some faith, then we tend to notice these miracles. If we do not believe, it is too easy to overlook them when they do happen.

Spiritual Practices

Four stages of Sufi practice

Ozak (1988) credits Ibn Arabi for describing four stages of practice and understanding in Sufism — *sharia* (exoteric religious law), *tariqa* (the mystical path), *haqiqa* (truth), and *marifa* (gnosis).

First is the *sharia*, which is found in all religions. *Sharia* consists of teachings of morality and ethics. It provides guidance for us to live properly in this world. Sufism is built on solid moral ethical principles. In Arabic, *sharia* means road. *Sharia* refers to the outer practice of religion, what one actually does. The *sharia* makes our outside clean and attractive. In many traditions, students are simply told what to do, without significant explanation of why. As a result, their practices tend to be shallow and mechanical.

Second is the *tariqa*, which refer to the inner practice of Sufism. *Tariqa* is the trackless path in the desert that the Bedouin would follow from oasis to oasis. This path is not clearly marked, nor is it even a visible road. The guide you need in order to find your way and to reach the destination is the Sufi teacher. The *tariqa* makes us clean and pure from within. A Sufi teacher once explained, "Anyone can learn the outer forms of prayer in a short time, but Sufi practice aims at developing a heart that can pray" (Quoted in Frager & Fadiman, 2007 : 464).

Third is *haqiqa,* or truth. *Haqiqa* refer to the personal understanding of the inner meaning of *sharia* and *tariqa* practices and guidance. Without this understanding, we are fated to follow blindly, to initiate mechanically those who know, those who have attained the station of *haqiqa.* The attainment of *haqiqa* conforms and solidifies the practices of the first two stages. Before *haqiqa* all practices is imitation. The third stage represents the experience developed in practice, an experience which may take years to deepen.

Fourth is *marifa*, or gnosis, a deep level of inner knowing, beyond *haqiqa*. It is the knowledge of reality, attained by few—the Messengers, the prophets, and the great sage and saints. This stage involves full understanding of a practice, because the individual has become transformed and has reached a state of knowledge and wisdom.

Ibn Arabi also explained these four stages as follows: *sharia* connotes "yours and mine." That is, the *sharia* guarantees individual rights and ethical relation between people. At the stage of *tariqa*, "mine is yours and yours is mine". Sufis are expected to treat each other as brothers and sisters. They open peoples' homes, their hearts, and their purses to each other. *Haqiqa* connotes "no mine and yours." The individual realize that all things from God has given us to benefit God's creation. Those who attain *haqiqa* have gone beyond attachment to possession, beyond attachment to externals in general, including fame and position. Those who reaches *marifa,* experience "no me and no you." The Prophet and saint have realized all is God, and nothing is separate from God.

In Sufism, what is lawful at one level of understanding may not be lawful at another. For example, the *sharia* requires only the outer practicing of fasting. However, according to the *tariqa*, an essential reason for fasting is to develop self-discipline and to control the insatiable ego. A fast that engenders pride in the one fasting is perfectly lawful in the *sharia* but would be considered a failure in the *tariqa.*

Other Sufi Practices

Sufism has no single practice. There are many other common practices which maintain the discipline of the heart. These practices support each other. As one begins to experience and move with heart, a world is discovered within of sensations that one may not have been allowing oneself to experience. Without Rumi's background, it is impossible to properly regard other Sufi spiritual practices involving movement, walking meditation and dance. To simply imitate certain whirling and circle movements in sacred dance performances without pursuing corresponding training in awareness and heart-awakening does nothing but introduce novelty and nervous energy into the psyche. Ritual dance and movement in Sufism do not begin with large expressions but with the smallest nuances of body awareness.

A. *Breathing*: Sufi teachers direct their students to experience the awareness of breathing as a link between where they feel limitation (*nafs*) and where they feel freedom (*fana*). When one feels ones' breathing centred in the heart, this sensation begins to represent the still-point, the place of silence within the conflicting demands one begins to feel. Awareness of breathing in all brings one an increasingly refined sense of body awareness. The student progresses from simple awareness of the breath while walking through awareness of the nuances of breath (its direction, duration and intensity), to a gradual release of the blocks to that inhibit movement and a fully human connection to life.

Breathing practices in the Sufi tradition both elicit greater awareness as well as interrupt habitual patterns that keep one separate from the breath of nature. In the use of these practices, one needs a teacher to ensure that one's habitual, neurotic patterns of breathing are not displaced onto the practice—thereby making the practice itself part of the problem. In the "dance of the breath", as well as the following movement practices, one aims to elicit altered states of awareness, which students then discover as elements of their natural awareness that they have enclosed or limited. The practices do not normally aim to produce "trance" (in the commonly understood sense), but at greater awareness of the interconnectedness of the divine, humanity and nature. In fact, in such states of awareness, the separate naming of these three becomes pointless.

B. ***Sound and Body Resonance*****:** As the breath becomes more perceptible and sensitive, one also becomes aware of the sensations in the body that occur as the breath becomes audible. Sufis place specific emphasis on feeling sound in heart area in order to integrate the feelings of above/below, known/unknown, light/dark. They believe that the resonance of certain phrases and words actually impels increasingly greater awareness of self and the divine. The Sufi science of *wazifa* (chanted phrases, including the 99 sacred "names" of Allah, the *sifat-i-Allah*) aims at engaging and awakening the feeling sense to small movements in the body which reveal both self and the divine within. These chants invoke qualities, like mercy, compassion and forgiveness, which can be awakened within one. The chants also include what Western psychology might call "shadow" qualities—shame, misdirection, confusion—in order to communicate with and acknowledge the whole range of feeling experienced by the *nafs*. According to one Sufi point of view, one misuses sound and chanting practices when they cause practitioners to enter trance states in which they become less aware of themselves as whole human beings.

C. ***Walking Meditation*****:** Murshid Samuel Lewis introduced modifications and refinements of traditional Sufi walking practices, which encouraged the ability to distinguish various states of awareness and control them. The walking meditation in the Sufi tradition encourages bridging the gap between the seemingly divine and seemingly commonplace. Teacher training in the Dances of Universal Peace always includes training in walking meditation. One source of these walking meditations is a traditional aphorism of the Naqshbandi Sufi order: "Look down and see whose feet are those that walk." In the introductory walking practices, the participant may be told simply to walk breathing "in the feet" or another part of the body, or to be aware of the rhythm of the breath. After becoming aware, one is enjoined to try a different rhythm by comparison, a different direction or intensity of breathing, or a different intention of feeling (for instance, walking toward a goal). One is asked to become aware of any changes in the inner state, and any thoughts or emotions that may arise.

The next step in refinement of the walking meditations involves concentration on breathing in different centres of the body or in attunement to the classical elements (earth, water, fire and air). This involves altering the direction, intensity and duration of the breathing and enlarging the body awareness to notice small differences of perception.

For instance, students may be encouraged to feel the elements as the body awareness of the bones/ligaments (earth), muscles/connective tissue (water), heart/lungs/bloodstream (fire) and skin (air). These somatic correspondences were adapted by Hazrat Inayat Khan (Khan, 1962) from traditional Sufi psychology. Research by the author has confirmed their usefulness in various therapeutic settings including substance abuse education. For instance, a heightened awareness of muscle/connective tissue seems to mimic the somatic effects of alcohol in some cases (Douglas-Klotz, 1986).

Advanced practice in walking meditation uses rhythms associated with the alchemical planets in combinations with elements. Further walking attunement practices encourage the experiences of *fana* by walking in a breath-movement connection with another person. All of these variations aim at releasing the natural breath and movement available to the participant, so that the devotion elicited by the dance and other practices is available in a useful way throughout life.

D. *Dance*: As one becomes aware of the movements within caused by breathing and sound, the prayers and sacred phrases so intoned or sung naturally cause one to begin to move the whole body in rhythm. This unity of intention and action is common to sacred dance in most spiritual traditions. In the Sufism tradition, one can categorize various types of movements and their effects.

The term "Sufi dancing" is a misnomer. The dances most often referred to were originally named the Dances of Universal Peace, and were first developed as a public form of sacred movement by the American

Sufi Ahmed Murad Chishti (Murshid Samuel L. Lewis, 1896-1971). The Dances of Universal Peace use movements derived from the practices of these orders as well as from a synthesis of spiritual dance techniques Lewis derived from his study with American sacred dance pioneer Ruth St. Denis (Lewis; 1986. St. Denis, 1996). Toward the end of his life, Lewis began to develop this form of circle dancing with awareness of breath, sound and movement, which he felt could be presented to the public as a means to expand one's sense of the self through devotion as well to promote "peace through the arts." In the later capacity, the Dances of Universal Peace use sacred phrases from most of the world's spiritual traditions, and participants are encouraged to feel the traditions uniting within themselves, in peace rather than at war. Variations of dances using folk-style partner movements encourage dancers to bring this experience into relationships with what the ego-self habitually sees as "others." This form of dance was done publicly and it is the form of imitation without feeling or training proliferated under the general rubric "Sufi dancing" The term "Sufi dancing" has sometimes come to mean any form of a circle dance with singing.

Sufi dancing demands training if pursued over a long period of time. Continued refinement of the breath and work with the personality is necessary. Proper teaching of each dance directs participants back to the feeling of the breathing and to the source of thoughts and emotions within.

Devotion must be transmuted from a dualistic experience to one in which the subconscious (*nafs*) is encouraged to develop in the atmosphere of acceptance, expansion and freedom that the dance creates. In this regard, specific applications of Sufi dances have been made for use therapeutically with various populations (for instance, developmentally disabled or substance abuse groups) or as well as in special education settings. The primary use of the Dances of Universal Peace remains that of an accessible form of devotional group dance in which the gap between participant and performer does not exist. From a psychological viewpoint, they combine movement, re-education, transpersonal therapy and community building in a unified form that transcends these names.

E. *Whirling and the Sema*: Most of the walking meditations developed by Murshid Samuel Lewis also have a counterpart turning practice. The act of turning or whirling with a certain concentration helps focus the breath and one's awareness of breathing within natural body awareness as the centre of balance. During turning, one can no longer visually spot without becoming dizzy, so attention is drawn to the centre or element upon which the awareness is focused. One develops by this an independent centre of balance that can lead to a sense of "being turned" rather than turning. As one proceeds further, this experience of "not-self" is again revealed to have a home within.

The Turkish Mevlevi order of Sufis also uses turning in a formalized ritual that has been exquisitely developed over the course of 600 years to commemorate the passing of the founding *pir* of the order, Jelaluddin Rumi. It was said that Rumi, upon learning of the death of his close friend and teacher, grabbed a pole in the marketplace and began to turn in both grief and ecstasy. Thereafter, he began to express the pinnacle of Persian mystical poetry in his writings.

In this formal turning or *sema*, one's attention must absolutely remain on the breath with a sub-vocalized form of *dhikr*. With arms upraised, one palm reaches up, the other down as the turning semazen presents the image of a funnel receiving from the heavens and giving to the earth. In his/her internal prayer, the semazen wishes to receive from the ultimate idealized divine and to bring this awareness fully into the body. The extensive training involved usually tests the subconscious *nafs* to the limit, but the beauty of the movement and music helps win its cooperation. As with other forms of Sufi movement, the so-called physical form of the Mevlevi turn is merely the doorway for exploring and re-evaluating one's beliefs, impressions and feelings about the self and God, as one goes through stages of *nafs* and *fana*. While this is the most "choreographed" of Sufi movement practices, its choreography is designed for inner effect first rather than its impression on the observer (Friedlander, 1975).

F. *Dhikr* (Remembrance): One of the Sufi spiritual practice is *Dhirkullah*, or Remembrance of God. *Dhikr* is a traditional form of chanting and movement practice used by most Sufi orders. Participants usually sing or chant some form of the Arabic phrase *La illahailla 'llahu* ("There is no god but God" or "There is no reality but Oneness") or portions thereof as a means of impressing the self with its origin and goal. *Dhikr* is performed in a variety of ways—seated, standing, moving in a circle or lines, and more or less vigorously depending on the Sufi order and the inspiration of the person leading the practice. Most orders reserve *dhikr* for initiates—those who have committed to a path of transformation through Sufism—although with more Sufi orders now establishing branches in the West, the practice is sometimes done publicly. Nevertheless, there are good reasons to be conservative in this regard. Because *dhikr* does not focus on qualities (like *wazifa*), but on the essence of unity, it may not be initially understood or assimilated by the subconscious and there may be more energy evoked than the body can assimilate without preparation.

Remembrance of God fuels our devotion and services. The Sufis seek constant remembrance, never forgetting that we are in God's presence, constantly feeling God within us. As God says in the *Qur'an,* "I am closer to you than your own jugular vein." Prayer is practiced of remembrance, as is mediation, spiritual chanting, and spiritual study. This practice varies with different Sufi orders, but it generally includes repetition of one or more of the ninety-nine Divine Names.

Devotion to God

Sufism has been called the "Path of the heart." Great Sufi Poets have written eloquently of the soul's love and longing for God, the Beloved. A Sufi master described this love as follows:

"The eye of the dervish who is true lover naught but God; his heart knows naught but Him. God is the eye by which he sees, the hand with which he holds, and the tongue with which he speaks....... were he not in love, he would pass away. If his heart should be devoid of love for as much as a single moment, the dervish could not stay alive. Love is the dervish's life, his health, his comfort. Love ruins the dervish, makes him weep; union makes him flourish, brings him to life."

The great Sufi poet Rumi described love as the only force that could transcend the bounds of reason, the distinction of knowledge, and the isolation of normal consciousness. The love he experienced was not sensual pleasure. It might be more aptly described as love for all things, for creation itself. Love is continually expanding capacity that culminates in certainty, in the recognition that in truth all beings are both loved and loving.

Since hearing of the world of love,
I have given my life, my heart,
And my eyes this way.
At first I believed that love
And beloved is different.
Now, I know they are the same. (Rumi)

The perception of God as the beloved, common to both Christian and Sufi writings, comes from mystical experience. As you channel your energy into loving God, there appears to be a response of being loved in return. Just as in a personal relationship saying, if you take two steps towards God, there appears to be a response of being loved in return. Just as in as personal relationship, the act of loving brings forth or awakens love in the other. According to an old Sufi saying, if you take two steps towards God, God runs to you.

A modern Sufi master observes: "The essences of God are love and the Sufi Path is a path of love.......love is to see what is good and beautiful in everything. It is to learn from everything, to see the gifts of God and generosity of God in everything. It is to be thankful for all God's bounties."

Sufis believe that when we come to certain point along the path of love, God reaches out and begins to assist us by drawing us toward God's presences. As this occurs, we stop striving and begin to surrender, to allow ourselves to be helped and be taken in.

Services

A service is the main practice in Sufism. As our hearts open with love of God, we realize that all hearts yearn for God, and God is hidden in every heart. Once we realize that every heart contains God, then, as an essential aspect of our spiritual journey, we have to service others.

One of the greatest services is to help heal the injured hearts of others. A Sufi master taught that every kind word or glance softens your hearts and every hurtful word or act close or harden your heart". To ignore God in the heart, of others is to separate ourselves from the union we so devoutly desire.

If someone sits with me
And we talk about the beloved,
If I cannot give his heart comfort,
If I cannot make him feel better
About himself and this world,
Then, Hafiz,
Quickly run to the mosque and pray—
For you have just committed
The only sin I know. (Hafiz in Frager, 1999 :187)

Conclusion

Sufism is an ancient tradition. It has not become so popular in the discipline of psychology because it is burdened with old ideas and practices, and it has taken so many forms. Sufism is presented here as a theory of Self and a way of spiritual practices. In the contemporary world, it seems to be responsive to new cultural demands. There is a need to modify its methods and to provide understanding to the new generation of psychologists who can involve themselves in the development of a theory of personality and to integrate spiritual practices into therapy.

In the concept of 'Self' in Sufism, we find a detailed and subtle view of the psyche. For this reason, grand psychological "theories of self" seem to fail as they either trivialize a profound reality that cannot fully be made conscious or else fabricate another orthodoxy that becomes philosophical dogma.

In India, Sufi practices are not limited to Muslims; rather these are practiced by people of all religious faith. In pluralistic societies, forms of *dhikr* have evolved which use a variety of movements appropriate to both men and women. Sufism is a well travelled route that anyone can follow. We need to adopt Sufi practices to understand and practice completely to become peace-loving men who can change the way we look at to maintain harmony. Sufism as a practice is an expression of love and gratitude. And love and gratitude are the qualities of the 'Loving Heart.'

References

Al-Ghazzali, M. (1972). *The Revival of Religious Sciences* (B. Behari, Trans.). Farnham, Surrey, England: Sufi.

Arasteh, A.R. (1973). Psychology of the Sufi way to individuation. In L.F. Rushbrook Williams (ed.), *Sufi Studies: East and West* (pp. 89-113). New York: Dutton.

Arasteh, A.R. and Sheikh, A. (1989). Sufism: the way to universal self. In A. Sheikh and Sheikh (Eds.), *Eastern and Western Approaches to Healing*. New York: Wiley.

Arberry, A.J. (1966). *The Doctrine of the Sufis*. Lahore, Pakistan: Shri Muhammad Ashraf. (Also, Cambridge: Cambridge University Press, 1977)

Beg, M.A. (1970). A note on the concept of self, and the theory and practice of psychological help in the Sufi Tradition. *Interpersonal Development, 1*, 58-64.

Douglas-Klotz, N. (1984). Sufi Approaches to transformational movement. *Somatics, 5*(1), 44.

Frager, R. (1999). *Heart, Self, and Soul: the Sufi Psychology of Growth, Balance, and Harmony*. Wheaton, IL: Quest Books.

Frager, R., and Fadiman, J. (2007). *Personality and Personal Growth*. Dorling Kindersley (India) Pvt. Ltd., Pearson Education in South Asia.

Friedlander, I. (1975). *The Whirling Dervishes*. New York: Collier Books.

Ibn 'Arabi, M. (1981). *Journey to the Lord of Power* (R. Harris, Trans.). New York: Inner Tradition.

Khan, H.I. (1962). *The Sufi Message* (Vols. 5). *Metaphysics*. Katwijk, Holland: Servire Publishers.

Lewis, S.L. (1986). *Sufi vision and initiation: Meetings with remarkable beings.* In N. Douglas-Klotz (Ed.). *Sufi Islamia/Prophecy*. San Francisco.

Lewis, S.L. (1991). *Spiritual Dance and Walk: An Introduction*, Seattle. Peace Works.

Nurbakhsh, J. (1992). *The Psychology of Sufism*. New York: Khaniqahi-nimatullahi.

Ozak, M. (Al-jerrahi). (1981). *The Unveiling of Love*. (M. Holland, Trans.). New York: Inner Tradition.

Ozak, M. (Al-jerrahi). (1987). *Love is the Wine*. (Edited and compiled by Sheikh R. Frager Al-jerrahi). Putney, VT: Threshold Books.

Qadri, M.A. (2003). What is Tasawwuf ? An answer by Hadrat Ali bin uthman al-Hajweri known as Hadrat Data Ganj Buksh, www.iecrcna.org/publication/articles/Tasawwuf_Data_Ganj_Baksh.pdf.

Rumi, Jalal al-Din. (1972). *Discourses of Rumi* (A.J. Arberry, Trans.). New York: Weister.

Ruth, St. Denis (1996). *Wisdom comes dancing: Selected writings of Ruth St. Denis and Kamae A. Miller* (ed.) Seattle: Peace Works.

Shafii, M. (1974). *The Development Stage in Man and Sufism and Psychoanalysis.* Unpublished manuscript.

Trimingham (1971). *El on Tasawwuf;* Hodgson (1974: vol. 2, pp. 201-54).

4

Ayodhya: Ramajanmabhumi *v/s* Babri Masjid Dispute Towards Peaceful Solution

Ram Kalap Tiwari

Introduction

Ayodhya is an ancient city of India, the old capital of Awadh, in the current Faizabad district of Uttar Pradesh. Ayodhya is the birthplace of Hindu God Shri Rama, and the capital of Kosala Kingdom. This Hindu holy city is described as early as in the Hindu Epics. During the time of Gautama Buddha the city was called *Ayojjha* (*Pali*). Under Muslim rule, it was the seat of the Governor of Awadh, and later during the British Raj the city was known as Ajodhya or Ajodhia and was part of the United Provinces of Agra and Oudh, it was also the seat of a small '*talukdari*' state. It is on the right bank of the river Sarayu. The Sarayu river winds its way from the Nepalese border across the plains of north India. Not long before its churning gray waters meet the mighty Ganga, it flows past the town of Ayodhya.

The word Ayodhya is Sanskrit for "not to be warred against". Some *Puranas* like the *Brahmanda Purana* consider Ayodhya as one of the six holiest cities in Hinduism. The ancient city of Ayodhya was one of the most ancient, largest and most magnificent of Indian cities and the holiest of the world. *Skand* and some other *Puranas* rank Ayodhya as one of the seven most sacred cities of India. It was the venue of many an event in Hindu history, today preeminently a temple town. This city was also a significant trade centre in 600 B.C.

Historical Evidence

The city of Ayodhya has undeniably been a city of great antiquity and a sacred spot to the Hindus for a long time. Giving the location of the city on the bank of river Sarayu, and describing its area, prosperity and glory, Valmiki has said in his *Ramayana*:

कोशलो नाम मुदितः स्फीतो जनपदो महान्।
निविष्टः सरयूतीरे प्रभूतधनधान्यवान्।।
अयोध्या नाम नगरी तत्रासील लोकविश्रुता।
मनुना मानवेन्द्रेण या पुरी निर्मिता स्वयम्।।
आयता दश च द्वे च योजनानि महापुरी।
श्रीमती त्रीणि विस्तीर्णा सुविभक्तमहापथा।।

Many *Puranas* attest the fact that Ayodhya was considered one of the six holiest of the holy cities. To quote one:

अयोध्या–मथुरा–माया–काशी–कांची ह्दवन्तिका।
एताः पुण्यतमाः प्रोक्ताः पुरीणामुत्तमोत्तमाः।।

In all Hindu scriptures since Valmiki, Ayodhya figures prominently and Lord Rama is referred to as an *avatar* of the Vishnu. Veda Vyasa incorporated the story of Rama through the *Ramopakhyana* in the *Vanparva* of his epic *Mahabharata*. The earliest sanskrit dramatist Bhasa who lived before the advent of Christ, wrote his dramas *Pratima* and *Abhisheka* based on the life of Rama. Identifying Rama with his *archanavatar*, he writes:

नमो भगवते त्रैलोक्यकारणाय नारायणाय
ब्रह्मा ते हृदयं जगतत्रयपते रूद्रश्च कोपस्तव
नेत्रे चन्द्रदिवाकरौ सुरपते जिह्वा च ते भारती।
सब्रह्मेन्द्रमरूद्रगणं त्रिभुवनं सृष्टं त्वयैव प्रभो
सीतेयं जलसम्भवालयरता विष्णुर्भवान् गृह्यताम्।।

The town's residents included both Muslims and Hindus. But most noticeable were the Hindu holy men known as *sadhus*, with painted foreheads, long beards and loose robes. They flocked there, as they do today.

According to the *Ramayana*, Ayodhya was founded by Manu, the law-giver of the Hindus. For centuries it was the capital of the descendants of the Surya dynasty, of which Lord Rama was the most celebrated king. Based on the records, it is said to have covered an area of 250 km^2 (96 square miles), and was the capital of the Hindu kingdom of Kosala (Kaushal), the court of the great king Dasaratha, the 63rd monarch of the Solar line. The opening chapters of the *Ramayana* recount the magnificence of the city, the glories of the monarch and the virtues, wealth and loyalty of his people. Dasaratha was the father of Rama, the seventh *avatar* of the Vishnu. It is here that Shri Rama was born.

Ayodhya, like other Indian cities, was the victim of pillage and sacking during the Ghaznavi raids and Ghori invasions. Hindu temples were allegedly looted or destroyed. The cultural fabric was totally destroyed. With Muslim rulers established around the city under Mohammed of Ghor, it lost its strategic and economic importance to Lucknow and Kanpur.

Ayodhya today is a small, rustic city with ancient Hindu architecture predominating, and with some Mughal influence. Its population is mostly Hindu with a minority of Muslims, Jains and Buddhists. However, its history and heritage hold an unequivocal importance for Hindus.

In the fifth century A.D., the town of Saketa was renamed Ayodhya by Gupta king, Skanda Gupta, who moved his residence there. Thus, what may have been the fictional Ayodhya of the epic poem was identified with Saketa quite late. This does not suggest that Gupta king was a *bhakta* of lord Rama. In bestowing the name of Ayodhya to Saket he was trying to gain prestige for himself by drawing on the tradition of Suryavamsi king, a lineage to which Rama is said to have belonged.

Archaeological Evidence

In 1949, as it is today, Ayodhya was a quiet town of temples, narrow byways, wandering cows and the ancient, mossy walls of *ashrams* and shrines. Our archaeological evidence comes from the excavations conducted in the area immediately south of and adjacent to the Babri mosque. Here the fieldwork was conducted from 1975 through 1980 by the Archaeological Survey of India under the direction of Prof. B.B. Lal. The excavations have revealed the existence of a series of burnt-brick pillar-bases at regular intervals. These are found arranged in parallel rows in the directional alignment in which a number of black-stone pillars are existing in the mosque. Archaeological evidence of "robber's trench" clearly proves that some of the bricks from the pillar-bases were intentionally removed by those who destroyed the temple. However, stratigraphical evidence proves that these pillar-bases were built in the 11th century and they continued to be in use till the end of the 15th century. From immediately below the topmost floor, which apparently belongs to the general floor of the mosque, archaeologists have recovered a variety of Islamic Glazed Wares which are dated to different periods between the 13th and 15th centuries. Evidently, the temple belonged to the period immediately before the construction of the mosque.

There is no archeological evidence to show that at this early time the region around present day Ayodhya was inhabited. The earliest possible date for settlement at the site are of about eighth century B.C. The archaeological remains indicate a fairly simple material life, more primitive than what is described in Valmiki's *Ramayana.*

Nobody can be certain about the historicity of Rama or the existence of Ayodhya in 4000 B.C. when Lord Rama is supposed to have lived, same applies to the location of Ayodhya. It will be worthwhile to note that the Rama cult in Ayodhya is a fairly late development. Ayodhya has been a focal point of many religions—Buddhism, Jainism and Hinduism. From about fifth century B.C. fairly large Buddhist community was living in Ayodhya. Though this religion suffered a setback during first millennium A.D. several remnants of its existence did survive. (Hiuen Tsang, Quoted in Hans Baker, 1986:38). According to Jain tradition Ayodhya was the birthplace of the first and fourth *Tirthankara.* The early places of Hindu worship of Ayodhya were of Shaiva or Vishnu provenance. The specific worship of Rama even as an *avatar* of the Vishnu is a much later development.

Rama was born precisely on that spot is a question of faith so temple should be built there operates entirely on different level. Faith cannot be the basis of history. The facts of history alone guide us about these issues. Resorting to faith can be a very dangerous game and there can be politically motivated faiths also as in this case there was no controversy on this issue before the British rule and also the same had died down after the independence. It was revived and given the coating of faith etc. for goals, which have nothing to do with the religion etc.

No evidence exists in the texts that before the 16th Century (and indeed before 18th Century) any veneration attached to the spot in Ayodhya for being the birth site of Rama. The legend that the Babri Masjid occupied the site of Rama's birth did not arise until late 18th century;

that a temple was destroyed to build the mosque was not asserted until the beginning of 19th century. The full-blown legend of destruction of the temple at the site of Rama's birth and Sita-ki-Rasoi is as late as the 1850s. Since then what we get is merely the progressive reconstruction of 'imagined history' based on faith.

Ayodhya was once projected as a symbol of grave assault on Hindu faith itself. By referring to Muslims as *Babur Ki Santan* (Children of Babur), the Muslim community as a whole was held responsible for acting against Hindu faith. Ayodhya thus became the site for constructing the Hindu solidarity and avenging the Muslim wrong.

The dispute over Ramajanmabhumi-Babri Masjid, it is said, is creation of the colonial rule. It is difficult to be very sure on how far direct is the hand of the colonial rule in inventing and or sustaining the dispute between some elements from both the communities. However, there is little doubt that the colonial rule benefited from the dispute and therefore, did not seem to take effective steps to see the dispute resolved. The authorities under the Colonial rule allowed the dispute over title of the land to acquire communal overtones. Whatever the former colonial masters did, or omitted to do, the post-Colonial state fared even worst in the matter. Post-Colonial State allowed the dispute over the land title to almost completely polarize the two communities. Essentially, a title suit between the plaintiffs and the defendants over a piece of land was allowed to acquire religious and communal colour with competing all India mobilizations by political leadership belonging to both the communities.

There are no two opinions that in the year 1528 a mosque was built by Mir Baqi by one of the Governors of the Mughal Emperor Babar. The Sangh Parivar maintains that this mosque was built after destroying a Ramajanmabhumi temple, which existed on the land whereas the Muslim political leaders as well as most reputed historians of integrity insist that there is no credible proof that there was any Ramajanmabhumi temple.

It must have been the best way to forget the effects of the politically motivated demolition of Babri mosque on 6th December, 1992. The demolition, a well planned offensive brought many tragedies not only to the country but also to the residents of Ayodhya. Since the launch of agitation to build Rama temple, the repeated campaigns disturbed the peace and amity in Ayodhya. While it is claimed to be the birthplace of Rama, there are ample records to show that Ayodhya was a sort of no war zone. It has been the place of importance for Muslims as they believe it is the place of two of their Major Prophets, Hazrat Shish and Hazrat Nuh. The Sufi shrines in this area are a place of major attraction for people of all the religions.

Many a social workers focused on Ayodhya to build the community bridges and in due course local platform for peace and amity made the voice of Ayodhya heard all-over the country. The local populations also pointed out that how can the communalists decide the fate of Ayodhya? It is they who live there and so the future plans of Ayodhya have to be drawn by them. While the loss of lives and property due to the post-demolition violence was difficult to heal, the focus was on peace in the city.

Apart from many other initiatives, the intercommunity mingling between Hindus and Muslims were promoted by Ayodhya ki Awaj, Asha, and many other Gandhian groups. This had remarkable effect on the city's life. It was best seen in the form of organization of *Roza Iftaar* at Hanuman Garhi temple, the temple of eminence in the city. This experiment in intercommunity living was a pleasant one for all except the communalists, who sowed the seeds of discord amongst the organizers and this experiment had to be stopped. But the seeds of amity sowed by this experiment of *Roza Iftar* at Hanuman Garhi temple went on and communities devised other mechanisms to live shoulder to shoulder. In the same direction, many a seminars, lectures and workshops were organized in Ayodhya, and this cemented the community bonds further, these acted to remove the misconceptions about each other and brought back the pre-demolition atmosphere of amity.

Matter of Faith

The issue in the title suit of the Ramajanmabhumi case was who owns the structure of, and the land on which Babri Masjid once stood. The RSS brought in the issue of faith as they were not confident of winning the title suit. It cannot be disputed that the Masjid was Waqf property for more than 420 years when the title suit was filed in 1949. Assuming that Lord Rama was born (only on the basis of faith of RSS and their affiliated organisations) on the spot where Babri Masjid stood and further assuming that there was a Ramajanmabhumi temple on the spot, law of adverse possession would come into play and the title would pass on to the Waqf Board on the ground that undisputedly, they have the possession of the land and the structure of Babri Masjid for over 12 years. The Sangh Parivar started forcefully contending only on the basis of their faith that Lord Rama was born on that very spot where there was a Ramajanmabhumi Mandir and the Mandir was demolished to construct Babri Masjid. The Sangh Parivar led mobilization did succeed in getting the Allahabad High Court to frame the issue of "whether there was a Ramajanmabhumi temple prior to the construction of Babri Masjid" for trial of the Title suit. The issue is otherwise irrelevant in deciding the Title suit. That is why the Archaeological Survey of India was ordered to dig Masjid precincts and their report has been submitted to the Court. However, it is doubtful if anything was found. Judgements of courts in secular states are not given on the basis of faith. If faith is made central to governance, conflicts will increase due to religious and sectarian diversity that exists in India. India with much more diversity has survived only because it did not make faith central to its governance.

The first suit regarding the structure was filed in 1885, when the Faizabad Deputy Commissioner refused to let Mahant Raghubar Das build a temple on land adjoining the mosque. Das then filed a title suit in a Faizabad court against the Secretary of State for India, seeking permission to build a temple on the Chabutra on the outer courtyard of the Babri Masjid. The legal battle over the title has gone on for over a century.

Dispute Progress

- **1859:** The British colonial administration erects a fence at the site to separate the places of worship. While the Muslims are allowed to use the inner court, the Hindus are allowed the outer court.
- **1885:** In January 1885, Mahant Raghubir Das files the first case, seeking permission to build a canopy on the Ramachabutra (a raised platform) outside the mosque. The plea is rejected by the Faizabad District Court.
- **1949:** Idols of Rama Lalla are placed surreptitiously under the central dome. Lord Rama's idols appear inside the mosque, allegedly placed by Hindu groups. Both sides file suits; the government declares the area as disputed and locks the gates to the premise.
- **1950:** Gopal Simla Visharad files first suit in Faizabad civil court for rights to perform *puja* to Rama Lalla.
- **1950:** Paramahansa Ramachandra Das files a suit for continuation of *puja* and keeping idols in the structure.
- **1959:** Nirmohi Akhara files third suit, seeking direction to hand over charge of the disputed site. U.P. Sunni Central Wakf Board files fourth suit in 1961 for declaration and possession and fifth in 1989 in the name of Ram Lalla Virajman for declaration and possession.

- **1961:** The Sunni Central Board of Waqf files a case against the placing of idols inside the mosque and claim that the mosque and surrounding land was a graveyard.
- **1984:** Hindu groups form a committee to spearhead the construction of the Rama temple at the Janmabhumi site. The temple movement gathers momentum. Bharatiya Janata Party (BJP) leader L.K. Advani takes over the leadership of the movement.
- **1986:** District judge orderes locks be removed. Site opened for Hindu worshippers.
- **1989:** The four suits pending were transferred to the High Court. The Vishwa Hindu Parishad (VHP) lays the foundation of a Rama temple on the land next to the Babri Masjid. Justice Deoki Nandan Agarwal, former VHP Vice-President, files a case asking for the mosque to be shifted elsewhere. Four suits that have been pending at the Faizabad court are transferred to a special bench of the High Court.
- **1990:** Volunteers of the VHP partially damage the mosque. The than Prime Minister Chandrashekhar intervenes and tries to resolve the issue through negotiations, but these fail. In September, Advani holds a *Rath Yatra* to educate people about the Ayodhya movement. He starts from Somnath in Gujarat, and ends his *Yatra* at Ayodhya.
- **1991:** U.P. Government acquires land around the structure for convenience of devotees who attend Rama Lalla darshan.
- **December 1992:** Babri Masjid demolished by a frenzied mob of *karsevaks*. Two FIRs filed in the Babri Masjid demolition case. Crime no. 197 deals with actual "demolition of the mosque by *karsevaks*." Crime no. 198 named L.K. Advani, Murli Manohar Joshi and others for 'communal' speeches before the demolition.
- **1993:** Government takes over 67 acres of land around the area, seeks SC's opinion on whether there existed a Hindu place of worship before the structure was built.
- **October, 1993:** CBI files a composite charge sheet and accuses Advani and other leaders of 'conspiracy'.
- **1994:** Case goes back to Lucknow Bench of HC, suits heard again from 1996.
- **May 4, 2001:** Special Judge S.K. Shukla drops conspiracy charge against 13 accused, including Mr. Advani and Kalyan Singh. Bifurcates Crimes 197 and 198.

- **May 20, 2010:** Advani, others absolved of conspiracy charges.
- **September 30, 2010:** Allahabad High Court awards two-thirds of Ayodhya site to Hindu parties, one-third to Waqf Board.
- **February, 2011:** CBI moves Supreme Court. Argues that "the actual demolition of the Babri Masjid and the continuous assault on media persons form a single connected transaction and can well be a concerted conspiracy".
- **May 9, 2011:** Supreme Court stays Allahabad High Court verdict on Ayodhya dispute.
- **December 25, 2014:** Oldest litigant Mohammad Farooq in Babri Masjid case passes away, a resident of Ayodhya, was one of the seven main litigants from Muslim side in the 1949 Babri Masjid case.
- **March 6, 2017:** Supreme Court indicates it may revive conspiracy charge and order a joint trial of crimes 197 and 198.
- **March 21, 2017:** Suggesting an out-of-court rapprochement among rival parties in the 68-year-old Ramajanmabhumi-Babri Masjid title dispute, Chief Justice of India J.S. Khehar advised peace negotiations instead of a pitched court battle, even offering help to settle the fight amicably.
- **March 23, 2017:** A Supreme Court Bench of Justices P.C. Ghose and Rohinton Nariman posted for detailed hearing the CBI appeal against the dropping of the criminal conspiracy charge against veteran BJP leader L.K. Advani and other top party leaders after two weeks.
- **April 6, 2017:** The Supreme Court indicated that it will use its extraordinary powers under Article 142 of the Constitution to transfer the Babri Masjid demolition related trial in Rae Bareilly against top BJP leaders L.K. Advani and Murli Manohar Joshi to Lucknow, where a CBI court is hearing conspiracy and other serious criminal charges against "lakhs of unknown *kar sevaks*" for the actual act of razing down the 15th century mosque.
- **April 19, 2017:** The Supreme Court revived conspiracy charges against L.K. Advani, Murli Manohar Joshi and 13 others in the 25-year-old Babri Masjid demolition case.
- **May 30, 2017:** L.K. Advani, Murli Manohar Joshi, Uma Bharti and Vinay Katiyar charged with criminal conspiracy in the Babri Masjid demolition case.
- **August 8, 2017:** Uttar Pradesh Shia Central Waqf Board tells Supreme Court that they would settle for a masjid located in a

"Muslim-dominated area at a reasonable distance from the most revered place of birth of Maryada Purushottam Sri Ram." They tell the Court that the Babri Masjid was a Shia waqf (endowment) and their Sunni counterpart, who have been at the frontline of the 70-year-old title dispute, were mere interlopers led by "hardliners, fanatics and non-believers" who do not want an amicable settlement with the Hindu sects involved.

- **August 11, 2017:** Supreme Court schedules hearing of 13 appeals in the Ramajanmabhumi-Babri Masjid title dispute on December 5, 2017, the eve of the 25th anniversary of the demolition of the 15th century mosque.

The need is to defeat communal politics and peace should be the outcome. Unless justice is done there is no peace. Justice must be done in accordance with the existing laws and not on basis of faith, as there are faiths and faiths, and all faiths must be equally respected.

References

Elst, K. (1990). *Ram Janmabhoomi* Vs *Babri Masjid*, Voice of India Pub., p. 173.

Elst, K. (1991). *Ayodhya and After: Issues Before Hindu Society*, Voice of India, p. 419.

Sharma, Y.D., *et al.*, (1992). *Ram Janma Bhoomi—New Archaeological Evidence*, Historians' Forum, New Delhi.

Justice Deoki Nandan. *Legal Aspects of RJB/BM issue*.

Ayodhya, Sacred Hinduism.

SECTION III
Hindu Culture and Acculturation

5

Triyoga and Triguna in Bhagavad Gita: An Empirical Validation

Anubhuti Dubey and *Laxmi Vajpeyi*

Introduction

In the course of development of psychology, in contemporary period a number of Asian, African, Russian, and South American psychologists set off confronting and rebuffing the supremacy of the self-pronounced universal, hegemonic, Euro-American, or Western Academic Scientific Psychology. The related observations have been articulated against the mainstream Indian Academic Psychology as it is also the imported, transplanted, and marginally adapted Western Psychology. The mounting discontentment with the radical behaviourist, purely empirical and exclusive natural science tradition in Western psychology has prompted the search for alternative paradigms. With the growing insight that many of the Western psychological concepts and methods are deficient in relevance to diverse cultural systems; the need for developing indigenous psychologies was recognized all-over the world (Kim & Berry, 1993).

In India, Psychology is known as *Manastattva*, *Manovijnana*, *Manovidya*, and/or *Manas-shastra*. The synthetic and comprehensive Indian psycho-spiritual worldview, derived from the *Vedas, Upanishads*, and the diverse Indian intellectual traditions, held that *"Mind is Brahman, the whole universe is in the mind only, and mind is all. Mind is everything, mind is all powerful, know the mind, control the mind, conquer the mind, and transcend the mind etc."*

Three marked tributaries of Indian Psychology justified to be identified as indigenous psychologies of India are—(1) the *Vedas,*

Upanishads, Puranas, Shastras, Gita, Ayurveda, Tantras, Jyotisha and *Kavyas* provide the foundation and intuition as the method for the classical Indian Psychologies; (2) the ages-old collective experiential knowledge base underlying the diverse mores and folkways, lifestyles, rituals and customs, attitudes, values, beliefs, totems and taboos, the folk literature and folk arts of the peoples of India provide the foundation for the Indian Folk Psychologies and (3) the indigenized academic psychology consists of importing the concepts, theories, and methods and replicating, adapting, standardizing and modifying them to fit to the local cultural context. Hence, in India, efforts have been executed to develop indigenous models and theories from the rich source of knowledge viz., the *Vedas, Upanishads,* the *Bhagavad Gita* and other philosophical texts. The Vedic narratives are full of knowledge about all spheres of human enterprises like from physics and psychology to medicine, art and aeronautics (Goswami, 1977). Thus, the pragmatic validation of the *Vedas* could uncover the warehouses of wisdom in many matters of life.

The various Indian schools of thought such as *Nyaya, Vaisheshika, Samkhya, Yoga, Mimamsa, Vedanta,* Buddhism, Jainism, Sufism etc. are a treasury of very rich analysis of psychological processes of mind-body interaction. In the past decades, much has been written and some had been done about the state, type, extent and sources of indigenization of psychology in India.

Indian Psychology is a complex subject variously viewed as esoteric and spiritual, philosophical and speculative, practical and ritualistic, and of course, as we believe, systematic and scientific understanding of human nature. Psychology in India is in such an apologetic state that it is widely felt that it needs to take a roundabout turn, look back into its own tradition, and learn from it; Western psychology itself is seen as being severely restrictive in its assumptive base and consequently unable to accommodate for study and investigation of a variety of phenomena of considerable human concern; some native Indian psycho-developmental techniques and personal transformation practices and strategies like meditation have become popular in the West, but they also have been subjected to serious scientific scrutiny, raising the expectation that what were once considered esoteric phenomena are now amenable for scientific investigation.

Indian Psychology is not merely conceptual or theoretical. Its therapeutic value is in its various teaching methods of mental integration. It prescribes systems of physical and mental discipline, which gradually stabilize the mind and integrate the emotions. This state of mind is considered essential because a restless mind cannot attain knowledge and a life of tensions is devoid of joy. The focus of most systems of psychology in Asia is the concern for emancipation of the seif. Systems differ in details.

Personality in Indian Psychology

Indian psychology holds that human personality goes deeper than what the empirical sciences have penetrated. Ancient Indian thinkers were characteristically synthetic in their views, intuitive in their approach, and, therefore, alive to the futility of purely empirical investigation. (See *Isha Upanishad*). *"It is the one God hidden in all beings and pervading all things. It is the self within all creatures, the ordainer/overseer of all actions, the dweller in all beings, the witness, the knower, the lonely, the one who is devoid of all qualities"*, says the *Shvetashvetara Upanishad.*

Thus, it can be stated that the concept of personality in Indian Psychology is a kind of dialectical advance that explicates remarkable promises and possibilities. The conception of personality as figured in different systems can give a very sound alternative paradigm to existing concept of personality and its realization. The Vedanta Psychology of Personality, the *Bhagavad Gita*, integrating and synthesize the essence of *Samkhya, Vedanta,* and *Yoga,* present unique classification of personality.

Concept of Triyoga

The *Bhagavad Gita* a major Indian text literally means *Song of the Absolute.* It is a conversation between Arjuna and Krishna that happens around 3000 B.C. in the combat zone of *Mahabharata.* Krishna epitomizes the Supreme Being and Arjuna symbolizes an ordinary creature similar to us. The entire science of *Yoga* is uncovered in the course of Arjuna's questions and Krishna's answers. It illustrates the concept of *Yoga* in a logical manner as it enlightens the people about how to go along with the *Yoga* processes and product of various practices as well. The *Bhagavad Gita* presents an elaborate analysis of the human mind from the context of a foundational philosophy of active living.

> "The language of the Gita, the structure of thought, the combinations and balancing of ideas belongs neither to the temper of a sectarian teacher nor to the spirit of a rigorous analytical dialectics cutting off one angle of the truth to exclude all the others; but rather there is a wide, undulating, encircling

movement of ideas which is the manifestation of a vast synthetic mind and a rich synthetic experience" (Aurobindo, 1970).

The *Bhagavad Gita* and other treatises have described at length the prototype of the person who has attained such a state. The person is said to characterize by such qualities as peace, happiness, calmness, contentment and compassion. This can be attained by controlling one's senses and desires, and by exercising restraint over one's mental activities. Such control makes possible the attainment of insight into the true nature of reality. In the words of Radhakrishnan (1977: 7): *The Gita is specially suited for the purpose, as it attempts to reconcile varied and apparently antithetical forms of the religious consciousness and emphasizes the root conceptions of religion which is neither ancient nor modern but eternal and belongs to the very flesh of humanity, past, present and future.*

Yoga has an elongated times of yore. It has been estimated that *yoga* dates back to Tantric civilization that was present all-over the world 10,000 years ago (Swami Satyananda Saraswati, 1996). Ever since, it has advanced incessantly up to contemporary era. Throughout this extensive span of time, the term 'yoga' has been utilized with diverse subtext (*see* Apte, 1970), and various kinds of *yoga* have come into existence. Possibly, the most primitive transcript, that deals with *yoga* in illustrious description, and furnishes taxonomy, is *Bhagavad Gita*. Some distinct manipulations of the term yoga are as follows—(i) to assign "a means of salvation or liberation", that is *yoga* as distinguished with *Samkhya*; (ii) as a suffix to refer to the "method or means", in *jñāna-yoga* which is also referred to *buddhi-yoga*) and *karma-yoga*; (iii) to signify "action, effort, and discipline"; (iv) to refer to a "state of equanimity"; and (v) as a "knack full act" (Edgerton, 1965; Rama, 1996). These diverse meanings have been employed in Indian tradition in various manuscripts and treatises, and thus the meaning of *yoga* is context-sensitive.

The title of each of the 18 chapters of *Bhagavad Gita* ends with the word *Yoga*, as each chapter deliberates a distinctive mode of uniting with the Supreme. These are as follows—

(1) ***Vishada Yoga*** — the Path of Dejection.
(2) ***Samkhya Yoga*** — the Path of Analysis.
(3) ***Karma Yoga*** — the Path of Action.
(4) ***Jnana Yoga*** — the Path of Knowledge.
(5) ***Karma-Vairagya Yoga*** — the Path of Renunciation of Action.
(6) ***Abhyasa Yoga*** — the Path of Practice (of Self-Control).

(7) ***Ashtanga Yoga*** — the Path of the Eightfold Mystic Processes [(e.g. *yama* (don'ts), *niyamas* (do's), *asana* (postures), *pranayama* (breath control), *pratyahara* (withdrawal of senses), *dharana* (concentration), *dhyana* (meditation) and *samadhi* (trance)].
(8) ***Paramahamsa Vijñāna Yoga*** — the Path of Realization of the Ultimate Truth.
(9) ***Akshara-Parabrahman Yoga*** — the Path of Imperishable Brahman.
(10) ***Raja-Vidya-Guhya Yoga*** — the Path of the Most Secret of Royal Knowledge.
(11) ***Vibhuti-Vistara-Yoga*** — the Path of Manifestation of Opulence (of the Absolute).
(12) ***Vishvarupa-Darshana Yoga*** — the Path of Vision of the Universal Form.
(13) ***Kshetra-Kshetrajna Vibhaga Yoga*** — the Path of Fields and the Knower of the Fields.
(14) ***Gunatraya-Vibhaga Yoga*** — the Path of the Three Divisions of Modes (e.g. *Sattva* or the mode of goodness, *Rajas* or the mode of passion and *Tamas* or the mode of ignorance).
(15) ***Purushottama Yoga*** — the Path of the Supreme Enjoyer.
(16) ***Daivasura-Sampad-Vibhaga Yoga*** — the Path of Divine and Demoniac Qualities.
(17) ***Shraddhatraya-Vibhaga Yoga*** — the Path of the Three Divisions of Faith (e.g. goodness, passion and ignorance).
(18) ***Moksha-Opadesha Yoga*** — the Path of Advice for Liberation.

Among all these *Yoga* systems, three are believed to be foremost, namely, *Jñāna Yoga, Karma Yoga,* and *Bhakti Yoga*. The first six chapters of *Bhagavad Gita* deal principally with *Karma Yoga*, the next six with *Bhakti Yoga* and the last six with *Jnana Yoga*.

Karma Yoga in Bhagavad Gita

"*Karma*" comes from the Sanskrit root *kri*, which means to act, do, or make. It is the same as the Latin verb *ago* from whose form, *actus,* we get our English words act and action. Both verbs are "all purpose" words—that is, they can be applied in many situations to express the idea of many forms of action both mental and physical. This is important to know so we can realize that *karma yoga* covers the entire range of human action that is beneficial. Lord declared *Karma yoga* to be the superior discipline in the *Gita* (Chapter 5, Verse 2). Lord Krishna further says (Chapter 2, Verse 48) that "*Karma yoga* is the denial of the fruit of action, as well as of attachment to the *karma* that is called detached action" (Bhave, 1981). *Karma yoga*, then, is the path of union with God through external action performed in a detached and selfless manner, dedicated to God alone who is seen as its origin and its goal. This includes the performance of one's own duty and service of humanity, but always in complete dedication to God. Real selflessness consists in surrendering the desire for all forms of fruit of *Karma*. Through such detached *Karma*, weaknesses like partially, prejudices are eradicated, and abnormality to which they generally lead are put a stop to. Therefore, it is the duty of every man to perform such detached action taking refuge under the feet of the Lord. "Your right is to work only, but never to its fruit. Be not instrument in making your actions bear fruit, nor let your attachment be too detached (*anasakta*). (*Gita* (Chapter 2, Verse 47).

The Path of action as taught in the *Gita* briefly consists in:

1. Discharging in the right way as a matter of duty the natural obligations that have been imposed on an individual by the 'Shastras' (Holy Text) in view of his or her grade in society, stage in life, temperament and circumstances.
2. Completely giving up all affinity, attachment and desire with regard to such actions and their fruit and remaining balanced in success and failure as well as in the matter of their reward and offering all one's actions and their fruit to God.
3. Performing all one's actions as enjoined by Him and under His prompting as an act of worship to Him.
4. Remaining supremely contended with every dispensation of God and contemplating all the time on His Name, excellence, glory, and real character.

Although *karma yoga* involves physical action, its focus is completely psychological. That is why Krishna says: "If you can understand and follow it, you will be able to break the chains of desire which bind you to your actions."

The *Karma yogi* in real sense is those who are *anasakta* means detached from action, perceive his work as duty, total absorption in the task and likely to discharge his duties scrupulously without mental attachment to the consequences, shows a lack of concern for the consequences of action. His behaviour will be guided by his own internal standards about correctness of conduct and excellence in performance.

Karma yogi always maintains an emotional equipoise in the face of positive as well as negative experiences.

Bhakti Yoga in Bhagavad Gita

Only those who offer exclusive and pure devotion to the Lord can speak on Devotion (*Bhakti*). Devotion is clearly emphasized here as the final and special teaching for Arjuna, and he has to lay it to his heart. Moreover, it is therefore that the Lord after teaching him the fundamental principles exhorts him thus: "Give your mind to Me, be devoted to Me, worship Me and bow to Me. Doing so you will come to Me alone, I sincerely assure you; for you are exceptionally dear to Me."("Resigning all your duties to Me, the all-powerful and all-supporting Lord, take refuge in Me alone. I shall absolve you of all sins, worry not" (Chapter 18, Verses 65-66).

The characteristics of *Bhakti yogi* as stated in *Bhagavad Gita* are— "*He* who is free from malice towards all beings, friendly and compassionate, rid of 'I' and 'mine', balanced in joy and sorrow, forgiving by nature, ever-contended and mentally united with Me, nay, who has subdued his mind, senses and body, has a firm resolve, and has surrendered his mind and reason to Me— that devotee of Mine is dear to Me" (Chapter 12, Verses 14-15). In the fifth and sixth chapters of *Gita* verses no. 10 and 47 respectively describe the qualities of a devotee. "He, who acts offering all actions to God, and shaking off attachment, remains untouched by sin, as the lotus leaf by water" (Chapter 5, Verse 10). "Of all *Yogis*, again, he who devoutly worships Me with his mind fixed on Me is considered by Me to be the best *Yogi*." This is the principal verse on Devotion (Chapter 6, Verse 47). Lord Krishna says to Arjun that "I consider them to be the best *Yogis*, who endowed with supreme faith, and ever united through meditation with Me, worship Me with the mind centred on Me" (*Gita*, Chapter 12, Verse 2).

Therefore, the best form of *Bhakti* for an individual is precisely that in which he is able to put his faith and pursue that very form with diligence. Those who are always truthful, non-violent, compassionate, gentle, modest, ready to forgive and free from malice and pride, called *bhakti yogis*.

Jnana Yoga in Bhagavad Gita

In the *Bhaghvad Gita*, the characteristics of *Jnana Yogi* are described as *Gunatita*" (Chapter 14, Verse 22). The fact is that recourse is taken to the method of marking out the distinctive nature of the functions of the mind of a *Gunatita* in order to understand what is meant by the term. *Srimad Bhagavadgita* characterizes a *Gunatita* thus:

"He, O Pandava, who abhorreth not perspicuity, activity, nor even infatuation, when actively present, nor longeth after them when they are no longer present." (Chapter-14, verse 22). In the verse reproduced above the word 'perspicuity' means transparency of mind and the cognitive senses, activity (बुद्धिशीलता) means voluntary effort (स्वैच्छिक चेष्टा), and infatuation (मोह) is interpreted as the tendency to sleep, lethargy or (सुस्ती) (not ignorance or moral delinquency) or a state very similar to profound sleep in the matter of worldly knowledge. Since, there is no ego identifying itself with the mind, in whom will 'abhorrence' (घृणा) and longing (साघ) inhere? The very fact of the mind being free from attachment and aversion (स्नेह/घृणा), delight and sorrow (आनन्द/दु:ख) and such other pairs of opposites prove that there is no ego identifying itself with the mind.

In nutshell those individuals are called *Jnana yogi* who control all their senses, and even-minded towards all, and devoted to doing good to all creatures, constantly adore as their very self the unthinkable, all-pervading, imperishable, ineffable, eternal, immobile, unmanifest and immutable God. He who is free from attachment, is beyond the feelings of friend and foe, honour and ignominy, heat and cold, pleasure and pain and ideas or thoughts.

Concept of Ṭriguna

The notion *triguna* is stated in one of four *Vedas* (Ancient Indian Philosophical literature), i.e. *Atharva Veda.* Though, it is in the *Sâmkhya* system of Indian philosophy, that this notion has earned the merit as a crucial illuminating paradigm. *Sâmkhya,* a dualistic philosophy, propose two inter-reliant but in sync existing reality, i.e. *purusha* (consciousness) and *prakriti* (nature or matter). The *purusha* forms the inner core of the personality and all the other things in the universe (both physical and psychological, including the mind) is supposed to be originated from *prakriti.* This *prakriti* encompasses three *gunas*, namely, *Sattva, Rajas* and *Tamas.* These *triguna* or three matters function concurrently and for no reason exist in isolation. They blend together as well as compete with each other resulting in the preponderance of one over the others. The extent of preponderance of one *guna* over other determines the personality type of the person concerned. Entrenched in this philosophical insight, personalities are categorized into three, viz., *sāâttvika, rājasika* and *tāmasika* types (Rao, 1966).

Indian Psychologists have examined the concept of *triguna* both theoretically and empirically (Boss, 1966; Parameshwaran, 1969; Parameshwaran, 1971; Uma, Lakshmi and Parameshwaran, 1971; Singh, 1972; Rao and Harigopal, 1979; Mohan and Sandhu, 1986, 1988; Das, 1987, 1991; Pathak, Bhatt and Sharma, 1992; Mathew, 1995; Sitamma, Sridevi and P.V.K. Rao, 1995; Kapur *et al.*, 1997; Marutham, Balodhi and Misra, 1998; Sharma, 1999; Sebastian and Mathew, 2002).

***Sattva*:** The term *sattva,* derived from the root verb '*as*' of Sanskrit language which means "to be", which is related to *asti* that is equivalent to "is". The word *sattva* is formed as '*sat + tva*' which is explained as '*sato bhâvaha*'.

***Rajas*:** The term *rajas,* derived from the root *ranj,* which means to be dyed, coloured, grow red, glow, moved, affected, excited, delighted, attracted so on as used by many. The sacred text *Bhagavad Gita* (Chapter 14.7) uses the term in this sense — *rajo rāgātmakam viddhi* (understand that *rajas* is of the nature of dyeing).

Tamas: The term *tamas* is derived from the root '*tam*' which means to gasp for breath, affecting, choke, exhausted, perish, be distressed or disturbed, become immovable or stiff, wish, desire.

The psychologists had attempted to relate *triguna* to already established conventional personality types (e.g., introversion-extraversion) and psychological processes (e.g., cognitions, ESP etc.). The findings are indicated that ***Sattvika* personalities** tend to be introverts (Uma, Lakshmi & Parameshwaran, 1971; Mohan & Sandhu, 1988); have clear cognitions and perceptions (Singh, 1972; Sitamma *et al.,* 1995); tend to be relatively less verbally aggressive (Wolf, 1988); are capable of ESP (Extra Sensory Perception) experiences (Sebastian & Matthew, 2002); and prefer self-growth (Sharma, 1999).

***Rājasika* personalities** tend to be extraverted (Uma, Lakshmi & Parameshwaran, 1971; Mohan & Sandhu, 1988), have clear cognitions and sharp perceptions (Singh, 1972); show high verbal aggressiveness and less satisfaction with life (Wolf, 1988); and experience less job satisfaction (Sharma, 1999).

***Tāmasika* personalities** show tendencies towards psychotics (Mohan & Sandhu, 1988); have poor cognition, defective memory and delusions (Sitamma *et al.*, 1995); experience less satisfaction with life (Wolf, 1998); and show low ESP abilities (Rao & Harigopal, 1979).

These *triguna* are always there in all beings, as well as the substances besieging us, but differ in their relative magnitudes. The *gunas* demonstrate our mental and spiritual position due to which we can appraise our susceptibility for psychological problems. The philosophy of *yoga* believes that somatic problems are nothing but a manifestation of an imbalance between three *Gunas* (*Sattva*, *Rajas* and *Tamas*) that go to constitute the body-mind complex of the individual (Goyandka, 1999). In a randomized, controlled, prospective study (Deshpande, Nagendra & Raghuram, 2008) in normal adults comparing the efficacy of *Yoga* (Y) with a control intervention of Physical exercise (PE) of eight weeks in 174 normal adults on changes in their personality (*guna*) and general health as assessed by Vedic Personality Inventory and GHQ respectively, it was that an increase in *Sattva scores* in both Y and PE groups and a decrease in *Rajas* and *Tamas* scores in the PE group. The scores for *Tamas* decreased significantly in seniors of both the groups (females in Y and males in PE). The increase in *Sattva* scores was higher in the Y group than in the PE group. The decrease in the *Rajas* scores was significantly higher in the PE than in the Y groups and this was seen in juniors and males. The GHQ revealed a significant improvement on all four domains and the overall health in both groups after the intervention. It can be seen from the GHQ scores that PE was more effective in reducing somatic symptoms, severe depression and anxiety and insomnia. There is a significant decrease in *Rajas* could be because of the inclusion of *Asanas* and *Pranayama* to the Meditation technique in the integrated *yoga* programme used in the present study.

The study by Venugopal, Mandal and Parimala (2011) investigated the effect of *yoga* practice on personality dimensions and mental health problems. For this purpose, a group of *yoga* practitioners (n=51, male=33, mean age=29.16 years) was compared with a group of non-practitioners (n=54, male=29, mean age=36.59 years) on measures of personality and mental health problems. Results indicated that compared to non-practitioners *yoga* practitioners were significantly high on *Sattva* aspect of personality and low on *Rajas* and *Tamas* aspects of personality. Further, *yoga* practitioners were found have significantly less emotional and behavioural problems, namely, anxiety/depression, somatic, aggressive, attention, rule-breaking and intrusive behaviours. It was also found that *Sattva guna* was negatively related to emotional and behavioural problems while *Rajas* and *Tamas* were positively related to. The findings of this study indicate the role of *yoga* practices in nurturing *Sattva* aspect of personality which can be a resilient factor against psychological problems. In a similar study Devi, Subrahmanyam and Singh (2016) tried to examine the efficacy of *yoga* practices on personalities (*Gunas*) of widows below 50 years of age (n=80). *Guna* (personality) was assessed before and after eight weeks using the self-administered "The Vedic Personality Inventory". The data analysis showed significant increase in *Sattva Guna* in experimental group whereas in control group there was no significant increase. There was significant reduction in *Tamas Guna* scores in experimental group as well as in the control group.

Apart from the studies seeing the effect of yogic practices in inculcating some researchers had tried to examine the effect of *triguna* in different life settings. Kumar and Thomas (2013) had conducted a study to see the effect of *Gunas* on creativity of managers. They found that *Sāttvika* mangers can handle any kind of situation, can be productive in their work, can achieve the goals with planning, effective utilization of the resources, and can perform well. *Rājasika* managers have the ability to be creative but are unable to have divergent thinking. Narayanan and Krishnan (2003) studied the relationship between *Gunas, Karma Yoga* and Transformational leadership and found that three *Sattva* dimensions, i.e. sympathy, motivation to work and accepting pain enhance transformational leadership and two *Rajas* dimensions, i.e. attribution, and right and wrong reduce *Karma Yoga*. Rastogi (2004) made an attempt to relate *Triguna* to seven constructs of psychological well-being from Western perspective. The seven constructs included self-acceptance, positive relation with others, autonomy, environmental mastery, purpose in life, satisfaction with life and personal growth. An important finding was that *Tamas* was found to be negatively and *Sattva* to be positively correlated with all the seven constructs of psychological well-being.

Objective of the Present Study

Mostly, in Indian studies, personality is measured through the personality inventories developed in Western socio-cultural context. Through this study, an effort has been made to assess personality orientations as outlined in different Indigenous literature. The researcher has taken one such treatise namely *Bhagavad Gita* for the same and taken two pertinent notion, i.e. *Triyoga* and *Triguna* and tried to find their relationship. Hence, the specific objective of the present investigation is to explore the relationship in personality orientations as depicted in *Bhagavad Gita* (i.e., *Jñāna, Bhakti* and *Karma*) and *Triguna* (i.e., *Sattva, Rajas* and *Tamas*).

Method

Sample: The sample consisted of 260 participants (200 Homemakers and 60 Saints) aged between 25 to 70 years. The homemakers were engaged in their household chores and the saints were serving God in different temples of Goddess Durga, Sai Baba and Radhey Krishna etc. All the participants were Hindu and residents of three districts of state of Uttar Pradesh. All of them were married, and their level of education was graduation and above.

Measures

(1) Triyoga Inventory—This inventory is developed by the present researchers and is based on the Hindu treaty *Bhagavad Gita*". This inventory is based on three *yogas* described in *Gita*, i.e. *Jyāna, Bhakti*, and *Karma*. After studying relevant literature, the present researchers have developed the operational definition of these personality orientations: **(i) Jñāna yogis:** The verses number 22 to 25 of chapter 14 enlighten the characteristics of *Jñāna yogis*. Based on those characteristics the researcher had defined the *Jñāna yogis* as—"*Those who are intellect, curious, firmness and one pointed are called Jyāna yogis*". **(ii) Karma yogis:** In the chapter 2 verses number 55 to 72 illuminate the characteristics of a *karma yogi* and based on those characteristics, the researcher has defined the *karma yogis* as—"*Those who are arrogant, free from will, self absorbed, full of self-consciousness, determined, harsh towards fellow creatures and given over to lust and anger are said to have demoniac minds, which are always truthful, non-violent, compassionate are called karma yogis*". **(iii) Bhakti yogis:** The *bhakti yoga* is precisely elaborated in verses 13 to 19 of the chapter 12. The researcher has developed the definition of *bhakti yogi* as—"*Those who are gentle, modest, ready to forgive and free from malice, pride, devoted, pure and religious are said to have divine minds are called bhakti yogis*".

Based on the qualities given in *Gita*, the researcher has made the items of *Triyoga* inventory. Firstly, researcher has made 220 items of inventory and has given to 10 experts for their judgement. Interaction with experts was useful for developing items, modifying and refining them. After the review of the experts, 25 items were dropped and the inventory with 195 items had been given to 30 participants with the instruction to rate themselves, as well as, about the language of the items. Derived from results of pilot study again, 38 items were dropped after the items analysis as these items had low discrimination power and inter item correlation. The final version of the inventory has 157 items.

These 157 items were related to *Jnana, Karma*, and *Bhakti yoga* orientations of personality. Some of the items in the inventory were positively worded and some are negatively. Therefore, the scoring for a positively worded item was (1) Totally disagree (2) Disagree, (3) Agree and (4) Totally agree and *vice versa*, for negatively worded items. *Jyāna yoga* domain consists of 68 items, *Karma yoga* domain consists of 41 items and *Bhakti yoga* domain consists of 48 items.

The Cronbach alpha for this inventory was moderately high for three domains. The co-efficient alpha for this scale was found to be 0.83. The Cronbach alpha for three personality orientations was—*Jyāna Yoga* (0.85), *Bhakti Yoga* (0.78) and *Karma Yoga* (0.72). Retest reliability (after 4 weeks of interval) was found 0.83. The examples of each personality orientations are given below:

> Generally, I am trying to concentrate myself in stressful situations (*Jñāna Yoga*).
> I never think about the result of those works, which I have done (*Karma Yoga*).
> I devoted all things happen in life to God (*Bhakti yoga*).

(2) Vedic Personality Questionnaire: In order to assess the personality in Indian context Wolf (1998) had developed the Vedic personality questionnaire. Pandey (1999) had developed the Hindi version of this scale. The present researcher had also made some minor changes in the language of the items of the Hindi version and had given it to experts of philosophy and psychology. Moreover, based on their opinion revised the scale. This scale consists of 84 items which were related to three dimensions namely Sattvika (30 items), *Rajas* (24 items), and *Tamas* (30 items). Participants were asked to give their responses on 4-point scale as Strongly Agree (4), Agree (3), Disagree (2) and Strongly Disagree (1). The Cronbach alpha of the revised version was found 0.89 and the Cronbach alpha for each of the three personality orientation was found *Sattva* (0.76), *Rajas* (0.71) and *Tamas* (0.79). The retest reliability after four weeks of interval was also found 0.77. The example of each personality orientations is given below:

> To attain my goal of life if any illegal method admits than I am ready for it (*Tamas*).
> I feel very happy to think about my personal properties (*Rajas*).
> I am not affected by the happiness and grieve of life (*Sattvika*).

Procedure: The process of data collection was started with contacting each participant personally. After their consent, the instructions were read to the participants and they were asked whether they were able to understand the instructions. After the completion of data collection process, each protocol was rechecked and scored and data analysis was done through SPSS version 16.

Results

To find out the relationship in *triyoga* and *triguna*, the coefficient of correlation was computed for homemakers and saint groups separately and presented in Table 5.1.

Table 5.1: Coefficient of Correlation in *Triyoga* and *Triguna*

Personality Orientations	*Groups*	*Jñāna*	*Karma*	*Bhakti*	*Sattviac*	*Rajas*	*Tamas*
Jyana	HM	—	0.54**	–0.04	0.35**	–0.40	0.27*
	S		0.10	0.31**	–0.05	0.14	–0.16
Karma	HM		—	0.06	0.34**	0.18**	0.30*
	S			0.36**	–0.10	0.01	0.05
Bhakti	HM			—	0.70**	0.33**	0.02
	S				0.36**	.05	0.09
Sattvika	HM				—	–0.04	0.24*
	S					0.09	0.01
Rajas	HM						0.11
	S						0.03
Tamas	HM						—
	S						

Note: **P<.01, *P<.05, HM = homemakers, S = *Sannyasi.*

Homemaker group—In this group, out of the three *yoga* domains two, i.e. *Jñāna* and *Karma* (r=0.54, p<.000) were positively and significantly related to each other. Conversely, the *Bhakti yoga* was not found to be correlated with either of the two. Subsequently, in this group the one domain of *Triyoga*, i.e. *Jñāna yoga* was positively correlated with both *Sattva guna* (r= 0.35, p<.01) and *Tamas guna* (r= 0.27, p<.01). In the same way, *Karma yoga* was significantly and positively correlated with all the three components of *Triguna,* i.e. *Sattva guna* (r= 0.34, p<.01), *Rajas guna* (r= 0.18, p<.01) and *Tamas guna* (r= 0.30, p<.01). But *Bhakti yoga* personality was not found to be significantly related to none of the three *gunas*. Hence, these findings suggested that *triyoga* and *triguna* are correlated to each other in different ways.

Saint group—However, in Saints group of participants *Jyāna yoga* was linked to *Bhakti yoga* ($r= 0.31$, $p<.01$) and *Bhakti yoga* is related to *Karma yoga* ($r= 0.36$, $p<.01$) as well which suggest that all three domains of *triyoga* was significantly and positively correlated to each other. However, among the three components of *triguna* only *Sattva guna* ($r=0.36$, $p<.01$) is positively and significantly related to one domain of *triyoga*, i.e. *Bhakti yoga.*

Discussion and Conclusion

Indian psychology is extensive, rich, complex, dynamic, and integrative. The Vedas and Upanishads lay the foundation for how to live a life. Nearly everyone has a personal belief system, whether culturally acquired or acquired through the process of an informed personal choice, which guides their understanding of God, self and the world around them—their physical and social reality. This belief guides their behaviour and interaction with the world. As much as a worldview is extremely personal, its ramifications are seen in the way we understand and deal with the world, not only at an individual, relational level, but also as a society, and in terms of how we explore and try to understand the world. These philosophies or belief systems, present us with a diversity of ideas and concepts. The Indian kaleidoscope contains within it many philosophies that need to be mined for the wealth of information that they contain within them. Of the many systems present, in this Chapter we investigated the Hindu religion-philosophical systems for their percepts on the concept of self. Self is the core of personality and its essence is pure cosmic consciousness as viewed in the Hindu scriptures.

It was thought that traditional beliefs determine individual's personality so in the present study the researcher takes two types of indigenous personality orientations as depicted in *Bhagavad Gita*. *Gita* describes *triyoga*, i.e. *Jyāna, Karma*, and *Bhakti* as three ways of life as well as the *triguna,* i.e. *sattva, rajas*, and *tamas* as three personality orientations. It was also expected that these personality orientations correlate with each other through different aspects of their characteristics. It was therefore, thought pertinent to investigate the relationship between psychological characteristics of these personality orientations in the present investigation. Total six personality characteristics were examined in people living life in two different ways, i.e. homemakers who are engaged in worldly affairs and saints, who had taken *sannyasa,* dissociated themselves from worldly affairs and serving to God in temples (*Sannyasa* means skip the householder and retirement stages, abandon worldly and materialistic pursuits and dedicate their lives to spiritual pursuits. It is a form of simplicity, is marked by renunciation of material desires and prejudices, represented by a state of disinterest and detachment from material life, and has the purpose of spending one's life in peaceful, love-inspired, simple spiritual life).

The research questions answered by this research are that *triyoga* and *triguna* are related to each other in homemakers and *Sannyasis* in their own ways. Apart from this, the three *yogas* and three *gunas* are interconnected to each one other in their own ways in two groups.

Jyāna Yoga and Triguna: Results showed that in homemaker group of participants *Jnana yoga* is positively and significantly related with *Sattva guna* and *Tamas guna.* In the *sannyasi* group *Jñāna yoga* had not showed any type of relation with any of the *guna.* The results represent that the psychological characteristics of *Jyāna yoga* are analogous to the characteristics of *Sattvika* and *Tamas guna. Sattva* also binds by attachment to knowledge. Because *sattva* is responsible for knowledge and knowledge is necessary for survival, it is easy to become attached to what you know or do not know. It so happens that the 'I'—consciousness—is not a knower. It illumines the knower, knowledge and the objects of knowledge. It illumines the absence of knowledge. Therefore, attachment to *sattva,* not *sattva* itself, stands in the way of self-knowledge. Self-knowledge removes doubt about the nature of the world because it reveals things as they are. When things are known as they are, the desire to have them be different subsides, freeing the mind from its need to have experience conform to its likes and dislikes, eliminating emotional suffering. Self-knowledge ultimately destroys desire, because it is clear that the bliss one seeks in objects, one already have as the self. It also eliminates fear, because the vision of non-duality means that there is no other. That is why the results also show the significant relation between *Jnana yoga* and *Sattvika guna.*

Karma Yoga and Triguna: The results of the present investigation indicate that *karma yoga* is significantly related with all the three *gunas* in the homemaker group of participants. *Karma yoga* is an action oriented path of life and a *karma yogi* always does his/her work to achieve his/her targets of life. But he/she sometimes becomes arrogant and harsh towards fellow creatures, sometimes he/she becomes an egoist that is why the *Tamas* and *Rajas guna* were found to be related with *Karma yoga.* Besides that, we see in the results that *Sattva guna* was highly correlated with *karma yoga* in comparison to other two *gunas*. These three energies (i.e. *Sattva guna*, *Rajas guna* and *Tamas guna*) the *guna* or ropes bind the soul, the indweller in the body, to habitual thoughts, feelings and actions. Each binds in a different way. *Rajas* bind by longing and attachment. Craving for things and attachment to things pressurizes one to become a doer and it ties up with *karma*. Furthermore, desire makes rule breaking tempting. If you push against the rules, the rules push back. Continual reaction to events is bondage. When a person is occupied with worldly affairs all these *gunas* are needed to some extent but the intensity of *sattva* to be more than rest of the two to deal with stress and positively cope with it. However, there was no relation in *karma yoga* with *sattva guna*, *tamas guna* and *rajas guna* in *sannyasi* group of participants.

Bhakti Yoga and Triguna: As we had seen in earlier two explanations that in saint group neither *Jyana* nor *Karma yoga* was found to be related with any of the *guna*, nevertheless *Sattvika guna* was only related to *Bhakti yoga* in *sannyasi* group. This finding is of very much importance that it revealed that people who take *sannyasa* are highly oriented towards *Bhakti yoga*, the path of Devotion, where one renounces everything and leaves everything to God. It is the easiest path and one needs to have faith in god to be able to walk this path. Faith is the driving factor; if one loses it his/her *Bhakti* is over. However, the *Bhakti yoga* is also associated with both *Jñāna* and *Karma yoga* with almost same magnitude. It suggests that the attainment of perfect Knowledge in the form of Self-realization is the result of spiritual effort on the lines of Knowledge and Action both. It may be concluded that in the path of knowledge (*Jyāna*) a person realizes his/her true self through knowledge and truth. This is said to be the most difficult of all as it is filled with hurdles and one needs the right path, which guides him through this maze, from darkness to light. The path of hard work, the journey in this path revolves around the work one does, his/her *karma*.

Conclusion: On the basis of above discussion we can conclude that a person is known by the kind of *karma* he does and with the right *karma*, he attains the eternal bliss. As per the common belief that one can choose any path, it is only a mix of all these paths that can lead one to the final truth that is he. As without *Jyāna* one would never know the final truth, without devotion, one will not be able to enjoy it, and without *karma* one will not be able to achieve it.

Limitations and Implications: Some limitations of the present study that is due to the sample size. Firstly, the number of participants in two groups varied. Besides this limitation, there are some important implications of this study. It is an unique attempt to develop an inventory based on *Triyoga* described in *Bhagavad Gita*. The personality orientations assessed in this study is purely indigenous. This study has attempted to investigate relationship in these variables in Indigenous perspective.

References

Apte, Vaman Shivram. 1970 [1890]. *The Student's Sanskrit English Dictionary*. 2nd ed. Delhi, India: Motilal Banarasidass Publishers.

Aurobindo, S. (1970). *Letters on yoga* (Vol. 1). Lotus Press (WI).

Bhave, V. (1981). *Talks on the Gita*. Varanasi: Sarva Seva Sangh. Original published 1932.

Boss, M. (1966). *A Psychiatrist Discovers India* (Henry A. Frey — Trans.). Calcutta: Rupa.

Das, R.C. (1987). The *Gita* typology of personality—An inventory. *Journal of Indian Psychology, 6*, 7-12.

Das, R.C. (1991). Standardization of the *Gita* inventory of personality. *Journal of Indian Psychology, 9*, 47-55.

Deshpande, S., Nagendra, H.R. and Nagarathna, R. (2009). A randomized control trial of the effect of *yoga* on *Gunas* (personality) and Self-esteem in normal healthy volunteers. *International Journal of Yoga, 2*, 13-21.

Devi, N.J., Subramanyam, K. and Singh, T.B. (2016). Efficacy of *yoga* on *triguna* in young widows: A randomized control trial. *International Journal of Arts, Humanities and Management Studies, 2* (7): 26-35.

Edgerton, F. (1965). *The Beginnings of Indian philosophy*. London: G. Allen & Unwin.

Goswami, S.D. (1977). *Readings in Vedic Literature: The Tradition speaks for itself.* Los Angeles: Bhaktivedanta Book Trust.

Goyandka, J. (1999). *Srimadbhagavad Gita Tattvavivecani*. 15th ed. Gorakhpur: Govind Bhavan Karyalaya, Gita Press, Gorakhpur, India.

Kapur, M., Hirisave, U., Reddy, M.V., Barnabas, L., and Singhal, D. (1997). Study of infant temperament: An Indian perspective. *Indian Journal of Clinical Psychology, 24*, 171-177.

Kim, U., Berry, J. (Eds.) (1993). *Indigenous Psychologies: Research and Experience in Cultural Context*. Newbury Park, CA: Sage Publications.

Kumar, K., and Thomas, T.M. (2013). Creativity and *Triguna* Personality of Managers. *Journal of Organisation and Human Behaviour, 2*(1): 1-6.

Marutham, P., Balodhi, J.P., and Mishra, H. (1998). *Sattva, rajas, tamas* (SRT) inventory. *NIMHANS Journal, 16(1)*, 15-19.

Mathew, V.G. (1995). *IAS Rating Scale*. Holigrative Psychology Institute, Thiruvananthapuram, Kerala, India. http://www.psychology4all.com

Mohan, V., and Sandhu, S. (1986). Development of scale to measure *sattvika, rajasika* and *tamasika guna*. *Journal of the Indian Academy of Applied Psychology, 12*: 46-52.

Mohan, V., Sandhu, S. (1988). *Samkhyan triguna* and Eysenck's dimension of personality. *The Vedic Path*, pp. 23-38.

Narayanan, J., and Krishnan, V. R. (2003). Impact of *Sattva* and *Rajas Gunas* on Transformational Leadership and *Karma Yoga*. *Journal of Indian Psychology, 21*(2): 1-11.

Parameshwaran, E.G. (1969). Indian psychology—the need for a breakthrough, an attempt. *Research Bulletin, 5*: 75-80.

Pathak, N.S., Bhatt, I.D., and Sharma, R. (1992). Manual for classifying personality on tri-dimensions of *gunas*: An Indian approach. *Indian Journal of Behaviour, 16*: 1-14.

Radhakrishnan, S. (1977). *Bhagavad Geeta*. New Delhi: Rajpal & Sons.

Rama, S. (1996). *Perennial Psychology of the Bhagavad Gita*. Honesdale, Pennsylvania: The Himalayan International Institute of Yogic Science and Philosophy of the USA.

Rao, K.B.R. (1966). *Theism in Pre-classical Samkhya*. Mysore: Prasaranga, University of Mysore, Karnataka, India.

Rao, P.V.K. and Harigopal, K. (1979). The three *gunas* and ESP: An exploratory investigation. *Journal of Indian Psychology, 2* (1), 63-68.

Saraswati, Swami Satyananda (1996). *Asana Pranayama Mudra Bandha* (New Edition). Munger; Bihar Yoga Bharati.

Rastogi, A. (2004). *Triguna and Psychological Well-Being*. Ph.D. Thesis, Lucknow University, Lucknow, Uttar Pradesh, India.

Sebastian, K.A., and Mathew, G.V. (2002). Three *gunas* and PSI experience; a study of PSI experience in relation to inertia, activation and stability. *Journal of Indian Psychology, 20* (2): 44-48.

Sharma, R. (1999). Self-concept and Job satisfaction in *sattva, rajas* and *tamas* personalities. *Journal of Indian Psychology, 17* (2): 9-17.

Singh, R. (1971). An inventory from *Mahabharata. Indian Journal of Psychiatry, 13*: 149-161.

Sitamma, M., Sridevi, K., and Rao, P.V.K. (1995). Three *gunas* and cognitive characteristics: A study of field—dependence—independence and perceptual activity. *Journal of Indian Psychology, 13*: 13-20.

Uma, K., Lakshmi, Y.S., and Parameshwaran, E.G. (1971). Construction of a personality inventory based on doctrine of three *gunas*. *Research Bulletin*, pp. 49-58.

Venugopal, D.V., Mandal, B.S.S. and Parimala, K. (2011). Effect of *yoga* practice on personality, emotional and behavioural problems. In S. Kumar and S.B. Yadav (Eds.) *Positive Psychology* (pp. 70-75), New Delhi: Global Vision Publishing House.

Wolf, D.B. (1998). The Vedic personality inventory: A study of the *gunas*. *Journal of Indian Psychology, 16*(1): 26-43.

6
Role of Astropsychology in Personality Making: An Empirical Validation

Bhagyashree Joshi and *Aradhana Shukla*

In these days considerable attempts have been made to explore the pattern of personality related to various areas of life experiences. The studies have laid their significant impact by revealing the relative efficacy of personality surrounded by many experiential factors. Most of the studies have followed Western concept and Indian concept are still to be explored. In additions to its personality have not been studied in Indian perspective whether it is present or past.

Astropsychology: A New Perspective

Planets are constantly in motion with respect to earth in the sky. The positions of Sun, Moon and some planets close to earth can give important clues about the fortunes of individual human beings and groups of human beings. *That* is the basic premise of astrology. How exactly we can make guesses about the fortunes of individual human beings and groups of human beings based on the positions of those planets in the sky is the question that we will attempt to answer here. While astrology is the subject that deals with this question, there are many theories and philosophies in vogue and they are significantly different from each other.

Sun sign astrology, for example, is based on categorizing people into 12 groups based on the solar month of birth. Some people may be convinced, based on their experiences, that people born in the same month share certain qualities. It is, however, not very logical from a rational perspective — there are just too many people in this world, who are totally different from each other. So, the month of one's birth is totally inadequate for guessing one's nature or fortune. Even the date and the hour of birth are not enough. We know that there are many twins in this world, who are significantly different from each other. It is like an "acid test" for any astrological doctrine. It is a known fact that there are many twins in this world, who are significantly different from each other and who lead totally different lives. Of course, some twins may have some common qualities between them, but the fact remains that several twins are significantly different. An astrological doctrine should be capable of explaining this fact in order to be considered as a meaningful subject. Most astrological doctrines of the world fail this acid test. If an astrological doctrine assumes, like in the case of many popular astrological theories of the world, that two persons born within a couple of hours in nearby towns will have the same fortune, then that doctrine is obviously lacking in completeness and inadequate for confident use in real-life. It fails the acid test of twins.

Indian Astrology

Materialistically speaking, India may not be a rich country today, but India has extremely rich cultural heritage. The depth of some of India's ancient knowledge (like astrology) is just amazing and it makes one wonder if the history of this great civilization is correctly represented in the pages of modern history. Astrology of India is the most comprehensive and complete system of astrology available today and it is the only one that comes close to answering the just mentioned "twins puzzle". India's astrology can explain how twins can be different. The principles used in India's astrology are so sensitive to changes in birthtime that people born within 1-2 minutes can be significantly different in some aspects and similar in some others. This approach distinguishes between what a person truly is, what a person wants to be, what he thinks he is and what the world thinks he is. It has enough parametres, tools, techniques and degrees of freedom to model the extremely complicated human life. This astrological approach is known in the world by many names. Early pioneers of modern Indian astrology, like Dr. B.V. Raman, called it "Hindu astrology", because this system was first taught by ancient Hindu sages. However, some people do not like this expression because "Hindu" is not a Sanskrit word. This word was later coined by the Western invaders from the name of a river flowing on the north-western border of India (river "Sindhu" or "Indus"). They used the word "Hindu" to describe the land and the people on the eastern side of this river. The religion practiced by a majority of Indians is known as "Hindu" religion today, but the fact is that there is no name for this religion in India's Sanskrit language, the language in which most of the literature of this religion — and astrology — appeared! Most other religions are known by the name of their main propagator, but India's ancient religion had no single propagator or prophet. This religion consisted of knowledge that revealed itself to spiritual masters of many generations. So, there was no name for this religion and the word "Hindu" coined by Western invaders was accepted by the world. However, as already stressed, this word finds no place in Sanskrit literature. Some people do not like using a non-Sanskrit word to describe India's astrology, considering that most of India's classical literature in astrology appeared in Sanskrit. Later day authors came up with the name — "Vedic astrology". The word "Vedic" means "pertaining to *Vedas*". *Vedas* are the sacred scriptures of, what is known today as, Hinduism and they are supposed to contain knowledge of *all* subjects. Moreover, astrology in particular is supposed to be a "*Vedaanga*" (which means a limb of *Vedas*). In particular, it is said to be the eye of the *Vedas*. So, the name "Vedic astrology" is becoming popular these days. We also suggest using "Vedic astrology" or "*Jyotish*" (meaning "science of light"). *Jyotishi* is a practitioner of *Jyotish*, i.e. a Vedic astrologer.

Nature of Astropsychology

The origins of psychological astrology can be traced to the writings of ancient Greek philosophers such as Thales, Plato, and Aristotle (especially his *De Anima* treatise). Their theories on the nature of the Soul were adapted to astrology by important historical astrologers such as Ptolemy and Al-Kindi. In the twentieth century, esoteric tradition inspired Carl Jung, Swiss psychiatrist and founder of analytical psychology, to formulate his archetypal hypothesis from Plato's theory of ideas or forms. In his research into the symbolic meaning of his patient's dreams, conversations and paintings, Jung observed recurring mythical themes or archetypes. He proposed that these universal and timeless archetypes channel experiences and emotions, resulting in recognizable and typical patterns of behaviour with certain probable outcomes. Jung claimed to observe a correlation between these archetypal images and the astrological themes or traditional 'gods' associated with the planets and signs of the zodiac. He concluded that the symbolic heavenly figures described by the constellations were originally inspired by projections of images created by the collective unconscious. Jung wrote "Astrology represents the sum of all the psychological knowledge of antiquity".

Grahas and *Nakshatras*: Basis of Astropsychology

Ancient Indian astrology is based on *nakshatra* system and it was the outcome of the deep insight and scientific understanding of Indian astrologers. During Vedic and *Mahabharata* period languages were interpreted in terms of *nakshatradaya* and the whole sky was divided in 27 parts from west to east according to Surya Palu. The basis of this classification was the revolve of moon. Moon is the mind owners and changes *nakshatra* everyday. It is the reason that the astrologers infer the *Phalita* (future forecast) on the ground of moon *nakshatra* interaction. Knowledge of *nakshatra* system and the interpretations of human past (*Gatita*) and future (*Phalita*) is the unique contribution of Indian astrologers.

Balancing *Nakshatras* and *Rashis*

There are 30 *anshas* in one *rashi*. It was found impossible to make a mathematical balance between 12 *rashis* and 28 *nakshatras*. Therefore, 27 *nakshatras* were remained and *Abhijit nakshatra* was left. One *rashi* was made by 2¼ (27÷12). In this way 27 *nakshatras* were divided in 108 qualities or/*pad/charanas* (27 × 4=108). Thus every *rashi* was consisted of a *charanas* (2¼ *nakshatras*), angular value of one *nakshatra* 360/27 =13 *ansha*, 20 *kala* and value of one *charanas*, i.e. 360/108=3 *ansha*, 20 *kala*. Therefore, 2¼ *nakshatras* were adjusted in one *rashi* commencing from *Ashwini*. The systematic flow chart of *nakshatras* and *rashi* is shown in Table 6.1.

In order to adjust 27 *nakshatra* 9 *rashis* were framed. First *mahadasha* at the time of birth is decided according to the sharp birth time and position of *nakshatra*. Different and many types of *mahadashas* appear at various stages of life. The time and duration of *mahadashas* varies person to person. People focus on different *mahadashas* according to the location and power of *grahas* according to Maharshi Parashar. Detail of the *mahadasha* of a *graha* up to 120 years of human life is shown in Table 6.2.

Table 6.1: *Rashis* and *Nakshatras*

S. No.	*Name Rashi/Swami*	*Western Name Nakshatras/Swami*	*Nakshatras Maya Charan*			*Total Charan*
			Nakshatras Name First Letter	*Nakshatras Name First Letter*	*Nakshatras Name First Letter*	
(1)	(2)	(3)	(4)	(5)	(6)	(7)
1.	Maish/Mangal	Aris/ 1. Ashwini Kumar 2. Yama 3. Agni	Ashwini Chu, Che, Cho La I II III IV	Bharani Li, Lu, Le, Lo I II III IV	Kritika Aa I	9
2.	Vrishabh/Shukra	Taurus/ 1. Agni 2. Brahma 3. Chandrama	Kritika EE, U Ai II III IV	Rohini Ao, Va, Vi, Vu I II III IV	Mrigashira Vai, Vo I II	9
3.	Mithun/Buddha Ketu	Gemini/1. Chandrama 2. Mahadeva 3. Aditi	Mrigashira Ka, Ki III IV	Aardra Ku, Gha, Ang, Chh I II III IV	Punarvasu Ke, Ko, Ha I II III	9
4.	Karka/ Chandrama	Cancer/ 1. Aditi 2. Brihaspati 3. Sarpa	Punarvasu Hi IV	Pushya Chhu, Chhai, Ho, Da I II III IV	Aashlesha Di, Du, De, Do I II III IV	9
5.	Singh/Sun (Surya)	Leo/ 1. Sarpa 2. Pitar 3. Sun (Surya)	Magha Ma, Mi, Mu, Me I II III IV	Pre Phalguni Mo, Ta, Ti I II III IV	Post Phalguni Te I II III IV	9
6.	Kanya/Buddha Rahu	Virgo/ 1. Sun (Surya) 2. Aaditya 3. Vishwakarma	Post Phalguni To, Pa, Pi II III IV	Hasta Pu Sha Na I II III IV	Chitra Ai, Po I II	9
7.	Tula/Shukra	Libra/ 1. Vishwakarma 2. Vayu 3. Indra	Chitra Ra, Ri III IV	Swati Ru, Re, Ro To I II III IV	Vishakha I II III	9

(*Contd.*)

Table 6.1: (*Contd.*)

(1)	(2)	(3)	(4)	(5)	(6)	(7)
8.	Vrishchik/Mangal	Scorpio/1. Indra 2. Mitra 3. Indra	Vishakha To IV	Anuradha Na, Ji, Nu, Ne I II III IV	Jyeshtha No, Ya, Yi, Yu I II III IV	9
9.	Dhanu/Brihaspati	Sagittarius/1. Rakshas 2. Jal 3. Vishwadeva	Mool Ye, Kshai, Bha, Bhi I II III IV	Pre Aashadha Bhu, Dha, Pha, Dha I II III IV	Post Aashadha Bhe I	9
10.	Makar/Shani	Capricorn/1. Vishwadeva 2. Vishnu 3. Ashtavasu	Post Aashadha Bho, Ja, Ji II III IV	Sharavan Khi, Khu, Khai, Kho I II III IV	Dhanishtha Ga, Gi I II	9
11.	Kumbha/Shani	Aquarius/ 1. Ashtavasu 2. Jal 3. Sun	Dhanishtha Gu, Gai III IV	Shatbhisha Go, Sa, Si, Su I II III IV	Pre Bhadrapad Sai, So Da I II III	9
12.	Meen/Brihaspati	Pisces/ 1. Sun 2. Sun 3. Rakshas	Pre Bhadrapad Di IV	Post Bhadrapad EE, Tha, Jha, Gyan I II III IV	Rewati De Do Cha Chi I II III IV	9

Table 6.2: Table of *Vinshottari Dashas*

Name of grahas	*Time*
Surya	06 years
Chandra	10 years
Mangal	07 years
Rahu	18 years
Guru	16 years
Shani	19 years
Buddha	17 years
Ketu	07 years
Shukra	20 years

Meaning of Personality

The word "personality" in English is derived from the Latin word "Persona". Originally, it denoted the mask worn by theatrical players in ancient Greek dramas; eventually, the term has come to encompass the actor's role as well. Thus, the initials conception of personality was that of a superficial social image that an individual adopts in playing life roles/ public personality that people display to those around them. This view is consonant with that of the contemporary layperson who equates personality with charms, social poise, and popularity, physical attractiveness and a host of other socially desirable characterstics.

Personality is the total pattern of characteristic ways of thinking and behaviour. It is the dynamic and organized set of characteristics processed by a person that uniquely influences his or her cognition, emotion, motivation and behaviour in various situations. Personality is defined as an individual's typical or consistent adjustment to his environment.

Personality also refers to the pattern of thoughts, feelings, and social adjustment and behaviour consistently exhibited over times. They strongly influence one's expectations, self-perception, values, and attitudes. It also predicts human reactions to other people's problem and stress.

Sixteen personality Factor Questionnaire Significant Measure of Personality

The **Sixteen Personality Factor Questionnaire** (or **16 PF**), is a multiple-choice personality questionnaire which was developed over several decades of research by Raymond B. Cattell, Maurice Tatsuoka and Herbert

Eber. Beginning in the 1940s, Cattell used the new techniques of factor analysis (based on the correlation coefficient) in an attempt to try to discover and measure the source traits of human personality (Cattell, 1946; Nevid, 2009).

The questionnaire measures the 16 primary traits, and the Big Five secondary traits which have become popularized by other authors in recent years. From early in his research, Cattell found that the structure of personality was multi-level and hierarchical, with a structure of interdependent primary and secondary level traits (Cattell, 1946, 1957). The sixteen primary factors were a result of factor-analyzing hundreds of measures of everyday behaviours to find the fundamental traits behind them. Then, they discovered the five global (or second-order) factors by factor-analyzing the sixteen primary traits themselves, to find the basic, organizing forces among the sixteen basic traits. Thus, the 16PF test gives scores on both the five second-order global traits which provide an overview of personality at a broader, conceptual level, as well as on the more-numerous and precise primary traits, which give a picture of the richness and complexity of each unique personality. A listing of these traits can be found in the article on the 16 Personality Factor Model. Cattell also found that there was a third-order level of personality organization that contained just two overarching, top-level factors (Cattell, 1957), but little time has been spent on defining this most abstract level of personality.

Relation Between Astrology with Personality

Essential Nature and Will

Just as the Sun is the central star of the solar system in astronomical terms, it also symbolizes the essential nature of a human being in astrology. Its position in the birth picture tells us something about our ego-consciousness, about our will and the way in which we shape our lives.

Feelings and Temperament

The Moon symbolizes the emotional, childlike/passive, and receptive principle. It stands for the needy part of us that would like to live according to its feelings and spontaneously reacts according to desire or reluctance. In this part of our personality, we are sensitive and impressionable, perceive moods, and need a sense of security and warmth. We can imagine this

Table 6.3: Primary Factors and Descriptors in Cattell's 16 Personality Factor Model.

Descriptors of Low Range	*Primary Factor*	*Descriptors of High Range*
Reserve, impersonal, distant, cool, reserved, impersonal, detached, formal, aloof (Sizothymia).	Warmth	Warm, outgoing, attentive to others, kindly, easy going, participating, likes people (Affectothymia).
Concrete thinking, lower general mental capacity, less intelligent, unable to handle abstract problems (Lower Scholastic Mental Capacity).	Reasoning	Abstract-thinking, more intelligent, bright, higher general mental capacity, fast learner (Higher Scholastic Mental Capacity).
Reactive emotionally, changeable, affected by feelings, emotionally less stable, easily upset (Lower Ego Strength).	Emotional Stability	Emotionally stable, adaptive, mature, faces reality calm (Higher Ego Strength).
Deferential, cooperative, avoids conflict, submissive, humble, obedient, easily led, docile, accommodating (Submissiveness).	Dominance	Dominant, forceful, assertive, aggressive, competitive, stubborn, bossy (Dominance).
Serious, restrained, prudent, taciturn, introspective, silent (Desurgency).	Liveliness	Lively, animated, spontaneous, enthusiastic, happy go lucky, cheerful, expressive, impulsive (Surgency).
Expedient, non-conforming, disregards rules, self-indulgent (Low Super Ego Strength).	Rule-Consciousness	Rule-conscious, dutiful, conscientious, conforming, moralistic, staid, rule bound (High Super Ego Strength)
Shy, threat-sensitive, timid, hesitant, intimidated (Threctia).	Social Boldness	Socially bold, venturesome, thick skinned, uninhibited (Parmia).
Utilitarian, objective, unsentimental, tough minded, self-reliant, no-nonsense, rough (Harria).	Sensitivity	Sensitive, aesthetic, sentimental, tender minded, intuitive, refined (Premsia).

(*Contd.*)

Table 6.3: (*Contd.*)

Descriptors of Low Range	*Primary Factor*	*Descriptors of High Range*
Trusting, unsuspecting, accepting, unconditional, easy (Alaxia).	Vigilance	Vigilant, suspicious, skeptical, distrustful, oppositional (Protension).
Grounded, practical, prosaic, solution orientated, steady, conventional (Praxernia).	Abstractedness	Abstract, imaginative, absent minded, impractical, absorbed in ideas (Autia).
Forthright, genuine, artless, open, guileless, naive, unpretentious, involved (Artlessness).	Privateness	Private, discreet, non-disclosing, shrewd, polished, worldly, astute, diplomatic (Shrewdness).
Self-Assured, unworried, complacent, secure, free of guilt, confident, self-satisfied (Untroubled).	Apprehension	Apprehensive, self-doubting, worried, guilt prone, insecure, worrying, self-blaming (Guilt Proneness).
Traditional, attached to familiar, conservative, respecting traditional ideas (Conservatism).	Openness to Change	Open to change, experimental, liberal, analytical, critical, free thinking, flexibility (Radicalism).
Group-oriented, affiliative, a joiner and follower dependent (Group Adherence).	Self-Reliance	Self-reliant, solitary, resourceful, individualistic, self-sufficient (Self-Sufficiency).
Tolerated disorder, unexacting, flexible, undisciplined, lax, self-conflict, impulsive, careless of social rues, uncontrolled (Low Integration).	Perfectionism	Perfectionistic, organized, compulsive, self-disciplined, socially precise, exacting will-power, control, self-sentimental (High Self-Concept Control).
Relaxed, placid, tranquil, torpid, patient, composed low drive (Low Ergic Tension).	Tension	Tense, high energy, impatient, driven, frustrated, overwrought, time driven. (High Ergic Tension).

part to be like a small child within us. If it gets what it needs, we feel good and lively. However, we often have to go through periods of stagnation and discontentment before we recognize and satisfy its needs. The Moon embodies the feminine principle and also stands for the aspect within us that, full of caring willingness, would like to be a "mother" in the broadest sense of the word. It wants to look after others and create a sense of security.

Communication and Thought

Mercury symbolizes the area of our personality related to thinking, information, and communication. The position of Mercury in a birth picture throws light on a person's way of thinking, preferred interests, and learning methods, as well as language and rhetorical abilities.

Relationships and Aesthetics

When Venus sparkles in the sky as the morning or evening star, it is an expression of harmony and beauty in terms of reality and as an astrological symbol. It stands for the need to be balanced and have things in common, for the striving to build bridges. It is a distinctly feminine and erotic principle and corresponds to the aspect within us that longs for a partner, seeks and creates relationships, and can be open for and enjoy all the beauty in life. The Venus in us chooses what is appropriate and agreeable for us from the diversity of people and things.

Actions and Assertion

Mars symbolizes masculinity and physical strength, as well as the capacity to take action and be assertive. It represents the part of our personality that is active in the outer world and wants to cause things to happen, that makes decisions and simply does things without asking, and that does not shy away from conflicts or confrontations. If something doesn't suit us, this is the part within us that defends itself and, if necessary, reacts with aggression and anger.

The Search for Meaning and Growth

Jupiter symbolizes the optimism in us, the part that wants meaning and expansion and sometimes gets out of control. It lets us look out for something higher and rise above the banalities of everyday life. It symbolizes the part in us that creates a relationship between things. It fills sober reality with a meaning by apportioning significance to each thing and imparting symbolic content to situations, words, and deeds.

The Search for Structure and Order

Saturn symbolizes the raised index finger within us, the inner authority with which we set ourselves boundaries and demand structure and responsibility from ourselves. The Saturn aspect within us is often very rigid, and then we block ourselves. However, if we have learned during the course of the years to reduce our fears and our standards of perfection, we will primarily experience Saturn as inner stability and security. In both the concrete and figurative sense, it symbolizes our backbone.

The Need for Change

Uranus symbolizes the "wind spirit" within us that strives for psychological growth through constant change. It stirs up an inner unrest that drives us to set out time and again, that lets us seek variety and new experiences, and that keeps us from psychological and physical stagnation. It represents the wanderer within us who does not settle down for long anywhere. When something has barely become a habit, he tears down his tents and surprises us with new ideas. His originality knows no limits, and the same applies to his non-committal nature.

The Longing for Liberation and Devotion

Neptune symbolizes our mystical side that continually dissolves the boundaries between our ego consciousness and the outside world, reminding us that we are part of a greater whole. This part lets us feel the longing for another world. It can equally be the motivation for reconnecting with something divine, for total devotion and a readiness to help, or for retreating from life and losing ourselves, which ultimately results in self-pity and chaos.

The "Dark" Side

Pluto symbolizes the most radical, energized, and passionate aspect of our personality that, especially because it is so bent on "all or nothing," also triggers fear. So we often feel this side of ourselves to be "dark" and inwardly turn away from it. Then we suppress this intensive part with somewhat the same effect as pressing a lid onto a pot with boiling water: We burn our fingers. We can only find an access to its power and liveliness when we accept this uncompromising and intensive part of ourselves and learn to deal with it. Then this aspect in particular can develop an enormous energy potential and lead us through and beyond profound crises.

Keeping these views in consideration this study was planned and it was aimed to find out the personality factors in Hindu and Muslim participants as derived from their *janam kundali* and 16PF.

Method

Sample: Twenty participants in the age range of 25-60 years served as participants. They were of both sexes., i.e. male and female and they were government employees hailing from Almora, Uttarakhand. They were educated between undergraduate to doctorate. They were efficient in Hindi and English

Measures

In this study following measures were taken in consideration.

Cattell's 16 Personality Factor

The **16 Personality Factor Questionnaire** (or **16 PF**): It is a multiple-choice personality questionnaire which was developed over several decades of research by Raymond B. Cattell, Maurice Tatsuoka and Herbert Eber. Beginning in the 1940s, Cattell used the new techniques of factor analysis (based on the correlation coefficient) in an attempt to try to discover and measure the source traits of human personality (Cattell, 1946; Nevid, 2009). The questionnaire measures the 16 primary traits, and the Big Five secondary traits which have become popularized by other authors in recent years. From early in his research, Cattell found that the structure of personality was multi-level and hierarchical, with a structure of interdependent primary and secondary level traits (Cattell, 1946, 1957). The sixteen primary factors were a result of factor-analysing hundreds of measures of everyday behaviours to find the fundamental traits behind them. Then, they discovered the five global (or second-order) factors by factor-analysing the sixteen primary traits themselves, to find the basic, organising forces among the sixteen basic traits. Thus, the 16PF test gives scores on both the five second-order global traits which provide an overview of personality at a broader, conceptual level, as well as on the more numerous and precise primary traits, which give a picture of the richness and complexity of each unique personality. A listing of these traits can be found in the article on the 16 Personality Factor Model. Cattell also found that there was a third-order level of personality organization that contained just two overarching, top-level factors (Cattell, 1957), but little time has been spent on defining this most abstract level of personality organization.

Birth chart: Participants were also studied on their birth charts. Birth charts of all participants whether Hindu or Muslim were prepared by computer after getting the exact date, time and place of birth by them. We can define birth chart (*Janam Kundali*) as the first thing that the Hindus do when a child takes birth. It is a chart that describes everything about a person. The astrologer is the person who knows how to read this chart. Birth chart of a person can describe the overall personality and characteristics of a person. It can predict the future of a person. Birth chart is the chart that can tell everything about persons including past, present and future. It is a complete analysis of a person's life and it is prepared as given below:

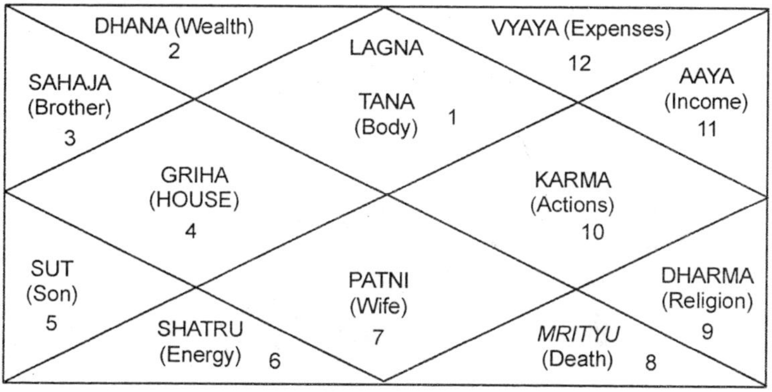

Chart 6.1 : A profile of Birth chart/*Janam kundali*

Procedure: At first the investigators contacted with a large group and made a proper rapport so that the data collection could be made properly. The 16PF test was administered on them and they were expected to provide their birth time, date and place, district. The birth charts were made after getting the related information. Data collection was done individually and best attempts were made to avoid external distractions.

Results

After data collection only two cases (one Hindu and one Muslim) were taken for consideration. As the data were analysed by case study so it was impossible to consider a large sample. So, only two cases were considered and they were analysed deeply by case study method. Results are given below:

Personality Factors of Hindus as Revealed by Their Janamkundalis and 16 Personality Factors:

- Name — A
- Age — 63 years
- Date of birth — 08-04-1954
- Place of birth — Almora
- Time of birth — 3:00 am

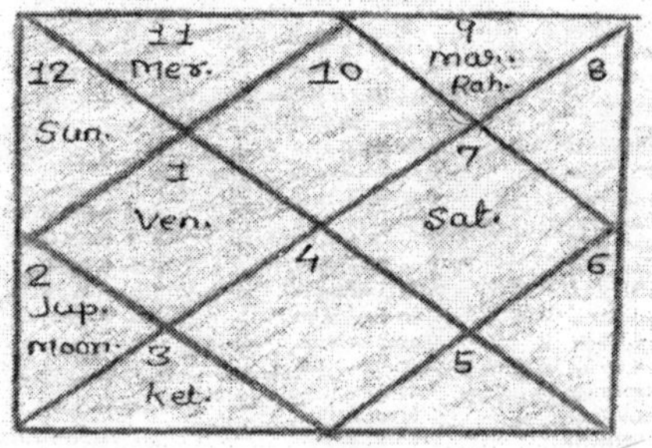

Chart 6.2: The Birth Chart of "A"

General characteristics: Due to lordship of Saturn he is intelligent and has very good retentive power. He has a broad outlook, human understanding are very outspoken unselfish and impersonal. He is silent worker in any society and club. He is always ahead with fresh ideas, new thoughts, new approach to problems, improved design for living.

Specific characteristics: He loves to travel. He is likely to be very emotional and a bit unstable at times. He has a very keen imagination but he should try to be more open and less self-centred.

Physical characteristics: The native tall with full structure. He is lucky and very handsome appearance.

Wealth characteristics: General indication for wealth is fairly good. He has a ability to acquire money with his own effort.

Educational characteristics: General indication for education is very excellent. He is very intelligent and love to read and study.

Health characteristics: The indications for health is fairly good.

Social characteristics: He is the type who needs intellectual stimulation and he is very choosy about friends. He is more mental and less emotional and has reforming tendencies towards friends.

Aspect consideration

- **Sun sextile Moon**—This is also a very good aspect in his birth chart. It indicates that he has good luck and luckily to be very successful. He will have harmony at home and enjoy physical well-being and good health.
- **Sun sextile Jupiter**—The combination of Sun and Jupiter makes him life loving and socially very popular. He has good executive power.
- **Sun square Uranus**—The planets Sun and Uranus thus aspect makes him highly unconventional and even tactless.
- **Sun opposite Neptune**—The combination of Sun and Neptune tends to move him towards escapism as he likes to live in dream world.
- **Moon square Mercury**—This aspect makes him high strung and unable to concentrate.
- **Moon sextile Pluto**—This combination of Moon and Pluto gives him success and achievement many a times.
- **Moon square Saturn**—This aspect of Moon and Saturn makes him subject to limitations and hardship and he find it very difficult to show his feeling many a time. He is jealous and critical and may have domestic difficulties.
- **Mars sextile Neptune**—This aspect indicates that he will be popular and has a charismatic personality.

Personality Factors

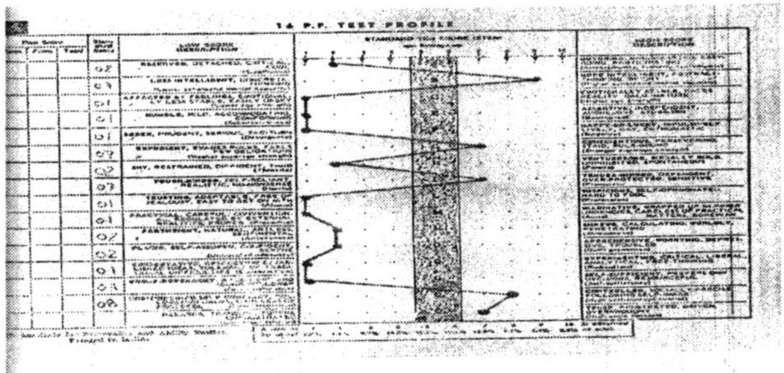

Fig. 6.1: The Personality Profile of "A"

- **Factor A—Reserved, Detached, Critical, cool (sizothymis)—** He is stiff, cool, skeptical and aloof. He likes things rather than people, working alone and avoiding compromise of viewpoints. He is likely to be precise and rigid in his way of doing things and in personal standard and in many occupations these are desirable traits. He may tend at times, to be critical obstructive or hard.
- **Factor B—More intelligent, Abstract thinking, Bright (Higher scholastic capacity)—**The person who scores high on factor B tends to be quick to grasp ideas, a fast learner, intelligent. There is some correlation with level of culture and some with alertness. High scores contraindicate deterioration of mental function in pathological condition.
- **Factor C—Affected by feelings, Emotionally less stable, easily upset (lower ego strength)—**The person who scores low on factor C tends to be low in frustration tolerance for unsatisfactory conditions, changeable and plastic, evading necessary reality demands, neurotically fatigued fretful. Easily emotional and annoyed, active in dissatisfaction, having neurotic symptoms.
- **Factor E—Humble, Mild, accommodating, conforming (submissiveness)—**The person who scores low on factor E tends to give way to other. He is often dependent, confessing, anxious, obsessional correctness. This passivity is part of many syndromes.
- **Factor F—Sober, prudent, serious, taciturn (desurgency)—** The person who scores low on factor F tends to be restrained, reticent, introspective. He is sometimes dour, pessimistic, unduly deliberate, and considered smug and primly correct by observers. He tends to be a sober, dependable person.
- **Factor G—Conscientious, Persevering, staid (stronger superego strength)—**The person who scores high on factor G tends to be exacting in character, descent sense of duty, preserver, responsible, painful, fills the unfurling minute.
- **Factor H—Shy, Restrained, Diffident, Timid (Threctia)—** He is shy, withdrawing, cautious retiring a wallflower, he usually has inferiority feeling. He tends to be slow and impeded in speech and in expressing himself, dislike occupation with personal contacts prefers one or two close friends, two large groups and it is not to given to keeping in contact with all that it is going on around him.
- **Factor I—Tender minded, Dependent, overprotected,**

Sensitive (premise)—The person who scores high on factor tends to be tender minded, day dreaming, artistic, fastidious, feminine. He is sometimes demanding of attention and help, independent, dependent, impractical. He dislikes crude people and rough occupation. He tends to slow up group performance and to upset group moral by unrealistic fussiness.

- **Factor L—Adaptable, Free of jealousy, Easy to get on with (alaxia)**—The person who scores low on factor L tends to be jealous tendencies, adaptable, cheerful, uncompetitive, concern about other people, a good team worker.
- **Factor M—Practical, careful, conventional, regulated by external realities, proper (praxernis)**—The person who scores low on factor M tends to be anxious to do the right things, attentive to practical matters and subject to the dictation of what is obviously possible, able to keep his head in emergencies, but sometimes unimaginative.
- **Factor N—forthright, natural, artless, sentimental (artlessness)**—He scores low on factor N, he tends to be unsophisticated, sentimental and simple. He is sometimes crude and awkward, but easily pleased and content with what comes, and is natural and spontaneous.
- **Factor O—Placid, self-assured, confident, serene (untroubled adequacy)**—The person who scores low on factor O tends to be placid, with unshakable nerve. He has a mature unanxious confidence in himself and his capacity to deal with things. He is resilient and resource, but to the point of being insensitive of when a group is not going along with him, so that he may evoke antipathies and distrust.
- **Factor Q1—Conservative, respecting established ideas, tolerant of traditions**—The person who scores low on factor Q1 is confident in what he has been taught to believe and accepts the "tried and true" despite inconsistencies, when something else might be better. He is cautious and compromising in regard to new ideas. Thus, he tends to oppose and postpone change, is more conservative in religious and politics and tends not to be interested in analytical intellectual thought.
- **Factor Q2—A joiner and sound follower (group adherence)**—The person who scores low on factor Q2 prefers to work and make decisions with other people, likes and depends on social approval and administrations. He tends to go along with the group

and may be lacking in individual resolution. He is not necessarily gregarious by choice rather he need group support.

- **Factor Q3—Controlled, socially precise, following self-image (high self-control)**—The person who scores high on factor Q3 tends to have strong control of his emotions and general behaviour, is inclined to be socially aware and careful, and evidences what is commonly termed "self-respect". and regard for social reputations. He sometimes tends however, to be obstinate. Effective leaders and some paranoid are high on Q3.
- **Factor Q4—Tense, frustrated, driven, overwrought (high agric tension)**—The person who scores high on factor Q4 tends to be tense, restless and impatient. He is often fatigued but unable to remain inactive. In groups he takes a poor view of the degree of unity, orderliness and leadership. His frustration represents an excess of stimulated, but undercharged drive.

Personality Factors of Muslims as Revealed by Their Janamkundalis and 16 Personality Factors

- Name—B
- Age—25 years
- Date of birth—20-07-1989
- Time of birth—5:35 am
- Place of birth—Almora

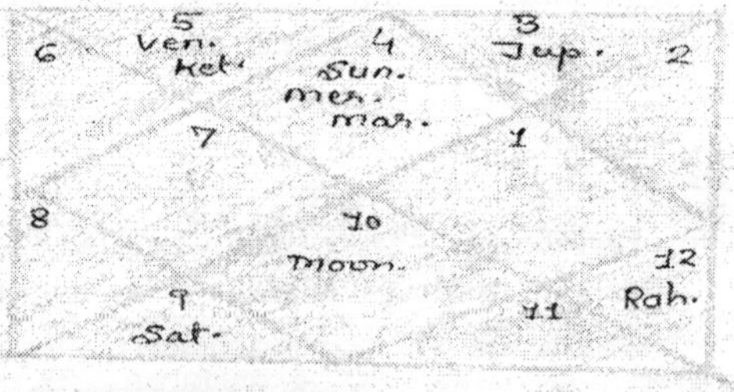

Chart 6.3: The Birth Chart of "B".

- **General characteristics**—Due to the lordship of moon, the native are remarkable for a changeful life. He has fertile imagination, delighting, in strange scenes and adventures. He is somewhat sentimental and talkative. He is very hard working and has artistic ability. He may miss good opportunities. His anger is shortlived and he holds no anger towards others.

- **Specific characteristics**—He has a strong urge to rule but he must learn to use power wisely.
- **Physical characteristics**—The native will be middle stature. He has a clumsy body, slender limbs and powerful claws. He has a large upper body, wide face and large mouth. His hairs may be brownish and complexion pale.
- **Wealth characteristics**—He will strive to process wealth and general indication for wealth are fairly good but he is one who will make and spend money with equal speed. Due to the rapid changes in fortune it is imperative that he learn to budget and save.
- **Education**—The position of Rahu indicates promise of a long life. The general indication for education are fairly good.
- **Health**—The position of Shukra indicates that he will normally enjoy very good health.
- **Social**—He has a few but very faithful friends.

Aspects Consideration

- **Moon Opposite Mars**—The Moon and Mars in this combination makes him temperamental and very moody. He is likely to be very rash and argumentative at times.
- **Moon square Jupiter**—Moon and Jupiter thus positioned makes him extravagant and emotionally rash.
- **Mars sextile Jupiter**—This aspect with Mars and Jupiter indicates that he enjoys financial protection.
- **Mars square Uranus**—This aspect between Mars and Uranus makes him temperamental. He may at times be totally frank and tactless. He may at times become irrational and even brutal.

Personality-Factors

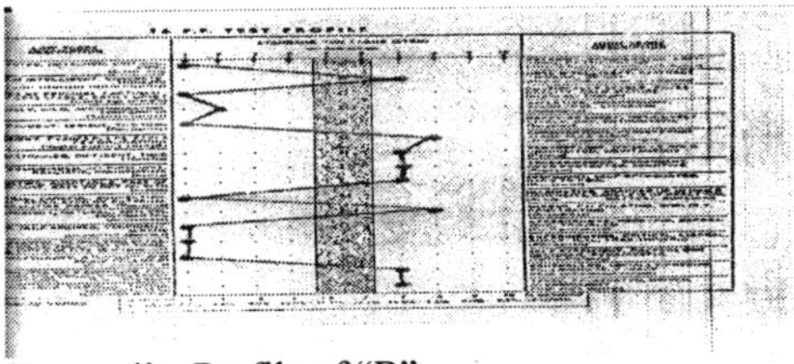

Fig. 6.2: Personality Profile of "B"

- **Factor A—Reserved, Detached, Critical, Cool (sizothymis)—** He is stiff, cool, skeptical and aloof. He likes things rather than people, working alone and avoiding compromise of viewpoints. He is likely to be precise and rigid in his way of doing things and in personal standard and in many occupations these are desirable traits. He may tend at times, to be critical obstructive or hard.
- **Factor B—More intelligent, Abstract thinking, Bright (Higher scholastic Capacity)**—The person who scores high on factor B tends to be quick to grasp ideas, a fast learner, intelligent. There is some correlation with level of culture and some with alertness. High scores contraindicate deterioration of mental function in pathological condition.
- **Factor C—Affected by feelings, Emotionally less stable, easily upset (lower ego strength)**—The person who scores low on factor C tends to be low in frustration tolerance for unsatisfactory conditions, changeable and plastic, evading necessary reality demands, neurotically fatigued fretful. Easily emotional and annoyed, active in dissatisfaction, having neurotic symptoms.
- **Factor E—Humble, Mild, accommodating, conforming (submissiveness)**—The person who scores low on factor E tends to give way to other. He is often dependent, confessing, anxious, obsessional correctness. This passivity is part of many syndromes.
- **Factor F—Sober, prudent, serious, taciturn (desurgency)—** The person who scores low on factor F tends to be restrained, reticent, introspective. He is sometimes dour, pessimistic, unduly deliberate, and considered smug and primarily correct by observers. He tends to be a sober, dependable person.
- **Factor G—Conscientious, Persevering, staid (stronger superego strength)**—The person who scores high on factor G tends to be exacting in character, donated sense of duty, preserver, responsible, painful, fills the unfurling minute.
- **Factor H—Venturesome, socially bold, spontaneous (parmia)**—The person who scores high on factor H is sociable, bold and spontaneous. He is always ready to try things. He tends to be pushy actively interested in the opposite.
- **Factor I—Tender minded, Dependent, overprotected, Sensitive (premise)**—The person who scores high on factor tends to be tender minded, day dreaming, artistic, fastidious,

feminine. He is sometimes demanding of attention and help, independent, dependent, impractical. He dislikes crude people and rough occupation. He tends to slow up group performance and to upset group moral by unrealistic fussiness.

- **Factor L—Suspicious, self-opinionated, hard to fool (pretension)**—The person who scores high on factor L tends to be mistrusting and doubtful. He is often involved in his own ego. He is usually deliberate in his action, unconcerned about other people, a poor team member.
- **Factor M—Practical, careful, conventional, regulated by external realities, proper (praxernis)**—The person who scores low on factor M tends to be anxious to do the right things, attentive to practical matters and subject to the dictation of what is obviously possible, able to keep his head in emergencies, but sometimes unimaginative.
- **Factor N—Shrewd, calculating, world Penetrating (shrewdness)**—The person who scores high on factor N tends to be polished worldly and shrewd. He is often analytical. He has an unsentimental approach.
- **Factor O—Placid, self-assured, confident, serene (untroubled adequacy)**—The person who scores low on factor O tends to be placid, with un shakable nerve. He has a mature unanxious confidence in himself and his capacity to deal with things. He is resilient and resource, but to the point of being insensitive of when a group is not going along with him, so that he may evoke antipathies and distrust.
- **Factor Q1—Conservative, respecting established ideas, tolerant of traditions**—The person who scores low on factor Q1 is confident in what he has been taught to believe and accepts the "tried and true" despite inconsistencies, when something else might be better. He is cautious and compromising in regard to new ideas. Thus, he tends to oppose and postpone change, is more conservative in religious and politics and tends not to be interested in analytical intellectual thought.
- **Factor Q2—A joiner and sound follower (group adherence)**—The person who scores low on factor Q2 prefers to work and make decisions with other people, likes and depends on social approval and administrations. He tends to go along with the group and may be lacking in individual resolution. He is not necessarily gregarious by choice rather he need group support.

- **Factor Q3—Controlled, socially precise, following self-image (high self-control)**—The person who scores high on factor Q3 tends to have strong control of his emotions and general behaviour, is inclined to be socially aware and careful, and evidences what is commonly termed "self respect" and regard for social reputations. He sometimes tends however to be obstinate. Effective leaders and some paranoid are high on Q3.
- **Factor Q4—Tense, frustrated, driven, overwrought (high agric tension)**—The person who scores high on factor Q4 tends to be tense, restless and impatient. He is often fatigued but unable to remain inactive. In groups he takes a poor view of the degree of unity, orderliness and leadership. His frustration represents an excess of stimulated, but undercharged drive.

Findings, in sum, reveal relationship between birth traits and personality factors.

Discussion

Result were derived from case analysis that the true qualities of participants obtained from their birth chart and 16 PF scores. It was found that a person has some characteristics or qualities from his birth and they are developed according to age and circumstances. They get modification with increase in age and are supported/suppressed by the circumstances. The attributes presented in the birth chart are only the signs or something more than the zero-point status of that particular quality or trait. They are firm developed, modified or hampered according to the social and/or personal circumstances. It is the responsibilities of the person under his/her trait and use them according to the demands. The attributes given in *janam kundali* are predicting forces that shape the personality characteristics and behaviour parameters.

- Our initial aim was to explore the personality profile of Hindus and Muslims through their 16 PF explanation and Birth chart.
- Personality is the total pattern of characteristic ways of thinking and behaviour, it is the dynamic and organized set of characterstics processed by a person that uniquely influences his or her cognition, emotion, motivation and behaviour in various situations. Personality is defined as an individual's typical or consistent adjustment to his environment. Personality also refers to the pattern of thoughts, feelings, and social adjustment and

behaviour consistently exhibited over times. They strongly influence one's expectations, self-perception, values, and attitudes. It also predicts human reactions to other people, problem and stress.

➢ Astrology is a tool meant to gain knowledge of the dynamics of our nature. Planets are constantly in motion with respect to earth in the skies. The positions of Sun, Moon and some planets close to earth can give important clues about the fortunes of individual human beings and groups of human beings. *That* is the basic premise of astrology.

Finding, in sum, reveal that if *Janam kundali* is properly prepared considering the accuracy of birth time, it predicts total truth of the person served. In addition, when the traits of *Janam kundali* are matched with personality test it is found same. In this way, it is proved that birth chart may be real predictor of psychological trait. Unfortunately, people of Hindu culture, where birth chart is considered very important, are forgetting or just avoiding its relevance. In Hindus system match of *kundali* between boy and a girl is found most important for the settlement and maintain happy married life. But people do not do it. They simply place the birth chart before the God and they think that they are blessed. Strangely, there are so many people who do not have birth chart.

This study has opened up many questions and touches wider issues, but there is a lot that is unexplored. After getting the result we can say that the birth chart, made by the help of birth date, birth time, birthplace represent the same qualities which we get by using psychological scales.

References

Adamson, Peter, "Al-Kindi", *The Stanford Encyclopaedia of Philosophy* (Spring 2011 Edition), Edward N. Zalta.http://www.aaperry.com/index.asp?pgid=64

Cattell, R.B. (1964). *The Description and Measurement of Personality*. New York: World Book.

Cattell, R.B. (1990). Advance in Cattellian Personality theory, In L.A. Pervin (Ed). *Hand Book of Personality: Theory and Research*. New York : Guildford.

Deneuve, C. (2006). *Personality Analysis with Psychological Astrology*. Paris.

Eysenck HJ and Nias DKB (1982). *Astrology: Science or Superstition*? Temple Smith, London, and St Martin's, New York.

http://www.skyscript.co.uk/synchronicity.html

http://www.cpalondon.com/history.html

7

Acculturative Strategies of Nepali Immigrants Living in India

Anubhuti Dubey and *Radha Maddhesia*

Introduction

Culture is reflected in the learned, shared beliefs, values, attitudes and behaviours, distinctiveness of a society or population. It is dynamic and ever-changing and is the process through which people organize, construct and adapt to their internal and external environment. Acculturation is a phenomenon in which groups of people and their individual members engage in intercultural contact, creating a potential for disagreement, and necessitate for its negotiation to achieve outcomes that are adaptive for individuals of both groups. It is the twofold process of cultural and psychological changes that takes place as a consequence of contact between two or more cultural groups and their individual members.

Understanding the processes and difficulties of acculturation could prove to be an important aspect of understanding cultural relations. Inferences are needed for policy recommendations that ease the process of acculturative adaptation but also for interventions that aim to reduce acculturative stress. Therefore, it is the purpose of this study to investigate which acculturative strategies are employed by the immigrants from Nepal residing in India on different social factors. Gorakhpur district is situated near the Indo-Nepal border. People from Nepal migrate to Gorakhpur for jobs in private sector as well as in Indian Army and Air Force as there is a Gorkha unit for Nepali people here in Gorakhpur, health care, studies As a consequence Nepali immigrants residing in these areas has mutual collaboration with each other culture, has occupational ties from last so many years. People from Nepal and India can move from and reside in each other's country as these countries do not have issues of visa and passport for individual of each other's country. Nepal has been unvoiced on the outpouring of its populace into India. Hence, it is difficult to count the number of Nepali citizens in India. However, it is estimated that almost six million Nepalese are working in India (Muni, 1996). In India in places like Darjeeling, Sikkim, Dharamsala, Dehradun etc. where colonies of those Nepalese have sprung up who have settled permanently here. Largely in the urban areas of India, one more group of Nepalese migrants are found whose stay is semi-permanent in nature and varies from six months to 10 years. The third group is of the seasonal migrants who migrate for three months during the winters (Jha, 1995). The movement of population towards India offers employment to Nepal's growing population on the one hand and facilitates in upkeep the families back at home by transfer of funds on the other. Those benefited with government employment in India obtain a pension on retirement which looks after them even after they have left for their country of origin. For instance, the military division of the Indian embassy in Kathmandu distributes pension not only to its ex-Gorkha soldiers but also to the Central and State Government pensioners.

Resemblance in the socio-cultural identities of the two countries supported the movement of people. The western border of Nepal, adjacent to Garhwal and Kumaon region of Uttarakhand, had inhabitants belonging to the same ethnic group as those across the border. Moreover, the segregation of borders between the two countries did not stop the movement of its population that sustained owing to economic exchanges and socio-cultural connections. The Terai border of Nepal positioned in proximity to the Indo-Gangetic plains of India has similar tribes, castes, languages, religious and social practices. The religious similarities have led to a greater suppleness in the attitudes of the people in agreeing to the movement of people from each other's country. For Example—the Hindus from India possess the temple of *Pashupati Nath* in Kathmandu, Nepal and Indian Hindus highly regard it as a place of pilgrimage, by tradition its head priest is always from Karnataka a state of India. In addition, the religious sentiments draw Hindus and Buddhists from Nepal to visit places of pilgrimage in India. Hence, the movement of people between the two countries carries on without termination. The Governments of India and Nepal have signed the *Treaty of Peace and Friendship* in 1950 and given a legitimate status to this visa free movement of citizens of both countries.

However, there are many factors that contribute to cultural differences among nations such as national heritage, language, traditions and rituals, food habits, race, geographical location, and historical events. Growing up in a particular culture leads to the internalization of shared ways of understanding the world (Kityama & Markus, 2000). Parents, schools, peers, and the media coach children in the way of their culture. Shared attitudes, norms, and values, contributes to the way people think, act and feel. Culture influences our goals and values, contributes to how we think about desirable and undesirable individual characteristics and behaviours, and sets normative expectations concerning the meaning and achievement of a successful life.

Acculturation refers to cultural alterations ensuing from primary contact between distinctive cultural groups (Redfield, Linton & Herskovits, 1936; Ward, 2006), predisposed by social customs of society on the one hand (Fuligni, 2001; Kim & Abreu, 2001; Montreuil & Bourhis, 2001; Sam, Vedder, Ward, & Hoarenczyk, 2006) and by an allegation of ethnic behaviours on others (Berry, 2005; Choi, 1997; Kim & Abreu, 2001; Kim & Omizo, 2006). Acculturation is the process by which an individual add in beliefs, behaviours and values from the new host culture into the context of beliefs, behaviours and values to the original culture (Constantine *et al.*, 2004; Noh & Kaspar, 2003). The acculturation process entails different levels of adjustment, endurance, adaptation, dominance, resistance and stress (Berry, 2006; Nwadiora & McAdoo, 1996). The process of acculturation is manifested by physiological and psychological changes owing to the adaptation requisite in diet, climate, housing, interaction styles, norms and values of a new society (Berry, 1997).

According to Ward (2001) there are two discrete dimensions of adapting to the host society. The first one phrased as psychological adaptation which implies to an individual's personal well-being and good mental health. And the second as socio-cultural adaptation, it refers to the individuals' social competence in maintaining their daily life functioning in the inter-cultural situation. Thus, acculturation basically necessitates learning to deal with a new cultural situation.

According to Berry and associates (1987) acculturation predispose to conceptualize individual changes moreover as a coping mechanism to a stressful situation provoked by the fall upon with an unfamiliar cultural context, or as a need on the part of an individual to learn specific cultural skills so as to prosper and endure in a given cultural context (Berry *et al.*, 1987). Two different factors are notable at the individual level: features prior to acculturation, like the age, gender, education, cultural distance and language, and features during the acculturation, such as acculturation strategies, attitudes and behaviours etc. (Berry, 2001).

Acculturation is the multidimensional, psychological and adaptive process that occurs when an individual interacts with other culture (Marin, 1992). Acculturation becomes the way in which an individual include values and behaviours of the new culture into currently held values and behaviours. It involves the maintenance of original culture identity and values as well as immigrant relationship with the dominant culture.

The adaptive process includes four acculturative attitudes, and they are integration, assimilation, marginalization and separation (Berry, 1998).

Integration takes place when the immigrants become proficient in the culture of the dominant group while retaining proficiency in the native culture. This is also phrased as biculturalism as the immigrants in this condition are highly acculturated (Berry, 1998). Integration is associated with abridged risk of acculturative stress and is increasingly accepted as the most adapted or well adaptive strategy (Berry, 1997; Ward & Kennedy, 1994).

Assimilations takes place when the individual reject the native culture and adapt to the dominant culture. They internalize the stereotypes negative concepts of their ethnic backgrounds (Sue & Sue, 1973). Individuals who adapt this strategy are caught between two cultural identities in a marginal position (Kim & Omizo, 2005) and they experience distress in the form of racial self-hatred and social isolation (Sue & Sue, 1973). Studies show that (Kagan & Cohen, 1990; Searle & Ward, 1990) assimilation strategy has shown expediency for social adaptation, as well as it has also negative impacts with regard to psychological adaptation. Assimilation is considered a risky orientation and likely to result in high levels of stress and anxiety, low self-esteem, difficulties in work or school, and low mood rating (Ward & Kennedy, 1994).

Separation occurs when the individuals only want to maintain their native culture with no intent to learn about the dominant culture. These individuals may experience difficulties when they have to interact with people outside of their ethnic background (Kim & Omizo, 2005) as they have strongly internalized the values, attitudes, beliefs and customs of their native culture. Immigrants adopting a separation strategy may acquire social support from their co-nationals and maintain their cultural identity. In a study Torres-Mastrullo (1976) measured it and found that lack of language (English) proficiency, has been associated with various problems such as depression, withdrawal and obsession compulsion, somatic symptoms, post-traumatic stress disorder and alcohol abuse/dependence (Escobar, Randolph, & Puente, 1983).

Marginalization occurs when individuals have no concern in maintaining or acquiring expertise in either the dominant culture or the culture of origin. Marginalization is exemplified by remarking out against the larger society and by feeling of alienation and loss of identity.

Researches with different immigrant groups shows that a tendency to isolate oneself from the host culture is associated with greater stress and that an integration strategy is usually the most adaptive strategy, while assimilation into the dominant culture is more likely to be related to psychological maladjustment and psychosomatic problems (Berry, 1997; Coll & Magnuson, 1997; Ward, 1996). Out of the four statuses separation and marginalization may be the most problematic since individuals in this status adhere to neither value systems (Kim & Omizo, 2005).

Cognitive flexibility is an enhanced awareness that in any problematic situation there are several alternative options available to solve the problem. And this also comprises the willingness to adapt to a situation; taking into consideration both linguistic and cultural differences (Martin & Rubin, 1995; Kim & Omizo, 2006). This relates to Lazarus and Folkman's (1984) cognitive appraisal process where stress is not always seen as such but is rather seen as temporary challenge that can be overcome by immigrants. The flexibility to interact and live with two cultures increases the capability to cope with problem and stress.

Among all four orientations of acculturation, acculturation theories contend that the integration or bicultural status is the healthiest status, followed by the assimilation status. These two modes of acculturative adaptation are helpful to the immigrant mental health (Berry, 1998). Lafromboise, Coleman & Gerton (1993) also supported that bicultural individuals exhibit increased cognitive functioning in the face of adversity. In order to reach the status of integration, the immigrants undergo a process of bicultural competence, a process in which the individuals are able to successfully meet the demands of the two distinct cultures. Bicultural competence includes (a) knowledge of cultural beliefs and values of both culture; (b) positive attitude towards both cultural groups; (c) bicultural efficacy or the belief that one can live in a satisfying manner within both cultures without sacrificing one's cultural identity; (d) communication ability in both cultures; (e) role repertoire or the range of culturally appropriate behaviours; and (f) a sense of being grounded in both cultures.

The integration style of acculturation is identified to serve as a resilient buffer against the development of psychopathology among adult immigrants, and the strategies of separation and marginalization produce poor adaptation in most circumstances (Berry, 1998). According to a study (Berry & Sam, 1997) individuals living in bicultural contexts tended to become maladjusted when they reject their culture of origin.

Markus and Kityama (1991) found that Asians are more interdependent than Westerners, i.e. they base their identities more on relationships with others. Lewis, Fernandez and Kleinman (1994) argue that because Western cultures view individuals as independent, self-contained, and autonomous, depressive symptoms are attributed to internal disturbances. In cultures that view individuals as interdependent, connected with others, and defined by the social context (e.g. Japan, China) these same symptoms may be attributed to interpersonal aspects (Markus & Kityama, 1991).

India and Nepal are the two Asian neighbour countries that are supposed to have interdependent relations with each other countries. From last so many years people of both countries can move freely within each other nations and share both social and psychological relations with members of each other country. The present study endeavours to find the effect of different social factors on acculturative strategies being adapted by the immigrants from Nepal residing near Indo-Nepal border areas.

Method

The study employed a descriptive research design. The purpose of the study was to examine the acculturative strategy used by Nepali immigrants for different social factors in their lives. The study used purposive sampling method.

Sample: The sample consisted of a total of 200 (100 male and 100 female) participants. They were recruited from the sites of bordering Indian city of Gorakhpur where Nepali immigrants reside. The participants were between the age-group of 25-50 years. All the participants were living in India for more than five years and earning their livelihood here. They frequently visit to their country of origin, i.e. Nepal.

Measures: Along with the some personal demographic information this study utilized an Acculturative Attitude Questionnaire (AAQ).

Acculturative Attitude Questionnaire—The questionnaire measures the attitude of people towards acculturation and it was developed by Mishra, Sinha & Berry (1996). The tool measures four acculturation orientations namely Integration, Assimilation, Separation and Marginalization. Originally, the items in this scale are related to 9 areas namely dressing style, friendliness, food, custom and rituals, residence,

Table 7.1: Frequency of Acculturation Strategies for different areas

Areas Assessed for Accultuative Attitude	*Acculturation Strategies*							
	Integration		*Assimilation*		*Separation*		*Marginalization*	
	M	*F*	*M*	*F*	*M*	*F*	*M*	*F*
Dressing Style	70	70	23	14	3	11	4	5
Friendliness	67	79	15	14	14	5	4	2
Food	71	75	10	5	18	18	1	2
Customs and Rituals	62	60	20	21	14	17	4	2
Residence	77	79	6	6	13	7	4	8
Cooperation	73	84	9	3	15	10	3	3
Naming the Child	47	59	30	19	18	18	5	4
Lifestyle	66	75	16	13	13	11	5	1
Community Relations	66	79	21	11	10	9	3	1
Sense of Security	59	71	26	10	11	14	4	5
Matrimonial Relations	56	61	29	29	10	8	5	2

Note: Male = M; Female = F

co-operation, naming of the child, lifestyle and community relationship. However, the present researchers have done an open-ended interview with the Nepali immigrants and content analysis was done with this interview data. On the basis of which two more areas namely sense of security and matrimonial relations were added to the origin scale with the permission of the original developers of the scale. For each of the 11 areas mentioned above four statements for the four orientation of integration, assimilation, separation and marginalization were framed. The participants had to select anyone of the four statements by expressing their judgements on a five point ladder scale. But in the present study, it was felt that some Nepali immigrants were unable to give responses on a five point ladder scale. Thus in the present study responses were taken only for the four acculturation orientations against each area.

Procedure—For the data collection the researcher went to the areas of Gorakhpur city where Nepali immigrants are mass living. The researcher explained the purpose of the study to the participants and asked them to partake in the self-administered study. The participants who wish to participate were asked to sign an informed consent. After getting signed, the informed consent form they were given Acculturation Attitude Questionnaire to complete. And once they were done questionnaire were taken back from them.

Results

Quantitative data analysis was employed in this study. Frequencies for each of the acculturation applied by the immigrants were computed and are presented in Table 7.1.

The respondents' acculturation orientation towards different social aspects is depicted in Table 7.1. The largest number of respondents (both male and female) showed integration strategy on all the dimensions mentioned. When the Nepali participants were asked about their attitude regarding dressing style, a large number of both male and female participants (140 out of 200 participants) had shown the Integration Strategy. This was found true for all the other areas assessed in the study namely, Friendliness (146 out of 200 participants); Food (146 out of 200 participants); Customs and Rituals (122 out of 200 participants); Residence (156 out of 200 participants); Cooperation (157 out of 200 participants); Naming the Child (106 out of 200 participants); Lifestyle (141 out of 200 participants); Community relations (145 out of 200 participants); Sense of Security (130 out of 200 participants); and Matrimonial relations (117 out of 200 participants). This suggests that most of the Nepali immigrants showed orientation towards integration.

It can be suggested from the table that in comparison to the participants showing orientation towards integration, only 37 participants out of 200 showed attitude towards assimilation when they were asked about their dressing style. It can be seen on all other areas as mentioned in the scale. In the area of Friendliness (29 out of 200), Food (15 out of 200), Customs and rituals (41 out of 200), Residence (16 out of 200), Cooperation (12 out of 200), Naming of the Child (49 out of 200), Lifestyle (29 out of 200), Community Relations (32 out of 200), Sense of Security (36 out of 200) and Matrimonial Relations (58 out of 200).

In comparison to the respondents showing attitude towards integration and assimilation less number of participants showed orientation towards separation. Moreover, 14 participants out of 200 showed orientations toward separation when they were asked about their dressing style. On all other areas as mentioned in the scale in the area of Friendliness (only 4 male while 2 female participants out of 200), Food (36 out of 200), Customs and rituals (31 out of 200), Residence (20 out of 200), Cooperation (25 out of 200), Naming of the Child (36 out of 200), Lifestyle (24 out of 200), Community Relations (19 out of 200), Sense of Security (25 out of 200) and Matrimonial Relations (18 out of 200).

It can be seen from the table that in contrast to the participants showing orientation towards integration, assimilation and separation less number of participants showed orientation towards marginalization. In addition, 9 participants out of 200 have showed orientation towards separation when they were asked about their dressing style. On all other areas as mentioned in the scale in the area of Friendliness (only 14 male while 5 female participants out of 200), Food (3 out of 200), Customs and rituals (6 out of 200), Residence (12 out of 200), Cooperation (6 out of 200), Naming of the Child (9 out of 200), Lifestyle (5 male and 1 female out of 200), Community Relations (4 out of 200), Sense of Security (9 out of 200) and Matrimonial Relations (7 out of 200).

It can be understood from the Table that there was not much differences between acculturation orientation of male and female respondents on different areas as mentioned in the questionnaire. Inclination towards integration was more in comparison to assimilation, separation and marginalization. While orientation towards assimilation, separation and marginalization kept on decreasing respectively.

Discussion

More than half of the respondents showed attitude towards integration in every aspect as mentioned in the questionnaire. Berry (1997) has also found in a study that integration ought to be the best orientation of acculturation strategy for cross-cultural adaptation while marginalization served to be the least used method. The findings of the study correspond to previous research based on the process of acculturation and bicultural competence (Berry & Kim, 1998). When immigrants have lived in the United States from the beginning and had lived there for a longer period of time, they become more accustomed and feel contented about the American culture, the English language, and the American learning and their teaching patterns. They have developed a secured social support system as well through years of living in this society. Consequently, they turn out to be more integrated into the American society and thus lowered level of acculturative stress. In a study Krishnan and Berry (1992) found integration as the most adaptive acculturation approach. There is a well-built correspondence between prospects of the host culture towards immigrants and the acculturation strategy being adopted. Such as an opportunity of assimilation can lead to a melting pot approach; burden of separation can result in segregation and marginalization can direct to exclusion from the host culture (Berry, 2001; Huntington, 2004). According to Lafromboise *et al.* (1993) immigrants who are oriented towards integration in acculturation, they are successfully able to meet the demands of American as well as their native culture and have attained bicultural competence. It can be said that when Nepali immigrants opt for integration (biculturalism) attitude it ease them to overcome obstacles that may arise due to differences between two cultures.

Immigrants from Nepal residing in India had orientation towards integration or biculturalism in preferring dressing style, friendliness, food, custom and rituals, residence, cooperation, lifestyle and community relationship. Comparatively they showed less orientation towards integration towards social factors such as naming of the child, sense of security and matrimonial relations. It indicates that they generally adapt to biculturalism in low social factors of daily living. But when it comes to sense of security, matrimonial relations and naming of the child they are less integrated and showed attitude towards assimilation too. While separation and marginalization were the least preferred strategy in this aspect. According to Berry (2003) immigrants resolve to come upon or adjust themselves towards defending them against threat *versus* embracing challenge will depend on several factors such as the motives for migration, the political conditions in the host society, the cultural differences or similarities between the sending and receiving societies, and the immigrants' dispositional qualities. Besides acculturation strategies used by immigrant's cross-cultural adaptation may be predisposed by social support (Berry, 1997; Berry & Sam, 1997).

Social indicators on different aspects as mentioned in the questionnaire suggest that most of the immigrants have integration as the acculturation strategy and least marginalization was depicted. The study correlates with previous studies (Berry *et al.*, 2006) showing that integration is the widely chosen process and turn out to be the best in the immigrant's adaptation during acculturation. Even though integration emerges as the most preferred acculturative strategy, it is alleged that the differences in the use of strategies might be based on differences in features existing prior to acculturation such as proximity between cultures, cultural plurality in the original culture, their level of education, perception of the native culture, language, age and gender.

The differences between two cultures may be accredited to the features of two distinct cultures. As much as there is closeness between the original and new culture it facilitates in the integration process and entails biculturalism. As immigrants from Nepal are able to easily move between the aura of both countries—Nepal and India and can have regular interactions with the people of native culture and dominant culture as well, makes them suffice to have bicultural competence. In a study Berry *et al.* (1987) found that nearness between two cultures produces less "behavioural shifts" and lessen the acculturative stress, as a consequence there are fewer levels of psychological problems.

Apart from social factors, abundant psychological factors may play a crucial role for individuals experiencing acculturation. Such factors include differences and similarities between factors of two cultures of immigrants which were present prior to contact with dominant culture, and those which developed during the process of acculturation. Certain experiences may predispose one to function more efficiently under acculturative pressures. These are prior knowledge of the new language and culture, prior intercultural encounters of any kind, motives for the contact (voluntary *versus* involuntary contact), and attitudes toward contact (that can range from positive to negative).

The findings of study is also confirmed with researches (Abe, Talbot, & Geelhoed, 1998; Hammer, 2002) that success of social adjustment to a new country is related to the quantity of both close and causal relationship immigrants have with people from the dominant culture. These interactions are also supportive to lessen acculturative stress (Olaniran, 1993).

Acculturation is a process that continues for as long as there are culturally different groups in contact, some longer-term adaptation to living in cultural-contact settings takes various forms usually resulting in some form of longer-term accommodation among the groups in contact. This often entails, for example, learning each other's languages, sharing each other's food preferences, and adopting forms of dress and social interactions that are characteristics of each group. Sometimes, these mutual adaptations take place rather easily (through processes of culture shedding and culture learning (Berry, 1992). Acculturative stress is always a probable outcome of acculturation, but its likelihood of occurrence can be much condensed if both participation in the dominant culture and maintenance of one's heritage culture are greeted by the policy and live out by the host culture.

Future quantitative as well as qualitative research on social predictors of acculturative strategies can build on this study. It is crucial to provide a better understanding of the social and psychological factors of Nepali immigrants residing in India so that it can be helpful in reducing acculturative stress and enhances their well-being and mental health.

References

Abe, J., Talbot, D.M., and Geelhoed, R.J. (1998). Effects of peer programme on international student adjustment. *Journal of College Student Development*, *39*, 539-547.

Berry, John; Kim, Uichol; Minde, Thomas and Mok, Doris (1987). Comparative studies of acculturative stress. *International Migration Review, 21,* 491-511.

Berry, J.W. (1992). Acculturation and adaptation in a new society. *International Migration, 30*, 69-85.

Berry, John. (1997). Immigration, acculturation and adaptation. *Applied Psychology: An International Review 46,* 5-34.

Berry, J.W. (1998). Acculturation and health: theory and research. In S. Kazarian, and D.R. Evans (Eds.), *Cultural Clinical Psychology* (pp. 39-57). New York: Oxford University Press.

Berry, J.W. (2001). A Psychology of Immigration. *Journal of Social Issues, 57*(3), 615-631.

Berry, J.W. (2003). Conceptual approaches to acculturation. In K. Chun, P. Balls-Organista, and G. Marin (Eds.), *Acculturation: Advances in Theory, Measurement and Applied Research* (pp. 17-37). Washington, DC: APA Press.

Berry, J.W. (2005). Acculturation: Living successfully in two cultures. *International Journal of Intercultural Relations, 29,* 697-712.

Berry, J.W. (2006). Acculturative stress. In Wong, PTP., Wong, LCJ., editors. *Handbook of Multicultural Perspectives on Stress and Coping.* Dallas: Spring Publications, pp. 287-298.

Berry, J., Kim, U., Minde, T., and Mok, D. (1987). Comparative studies of acculturative stress. *International Migration Review, 21,* 491-511.

Berry, J.W., and Sam, D.L. (1997). Acculturation and adaptation. In J.W. Berry, Y.H. Poortinga, and J. Pandey (Eds.), *Handbook of Cross-cultural Psychology* (pp. 291-326). Boston: Allyn & Bacon.

Berry, J.W., and Sam, D.L. (1997). Acculturation and adaptation. In J.W. Berry, M.H. Segall, and C. Kagitcibasi (Eds.), *Handbook of Cross-cultural Psychology, Vol. 3: Social Behaviour and Applications* (pp. 291-326). Needham Heights, MA: Viacom.

Berry, J., Phinney, J., Sam, D., and Vedder, P. (2006). Immigrant youth: acculturation, identity, and adaptation. *Applied Psychology: An International Review, 55,* 303-332.

Choi, G. (1997). Acculturative stress, social support, and depression in Korean American families. *Journal of Family and Social Work, 2*(1), 81-97.

Coll, C.G., and Magnuson, K. (1997). The psychological experience of immigration: A developmental perspective. In A. Booth, A. Crouter and N.S. Landale (Eds.), *Immigration and the Family: Research and Policy on U.S. Immigrants* (pp. 91-131). Hillsdale, NJ: Erbaum.

Constatntine, M., Okazaki, S., and Utsey, S. (2004). Self-concealment, social self-efficacy, acculturative stress, and depression in African, Asian, and Latin American International College Students. *American Journal of Orthopsychiatry, 74*(3), 230-241.

Fuligni, A.J. (2001). A comparative longitudinal approach to acculturation among children from immigrant families. *Harvard Educational Review, 71*(3), 66-78.

Huntington, S.P. (2004). *Who are We? The Challenges to America's National Identity.* New York, NY: Simon & Schuster.

Jha, N. (1994). Minorities, Immigrants and Refugee Issues in the Context of Indo-Nepal Relations" in Kalim Bahadur, Mahendra P. Lama, ed., *New Perspectives on India-Nepal Relations* (New Delhi: Har-Anand Publication, 1995), p. 24.

Kagan, H., and Cohen, J. (1990). Cultural adjustment of international students. *Psychological Science, 1*, 133-137.

Kim, B., and Abreu, J.M. (2001). Acculturation measurement: Theory, current instruments, and future directions. In J.G. Ponterotto, J.M. Casas, L.A. Suzuki, and C.M. Alexander (Eds.), *Handbook of Multicultural Counselling* (2nd ed., pp. 394-424). Thousand Oaks, CA: Sage Publications.

Kim, B., and Omizo, M. (2006). Behavioural acculturation and enculturation and psychological functioning among Asian American college students. *Cultural Diversity and Ethnic Minority Psychology, 12*(2), 245-258.

Kim, B.S.K., and Omizo, M.M. (2005). Asian and European American cultural values, collective self-esteem, acculturative stress, cognitive flexibility, and general self-efficacy among Asian American college students. *Journal of Counselling Psychology*, *52*, 412-419.

Kim, Y. (2008). Intercultural personhood: Globalization and a way of being. *International Journal of Intercultural Relations, 32*(4), 359-368.

Kitayama, S., and Markus, H.R. (2000). The pursuit of happiness and the realization of sympathy: Cultural patterns of self, social relations, and well-being. In *Culture and Subjective Well-being.* Eds. Diener, E., Suh, E.M. Cambridge, M.A. MIT Press. pp. 113-1621.

Krishnan, A., and Berry, J.W. (1992). Acculturative stress and acculturation attitudes among Indian immigrants to the United States. *Psychology and Developing Societies, Special Issue: Immigrant Mental Health, 4*(2), 187-212.

LaFromboise, T., Coleman, H.L.K., and Gerton, J. (1993). Psychological impact of biculturalism: Evidence and theory. *Psychological Bulletin, 114*, 395-412.

Lazarus, R.S., and Folkman, S. (1984). *Stress Appraisal and Coping.* New York: Springer.

Lewis-Fernandez, R. and Kleinman, A. (1994). Culture, personality and psychopathology. *Journal of Abnormal Psychology, 103* (1), 67-71.

Marin, G. (1992). Issues in the measurement of acculturation among Hispanics. In K.F. Geisinger (Ed.), *Psychological Testing of Hispanics* (pp. 235-251). Washington, DC.: American Psychological Association.

Markus, H.Z., and Kitayama, S. (1991). Culture and the Self: Implications for the Cognition, Emotion, and Motivation. *Psychological Review,* Vol. 98, *(2),* 224-253.

Martin, M., and Rubin, R.B. (1995). A new measure of cognitive flexibility. *Psychological Reports, 76,* 623-626.

Mishra, R.C., Sinha, D., and Berry, J.W. (1996). *Ecology, Acculturation and*

Psychological Adaptation: A study of Adivasis in Bihar. New Delhi: Sage Publications.

Montreuil, A., and Bourhis, R. (2001). Majority acculturation orientation toward "valued" and "devalued" immigrants. *Journal of Cross-Cultural Psychology, 32,* 698-719.

Muni, S.D., and Baral, L.R. (1996). *Refugees and Regional Security in South Asia*. New Delhi: Konark Publishers, p. 17.

Nwadiora, E., and McAdoo, H. (1996). Acculturative stress among Amerasian refugees: Gender and racial differences. *Adolescence, 31,* 477-486.

Olaniran, B.A. (1993). International students' network patterns and cultural stress: What really counts?*Communication Research Reports, 10*, 69-83.

Redfield, R., Linton, R., and Herskovits, M.J. (1936). Memorandum on the study of acculturation. *American Anthropologist, 38,* 149-152.

Sam, D.L., Vedder, P., Ward, C., and Hoarenczyk, G. (2006). Psychological and socio-cultural adaptation of immigrant youth. In J.W. Berry, J.S. Phinney, D.L. Sam, and P. Vedder (Eds.), *Immigrant Youth in cultural transition: Acculturation, Identity and Adaptation across National Contexts* (pp. 117-141). London: Lawrence Erlbaum.

Searle, W., and Ward, C. (1990). The prediction of psychological and socio-cultural adjustment during cross-cultural transitions. *International Journal of Intercultural Relations, 14*(4).

Sue, S., and Sue, D.W. (1973). Chinese American personality and mental health. In S. Sue, and N. Wagner (Eds.), *Asian-Americans: Psychological Perspectives* (pp. 111-124). San Francisco: Science and Behaviour Books.

Ward, C. (1996). Acculturation. In D. Landis and R.S. Bhagat (Eds.), *Handbook of Intercultural Training* (Vol. 2, pp. 124-147). Thousand Oaks, CA: Sage Publications.

Ward, C. (2006). Acculturation, identity and adaptation in dual heritage adolescents. *International Journal of Intercultural Relations, 30*(2), 243-259.

Ward, C. (2001). The A, B, Cs of acculturation. In David Matsomoto (Ed.), *The Handbook of Culture and Psychology* (pp. 411-445). Oxford: Oxford University Press.

Ward, C., and Kennedy, A. (1994). Acculturation strategies, psychological adjustment and socio-cultural competence during cross-cultural transitions. *International Journal of Intercultural Relations, 1*, 329-343.

8

Culture, Family and Cognitive Behaviour

Aradhana Shukla

In these days considerable attention is being made on various aspects of culture and its variation. It has been observed that culture prevails in that particular area where it is rooted. So, it is necessary to explore the essence of various cultures at the place of emergence. People, if, they do not leave their places and reside in this culture specific environment, it affects their behaviour. In this study pattern of family climate and cognitive behaviour (metamemory) was studied in *Bhotia, Tharu, Raji* and *Buxa* tribals and General Kumaunies as affected by their cultural variation, gender and age. Delineation of concepts is as follows:

Culture

Culture is defined as a dynamic system of rules, explicit and implicit, established by groups in order to ensure their survival, involving attitudes, values beliefs, norms and behaviours, shared by a group but harboured differently by each specific unit within the group communicated across generation, relatively stable but with the potential to change across time.

The dynamics of the cross-cultural experience at the personal level represents the process of positive disintegration. Such experiences can occur whenever new environments of experience and perception are encountered. Although many different reactions and responses, can take place in this confrontation of cultures, the greatest shock may be the encounter with one's own cultural heritage and the degree to which one is a product of it. In the encounter with another culture, the individual gains new experiential knowledge becoming to understand the roots of his or her own ethnocentrism and by gaining new perspectives and outlooks on the nature of culture and its experiences. Throughout the transitional experience, the individual is presented with differ ences and complexity. When differences cannot be ignored, they become distorted. This distortion gives rise to emotions that each person must come to understand experientially so doing, learning, self-awareness and personal growth takes place. Anecdotal evidence suggests that such inspirational personal outcomes can emerge from the intercultural encounter. Certainly, the hope of such change motivates some exploration across cultures, and fuller scientific documentation of it would be most useful in helping us to understand the cross-cultural experience.

Yang (1988) has synthesized the results from both the cross-cultural and intercultural studies and produced the following profile of the modern cultured person:

- A sense of personal efficacy (anti-fatalism),
- Low social integration with relatives.
- Egalitarian attitudes towards others.
- Openness to innovation and change.
- A belief in sex equality.
- High achievement motivation. Independence or self-reliance.
- Active participation in social organizations.
- Tolerance of and respect for others.
- Cognitive and behavioural flexibility.
- Strong future orientation.
- Empathetic capacity.
- A high need for information.
- Propensity to take risks in life.
- A preference for urban life.
- An individualistic orientation towards others.
- A non-local orientation.

Family Climate

The term climate has been regarded as providing a network of forces and factors which surround, engulf and play on the individual (Bloom, 1968). According to Stott (1974) the term environment in its usual sense, encompasses all of the influences upon development which come from outside the individual. Good (1973), *Biswas* and Aggrawal (1971) and Wolman (1977) have also given similar definition to the term environment.

Different authors have also defined the home or family. Murdock (1949) states that "the family is as social group characterized by common residence, economic co-operation and reproduction, it include of both sexes, who maintain a socially approved sexual relationship and one or more children, own or adopted of the sexual co-habituating pair" the international dictionary of education mentions that "family is a primary social group of parents, offsprings and possibly other members of household".

Maslow (1941) in contrast, stated that, "A good home is said to be one in which the child is given fullest opportunity for self-expression within the limits of parental affection and supervision." Malm and Jamisom (1952) characterized, "a good home" with affection; democracy; lack of conflict; comradeship; good personal adjustment; security and appropriateness of attitude". Douvan and Adelison (1966), defined a democratic family as one "in which the child is allowed a fair degree of autonomy; is included in important discussion massing and is controlled primarily by reasoning and verbal discipline." On the other hand, an authoritarian family is that in which rules are set without consulting the children. Autonomy is limited and discipline is made by physical resources.

According to Chronbach (1977) "Home differs in many respects; warmth, encouragement of independence, pressure for achievement and so on. Warm parents express their own love and encourage the child to express his feeling. Family members react to each other on emotional level. Other extreme is hostile rejection. The parents dislike children and are continuously critical and punitive. In some homes the child has little influence and freedom while other homes are often caused by democratic practices. Here, policies are worked out between parent and child or explained carefully." Danesh (1978) pointed out "authoritarian families are power oriented, tend to have dichotomous conceptions, have emotional and intellectual rigidity. In contrast, democratic homes and permissive home bows to the whims of the child."

Metamemory

Metamemory is the insight or awareness of an individual's own memory functioning (Troyer & Rich, 2002). Metamemory includes the components of contentment ability and strategies produced from factor analysis conducted by Troyer and Rich (2002). Contentment is the confidence, concern and satisfaction in the ability to remember things ability refers to the ease in remembering events and information. Strategies involve asking someone to remember, creating rhymes and visual images, organizing, saying out loud, making a list, and elaboration.

The relationship between memory and the writing process has been investigated only recently. Metamemory as a strategy has shown influence over language proficiency but not isolating written proficiency as a dependent measure (Ehrman & Oxford, 1995; Goh & Foong, 1997; Ku, 1997; Mullins, 1992; Oxford, 1995; Politzer & McGroarty, 1985). In students done by Bedell and Oxford (1996), Rong (1999) and Bremner ***(1999),*** it is found as the least useful strategy employed in language learning with Chinese students as their participants. Memory as a strategy in language proficiency is commonly used as individuals' need to retain English vocabulary and construction overtime to be able to use it when necessary. This has been illustrated in some researches where learners are more likely to remember the items that they have just generated on their own than the ones presented or read (Kinjo & Snodgrass, 2000; Moshfeghi & Sharifian, 1998; Slamecka & Graf, 1978). It can also be explained that as the level of proficiency in second language increases, cognitive processes such as memory also approximates development (Sharifian, 2002).

The link between memory and the writing task was explained by Olive (2004) using the dual-task technique. It was explained that in writing during the planning stage, writers construct a preverbal message that corresponds to idea that they want to communicate. The ideas are retrieved from the long term memory and organized. The preverbal message is then transformed into a verbal message. During the transformation, the plan is grammatically encoded by retrieving the mental lexicon, the meaning of words and rules for word formation. The written text is then improved by comparing the mental representation and the text already written. Lastly, during the psychomotor level, there is the execution or graphic representation of the linguistic message producing handwriting. From this model, writing is viewed as a cognitive task where information is retrieved from memory, and then the execution of writing takes place. It can be noted that memory takes an important role in writing since morphology, syntax and semantics are accessed in memory.

Keeping these views in consideration this study was planned and it was aimed to find out the impact of cultural variation and gender on experiential supportiveness of family climate and cognitive behaviour in developmental perspective. It was contended that:

- Variation in culture would cause variation in experiential supportiveness of family climate and cognitive behaviour.
- Boys and girls would evince difference in relation to their scores on experiential supportiveness of family climate and cognitive behaviour.
- Variation in experiential supportiveness of family climate and cognitive behaviour would also be caused by age related variation.

Method

Coverage of the study: In this study four tribal races namely, *Bhotia, Tharu, Raji* and *Buxa* were taken in consideration and they were taken from Uttarakhand, India.

Sample: Two hundred and forty participants aged 7-12 years hailing from various sub-cultural segments of Uttarakhand, India served in this study and were arranged according to the requirements of 3 way factorial design with 5 types of cultural groups *(Bhotia, Tharu, Raji, Buxa and general Kumauni)* 2 gender (boys and girls) and 2 levels of chronological age (7-9 years and 10-12 years), i.e. 12 participants per cell. The schematic presentation of experimental design is shown in Table 8.1:

	A1		A2		A3		A4		A5	
	B1	B2	B1	B2	B1	B2	B1	B2	B1	B2
C1	12	12	12	12	12	12	12	12	12	12
C2	12	12	12	12	12	12	12	12	12	12

Table 8.1: Schematic Presentation of Experimental Design.

Legends

A = Cultural variation
A1 = Bhotia
A2 = Tharu
A3 = Raji
A4 = Buxa
A5 = General Kumauni

B = Gender
B1 = Boys
B2 = Girls

C = Age
C1 = 7-9 years
C2 = 10-12 years

Measures: In this study two measures were considered and their description is as follows:

Home Environment Scale

In order to assess the pattern of family climate, the HES was employed. Constructed by Dhaundiyal (1993) this measures has 74 items and it deals with ten dimensions namely, *1-Attention and care 2-facilities 3-impartiality 4-parental approval of adolescents' activities 5-sharing of ideas 6-trust 7-confidence 8-decision making 9-parental support and encouragement and 10 harmony among family members.* It is a questionnaire of True-False items. Two scores are given for the true items and one score for false item. Thus, the score ranges between 74-148. Low score indicates supportive family climate and high *vice versa.* Split half reliability is .79 and test retest reliability .70.

Measure of meta memory: In order to measure the pattern of meta memory two question papers were framed. Since 7-9 years old were the students of IInd class and 10-12 years old were the students of Vth class so two question papers were framed. Each question paper was consisted of 5 questions of arithmetic having 50 total marks, i.e. 10 marks per question.

Procedure: At first the researcher contacted some villages where the tribal used to live. After establishing proper rapport with the *Gram Pradhan* and villagers, she came in the contact of participants of the target age group on whom measure of family climate and meta memory were administered. Data collection was done individually/in group as per her convenience and ability of the participants and best attempts were made to avoid external distractions.

Results

Data was analyzed by 3 way analysis of variance and interpreted in terms of sub-cultural variation, gender and age as affectors of *(i) experiential family climate* and *(ii) meta memory.* Findings are presented in two sections and they are as follows:

Section one

I. Impact of cultural variation, gender and age on experiential family climate: Data were analysed by 3 analysis of variance and they are reported in Table 8.2.

Table 8.2: Summary table of analysis of variance showing the impact of cultural variation, gender and age on family climate

Sources of Variation	*Ss*	*df*	*MS*	*F*
A	13.24	4	3.11	8.49
B	1.59	1	1.59	4.10
C	.37	1	.37	.094
AB	13.97	4	3.49	8.96
AC	14.19	4	3.55	9.10
BC	1.63	1	1.63	4.19
ABC	16.47	4	4.11	10.56
Error within	55.80	220	.39	
		239		

Table 8.3: Summary table of analysis of variance showing the impact of cultural variation, gender and age on metamemory.

Sources of Variation	*Ss*	*df*	*MS*	*F*
A	105.71	4	26.42	7.40
B	.098	1	.098	.35
C	.059	1	.059	.21
AB	9.96	4	2.49	8.90
AC	9.17	4	2.29	8.19
BC	115	1	115	4.12
ABC	10.27	4	2.57	9.17
Error within	61.60	220	.28	
		239		

A close perusal of the table reveals that the main effect of cultural variation was significant (F, 4, 239 = 8.49 P < .01). Mean values pooled across gender and age were respectively for *Bhotia, Tharu, Raji, Buxa* and General Kumauni population. The next main effect of sex was also significant (F, 1,239 = 4.410 P < .05) and it was found that boys experienced supportiveness for home environment (X = 27.80) than girls (X = 36.50). The next main effect of chronological age was insignificant (F, 1,239 = .94 P > .05). It was found that participants of 7-9 years (X = 33.00) and 10-12 (X = 31.30) were almost equal in relation to their scores on home climate.

The cultural variation × gender interaction was significant (F, 4,239 = 8.96 P < .01) and it is presented in Fig. 8.1.

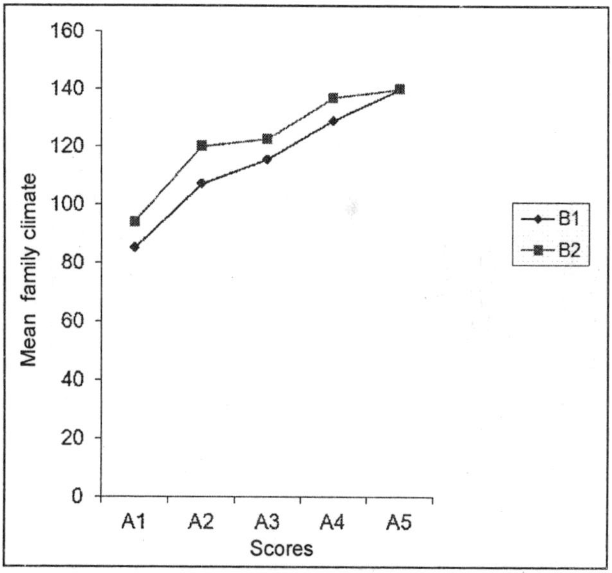

Fig. 8.1: Mean scores showing the impact of cultural variation and age on family climate

Legends

***A* = Cultural variation**	***B* = Gender**
A1 = Bhotia	B1 = Boys
A2 = Tharu	B2 = Girls
A3 = Raji	
A4 = Buxa	
A5 = General Kumauni	

Figure reveals cultural variation and it was commonly shared by both gender. The cultural variation × chronological age was also significant (F, 4,239 = 9.10 P < .01) and it is mentioned in Fig. 8.2. Figure reveals that general Kumaunies showed highest discrepancy and it was evident at both age groups. Also, gender related discrepancy was more pronounced in general Kumaunies.

The sex age × interaction was significant (F, 1,239 = 4.19 P < .05) and it is shown in Fig. 8.3. Figure shows sex related difference in older age group.

The three way interaction of cultural variation × sex × age interaction was significant (F, 4,239 = 10.56 P < .01) and it is reported in Fig. 8.4.

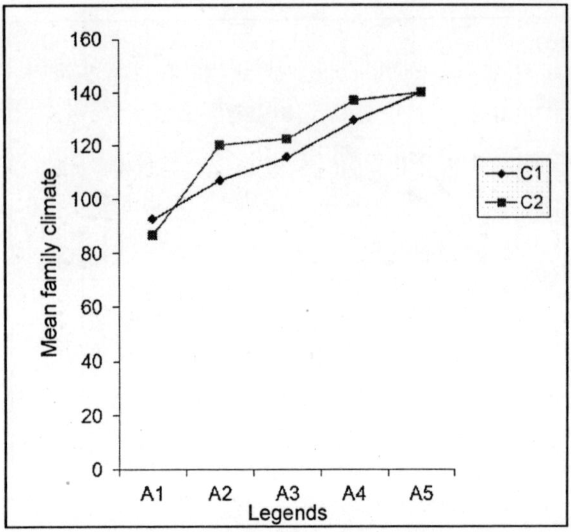

Fig. 8.2: Mean scores showing the impact of cultural variation and age on family climate

Legends

A = Cultural varlation	***C = Age***
A1 = Bhotia	C1 = 7-9 years
A2 = Tharu	C2 = 10-12 years
A3 = Raji	
A4 = Buxa	
A5 = General Kumauni	

Figure shows that all variables laid their impact on family climate experience.

(ii) Impact of cultural variation, gender and chronological age on metamemory: Obtained data were analyzed in 3 way analysis of variance and they are presented in Fig. 8.5.

A close perusal of the table reveals that the main effect of cultural variation was significant (F, 4, 239 = 7.40 P < .01). It was found that variation is climate caused variation in the magnitude of meta memory. Mean values pooled across sex and ages were: 9.00, 7.00, 7.25, 8.75 and 4.50 respectively for *Bhotia, Tharu, Buxa, Raji and General Kumauni* participants. The next main effect of sex was insignificant (F, 1,239 = .35 P > .05). It was noted that boys (X = 7.20) and girls (X = 7.50) were

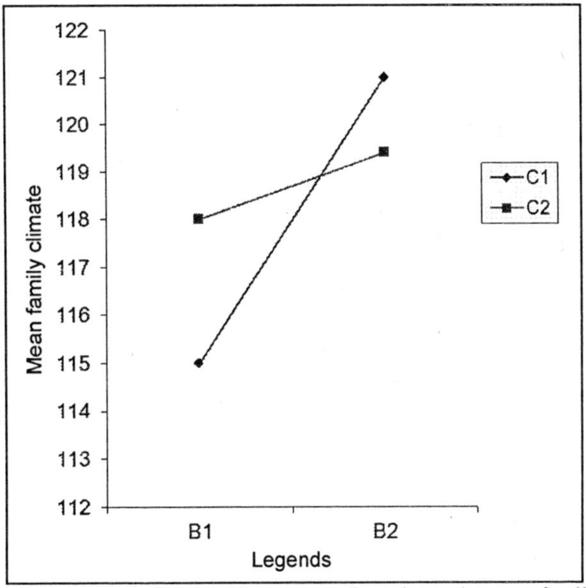

Fig. 8.3: Mean scores showing the impact of gender and age on family climate

Legends

B = Gender ***C = Age***

B1 = Boys C1 = 7-9 years

B2 = Girls C2 = 10-12 years

almost equal in relation to their scores on metamemory. The last main effect of chronological age was also insignificant (F, 1,239=.21 P>.05). It was found that 7-9 years old (X = 7.50) and 10-12 years old (X = 7.00) participants were almost equal in metamemory.

The cultural variation × sex interaction was significant (F, 4,239 = 8.90 P < .01) and it is reported in Fig. 8.5.

Figure shows that unsimilarity in boys and girls showed reversed trend in metamemory. The cultural variation × age interaction was also significant (F, 4,239=8.19 P<.01) and it is shared by Fig. 8.6.

The gender × age interaction was also significant (F, 1,239=4.12 P<.05) and it is depicted in Fig. 8.7. A reversed trend in both groups was shown by them.

The three way interaction of cultural variation × sex × age was also significant (F, 4,239=9.17 P<.01) and it is appeared in Fig. 8.8. Figure shows that all variations laid their impact on metamemory.

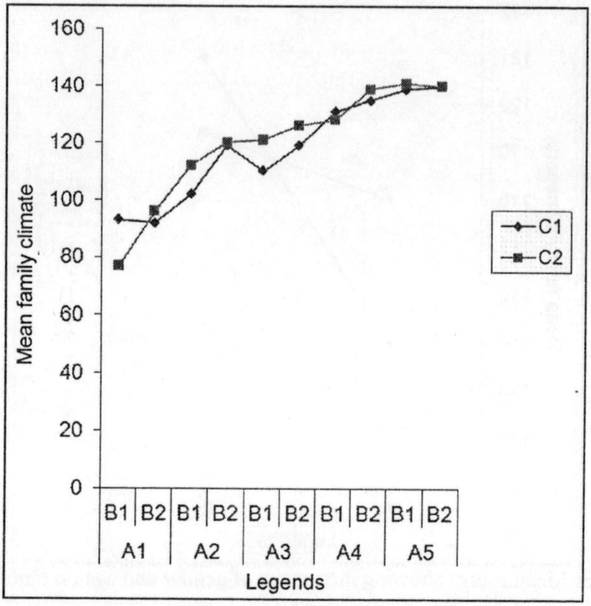

Fig. 8.4: Mean scores showing the impact of cultural variation, gender and age on family climate

Legends

A = Cultural variation	***B = Gender***
A1 = Bhotia	B1 = Boys
A2 = Tharu	B2 = Girls
A3 = Raji	***C = Age***
A4 = Buxa	C1 = 7-9 years
A5 = General Kumauni	C2 = 10-12 years

Discussion

Obtained data were analysed by three way ANOVA and interpreted in terms of cultural variation, sex and age as affectors of family climate and metamemory. It was focused that both variables were significantly influenced by cultural variation, gender and age. In sum, we can say that family climate and metamemory both are important variables and they develop differently in various societies, age groups and separately in boys and girls.

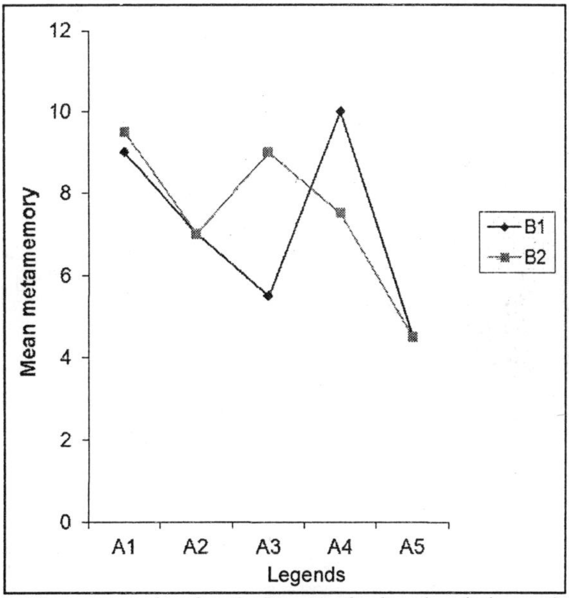

Fig. 8.5: Mean scores showing the Impact of cultural variation and gender on metamemory

Legends

A = Cultural variation	***B = Gender***
A1 = Bhotia	B1 = Boys
A2 = Tharu	B2 = Girls
A3 = Raji	
A4 = Buxa	
A5 = General Kumauni	

Prior to the inception of the study some hypotheses were formulated and the findings will be discussed accordingly.

(i) ***Variation in culture would cause variation in experiential family climate supportiveness and metamemory***: Our first and foremost Norton was related with the impact of cultural variation on family climate and metamemory. It was contended that differentials in cultural set up would evince difference in the magnitude of experiential supportiveness of home climate and metamemory. It was found non-tribals General Kumauni were far better in metamemorial functioning and they experienced

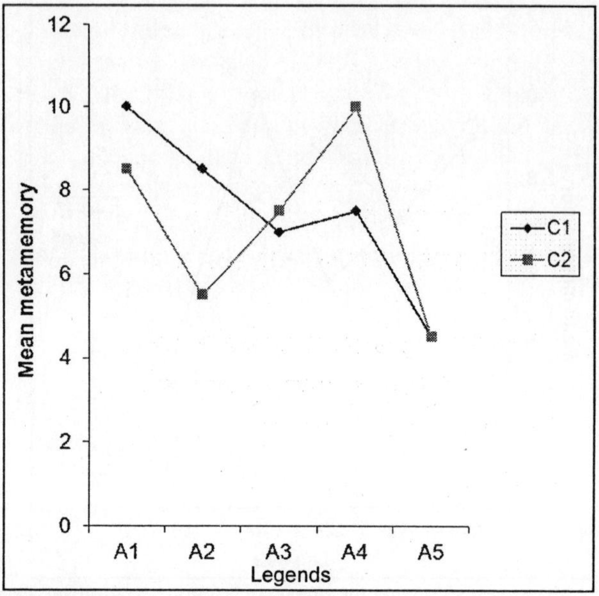

Fig. 8.6: Mean scores showing the impact of cultural variation and age on metamemory

Legends

A = Cultural variation	***C = Age***
A1 = Bhotia	C1 = 7-9 years
A2 = Tharu	C2 = 10-12 years
A3 = Raji	
A4 = Buxa	
A5 = General Kumauni	

their family climate more supportive as compared to their tribal counter-parts. So far as the matter of intertribal group was concerned, Bhotia tribals were found more superior than other tribals.

It was also noted that there was nominal difference in boys and girls in relation to their scores on experiential supportiveness towards school climate and metamemory. Also, it was noted that age related gap was not so dominant. It was higher in metamemory scores than the scores of experiential supportiveness towards family climate.

Characteristics of home environments are related to children's cognitive developments (Gottfried, 1984). It follows that cross-national

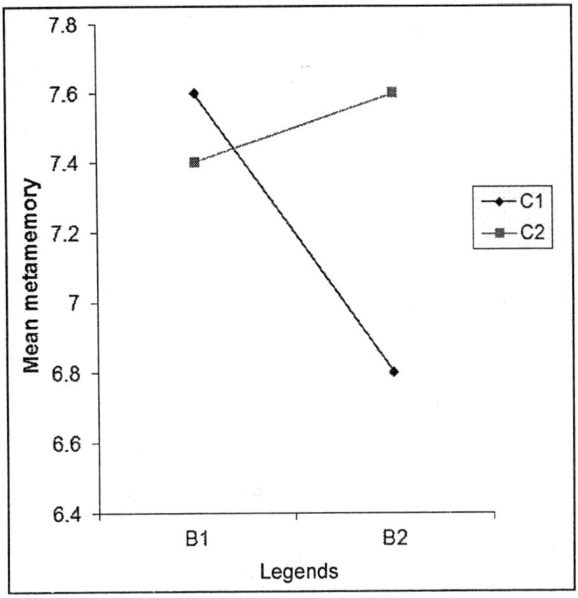

Fig. 8.7: Mean scores showing the impact of gender and age on metamemory

Legends
B* = *Gender* *C* = *Age
B1 = Boys C1 = 7-9 years
B2 = Girls C2 = 10-12 years

differences in parenting and children's should be directly linked to individual differences in children's performances. Research has illustrated that metacognitive knowledge is enhanced in school settings by teachers who include information about how and why to use strategies as part of their regular instruction (Moely, *et al.*, 1986). Teachers show considerable variability in amount and type of strategy instruction and some tailor their instruction to make strategies age appropriate (Hart, Leal, Burney and Santulli, 1985; Moely *et al.*, 1986). Metacognitive skills are probably further developed in school settings because the demands of school curricula accentuate the value of being strategies and of using efficient executive skills such as monitoring (Brown, 1979).

Similarly, parent's instruction at home and the problem solving situation to which they expose their children influence the pace and pattern of children cognitive and metacognitive development. Parents provide the groundwork for metacognitive development prior of child entry into

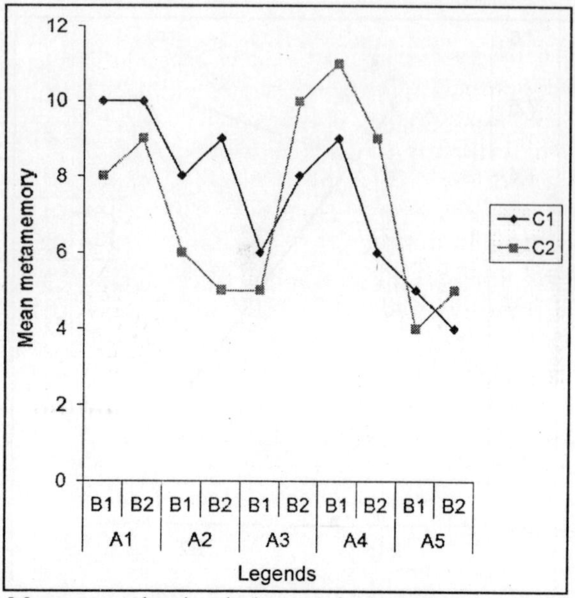

Fig. 8.8: Mean scores showing the impact of cultural variation, gender and age on metamemory

Legends

A = Cultural variation
A1 = Bhotia
A2 = Tharu
A3 = Raji
A4 = Buxa
A5 = General Kumauni

B = Gender
B1 = Boys
B2 = Girls

C = Age
C1 = 7-9 years
C2 = 10-12 years

school (McCombs, 1986). They influence school achievement by providing important learning experiences and encouraging their children of strategies (Sigel, 1982). Parents respond flexibly to their children's developing skills; for instance, they decrease the amount of task instruction as their children develop and internalize metacognitive information (Moore, Mullis and Mullis, 1986; Wertsch, McNamee, McLane and Budwig, 1980). Hence, parents can make unique contributions to their chiidren's metacognitive development by providing enriched home environment and stimulating learning experiences.

The other variable that was focused here was metametamory, i.e. the awareness of one's own potential memory.

By the end of the pre-school period, children appear to have acquired some important truths about the mental state of knowing. They realize that the word know expresses more speaker certainty than think or guess and is a surer guide to the true state of affairs. Unlike young pre-schoolers and young elementary school children are good at knowing how and when they came to know some recently acquired fact, for example, by witnessing it firsthand rather than by hearing about it from someone else. Although young pre-schoolers may have some minimal understanding of knowing (O. Neill, 1996), in general they seem to have only a hazy conception of what it means for someone to know something and about how knowledge is acquired. Surprisingly, even 4- and 5-year-olds will claim that they have always known information that they have just learned during the experimental session. In the late pre-school and middle-childhood periods, children discover that to acquire knowledge through exposure to perceptual information, that information has to be adequate as well as merely present. In contrast to younger children, for example, they realize that one cannot know an objects' colour merely by feeling the object, that one often cannot be certain of an object identity when only a little bit of it is visible, and that one's interpretation of an impoverished or ambiguous perceptual input may be influenced by one's biases or expectation, this refers the age related pattern of metamemory.

Findings, in general, reveal the relative efficacy of cultural variation, age and sex. So, it can be concluded that metamemory enrichment training programmes should be implemented. It will narrow gap between metamemory and potential memory. Moreover, better environment in home can also be prevailed and patently should be counselled properly. It will prove the empirical validation of the study.

References

Bedell, D.A. and Oxford, R.L. (1996). Cross-cultural comparisons of language learning strategies in the People's Republic of China and other countries. In R. Oxford (Ed.), *Language Learning Strategies around the World: Cross-cultural Perspectives* (pp. 47-60). University of Hawaii at Manoa: Second Language Teaching and Curriculum Centre.

Bloom, M. (1968). *Stability and Change in Human Characteristics*, John Wiley & Sons, New York.

Biswas, A. and J.C. Aggarwal (1971). Encyclopedic Dictionary and Directory of Education, Vol. I, Academic Publishers, New Delhi.

Bremner, S. (1999). Language learning strategies and language proficiency:

Investigating the relationship in Hong Kong. *Canadian Modern Language Review, 55*, 1-15.

Brown, A.L. (1979). Theories of memory and the probiem of development: Activity, growth, and knowledge. In L.S. Cermak and F.M. Crick (Eds.), *Levels of Processing in Human Memory*, Hillsdale, NJ: Erlbaum.

Danesh, H.B. (1978), "The Authoritarian Family and Its Adolescents", *Canadian Psychiatric Association Journal,* 23, 7, pp. 479-485.

Douvan, E. and J. Adelson (1966). *The Adolescent Experience,* Willey, New York, pp. 95-98.

Ehrman, M. and Oxford, R. (1995). Cognition plus: Correlates of language learning success. *Modern Language Journal, 76*, 67-89.

Goh, C.C.M. and Foong, K.P. (1997). Chinese ESL students' learning strategies: a look at frequency, proficiency, and gender. *Hong Kong Journal of Applied Linguistics, 2*, 39-53.

Good, C.V. (1973). *Dictionary of Education,* IIIrd Ed., McGraw Hill Co., New York.

Gottfried, A.W. (1984). Issues concerning the relationship between home environment and early cognitive development. In Gottfried (Ed.), *Home Environment and Early Cognitive Development,* London: Academic Press.

Gottfried, A.E., Gottfried, A.W., and Guerin, D. (1986, April). Environmental predictors of cognitive development and early school success: A longitudinal study. *Paper presented at the annual meeting of the American Educational Research Association*, San Francisco.

Hart, S.S., Leal, L., Burney, L., and Santulli, K.A. (1985, April). Memory in the elementary-school classroom: how teacher encourage strategy use. *Paper presented at the meeting of the Society for Research in Child Development*, Toronto.

Kinjo, H. and Snodgrass, J.G. (2000). Does the generation effect occur for pictures? *American Journal of Psychology, 113*, 95-117.

Ku, P.Y.N. (1997). *Predictors of strategy choice by EFL students in Taiwan.* Paper presented at RELC Seminar, Singapore, April 1997.

Malm, M. and O.G. Jamison (1952). *Adolescence,* McGraw Hill Co., New York, pp. 282-83.

Maslow, A.H. (1941). The Dynamics of Psychological Security and Insecurity, *Character and* Personality, 10, pp. 331-34.

McCombs, B.L. (1986, April). The role of the self-system in self-regulated learning. *Paper presented at the annual meetings of the American Educational Research Association,* San Francisco.

Moely, B.E., Hart, S.S., Leal, L., Johnson, T., Rao, N., and Burney, L. (1986). How do teachers teach memory skills? *Educational Psychologist, 21*, 55-71.

Moore, J.J., Mullis, R.L., and Mullis, A.K. (1986). Examining metamemory within the Educational context of parent-child interactions. *Psychologist, 21*, 55-71.

Moshfeghi, F. and Sharifian, F. (1998). Generation effect and associative learning. *Journal of Education and Psychology Research, 1*, 1-20.

Mullins, P. (1992). *Successful English language learning strategies of students enrolled in the faculty of arts, Chulalonkorn University, Bangkok Thailand.* Unpublished doctoral dissertation, United States International University, San Diego, CA.

Murdock, G.P. (1949), *Social Structure,* McMillan Co., New York.

Olive, T. (2004). Working memory in writing: Empirical evidence from the dual-task technique. *European Journal, 9*, 32-42.

Politzer, R.L. and Groarty, M. (1985). An exploratory study of learner behaviour and their relationship to gain in linguistic and communicative competence. *TESOL Quarterly, 19*, 103-123.

Rong, M. (1999). Language learning strategies of a sample of tertiary-level students in the P.R. China. *Guidelines, 21*, 1-11.

Sharifian, F. (2002). Processing hyponymy in L1 and L2. *Journal of Psycholinguistic Research, 31*, 421-436.

Sigel, I.E. (1982). The relationship between parental distancing strategies and the child's cognitive behaviour. In L.M. Losa and I.E. Sigel (eds.), *Families as Learning Environment for Children,* New York: Plenum Press.

Stoott, L.H. (1974). *The Psychology of Human Development,* Holt, Rinehart and Winston, New York, p. 208.

Troyer, A. and Rich, J.B. (2002). Psychometric properties of a new metamemory questionnaire for older adults. *The Journal of Gerontology, 57B*, 19-27.

Wertsch, J.V., McNamee, G.D., McLane, J.B., and Budwig, W.A. (1980). The adult-child dyad as a problem-solving system. *Child Development, 51*, 1215-1221.

Wolman, B.B. (1977), *International Encyclopedia of Psychiatry, Psychology, Psychoanlysis and Neurology,* Van Nostrand Reinhold Co., New York.

Yang, K.S. (1982). Causal attributions of academic success and failure and their affective consequences, *Chinese Journal of Psychology,* Taiwan, *24*, 65-83.

9

Asian Female Foreign Domestic Workers as Migrants in Hong Kong

Diane C. Zelman, Cecile Valantin and *Michele Bland*

The Context of Gendered Domestic Work in Hong Kong

Asian foreign domestic workers are a recognized mainstay of the labour force in a number of developed Asian countries. Although foreign domestic workers are impelled by economic need and the promise of salaries five to fifteen times greater than can be found in their home countries, they sacrifice much. They leave their homes, daily life with their families, their culture, the social status of prior education or careers, and the safety net of their communities, to care for others' homes and children in foreign countries, where they must adapt to a new culture and learn a new language.

Currently, approximately 3,00,000 female foreign domestic workers are employed in Hong Kong, almost evenly divided between workers from the Philippines and Indonesia. These are both countries for which export of workers serves a national economic strategy to buffer the impact of global economic crisis (Carney, 2012; Drew, 2012). During the 1970s, Hong Kong's profound need for a domestic workforce was filled by Filipina migrants when the Marcos regime wished to reduce the impact of trade deficit and unemployment; worldwide remittances by Phiiippine migrant workers now exceed US$1.5 billion per month (Adriano, 2009; Leahy, 1990). In Indonesia, the strategic export of foreign workers to Asia and the Middle East began during the latter part of the Suharto regime in the 1990s, also to buoy up a failing economy (Sim, 2009). Thus, it is notable that although individuals choose to migrate for various personal reasons, they are permitted to migrate due to a national strategy crafted primarily to support the economies of their countries of origin.

The demand for inexpensive household help in Hong Kong has converged with the rise of an affluent expatriate community and the growing Hong Kong Chinese middle and upper middle class. Since the 1970s, there have been increasingly more women in Hong Kong employed outside of the home and fewer local women who are willing to take on work of low status and pay. Sarah Jaffe and others note that although there is much attention to the "glass ceiling" encountered by women in various cultures who wish to enter high-status jobs, there is a profound need for attention to the dynamic by which women of lower socio-economic class, especially those from developing countries, are hired to mind the homes of those same women who seek higher professional status (Akalin, 2007; Jaffe, 2013).

Hong Kong visas for domestic work are governed by strict residency and employment rules, such as a two-year limited contract to work with a specific family that must be obtained *via* a recognized recruitment agency, at cost to the worker and employer. Minimum salary is only US$500 per month (Roncesvalles, 2012). Foreign domestic workers must work full-time, 6 days a week, and may not "moonlight", they must reside with their domestic employer, they are not eligible for permanent resident status in Hong Kong, and they cannot bring other family members to Hong Kong (*Asian Migrant Yearbook*, 1997). Under the "New Conditions of Stay", also referred to as the Two Week Rule, if their contract is terminated for any reason other than documented abuse or exploitation, a foreign domestic worker must find a new contract or leave the country within 2 weeks of termination of employment (*Immigration Department of HKSAR*, 2008). However, foreign domestic workers often refrain from reporting violations such as sexual or physical abuse, due to the requirement that they not work nor receive any income or financial compensation during the process of adjudication, or out of fear that they will be compelled to return home under the Two Week Rule. Legal actions may be costly, time consuming, and favour the employer (Benitez, 2007). Legal and advocacy efforts on behalf of foreign domestic workers to change the Two Week Rule, and to offer permanent residency to foreign domestic workers after 7 years, have been unsuccessful, leading some to assert that such laws constitute institutionalized oppression that unfairly targets those immigrants who are domestic workers (BBC, 2013; Drew, 2012).

The Indonesian and Filipina foreign domestic worker populations are demographically distinct, which leads to different life trajectories in Hong Kong. Filipino workers, on average, are older, are likely to have some post-secondary education, and are much more likely to come to Hong Kong with English language proficiency. Many are already skilled workers, such as nurses, teachers, or office workers, who are willing to trade loss of status for higher salaries as domestic workers in Hong Kong (Tillu, 2005). Filipina foreign domestic worker activists have established many of the existing Hong Kong migrant labour support organizations.

In contrast, Indonesian foreign domestic workers are on average younger and less well-educated than their Filipina counterparts. The Indonesian government requires them to serve a period of residency away from their family at migrant training camps, where conditions have been described as substandard and personal safety is often compromised (O'Connor, 2012). Workers are expected to incur the high cost of their travel and training, so that they often arrive in Hong Kong needing to work off considerable debt. In this way, institutions in Indonesia may contribute to the vulnerability of their own country's women migrants. O'Connor (2012) noted that Indonesian foreign domestic workers are more likely than Filipina domestic workers to be paid below the minimum required salary, and without English or Cantonese language skills, they may be unable to exercise their legal rights. Thus, they can appear more attractive to some prospective employers who are looking for more submissive household help. The contrast in experience between Filipina and Indonesian foreign domestic workers is a powerful illustration of the vulnerability to exploitation that comes from economic hardship, lack of education, lack of local language skills and lack of advocacy by an established community (Raj & Silverman, 2002).

Hong Kong is generally a more desirable destination for foreign domestic workers than the Middle East or other Asian nations, due to a stronger tradition of protective labour laws, despite these laws being sometimes insufficiently enforced (*Asian Migrant Yearbook*, 1997, Constable, 2007/1997). The Mission for Migrant Workers (MFMW), Hong Kong's oldest social services organization for foreign domestic workers, reported that in 2010 and 2011, the chief presenting complaints of foreign domestic worker clients were unfair practices of recruitment agencies (36%), poor labour conditions and other disputes with employers (45%), legal concerns (8%) and indebtedness (5%). Clients reported working 16-17 hours a day, 6 days per week, and expressed the following additional current concerns: insufficient food provided for the foreign domestic worker at home (34%), having no private room (56%), being expected to perform illegal work or problems with illegal work (9%), maltreatment (18%), physical/sexual assault (12%) and underpayment (11%).

Power Relations in Foreign Domestic Work in Hong Kong

In a series of insightful ethnographies of foreign domestic workers in Hong Kong, the anthropologist Nicole Constable (2007/1997) has explored the power relations inherent in domestic care in Hong Kong. Referencing the work of Michel Foucault, she showed how the commodification of workers begins during the recruitment process and continues throughout employment in the form of both implicit and explicit control of the bodies and behaviours of foreign domestic workers. Recruitment agencies ask personal questions of prospective foreign domestic workers that would be considered illegal areas of inquiry in the U.S., and applicants adapt their responses to fit the portrait of docile prospective employees. As such, in order to "sell" an applicant to a family, both the agencies and prospective employees consciously craft a false identity consistent with the kind of stereotypical female role described in classic feminist psychology texts: subordinate, eager and without alternate options (Miller, 1986). For example, applicants underreport their education and occupational attainments in order to appear less threatening to employers.

At the same time, foreign domestic workers are advised or required to change their appearance in ways that are de-feminizing; for example, they may be asked to cut their hair, refrain from wearing make-up, and to conform to strict standards concerning length and fit of clothing. These restrictions reflect a prevailing view of the foreign domestic worker as a sexual rival who might wish to seduce the male of the house to secure permanent residency in Hong Kong or to obtain financial gain. In our clinical practice (Cecile and Michele) our clients were very much aware of such attitudes; some of our clients have asserted that they are devout Catholics or Muslims and in particular have expressed rage at rumours that foreign domestic workers come to Hong Kong only to work in the sex trade. They have been advised by friends and employment agencies that in order to keep their job and to avoid any suggestion of immoral motives, they should interact as little as possible with the man of the house, thus implicitly colluding with the image of domestic worker as seductress. It has been commented that portrayal of women of colour as promiscuous or predatory serves the purpose of reinforcing existing power structures and assuaging the guilt of those with greater resources (Bullock, Wyche and Williams, 2001; Greene, 1994).

Constable (2007/1997) described other ways in which behaviour of foreign domestic workers is tightly regulated by some employers, such as by lack of privacy and highly detailed daily work schedules that dictate when they must eat, sleep and bathe, as shown below in a vignette from a client at the setting in which we provide therapy:

> On her first day of work, Flora was handed a long list of rules, with a minute-by-minute daily work schedule that required all tasks and meals to be performed in a particular way at a specified time. All household items had a "correct" place, and she would be scolded if she did not return the items to their proper place and position. Flora reported that her employers were always at home and monitored and criticized her. Although, she had no other job and needed to send most of her salary back to her family to pay for her children's school fees and food, she thought she would go "crazy" if she stayed. She resigned after 2 months, but according to the Two Week Rule, she was expected to return home immediately. In defiance of her visa, she moved in with a friend, took on illegal work, and sought help from a support organization, who helped her find a new legal contract.

Flora described feeling powerless, infantilized, and imprisoned. Micro-management in work settings breeds passivity, token behaviour, inefficiencyand low self-esteem among employees; in home settings, it is part of the spectrum of coercive control in domestic abuse (Cangemi, 2000; Lombard & McMillan, 2013). Working and living in the same residence, along with labour laws that constrict residential and employment options, can create a loss of boundary that transforms the domestic worker into a "fictitious family member" and creates risk for exploitation (Akalin, 2007).

Empowering Influences

Constable (2007, 1997) encourages readers to resist essentializing foreign domestic workers in terms of victim-oppressor mentality, and to tune in to the spectrum of ways, from very subtle to very public, in which foreign domestic worker simplicitly exert power and resistance in their daily lives. This is demonstrated in the following clinical vignette of a client served at our agency:

> Malaya, a Filipina foreign domestic worker, was able to use the encouragement she received from our support services agency to "take on" a recruitment agency that refused to reimburse her for an airplane ticket. Malaya contacted the police and ultimately got her money back. She became an advocate for other domestic workers facing labour or agency disputes.

In the vignette above, Malaya initiated contact with migrant support services neither as a consciously political nor apolitical person; she needed to address an immediate financial crisis. Her experiences of support and advocacy emboldened her to provide the same to others. Anna Stetsenko (2012) proposed that taking on an activist stance is part of a developmental path to personhood; she notes that by engaging in such roles, people become "agents not only for whom 'things matter' but *who themselves matter* in history, culture and society" (Stetsenko, 2012: 144).

When personal identity is reaffirmed by foreign domestic workers, notes Constable, this serves as counterpoint to the social control mechanisms inherent in their employment the other 6 days of the week. One of these is the ubiquitous Sunday rest day, during which thousands of foreign domestic workers congregate in the elite commercial areas and parks of Hong Kong, essentially "privatizing" public space for rest, parties, prayer groups, commerce and social activism (O'Connor, 2012; Tillu, 2011). The use of mobile phones can also be seen as a mechanism to reinforce personal identity; social media is now heavily used to strengthen connections with family and other foreign domestic workers, to strategize ways to set reasonable limits with employers, and to mobilize activist efforts (Tillu, 2011). An example of subtle resistance is sharing humour that ridicules their employers or local citizens. Carol Gilligan has similarly emphasized the value of social connection as "a manifestation of a more general resistance to losing the grounds of our humanity" (Gilligan, 2011: 12). Rina, a client who joined a support group at the agency in which we work, eventually found such relatedness and personhood on her Sunday rest day:

> Aara grew up in a small Muslim village in Indonesia and moved to Hong Kong for domestic work. In Hong Kong, she changed her name to Rina when she became a Christian. On her Sunday

> rest day, Rina gets up early and goes to the church to help set up for the day's activities. She brings family leftovers and other food to share; she sings in the worship team and leads a small Bible study group. In the afternoon she remains at the church and takes additional classes in English, Bible studies, and cooking. Rina says that this is her most important time each week; she returns to her job happy to have spent time with friends and learning about God.

Romantic Relationships and Sexuality

Amy Sim's innovative body of work has focused primarily on Indonesian foreign domestic workers, including their sexual identity in relationship to sexual and gender politics in both Indonesia and Hong Kong (Sim, 2009). Sim's cautioned against limiting public discourse on foreign domestic worker sexuality to stereotypes, such as the foreign domestic worker as victim of sexual abuse, promiscuous female, threatening lesbian, or temptress of the male of the house. The following clinical vignette demonstrates the complex relationship between power, sexuality, motherhood and disenfranchisement for a foreign domestic worker who received services at our clinic:

> Viti has been working for 10 years in Hong Kong as a domestic helper and had saved enough money to support her family and buy a land in Indonesia for a house. She has an on-and-off relationship with a married Pakistani man, and is now pregnant by him. Viti is desperate. She has become isolated from her only social support network because she avoids her Indonesian friends due to fear of gossip and stigma, and she has also lost her job because of the pregnancy. When she asked her family to sell the property she owned, she discovered that her father had already sold it and the money had gone to pay gambling debts. Her family also made it clear that she and her baby born out of wedlock would be unwelcome. In Hong Kong, her boyfriend told her that he might help support her but only if the baby is a boy and only if she returns to Indonesia.

By entering motherhood, Viti lost her financial independence and became an "overstay" on her visa. She became alienated from her Indonesian family and her own friends: once an independent woman providing for a whole Indonesian family, she now experiences her fate as determined by two men: her father and the father of her baby. Sheentered psychotherapy to manage overwhelming affect in the face of profound personal decisions, and she spent her counselling sessions making lists of pros *vs*. cons that exemplified the limited choices she faced. Viti began her romantic relationship out of what appeared to be lasting mutual affection, her partner did not wish to use condoms and she had limited understanding of their use; her boyfriend married a woman of his own ethnicity and continued his relationship with Viti. Her employer (illegally) terminated her foreign domestic worker contract due to her pregnancy, so that under the Two Week Rule she was now illegally living in Hong Kong, however, she was energetic and resourceful and wished to find a way to earn money, in order to avoid returning home and facing likely rejection by her family in Indonesia. The benefits of focusing on women like Viti as exemplars of the victimization of foreign domestic workers are obvious; such awareness might ultimately mobilize needed public support, advocacy, and education. However, viewing a client like Viti primarily as victim (as warned by Constable, 2007) may make it difficult for her psychotherapist to fully empathize with the complex factors that lead women to enter into such relationships.

Sim (2009) argued that in much of Indonesia, women are considered powerful only in the context of supporting local and national agendas for creating, raising, caring for, or educating the next generation. Such perspectives are reminiscent of the concept of the *motherhood mandate* (Russo, 1976) by which a culture frames the success of females only in terms of procreation. Sim (2009) described long standing traditions in Indonesia that shape female submissiveness around sexuality that extend to restricted access to knowledge about the female body, female sexuality, contraception, and protection from sexually transmitted diseases. She noted, for example, that unmarried women in Indonesia are generally unable to acquire contraception without special permission. Lynn Freedman describes the state-controlled restriction of information about sexuality as a method by which women "become instruments or tools of state policies....that deprive them of the ability to express their sexuality safely...it thus involves state control over some of the basic elements of what it means to be human" (Freedman, 1995: 1).

Although many Indonesian foreign domestic workers primarily migrate for economic opportunity, they also seek the novelty of exploring life in an international city with its attendant anonymity, social freedoms, and opportunity for romantic and sexual exploration. Relationships may fulfil needs for intimacy, security, and exploration, but many of these go badly, with high risk of sexually transmitted disease, domestic violence, and unwanted pregnancy (which usually implies illegal termination from the foreign domestic worker contract) and entering the illegal labour force.

As the Indonesian domestic workforce is almost entirely female, many heterosexual romantic relationships in Hong Kong occur between Indonesian women and other immigrant men, most commonly South Asian and African men, often of Muslim faith. These relationships are often complicated by both partners' marginal immigration and social status, the man's marital status in Hong Kong or in his home country, and expectations of sex, often unprotected. This is a sensitive area to broach, as certainly lasting relationships are formed; however, the Indonesian foreign domestic worker community and our mental health practice abound with stories of the disastrous impact of sexual transgression (Sim, 2009).

Recent popular press has also explored the topic of Lesbian foreign domestic workers in Hong Kong (Fenn, 2010; Tam, 2012). An oft-quoted statistic is that as many as 20 per cent of Indonesian foreign domestic workers are Lesbian, but this statistic appears to have been frequently cited from anecdotal accounts referenced in Fenn's (2010) newspaper article rather than from any systematic study. For Filipino foreign domestic workers, there are established gathering spaces on the Sunday rest day in the Central District of Hong Kong where Lesbian women can meet. Filipino foreign domestic worker Lesbians have formed a support network, *Filguys,* which began as a small social organization in 2007 and has grown to a local and international support network of over 300 members; *Filguys* also raises consciousness about gay and lesbian needs in the foreign domestic worker community (Tam, 2012).

Sim (2009) asserted that it is not appropriate to understand these relationships from a Western perspective, which considers such relationships as primarily an outgrowth of desire for same-sex emotional and sexual intimacy. Sim (2009) explained that lesbian identity among foreign domestic workers, as an identity in itself, is only a nascent phenomenon. She indicated that many women involved in lesbian relationships had no lesbian relationships in Indonesia and do not consider themselves lesbian, but they are described as such by non-lesbian friends. Based on her interviews with lesbian Indonesians foreign domestic workers, she traced lesbian relationships to a wish for romantic contact in an environment in which predatory behaviour of males is common, physical intimacy is seeded by close spaces in the domestic worker camps, and fear of pregnancy. She also described a "trendiness" associated with lesbian sexuality that can be considered in the context of self-definition and freedom from male definition and domination. Some lesbian women interviewed by Sim indicated that they prefer to date foreign domestic worker *tombois,* women who dress with masculine clothing and hair, because they were more compassionate, safer and less exploitative mates than men.

Not much is known about the sexuality of foreign domestic workers when they return to their home country, although Sim (2009) reported anecdotal evidence that some women who were romantically involved only with other women, enter into traditional heterosexual marriages. What is fairly certain is that Indonesian women who have had lesbian relationships in Hong Kong return to a homophobic society in which such relationships are closeted and stigmatized, and that unmarried heterosexual women who return with children or sexually transmitted diseases, face disgrace and exclusion.

Mental Health Concerns

A recent text on mental health among migrants has noted that foreign domestic workers worldwide are a highly psychologically vulnerable population due to discrimination, marginalization, abuse, hard work, and isolation (Bhugra & Gupta, 2011). Bhugra and Gupta (2011) noted that although the media portrays the most egregious cases of chronic labour abuse and domestic violence, the most typical stress for foreign domestic workers in Hong Kong is either relational, such as family, romantic and friendship problems, or chronic work-related stress.

A retrospective chart review of three Hong Kong hospitals delineated the psychiatric problems and life stressors among 27 Filipino and 14 Indonesian female foreign domestic workers who had a first inpatient psychiatric admission in Hong Kong (Lau, Cheng, Chow, Ungvari, & Leung, 2009). The most common ICD-10 diagnosis (approximately 64 per cent of both samples) was acute and transient psychotic disorder, a brief psychotic episode characterized by hallucinations, delusions, and/or incoherence, which usually subsides with brief psychosocial and medication intervention (Marneros & Pillman, 2002). Significant recent psychosocial stressors were reported for almost 90 per cent of the sample, with death or illness of relatives reported in about one-half, marital and other romantic concerns in one-third, and job-related concerns in approximately one-quarter of the sample. Typical acute stressors included concerns about the upcoming renewal of the two-year worker contract, financial problems, and abuse and exploitation by employers. Suicidal ideation was reported in 7.1 per cent and 22.2 per cent of the Filipino and Indonesian psychiatric samples.

Two recent studies (Chen, Benet-Martinez, & Bond, 2008; Chen, Benet-Martinez, Wu, Lam, & Bond, 2013) considered the role of bicultural identity integration, instrumental acculturative skills, such as language proficiency, and acculturative stress on the psychological adjustment of several samples of individuals in Hong Kong, including Filipino foreign domestic workers. Bicultural identity integration was defined as the ability to integrate two cultures into one's behaviour and identity, and acculturative stress was measured based on perceived discrimination and problems in intercultural interactions. The strongest predictors of poor psychological adjustment were trait neuroticism, poorer English and Chinese skills, and higher acculturative stress (Chen *et al.*, 2008). Bicultural identity was unrelated to psychological adjustment, leading the authors to speculate that for pragmatic intercultural skills such as language ability exerted more impact on psychological adjustment than bicultural identity.

These studies show that when severe psychiatric conditions emerge, it is often at times of family, relationship, and work crises. In our (Michele and Cecile) practice, we note that stress related to the Two Week Rule is a common presenting problem; it creates cycles of anxiety and depression at time of contract renewal or during time of dissatisfaction with a current employer; leading to a desperation to obtain the first available new contract even if it does not seem satisfactory. Becoming an "overstay" and taking illegal jobs puts her at risk of exploitation, legal action, jail and deportation. The direct impact of Hong Kong residency rules on mental health cannot be ascertained, but they create predictable crises associated with psychiatric risk, risk that might be reduced if attempts to broaden immigration privileges for foreign domestic workers are instituted. Remoteness from loved ones at times of death or crisis in the family are also a time of emotional risk that can be addressed if family leave policies permit foreign domestic workers to return home during crisis without risking loss of contract. The studies of Chen and colleagues described above suggest that minority stress among foreign domestic workers is compounded by lack of language proficiency and instrumental cultural skills and experiences of acculturative/intercultural stress. This research suggests that interventions that provide "training" that includes language education and combatting anti-immigrant discrimination would improve the mental health and psychological functioning of foreign domestic workers. Such programmes are offered at a number of support missions in Hong Kong, yet these are underutilized.

The following depicts a successful therapeutic encounter at the agency in which we (Michele and Cecile) work, when timely help was initiated by a client's employer:

> In Indonesia, after learning that her fiancé was actually married, Lia started going out, drinking and smoking; she considered suicide, and she made cuts on her arms with sharp objects. After a few months, her family convinced her to work abroad, and she moved to Hong Kong to work as a domestic helper for a local Chinese family. Despite her determination to do a good job, she started drinking again. Her employer noticed that something was wrong and found her a therapist. Lia saw me (Michele) every week for 3 months and said that what she most appreciated was that "we talked a lot." She said she learned to notice when she had negative thoughts about her ex-boyfriend and to deal with them before they affected her feelings and behaviour. Now, when she feels angry at people, she knows she needs to express her concerns, remove herself from the situation, and calm herself, by saying a prayer. She said that this simple technique has helped her through some tough times.

Lia came to Hong Kong already in considerable emotional distress when she learned that her boyfriend in Indonesia was married, distress that could in turn be traced to dismissive attitudes towards women in her host country, her self-blame and shame in the eyes of her family and community, and her use of alcohol to manage these feelings. It is notable that so much of her successful counselling focused on recognition and management of anger, which is described by Jean Baker Miller as a core experience of individuals of subordinate groups (Miller, 1985). This therapy legitimized Lia's anger and encouraged her to find ways to express it or manage it without self-harm. Miller (1985) noted that women live in both relational and economic dependency which makes them vulnerable to both fear of relational loss as well as anger. She recognized that dominant groups in a society do not consider the need to care for the personhood of those with less power. In Lia's situation, a compassionate employer, available support services and her own efforts and insight helped her regain resilience.

Providing Mental Health Intervention for Foreign Domestic Workers in Crisis

Two of us (Michele and Cecile) have provided services in a shelter and social services setting for foreign domestic workers who are pregnant or who have recently had babies while working in Hong Kong. The goal of the organization is to help clients to access legal, educational, and other support services for themselves and their child. Their pregnancy made our clients particularly at risk for social, legal, and emotional problems, and some have HIV+ status. Many of our clients have been terminated from their foreign domestic worker contracts due to their pregnancies. Although the Two Week Rule may require a return to their home country, some anticipate poverty and family rejection if they return with HIV+ status, pregnant or with a child born out of wedlock, especially if the child is of mixed race. Describing the severe ostracism, sexism and racism she expected to encounter in Indonesia, one of our clients explained that "women with HIV+ are sent away to a place in the mountains where someone brings food to you." Others may wish to stay in Hong Kong with the father of their child, even if the relationship is not satisfying or if one or both of them face potential deportation. Although our clients may have temporary shelter, they have few financial resources, and by the time they locate support organizations, they have often overstayed their visa and entered into undocumented status. Some women, based on their experiences in Hong Kong and anticipated treatment in their home country, make asylum and torture claims at the United Nations High Commissioner for Refugees. The inquiry for such claims usually takes between 1 and 3 years. During that time, they get help from the International Social Services, an International non-governmental social services organization with a migrant programme under the Hong Kong Social Welfare Department that provides food, shelter, and basic health needs to asylum and torture claimants.

Social workers or case workers initially help our clients obtain concrete help such as housing, clothing and food, and assist with visa applications or other legal procedures. Clients are referred for counselling if the social worker believes it will be beneficial. Few clients request to speak with a psychotherapist, and if they do, it is for a very specific need. Clients seek practical advice such as information on baby care and parenting, help with problem solving and decision-making, romantic concerns and relational problems with friends and family. Clients may also come to therapy with severe anxiety, depression, and thoughts of harming themselves, and rarely, they use drugs or alcohol to manage unendurable life circumstances.

Our Indonesian clients can seem to be passive and submissive or passive-aggressive with their partners. Their descriptions of their current relationships correspond with patterns often seen in cycles of domestic violence; they experience beatings, threats, and extreme control over their behaviour by their partner, with periods of calm and superficial resolution. They often condemn themselves for their predicament or assume that God is punishing them for sins, such as having sex outside of marriage. We were at first surprised at how little agency these clients exert in their romantic relationships, because they are often quite resourceful in other aspects of their lives: they start small businesses, they assist friends and relatives, and despite extremely limited means, they care well for their babies. But, at least from a Western woman point of view, they seem to relinquish all their agency and independence when they enter a romantic relationship, and adopt a new identity, one of a submissive and obedient wife whose life is entirely ruled by her partner. After seeing several clients with this similar pattern of behaviour, what emerged was that male domination was so deeply embedded in the Indonesian culture, where men can marry up to four wives, that women accepted it as the inevitable norm and obligation.

Most of our clients are unfamiliar with psychotherapy, or think of it only as "talking about my problems." They do not share our conceptualization of psychotherapy as a gradual process of expression, reflection, catharsis, and working through over time, nor do they experience those featuresas particularly relevant to their problem-saturated daily lives. This is consistent with research findings that women of low socio-economic status do not typically utilize psychotherapy (Azocar, Miranda & Dwyer, 1996). Even for presenting problems such as physical or emotional abuse, pregnancy loss, or considering placing their baby for adoption, the modal number of sessions at our clinic is one or two. Notably, Laura Smith (Smith, 2005) identified the idea that poor people are too overwhelmed to utilize psychotherapy as "essentially classist while containing a grain of truth" (p. 691). She recommends that feminist therapists carefully reflect on ways in which distancing themselves from the poor contributes to underutilization of care, and recommends a more flexible, psychoeducational, and community based therapeutic practice. We agree, and note that a supportive therapist can provide validation and catharsis, help with managing strong feelings, education, advocacy, crisis intervention, assistance in locating resources, and practical problem-solving.

We have found that in the context of one-or two-session interventions, therapists may be tempted to try to cover too much; they need to orient their efforts towards providing help in a single brief interaction. That being said, one of us (Michele) led a successful support group with full attendance for several sessions, and we believe that short-term skills or problem-focused small groups may best engage the clients to help one another, consistent with recommendations of others that for clients of low income and highly stressful lives, group therapies often mobilize greater continuity and attendance (Grote *et al.*, 2007). Short-term workshops are also popular; among the workshops offered at our centre, our clients report a preference for topics related to relationships and emotional management.

Therapy begins with an assessment of immediate needs or crisis (e.g., safety, food, shelter, intervention for suicidal ideation). Because of the high cost of business space and the limited funds available for private therapy rooms and childcare, our sessions sometimes feel chaotic; a clients' child is crying and walking around, we are meeting in the corner of a room with a simple curtain drawn for privacy, we speak in low tones on a sofa with others walking by, the client is holding back tears while telling of a beating or of a recent loss. One client asked to be seen at a local McDonald's rather than at the organization proper, because the noise and anonymity of the setting felt more comfortable to her. Still, when we can, we try to cultivate an atmosphere of calm, which is the foundation for reflection, clear thought, and problem solving. Calm can be found by sitting quietly, by encouraging a moment of silence, or by meditation. Sometimes a client has a personal ritual or prayer ritual (e.g., Muslim or Christian) that she associates with feelings of calm. Being able to access this calm state can also help her at other times when she is trying to manage anxiety and anger or when she in need of quickly assessing and managing a dangerous situation.

Therapists working with foreign domestic workers need to be aware of, and have an outlet to explore, their countertransference experiences. Clients often miss sessions and end therapy without termination. Therapists who are accustomed to growing trust and relatedness with clients over time may be disappointed if little relationship building occurs. These interactions can sometimes leave the therapist wondering about their purpose and their impact. One of us (Cecile) learned early in training that our value to our client might be conditional on our willingness to step out of our typical office role:

> Annisa had seen me several times, when she phoned, very upset, because the International Social Services officer would not give her baby formula. She was breastfeeding but felt that it was unfair since her friends got it whether they were breastfeeding or not. She wanted my help immediately. My first thought was that this was not my role, and I recommended she call her social worker. You can imagine how useful she thought I was after that! It took the strong recommendation from her social worker to get her back in therapy with me.

We experience helplessness and rage towards the men who victimize our clients. It is common for therapists to feel overwhelmed with the complexity of their clients' life problems and to wish to address everything at once as one of us (Cecile) experienced,

> One of my clients, Nenita, was a new mother with HIV. She couldn't find a job because potential employers would turn her down when they learned she was HIV+. I struggled not to try to find her a job. Iimagined employing her myself or giving her money. I was horrified to hear about the man who infected her. I wanted to post signs on every building to warn women to beware of this destructive man. I wanted to install condom machines and posters explaining about safe sex. Each time I met with her, I would first breathe deeply and remind myself to just try to do at least one helpful thing.

We have found it useful to remember that although psychotherapy is generally time-limited and focused on immediate problems, successful resolution of a single problem can empower a client to solve other problems in their lives or to advocate for other foreign domestic workers. We also focus on the strength and resourcefulness of our clients in other spheres of their lives. Over time, the clients at our agency form their own supportive subculture, meeting at weekly psychoeducational talks and for outings and play dates with their children, even accompanying each other to speak with employers or agencies.

We have found that Indonesian foreign domestic workers often present a calm and dignified demeanor, with a tendency to be resigned to the hardship of their current situation, which leads them to adopt behaviour that can appear passive. For example, they can wait in Hong Kong for months or years in extremely precarious conditions hoping for change in their romantic partners instead of identifying or acting on their best options. This seemingly passive behaviour can be bewildering at first, especially in times of crisis. Therapists working with these clients, therefore, need to keep in mind that this behaviour does not preclude our ability to work with them on decision-making and problem solving strategies. We have realized that a key to supporting and empowering our clients is to acknowledge their approach to life problems and accompany them in their reflections, rather than to try to make them adopt our own ways of reasoning that we would qualify as rational. For instance, understandably, they resent being told that they need to go back to Indonesia, not because it is not true, but simply because they need to own that decision.

Conclusion

When foreign domestic workers move to Hong Kong, they do so as part of a national economic strategy to strengthen their home country. In many ways they leave behind what little power and privilege that they once had, and they attempt to reassert their status, with varying degrees of success (Constable 2007/1997). They embody an intersectionality of disempowered identities and they experience multiple jeopardy of oppression and exploitation (Crenshaw, 1991). This is because they are women who move from one patriarchal culture to another, because they are from minority cultures in the countries to which they migrate and therefore are likely to experience ethnic discrimination, because they have come because of dire economic need, and because their nationality, language and immigrant status leave them vulnerable to anti-immigrant sentiment and exploitation.

Supporting the psychological health of foreign domestic workers will require continued efforts on numerous levels in Hong Kong, including working towards changing labour and immigration laws, as well as public health and social services intervention. Lau and colleagues (Lau *et al.*, 2009) emphasized that in order to reduce mental health risk, it is necessary to improve the social status and working conditions of foreign domestic workers. In Hong Kong, this would include "relaxing the regulations against family reunification, lifting restrictions to live-in domestic work and allowing temporary settlement on overseas labour contracts" (Lau *et al.*, 2009: 575). The fact that severe psychiatric illness occurs within the context of severe psychosocial stress suggests the need for community outreach to help those facing personal crises. Increased utilization of social service centres indicates that these facilities can also function as first-line response or referral centres for mental health screening and intervention. Additional research is needed on the prevalence of mental health concerns among foreign domestic workers and the most effective counselling strategies for treating them. Focused training on short-term counselling interventions could increase the effectiveness of trainees and therapists who are new to work with foreign domestic workers. Utilizing lay therapists within the foreign domestic worker population and group interventions can extend the effectiveness of social service agencies and potentially provide more culturallysensitive care.

References

Adriano, J.D. (2009, August 11). *Remittances save the Philippines. Asia Times Online.* Retrieved from http://www.atimes.com/atimes/Southeast_Asia/KH11Ae01.html

Akalin, A. (2007). Hired as a caregiver, demanded as a housewife: Becoming a Migrant Domestic Worker in Turkey. *European Journal of Women's Studies, 14,* 209-225.

Azocar, F., Miranda, J. and Dwyer, E.V. (1996) Treatment of depression in disadvantaged women. *Women and Therapy, 18,* 91-105.

BBC. (2013, March 25). *Hong Kong court denies workers residency.* Retrieved from http://www.bbc.co.uk/news/ world-asia-china-21920811

Benitez, M.A. (2007, August 20). Rough justice. *South China Morning Post,* p. A 14.

Bhugra, D., and Gupta, S. (2001). *Migration and Mental Health.* United Kingdom: Cambridge University Press.

Bullock, H.E., Wyche, K.F., $ Williams, W.R. (2001). Media images of the poor. *Journal of Social Issues, 15,* 226-246.

Cangemi, J.P. (2000) Leadership and micro-managing: what are the consequences? *IFE Psychologia: An International Journal,* 8,212-218.

Carney, J. (2012, November, 11). Adviser says number of Indonesian maids will tumble in next five years. *South China Morning Post.* Retrieved from http://www.scmp.com/news/hong-kong/article/1079602/adviser-says-number-indonesian-maids-will-tumble-next-five-years.

Chen, S.X., Benet-Martinez, V., and Bond, M.H. (2008). Bicultural identity, bilingualism, and psychological adjustment in multicultural societies: Immigration-based and globalization-based acculturation. *Journal of Personality, 76,* 803-38.

Chen, S.X., Benet-Martinez, V., Wu, W.C. H., Lam, B.C.P., and Bond, M.H. (2013). The role of dialectical self and bicultural identity integration in psychological adjustment. *Journal of Personality, 81:* 61-76. doi: 10.1111/ j.1467-6494.2012.00791.x

Constable, N. (2007). *Maid to order in Hong Kong: Stories of Migrant Workers* (2nd ed.). Ithaca NY: Cornell University Press. (Original work published 1997).

Cortes, P., and Pan, J. (2009). *Outsourcing Household production: The Demand for Foreign Domestic helpers and native labour supply in Hong Kong.* Retrieved from http://harris.princeton.edu/seminars/pdfs/Cortes.pdf

Crenshaw, Kimberlé W. (1991). Mapping the Margins: Intersectionality, Identity Politics, and Violence against Women of Colour, *Stanford Law Review*, Vol. 43, No. 6, pp. 1241-1299.

Drew, K. (2012, March 28). Hong Kong court overturns ruling on domestic workers. *The New York Times*. Retrieved from http://www.nytimes.com/ 2012/03/29/world/asia/hong-kong-court-overturns-ruling-on-domestic-workers.html?_r=0

Fenn, A. (2010, October 19). Indonesian maids in Hong Kong blur the borders. *Jakarta Globe*. Retrieved from http://www.thejakartaglobe.com/ lifeandtimes/indonesian-maids-in-hong-kong-blur-the-borders/402153

Freedman, L.P. (1995). Censorship and manipulation of reproductive health information. Chapter 1 in S. Coliver (Ed.) *The Right to Know: Human Rights and access to reproductive health information.* Philadelphia: University of Pennsylvania Press.

Gilligan, C. (2011) *Joining the Resistance*. Cambridge, UK: Polity Press.

Greene, B. (1994). *African American Women*. In L. Comas-Diaz and Greene, B., *Women of Colour: Integrating ethic and Gender identities in Psychotherapy*. NY: Guilford Press.

Grote, N.K., Zuckoff, A., Swartz, H., Bledsoe, S.E., and Geibel, S. (2007). Engaging Women Who Are Depressed and Economically Disadvantaged in Mental Health Treatment. *Social Work. 52*, 295-308.

Ignacio, E., and Mejia, Y. (2008). *Managing Labour Migration: The case of the Filipino and Indonesian Domestic helper market in Hong Kong.* Retrieved from John F. Kennedy School of Government, Harvard University, http:// www.innovations. harvard.edu/showdoc.html?id=124761

Immigration Department of HKSAR. (2008). *Quick Guide for the Employment of Domestic helpers from abroad* (ID 989). Retrieved from http:// www.immd.gov.Hong Kong/ehtml/ID (E)989.html.

Jaffe, S. (2013) Trickle-down feminism. *Dissent, Winter 2013.*

Lau, P.W.L., Cheng, J.G.Y., Chow, D.L.Y., Ungvari, G.S., and Leung C.M. (2009) Acute psychiatric disorder in foreign domestic workers in Hong Kong: A pilot study. *International Journal of Social Psychology, 55,* 569-76.

Leahy, P. (1990). *Female migrant labour in Asia: A case study of Filipina Domestic workers in Hong Kong*. (Masters thesis, University of Hong Kong). Retrieved from http://hub.Hong Kongu.Hong Kong/bitstream/ 10722/28106/1/ FullText.pdf?accept=1 Leahy

Marneros, A., and Pillman, F. (2002). Acute and transient psychotic disorders. *Ψυχιατρική*, 13, 276-286.

Miller, J.B. (1985) The construction of anger in women and men. *Work in Progress*, Number 4 Wellesley, MA: The Stone Centre Working Paper Series.

Miller, J.B. (1986). *Toward a New Psychology of Women* (2nd ed.). Boston: Beacon.

Mills, M.B. (2003). Gender and inequality in the global labour force. *Annual Review of Anthropology, 32,* 41-62. doi: 10.1146/annurev.anthro.32.061002. 093107Mission for Migrant Workers. (2011). *Data and statistics on mission clients.* Retrieved from http://www.migrants.net/_resources/files/ MFMW_Statistics_Booklet_2011.pdf

O'Connor, P. (2012). *Islam in Hong Kong: Muslims and Everyday Life in China's World city.* Hong Kong: Hong Kong University Press.

Raj, A. and Silverman, J. (2002). Violence against immigrant women: the roles of culture, context and legal immigrant status on intimate partner violence. *Violence Against Women, 8,* 367-398. doi: 10.1177/10778010222183107

Roncesvalles, C. (2012, September 20). Hong Kong government raises salary of domestic helpers. *The Philippine Star.* Retrieved from http://www.abs-cbnnews.com/global-filipino/09/20/12/hong-kong-raises-salary-domestic-helpers

Russo, N.F. (1976). The motherhood mandate. *Journal of Social Issues, 32,*143-153.

Sim, A. (2009). *The Sexual Economy of desire: girlfriends, boyfriends and babies among Indonesian women migrants in Hong Kong.* Unpublished manuscript. University of Hong Kong.

Smith, L. (2005). Psychotherapy, classism and the poor: conspicuous by their absence. *American Psychologist, 60,* 687-696.

Stark, E. (2013). Coercive control. Chapter 1 in Nancy Lombard and Lesley McMillan, *Violence against Women: current theory and practice in Domestic Abuse.* London, UK: Jessica Kingsley Publishers.

Tam, A. (2012, January 17). Girl-on-girl power. *Time Out, Hong Kong.* Retrieved from http://www.timeout.com. Hong Kong/gay-lesbian/features/48226/girl-on-girl-power.html

Tillu, J.S. (2011). *Spatial Empowerment: The Appropriation of Public spaces by Filipina Domestic workers in Hong Kong* (Doctoral dissertation Massachusetts Institute of Technology).

10

Social Identity and Acculturation Attitudes among Different Tribal Groups of Jharkhand, India

Dhananjay Kumar

Introduction

In a culturally plural society, a number of different cultural groups reside together with a shared social and political framework (Skeltone & Allen, 1999). There will be few examples of societies in which one culture, one language, one religion and one single identity characterize the whole population. Usually, many cultural groups live together in a society. Berry (1998 b) had talked about two contrasting view of plural societies; first the mainstream—minority framework in which there will be a single dominant or mainstream society and on the margins of which there exist various minority groups. Second view is a multicultural one that can be best understood by an example of a "mosaic" of ethno-cultural groups which refrain a sense of their cultural identity, and live in a social framework that is characterized by some shared norms. People define and characterize themselves in terms of the group to which they belong. People develop their collective self-concept and a social identity by the groups to which they belong. Thus, people can have many social identity by the groups to which they feel they belong (Hogg, 2001; Hogg & Williams, 2000). Tajfel and Turner (1986) said that individuals strive for a positive self-image. Such a positive self-image can be obtained through groups to which one belongs. Individuals define and evaluate themselves, to an extent, they belong to groups and groups can be positively or negatively valued. They have posited that individual's self-concept derives from his knowledge of his membership of a social group or groups along with the value and emotional significance attached to that membership" (Tajfel, 1981). Individuals strive for a positive social identity and they try to attain this by comparing their own group with a relevant other group on a dimension which is important for social comparison. If the outcome of this comparison is favourable it means that one's group distinguishes itself positively from the other group on that important dimension and a positive social identity is experienced.

Group members can also experience a negative social identity when an intergroup comparison on an important dimension results in negative social identity. Group members with negative social identity try to leave or dissociate from the group to which they belong. This is a purely individual action and Tajfel and Turner (1986) have labeled it as individual mobility. Another possibility is that group members choose another dimension of comparisons. They could change their evaluation of the discovered negative characteristics of their own groups as well as of comparison groups. A third behavioural option is social competition. Here, group members may directly confront the comparison group on some dimensions. These three behavioural options are called social creativity by Tajfel and Turner (1979). Salience of the social identity strategy is situation dependent, but which situational factors foster salience is not yet known. Moreover, the conditions under which individuals or group adopt different strategies to bring social change have not been explored (Taylor & Moghaddam, 1994). Brown (1986) has pointed out, that sometimes groups do not express dislike or hostility towards the out group.

Acculturation is one of the many forms of culture change process (Berry, 1980; Segall *et al.*, 1999). Acculturation is second-culture acquisition, in contrast with "enculturation", a first-culture acquisition. At the societal level, acculturation leads to processes by which culture change (Redfield *et al.* (1936), defined acculturation as a process when—*groups of individuals having different cultures come into continuous first-hand contact, with subsequent changes in the original culture patterns of either or both groups....* ".

Acculturation is referred as culture change that is initiated by the conjunction of two or more autonomous cultural system. In cross-cultural psychological researches the distinction has been made between individual and group level of acculturation. Acculturation strategies were earlier termed as acculturation attitude by Berry (1990). But now, these are not used interchangeably.

Some of the key elements of the definitions of acculturation are as follows: (i) there must be first hand contact or interaction between cultures and that should be continued. It means that short term accidental contact will not be a sufficient condition to qualify as acculturation process and single cultural practices over long durations are not adequate for acculturation process. (ii) Some changes in the cultural practices or psychological makeup among the people in contact, usually, continue for generations. (iii) Taking these two aspects jointly there is activity during and after contact which is dynamic and the long term result of this process may be relatively stable. This outcome may include not only changes to existing phenomenon, but also some other moral phenomenon that are generated by the process of this cultural interaction.

The first full psychological theory of acculturation was proposed by Thomas and Znaniecki (1918). Based on their empirical studies of immigrants of Chicago, they theorized that a minority group's culture is defined by shared attitudes and habits, called schemas, adaptive to one's family, ethnic community and occupation. Bartlett (1923/1970) was probably the first to argue that attitudes of the minority toward the dominant culture are of particular importance. Blending of two cultures is possible, when neither of them is dominant, where a dominant can cause the complete cultural assimilation of one group or can cause chronic "compromise formations" to arise. Bartlett argued that cultural similarities facilitate acculturation, especially of emotional meanings can be easily transferred from old practices to new.

Graves (1967) coined the term "psychological acculturation" which refers to the changes that an individual experiences during the contact with other cultures, participating in the process of acculturation that his or her cultural or ethnic group is undergoing. Group level acculturation and psychological acculturation processes are distinct to each other. At group level changes take place in social structure, economic base and political organization, while at the individual level the changes occur at the level of identity, values and attitudes. There are individual differences in participating in the collective changes that are under way in their group. Culture influence each other, but some cultures tend to dominate the other and this make distinction between dominant and non-dominant groups (Most, 1995). The contact and influence result in the transformation of certain aspects of non-dominant group. Acculturation is neither passive nor colourless absorption. It is a culture producing and culture receiving process (Mishra, Sinha & Berry, 1996). Sazapocznik and Kurtines (1993) point out that acculturation process is a type of accommodation which take place in a cultural context that may be either uni-dimensional or multi-dimensional. It depends on the type of cultural context and the quality of the relationship of the cultural groups.

Acculturation is not simply an external process, but it also creates a dynamics at the internal level for concerned cultural groups. The impetus for change is derived from external source; however, the actual process of acculturation is carried on with dynamic resources (Berry, 1980a).

People may have different views about how they want to live following the inter-cultural contact. Everyone belonging to such an interacting group does not want such contact and among those who do not seek to change his/her culture and behaviour to be more like the other group. Therefore, assimilation is not the only form of acculturation; there are other strategies identified by researchers working in the field of cross-cultural psychology (Berry, 1990, 1997; Nguayn *et al.,* 1999; Sayegh & Lasry, 1993; Phinney, 1990). Largely, based on the work of Berry (l997a), the two dimensional models of acculturation recognize two dominant aspects of acculturation (i) preservation of one's heritage culture; and (ii) adaptation to host society. These two aspects are conceptually distinct and independent (Liebkind, 2001). On the basis of these two aspects, Berry (1990) had asked two questions to identify the acculturation strategies. First is how valuable is to maintain one's cultural heritage? And second, what value is to develop relationship with the dominant culture? Hence, four acculturation strategies, assimilation, integration, separation and marginalization have been emerged by answering the yes and no to these questions.

Integration: From the point of view of non-dominant ethno-cultural groups, when individuals value both, maintaining one's original culture and interaction with people of other culture in daily life and business with equal magnitude, this is called the integration strategy.

Assimilation: When individuals do not value the maintenance of their cultural identity and seek daily interaction with other cultures, this is identified as assimilation strategy.

Separation: In contrast to the assimilation strategy when individuals place a value on maintaining their original culture and at the same time do not give value to interaction with other, this is known as separation strategy.

Marginalization: When individuals do not value their own culture and at the same time, show little interest in having relations with others then it is defined as marginalization strategy (Berry 1970a, 1974b, 1980a).

Mutual accommodation is necessary for integration to be adopted. Acceptance is a condition for both dominant and non-dominant groups to live in a culturally different manner in the same society. The non-dominant group has to accept the basic value of the larger society. Many studies have examined the acculturation strategies used by non-dominating acculturating groups.

Most of the studies concluded that integration is the most favoured strategy over the other three strategies with marginalization being the least preferred. An exception is that of Turks in Gennany (Piontkowski, Florack, Hoelker & Obrzalek, 2000), and lower socio-economic status Turks in Canada (Berry & Ataca, 2000), who preferred separation over integration. Mishra and Chaubey (2002) had studied the acculturation attitude of Kharwar and Agaria tribal groups living in Sonabhadra region of Uttar Pradesh using Berry's model of acculturation. Agaria tribe displayed a significant stronger separation attitude than the Kharwar tribe. The contact-acculturation was emerged as significant predictor of integration and separation attitudes.

Kertanguy, Salaun and Anne (2004) using the Rorschach technique on the sample of the Adivasi tribes from the state of Kerala in the south-west of India. The results revealed that Adivasi people have deep awareness of a grave crisis with respect to their cultural identity. Studies conducted on immigrants' acculturation strategies have showed that integration is the most preferred acculturation strategy. Krishnan and Berry (1992) demonstrated that both adults and adolescents have given preference for integration. This trend was found in a multi-cultural society (Berry *et al.,* 1989), and also in a relatively more cultured society (Partridge, 1988). In a series of studies conducted in Canada on different immigrant groups, Berry *et al.* (1989) found integration to be the most preferred attitude. However, it was also revealed that among first generation Hungarian-Canadian, separation is the second most preferred acculturation strategy, while assimilation is the second most preferred strategy among the second generation.

In another study, involving Westerners living in Japan, and immigrants from developing countries living in Norway, separation was the second most preferred acculturation strategy (Partridge, 1988; Sam, 1995) Kim, Lujon and Dixon (1998) studied the identity experience of American Indians in Oklahoma, USA, and found that predominance of integrative identity mixed with varying degrees of separatist orientation.

Objective: Major objective of the present research was to investigate the relationship among social identity and acculturation attitudes among different tribal groups.

Method

Sample: The sample comprises of 300 tribal participants of three different tribes namely, Oraon, Parhaiya and Birjia, 100 participants belonging each of the three tribal groups. These tribes are basically residents of Jharkhand state. The sample was drawn from Palamau, Gumla and Latehar districts of Jharkhand state. Because of some local social and political dynamics only male participants were selected. Due to some regional socio-political issues and violence in these areas, the present researcher could not make it possible to select sample through randomization. Because of extremist violent social movements, it was not possible to approach some areas. Hence, to reach these tribal people help of locals were sought. Some affected areas were dangerous and likely to have some real and potential danger and life threats for outsiders. Range of the sample was 20-50 years. The mean age of the sample of Oraon was 30.91 years, Parhaiya was 31.27 years and of Birjia was 32.68 years.

Measures:

1. **Social Identity Measure:** This scale was developed to measure two factors namely Ethnic Identity search (A developmental and cognitive component), and Affirmation (An affective component), dimensions, originally found in Phinney's Multi-group Ethnic Identity Measure. This test has 12 items. To assess the psychometric properties, the test was administered on a sample of 40 (20 Gond and 20 Tharu), tribal people of Balrampur district of Uttar Pradesh. The test-retest reliability of this version was found to be 0.90. The responses elicited on a four point scale ranging from strongly agree to strongly disagree.
2. **Acculturation Attitudes Questionnaire:** It was developed by Mishra, Sinha and Berry (1966). The scale is partially based on the scale of Sommerland and Berry (1970) who had developed a similar kind of attitude scale for the measurement of attitude towards modes of group relation, and used it with the Australian Aboriginal population. The tool measures four acculturation orientations namely Integration, Assimilation, Separation and Marginalization. The items in this questionnaire are related to nine areas namely, dressing style, friendship, food, customs and rituals, residence, co-operation, naming of the child, lifestyle and community relationship. For each of the nine areas mentioned above four statements for the orientation of integration, assimilation, separation and marginalization, were framed. The participants had to select anyone of the four statements by expressing their judgements on a five point ladder scale. But in

the present study, it was felt that some tribal people were unable to give response on a five point ladder scale. So, responses were taken only for the four acculturation orientations against each area. It means that each participant had to give one response among the four statements of an acculturation orientation area. Total nine responses were obtained from each participant, knowledge about anyone of the acculturation attitude for each of the nine areas can be ascertained.

Procedure: The subjects were contacted individually, after taking their consent, research materials were given to each of the participants with the help of a local bilingual helper. The responses were given by the participants in their own languages. It was transcribed by the local bilingual helper into Hindi which was noted by the investigator on a separate sheet of paper. Participants were thanked to give their response.

Results and Discussion

The inter-correlations among the dimensions of social identity, i.e. ethnic identity search and affirmation, as well as, the dimensions of acculturation attitude was computed and presented in Table 10.1.

Table 10.1: Inter-correlations among Social Identity (total score) and its components in three tribal groups

	Groups	*Social Identity (Total)*	*Ethnic Identity Search*	*Affirmation*
	Oraon		.65**	.81**
Social Identity (Total)	Parhaiya	—	.46**	.81**
	Birjia		.57**	.83**
	Oraon			.08
Ethnic Identity	Parhaiya	—		—
	Birjia			–.03
	Oraon			
Affirmation	Parhaiya	—	—	—
	Birjia			

Note: $P<.01^{**}$ $P<.05^{*}$

It is clear from Table 10.1 that in all groups (Oraon, Parhaiya and Birjia), the affective component (affirmation) has salience over cognitive component (ethnic identity search). In all the three tribal groups, social identity total score was significantly correlated with affirmation, as well as, ethnic identity search.

Table 10.2: Inter-correlations among dimension of Acculturation Attitude

Dimensions of Acculturation Attitudes	*Groups*	*Assimila-tion*	*Integration*	*Separation*	*Marginali-zation*
	Oraon		0.09	.0 0	–0.06
Assimilation	Parhaiya	—	–0.66**	–0.19	–0.27**
	Birjia		–0.06	–0.25	–0.34**
	Oraon		—	–0.14	–0.78**
Integration	Parhaiya			0.14	–0.23*
	Birjia			–0.42	–0.54**
	Oraon		—	—	–0.20
Separation	Parhaiya				–0.16
	Birjia		—	—	–0.27**
	Oraon				
Marginalization	Parhaiya		—	—	—
	Birjia				

Note: P<.01** P<.05*

Table 10.2 presents the inter-correlations among dimensions of acculturation attitude in the tribal groups which showed significant negative correlations between integration and marginalization and assimilation and marginalization. Separation has not been correlated with any of these acculturation attitudes accept in the case of Birjia where a negative correlation has been found between separation and marginalization. In Parhaiya tribe a negative correlation has been found between assimilation and integration attitudes.

In order to observe the relationship between social identity and the acculturation attitude a correlation was computed for total score of social identity and the four dimensions of acculturation attitude for each of the three tribal groups. There is an indication from Table 10.3 that positive correlation emerged between social identity and integration dimension in all tribal groups. The correlation between social identity and integration was largest in Parhaiya group (r = 0.61**) followed by with Oraon (r = 0.57**) and with Birjia (r = 0.35**). A significant but negative correlation occurred between social identity and marginalization in Oraon and Birjhia group (r = –0.56** and –0.27**).

Similarly, a negative but significant correlation was found between social identity and assimilation in Parhaiya group (r = –0.51**) but not in Oraon and Birjia groups.

Apart from these another inter-correlation was computed among social identity and acculturation attitude comprising total sample of all

Table 10.3: Inter-correlations among Social Identity and Acculturation Attitude in three tribal groups

Social Identity	*Groups*	*Assimila-tion*	*Integration*	*Separation*	*Marginali-zation*
	Oraon	0.12	0.57**	0.02	–0.56**
Social Identity (Total)	Parhaiya	–0.51**	0.61**	0.10	0.01
	Birjia	–0.30	0.35**	–0.07	–0.27**

Note: P<.01** P<.05*

three tribal group of participants. The observation of Table 10.4 suggested that only integration acculturation attitude have been positively correlated with social identity total score and its two components namely, ethnic identity search and affirmation. However, marginalization has found to be negatively correlated with social identity and its components.

Table 10.4: Inter-correlations among Social Identity and Acculturation Attitude in total group

	Acculturation Attitude			
Social Identity	*Assimilation*	*Integration*	*Separation*	*Marginalization*
Social Identity (Total)	–.01	.49**	–.13*	–.34**
Ethnic Identity Search	.01	.30**	–.08	–.24**
Affirmation	.04	.37**	–.09	–.26**

Note: P<.01** P<.05*

The results of inter-correlations among social identity and its two components, affirmation (affective component) and ethnic identity search (components) clearly showed that affirmation was highly and significantly correlated with social identity. However, ethnic identity search too was significantly correlated with social identity. But the values of correlations showed the primacy and salience of affirmation (affective component) over ethnic identity search, i.e. cognitive component. The results are self-explanatory in the sense that emotional and affective state of individual largely determines and shapes the social identity in comparison to cognitive state.

The inter-correlations among four dimension of acculturation attitude showed that there were highly significant negative correlations between assimilation and integration in Parahiya tribal group, between assimilation and marginalization in Parhaiya and Birjia tribal groups, between integration and separation in Birjia tribal group, between integration and marginalization in all the three tribes, i.e. Oraon, Parahaiya and Birjia and between separation and marginalization in Birjia tribal. These results were pointing out the fact that most of the dimensions of acculturation attitude are variedly opted as a choice of their attitude towards acculturation.

The results of inter-correlation among social identity and acculturation attitude in the three tribal groups showed highly significant correlation between social identity and integration in all the three tribal groups while significant negative correlation was found between social identity and assimilation in Parahaiya tribal and between social identity and marginalization in Oraon tribal group.

Findings are supported by the studies which concluded that integration is the most favoured attitudes over the other three attitudes with marginalization being the least preferred. However, some exception has also been found (Piontkowski, Florack, Hoelker & Obrzalek, 2000), (Berry & Ataca, 2000), when some groups preferred separation over integration. In another study conducted in India, Agaria tribal group displayed a significant stronger separation attitude than the Kharwar. The contact-acculturation was emerged as a significant predictor for both integration and separation attitudes (Mishra & Chaubey, 2002).

In the study of Krislman and Berry (1992) both adults and adolescents have given preference for integration. This trend was found in several other studies with varied groups (Berry *et al.,* 1989), (Partridge, 1988). In a series of studies conducted in Canada on different immigrant groups, Berry *et al.* (1989) found integration to be the most preferred attitude. However, it was also revealed that among ûrst generation Hungarian-Canadian, separation is the second most preferred acculturation strategy, while assimilation is the second most preferred strategy among the second generation.

In another study, involving Westerners living in Japan, and immigrants from developing countries living in Norway, separation was the second most preferred acculturation strategy (Partridge, 1988; Sam, 1995).

Overall findings suggested that social identity and integration go together and are complementary to each other in a multicultural situation. Contrary to this, social identity and marginalization hinders each other and seem two poles apart.

References

Bartlett, F.C. (1970). *Psychology and Primitive Culture*, West Port, CT: Greenwood Press (Original work published, 1923).

Berry, J.W. (1970a). Marginality, Stress and identification in an acculturating Aboriginal community. *Journal of Cross-Cultural Psychology, 7,* 415-18.

Berry, J.W. (1974b). Psychological Aspects of Cultural Pluralism. *Topics in Culture Learning, 2,* 17-22.

Berry, J.W. (1980a). Acculturation as varieties of adaptation. In A. Padilla (Ed.), *Acculturation: Theory Models and some new findings* (pp. 9-25), Boulder, CO: Westview.

Berry, J.W., Kim, U., Power, S., Young, M. and Bujaki, M. (1989). Acculturation attitudes in plural Societies, *Applied Psychology, 38,* 185-206.

Berry, J.W. (1990). Psychology of acculturation: understanding individuals moving between cultures. In R.W. Brislin (Eds.), *Applied Cross Cultural Psychology*. Thousand Oaks, CA: Sage Publications.

Berry, J.W. (1990a). Psychology of acculturation. In J. Berman (Eds.), *Cross-cultural Perspectives: Nebraska Symposium on Motivation* (Vol. 37, pp. 201-34). Lincoln, NE: University of Nebraska Press.

Berry, J.W. and Kalin, R. (1995). Multicultural and Ethnic attitudes in Canada: Overview of the 1991 Survey. *Canadian Journal of Behavioural Science, 27,* 301-20.

Berry, J.W. (1997a). Immigration, acculturation and adaptation. *Applied Psychology: An International Review, 46,* 5-68.

Berry, J.W. (1998b). Social psychological costs and benefits of multiculturism, *A view from Canada, Trames, 2,* 209-33.

Berry, J.W., Ataca, B. (2000). Cultural factors in stress. In G. Fink (Ed.). *Encyclopaedia of Stress.* San Diego: Academic Press.

Brown, R. (1986). *Social Psychology* (2d Ed.), New York: The Free Press.

Graves, T.D. (1967). Psychological acculturation in a tri-ethnic community. *Southwestern Journal of Anthropology, 23,* 337-50.

Hogg, M.A. (2001). Social Identity and Sovereignty of the Group: A Psychology of Belonging; in C. Sedikides and M.B. Brewer (eds.) *Individual self, Relational Self and Collective Self: Partners, Opponents, or Strangers,* Philadelphia: Psychology Press, pp. 123-143.

Hogg, M.A. and Williams, K.D. (2000). From I to We: Social Identity and the Collective Self I Group Dynamics Theory. *Research and Practice, 4;* 81-87.

Kertanguy, Salaun, H., Anne, A. (2004). Reaction to Tragic loss of socio-cultural environment in the Adivasi Tribes: A Rorschach Study. *Rorschactiana,* Vol. *26(1)*, 11-25.

Kim, Y.Y., Lujon, P. and Dixon, L.D. (1998). "I can Walk Both Way" Identity Integration of American Indians in Oklahoma. *Human Communication Research, 25,* 252-274.

Krishnan, A. and Berry, J.W. (1992). Acculturative Stress and Acculturation attitudes among Indian immigrants to the United States. *Psychology and Developing Societies, 4,* 187-212.

Liebkind, K. (2001). Acculturation in R. Brown and S. Gaerturner (Eds.) *Blackwell Handbook of Social Psychology I Intergroup Processes* (pp. 386-406). Oxford, U.K.: Blackwell.

Mishra, R.C., Sinha, D. and Berry, J.W. (1996). *Ecology, Acculturation and Adaptation: A Study of Adivasi in Bihar*. New Delhi: Sage Publications.

Mishra, R.C. and Chaubey, A.C. (2002). Acculturation attitudes of Kharwar and Agaria Tribal Groups of Sonebhadra. *Psychology and Developing Societies,* Vol. 14 (2), 201-220.

MOST (Management of Social Transformations Programme) 1995. Multiculturalism: A Policy response to diversity, Paris: UNESCO.

Nguyen, H., Messe, L. and Stollak, G. (1999). Toward a more complex understanding of acculturation and adjustment: Cultural involvements and psychosocial functioning in Vietnamese youth. *Journal of Cross-cultural Psychology, 30*, 5-31.

Partridge, K. (1988). Acculturation Attitudes and Stress of Westerners living in Japan. In J.W. Berry and R.C. Annis (Eds.). *Ethnic Psychology*, Amsterdam: Swets and Zeitlinger.

Piontkowski, U., Florack, A., Hoelker, P., and Obdrzalek, P. (2000) Predicting acculturation attitude of dominant and non-dominant groups. *International Journal of Intercultural Relations, 24,* 1-26.

Phinney, J. (1990). Ethnic identity in adolescents and adults: A review of research. *Psychological Bulletin, 108,* 429-514.

Redfield, R., Linton, R. and Herskovits, M.J. (1936). Memorandum on the study of acculturation. *American Anthropologist, 38,* 149-52.

Sam, D.L. (1995). Acculturation Attitudes among Young Immigrants as a function of Perceived Parental Attitudes to Cultural Change. *Journal of Early Adolescents, 15,* 238-258.

Sayegh L. and Lasry, J.C. (1993). Immigrants' adaptation in Canada: Assimilation, acculturation and orthogonal identification. *Canadian Psychology, 34(1),* 98-109.

Segall, M.H., Dasen, P.R., Berry, J.W. and Poortinga, Y.H. (1999). *Human Behaviour in Global Perspective: An Introduction to Cross-cultural Psychology* (rev. 2nd ed.) Boston, M.A. Allyn & Bacon.

Skelton, T. and Allen, T. (Eds.) (1999). *Culture and Global Change*, Routledge & Keagan Paul, London.

Social Science Research Council (1954). Acculturation: An exploratory formulation. *American Anthropologist, 56,* 973-1002.

Sommreland, E. and Berry, J.W. (1970). The role of ethnic identification in distinguishing between attitudes towards assimilation and integration of a minority racial group. *Human Relations, 23,* 29-9.

Szapocznik, J., & Kurtines, W.M. (1993). Family Psychology and cultural diversity. Opportunities for theory, research and application. *American Psychologists, 48(4)*, 400-440.

Tajfel, H. (1981). Social Stereotypes and Social groups in J.C. Turner and H. Giles (Eds.). *Intergroup Behaviour.* Oxford: Blackwell. pp. 144-167.

Tajfel, H. and Turner, J.C. (1979). An Intergrative theory of intergroup conflict. In W.G. Austin and S. Worchel (Eds.), *The Social Psychology of Intergroup Relations* (pp. 33-47). Monterey, C.A.: Brooks/Cole.

Tajfel, H. and Turner, J.C. (1986). The social identity theory of intergroup behaviour. In S. Worchel, W.G. Austein (Eds.), *Psychology of Intergroup Relations* (pp. 07-24). Chicago: Nelson-Hall.
Taylor, D.M. and Moghaddam, F.M. (1994). Theories in intergmup relations: *International Social Psychological Perspectives,* Westport, C.T.: Praeger.
Thomas, W.I. and Znaniecki, F. (1918). *The Polish Peasam in Europe and America*, New York: Dover (Original work published in 1918).

SECTION IV
Psychological Facilitators of Mental Health in Asia

11

Sources of Happiness

A Qualitative Analysis

Anubhuti Dubey and *Garima Singh*

Introduction

The search for happiness and a good life has been one of the primary and persistent concerns among all civilizations. Still, happiness is a nebulous concept and thus defining it can be as elusive as achieving it. Happiness, as found in psychological researches, is an overall feeling of satisfaction with life that pervades and abides over longer duration of time. The concept of happiness has been clearly related with the question that what does one wants in life, as Dalai Lama sets that the main purpose of life is happiness.

Happiness is a subjective concept and thus it has been defined in variety of ways and has been identified in numerous sources. But, according to positive psychology happiness is the state of mind or feeling characterized by contentment, love, satisfaction, pleasure, or joy. Happiness is being aware not only of the positive events that occur in our life but also that we ourselves are the cause of these events that we can create them, that we control their occurrence, and that we play a major role in the good things that happen to us.

Happiness is the subjective evaluation of life. It is a mental state of well-being characterized by positive emotions ranging from contentment to joy. Within the field of psychology, interest in happiness emerged in the 1960s with the growth of the human potential movement, and more recently with the rise of positive psychology. Researchers often use "happiness" interchangeably with other terms such as subjective well-being and quality of life. In all these uses, the common thread is cognitive evaluation of the affective quality of life and the extent of satisfaction enjoyed by people.

Conceptually two main kinds of happiness, hedonic or utilitarian, and eudaimonic, are distinguished. Hedonism emphasizes maximization of pleasure and minimization of pain and it nurtures self-interest (Kahneman, Diener, and Schwarz 1999). The other view relates happiness to the search for values. As Waterman (1993) observed, happiness involves living with the true self and allowing for personal expression. According to Ryff and Keys (1995) the eudaimonic view focuses on autonomy, personal growth, self-acceptance, life purpose, and having positive relationships. According to Seligman (2002), positive psychology findings state that humans seem happiest when they have in their lives: Pleasure, Engagement, Relationships, Meaning, and Accomplishments (PERMA). In his book *Authentic Happiness*, Seligman (2002) identifies three levels of happiness, they are:

1. *Pleasure:* the delights that have clear sensory and strong emotional components.
2. *Engagement:* these activities absorb us much more fully than simple pleasures but are not necessarily accompanied by raw feelings; like enjoying a great conversation, rock climbing, playing chess etc.
3. *The Meaningful Life:* this involves using our signature strengths in the service of a higher cause.

Hedonic Happiness

Happiness seems to be an important part of how people define a good life. Defining the good life in terms of personal happiness is the thrust of the hedonic view of well-being (Kahneman, Diener, & Schwarz, 1999; Ryan & Deci, 2001). Hedonic psychology parallels aspects of the philosophy of hedonism. While there are many varieties of philosophical hedonism dating back to the ancient Greeks, a general version of hedonism holds that the chief goal of life is the pursuit of happiness and pleasure. Within psychology, the view of well-being is expressed in the study of subjective well-being (Diener, *et al.*, 1999). Subjective well-being takes a broad view of happiness, beyond the pursuit of short-term or physical pleasures defining a narrow hedonism. Subjective well-being is defined as life satisfaction, the presence of positive affect, and a relative absence of negative affect. Together, the three components are often referred to as happiness.

Eudaimonic Happiness

Pleasure, disconnected from reality, does not affirm or express our identity as individuals. Still, there is more to life than happiness and subjective pleasure; or as Seligman (2002) describes it, there is deeper and more "authentic happiness". Much of classic Greek philosophy was concerned with these deeper meanings of happiness and the good life. Waterman (1993) describes two psychological views of happiness distilled from classical philosophy. Hedonic concept of happiness describes happiness as the enjoyment of life and its pleasures. The hedonic view captures a major element of what we mean by happiness in everyday terms.

In contrast, eudaimonic conceptions of happiness, given fullest expression in the writings of Aristotle, define happiness as self-realization, meaning the expression and fulfilment of inner potentials. From this perspective, good life results from living in accordance with your *daimon* (your true self). That is, happiness results from striving toward self-actualization—a process in which our talent, needs, and deeply held values direct the way we conduct our lives. "Eudemonia" or happiness results from realization of our potentials. We are happiest when we follow and achieve our goals and develop our unique potentials. Eudaimonic happiness has much in common with humanistic psychology's emphasis on the concepts of self-actualization (Maslow, 1968) and the fully functioning person (Rogers, 1961) as criteria for healthy development and optimal functioning.

Waterman (1993) argued that eudaimonic happiness results from experiences of personal expressiveness. Such experiences occur when we are fully engaged in life activities that fit and express our deeply held values and sense of who we are. Under these circumstances, we experience a feeling of fulfilment, of meaningfulness, of being intensely alive—a feeling that is who we really are and who we were meant to be.

Indian Perspective on Happiness

The Indian tradition holds an exclusively materialist view where fulfilment of desires, predominantly of sensory nature, is the exclusive norm for well-being that finds path in course of pleasure. Much of the accepted wisdom regarding quality of life and well-being in the Indian culture today has been drawn from Vedic and Upanishad periods. The Vedic and Upanishad oracles highlightthe eternal (*nitya*) and permanent (*satya*), instead of focusing on momentary things (*kshanika*) or destructive (*kshara*) or transitory things (*mithya*). They recognized the ultimate truth concerning with that which is permanent and eternal rather than that which is impermanent and ephemeral. Their understanding of everything in the universe, be it physical, psychological, biological, moral, revolves around this ultimate truth. The difference created between good and bad, worthy and unworthy, moral and immoral, all had its basis in the same philosophy. So, was their conceptual understanding of happiness and well-being. The ancient Indian philosophy, thus, views happiness in things and notion that are permanent and eternal and lacking the same in momentary possessions.

Theories of Happiness

Theories of happiness have been divided into three types: nee/goal satisfaction theories, process/activity theories, and genetic/personality predisposition (Diener, *et al.*, 2002).

In regard to need/goal satisfaction theories, the leaders of particular schools of psychotherapy proffered these ideas about happiness. For example, psychoanalytic and humanistic theorists (Sigmund Freud and Abraham Maslow, respectively) suggested that the reduction of tension or the satisfaction of need leads to happiness. In short, it was theorized that we are happy because we have reached our goals. Such "happiness as satisfaction" makes happiness a target of our psychological pursuits.

In the process/activity camp, theorists posit that engaging in particular life activities generates happiness. For example, Mike Csikszentmihalyi proposed that people who experience flow (engagement in interesting activities that match or challenge task-related skills) in daily life tend to be very happy. Indeed, Csikszentmihalyi's (1990, 2000) work suggests that engagement in activity produces happiness. Other process/activity theorists (*e.g.*, Emmons, 1986; Snyder, 1994) have emphasized how the process of pursuing goals generates energy and happiness.

Those who emphasize the genetic and personality predisposition theories of happiness (Diener & Larsen, 1984; Watson, 2000) tend to see happiness as stable, whereas theorists in the happiness-as-satisfaction and process/activity camps view it as changing with life conditions. On this latter point, Costa and McCrae (1988) found that happiness changed little over a six year period, thereby lending credence to theories of personality-based or biologically determined happiness. Demonstrating this link between happiness and personality, Lucas and Fujita (2000) showed that extraversion and neuroticism, two of the Big Five factors of personality, were closely related to the characteristics of happiness.

Studies of the biological or genetic determinants of happiness have found that up to 40 per cent of positive emotionality and 55 per cent of negative emotionality are genetically based (Tellegen, *et al.,* 1988). Obviously, this leaves about 50 per cent of the variance in happiness that is not explained by biological components. Overall, therefore, a thorough understanding of happiness necessitates an examination of genetic factors and the variables suggested by need/goal satisfaction and the activity/process theorists.

Measuring Happiness

Happiness is defined as the degree to which an individual judges the overall quality of his life-as-a-whole positively, or in short: how well one likes the life one lives. In this way, happiness belongs to a wider class of subjective appraisals of life, which is usually referred to as 'subjective well-being' (SWB) or 'life satisfaction'. Considering the definition of happiness, the obvious way to measure it is to ask the individual to give his or her opinion on one's own happiness situation.

Different quantitative methods have been used to measure happiness. Diener and his collaborators (1984) presented a method to measure happiness based on the idea that individuals can consistently identify their level of satisfaction with life on a scale, and as such, what must be done is to ask people questions. Another method for measuring happiness is based on the sampling of experiences developed by the psychologist Csikszentmihalyi and several researchers (1990). This method consists of using locators (beepers) and afterwards using computers to contact individuals at random and ask them about their mood. A different approach is followed by a group of researchers led by Kahneman (1999). They created a method for measuring happiness based on following or reconstructing what people do at each moment of the day and asking them how they feel. The main findings of this research specify that the three basic components of happiness are pleasure, commitment and meaning.

Following this method and using messages on mobile telephones as an instrument of communication with those surveyed, Killingsworth (2000) identified happiness associated with a wide range of activities.

He points out that, until recently; researchers had to trust the assessments and appraisals that people made about their average emotional states over long periods of time. This inconvenience is avoided when following the method based on reconstructing what people do at different moments every day. Recently, and amidst the impressive growth of social networks, there has emerged a new method for measuring happiness. This method consists of inferring the feelings of social network users on the basis of a semantic. Specifically, the researchers Dodds and Danforth (1998) have developed a method that by incorporating the direct human evaluation of words, allows us to quantify levels of happiness on a continuous scale from a diverse collection of texts. The method is transparent and able to quickly process texts from the Internet.

Methods of quantifying happiness

1. *Survey studies:* Measuring happiness for social scientific purposes is usually realized as a part of a 'survey' in which a lot of people answer the same questions, either in face-to-face interviews or on questionnaires presented on the web. The way questions are presented to the respondents is adjusted to this technique, and that means typically that question are answered selecting from a limited number of response options (so called 'closed' questions).

2. *Survey questions:* To all members of a sample that is considered to be representative for the target population of the study, one or more closed questions are presented with a limited number of response options. This combination of the question and all response options together is referred to as a *primary scale of happiness measurement.*

3. *Self-report using multiple questions:* This includes:

- *Affect balance scales*, such as Bradburn's Affect Balance Score (ABS)
- *Life satisfaction questionnaires*, such as Diener's Satisfaction With Life Scale (SWLS)

4. Repeated single questions on happiness of the moment, such as:

- *Experience Sampling Method* (*ESM*) *e.g.* Wessman and Ricks Personal Feeling Scale.
- *Day Reconstruction Method* (*DRM*), e.g. Veenhoven's Happiness Diary.

5. *External Judges:* Estimating happiness by *external judges* on the basis of observation of the subject's behaviour, which is assumed to be related to his/her happiness.

- Rating of cheerful behaviour: *e.g.* Webb's rating of pupils by teachers.
- Rating on multiple indications of mood, *e.g.* well-being subscale of Baker and Dowling Interact schedule.
- Rating by interviewer of non-verbal behaviour during the interview, *e.g.* Allensbacher rating of cheerful appearance.
- Time sampling of happy and unhappy utterances, part of Bailey observation schedule for babies.

Qualitative Analysis of Happiness

1. *Narrative self-report:* These are descriptions of individuals about happiness which are coded afterwards and includes:

- Content analysis of open interviews, *e.g.* Mussen's rating of trait cheerfulness.
- *Content analysis of life reviews*, *e.g.* Danner's rating of happiness in autobiographies.
- *Content analysis of diaries, e.g.* Newman Langner scale of post-divorce adaptation.

Happiness, when measured is as a discrete variable at the *ordinal level of measurement*, not only if verbal scales are used, but also for numerical scales. The digits of numerical scales are code numbers in principle. A variable is called *discrete* if it can adopt a very limited number of values only.

Rationale and Objective of the Present Study

Method

Sample: The sample consisted of 40 students of undergraduate courses of D.D.U. Gorakhpur University. The students were equally divided in two groups on the basis of gender, i.e., 20 males and 20 females. The students were in the age range of 19 to 22 years.

Interview Schedule: A semi-structured interview schedule was prepared to understand the concept and meaning of happiness in students. The interview focused on as to how the students relate their happiness to: materialistic things, situations in life, relationships with others, and the general meaning of happiness for them.

Procedure: The study was conducted in classroom setting. The students were briefed about the objective of study and their consent was taken. Thereafter, a semi-structured interview was conducted one-by-one. The data was collected individually and it took around 10-15 minutes with each of the participant. After taking their responses they were thanked and the obtained data was put to content analysis.

Results and Discussion

The narratives were analyzed using content method. Particular texts relevant to the research questions were analyzed, thereby initial codes were generated, i.e., patterns were identified and coded. Further, themes were adopted as a recording unit. For each of the four sources of happiness (Materialistic Things, Relationships, Situations and General Meaning), various major themes and subthemes under them were found. These themes and subthemes were tabulated (Table 11.1) with their respective frequencies.

Materialistic Things: Happiness in today's scientific and media world depends more on materialistic things. From Table 11.1, it is clear that boys prefer electronic devices the most, while girls prefer books the most. One of the responses from a boy was: *getting any gadget as a gift leads to happiness*. Similarly, a girl student responded that *happiness is getting books and novels*. Among other major responses of boys included books, clothes or shoes, land or property and sports good. While, major adores of girls included electronic devices, clothes, shoes and vehicle. In today's scenario, technological devices and other luxuries form a part of basic need, especially for youngsters. Thus, the role of income in fulfilling the basic needs helps explain the importance of money for people. Although, a number of studies suggest that income has a small correlation with happiness and life satisfaction that is independent of many individual and social variables. Rising expectations are one major reason why more money does not bring happiness. Diener and Biswas-Diener (2002) argue that rising expectations create a perpetual gap between material aspirations and current material possessions.

Situations in Life: Happiness is a feeling that is solely context-dependent and thus situations in life determine it in various ways. For both, boys and girls gaining achievements in career governs their

Table 11.1: Sources of Happiness

	Sources of Happiness		*Male*	*Female*
Major Themes	*Exemplars*	*Sub Themes*	*f*	*f*
Materialistic Things	• Receiving first gift from mother • A peacefully located house • Electronic gadget • While using laptop	Books	09	14
		Clothes/Shoes	08	10
		Electronic Devices	13	11
		Gifts	02	02
		Land/Property/Vehicle	08	04
		Money	03	00
		Sport Goods	05	03
		Food	01	03
Situations in Life	• Admission to new course • Establish a career • Get the aim of life • Falling in love	Achievements in career	15	18
		Family time	03	04
		Time spent with friends	02	04
		Success of family member	00	02
		Marriage	03	00
		Helping others	01	00
		Love	06	00
Relationships	• Love from parents • Making good friends	Mother	13	12
		Father	13	10
		Friends	14	11
		Siblings	09	10
		Family members	03	04
		Relatives	04	03
		Teachers	03	02
		Neighbour	01	01
		Poor/ Orphan/Old people	00	01
		Life partner	03	01
		Pets	00	01
General Meaning of Happiness	• Working for a social cause like helping orphans, old age people. • Happiness is mental peace • Helping others is happiness • Happiness is when others are happy	Helping others	07	09
		Happiness of family	03	05
		Achieving the goal of life	10	04
		Other people's happiness	02	04
		Prestige	00	01
		Money	02	00
		Life	00	01
		Friends	00	01
		Praise from others	00	01
		Development of Nation	00	01
		Recreational Activities	03	00
		Fulfilment of basic needs	01	00
		Satisfaction/Mental Peace	02	00
		Being in love	02	00

happiness, like one of the responses was *getting a job after studies is happiness*. Situations like finding love, marriage and time spent with family are other factors of happiness in boys; while for girls, time spent with family and friends, and success of family member bring happiness to them. Unemployment makes people unhappy and thus achievements in career are linked to happiness in students. In a recent study (Knabe, *et al.*, 2010), the well-being effect of unemployment in Germany was studied. The results indicated life satisfaction was greater in employed people as compared to unemployed people. Studies also show that married people tend to be happier and healthier than singles.

Relationships: As human-beings, we are fundamentally social animals whose connections to others are vital to our health and happiness. Relationships with mothers govern happiness in girls, while for boys relations with friends are associated with their happiness. A girl responded that *love and care from parents shows way to happiness*, while a boy responded *happiness is getting good friends*. Other relationships that are associated with happiness for both, boys and girls include father, relatives, neighbours and teachers. The evidences connecting well-being to relationships is overwhelming. Myers (1992) referred to contribution of relationships to health and happiness as a "deep truth". According to Diener and Diener (1995) of the many factors that contribute to well-being, only social relationships consistently predict happiness across widely different cultures.

General Meaning: Happiness is an abstract concept and thus the general meaning of it varies from one person to other. Like, for boys happiness equals getting the goal of life, while for girls, helping other people means happiness. Other meaning of happiness for boys lies in helping others, recreational activities and mental peace. Whereas, for girls, meaning of happiness lies in happiness of family, achievements and other people's happiness. Some of the responses were: *helping others gives immense pleasure* and *happiness for oneself is where others tend to be happy.* Our definition of good life or happiness is reflected in our cultural images and the society we wish to have.

The ultimate aim of all human activity can be broadly described as an ongoing quest for greater happiness. To be happy is the very core of all human motivation. People in general across the world report that they would need following, in order of priority, for their lives to be completely happy: material living conditions, happy family life, personal or family health, interesting job and personal characteristics such as emotional stability, self-discipline etc. (Easterlin, 2004). The influence of culture is also suggested across countries by the varying interpretations and meanings of happiness in different cultures.

References

Argyle, M. (1999). *Causes and Correlates of Happiness*, in Kahneman, Diener and Schwarz (eds.): Well-Being: The foundations of hedonic psychology. New York: Russell Sage Foundation, *op. cit.,* pp. 353-373.

Baumgardner, S.R., and Crothers, M.K. (2009). *Positive Psychology*. Upper Saddle River, N.J.: Prentice Hall.

Dalal, A.K., and Mishra, G. (2011). *New Directions in Health Psychology.* SAGE Publications, New Delhi.

Diener, E. (2000). Subjective well-being: The science of happiness and a proposal for a national index. *American Psychologist, 55*, 34-43.

Diener, E., and Seligman, M.E.P. (2003). Beyond money. *Psychological Science in Public Interest, 5*, 1-31.

Diener, E., Diener, M., and Diener, C. (1995). Factors predicting the subjective well-being of nations. *Journal of Personality and Social Psychology, 69*, 851-864.

Kiran Kumar, S.K. (2006). Happiness and well-being in Indian tradition. *Psychological Studies, 51*, 105-112.

Lambert, C. (2009). *The science of happiness*. Retrieved from http://harvardmagazine.com/2007/01/the-science-of-happiness.html

Lu, L., and Gilmour, R. (2004). Culture and conceptions of happiness: Individual oriented and social oriented SWB. *Journal of Happiness Studies*, 5, 269-291.

Markus, H.R., and Kitayama, S. (1998). The cultural psychology of personality. *Journal of Cross-Cultural Psychology, 29*, 63-87.

Myers, D.G. (2000). The funds, friends and faith of happy people. *American Psychologist, 55*, 56-67.

Oishi, S., Koo, M., and Akimoto, S. (2008). Culture, interpersonal perceptions, and happiness in social interactions. *Personality and Social Psychology Bulletin*, 34, 307-320.

Ryan, R.M., and Deci, E.L. (2001). On happiness and human potentials: A review of research on hedonic and eudemonic well-being. In S. Fiske (Ed.), *Annual Review of Psychology* (pp. 141-166). Palo Alto, CA: Annual Reviews, Inc.

Ryff, C.D. (1989). Happiness is everything, or is it? Explorations on the meaning of psychological well-being. *Journal of Personality and Social Psychology, 57*, 1069-1081.

Snyder, C.R., and Lopez, S.J. (2009) *Positive psychology: The Scientific and Practical Explorations of Human Strengths*. SAGE Publications, New Delhi.

Tam, K.P., Lau, H.P.B., and Jiang, D. (2010). Culture and subjective well-being: A dynamic constructivist view. *Journal of Cross-Cultural Psychology, 20*, 1-9.

Waterman, A.S. (1993). Two conceptions of happiness: Contrasts of personal expressiveness (eudaimonia) and hedonic enjoyment. *Journal of Personality and Social Psychology, 64*, 678-691.

Wierzbicka, A. (2009). What makes a good life: A cross linguistic and cross-cultural perspective. *Journal of Positive Psychology, 4*, 260-272.

12

What Does Happiness Mean

An Indigenous Psychological Analysis on College Students' Sources of Happiness in Semarang, Central Java, Indonesia

Anggun Resdasari Prasetyo, Erin Ratna Kustanti and *Dinie Ratri Desiningrum*

Introduction

Scientific study on positive psychology has been increasingly popular to be applied in human development because it observes the positive sides of human being. The paradigm of positive psychology applies more positive perspective compared to psycho-analysis theory. Positive psychology establishes that in the midst of human helplessness, they always have a chance to see life more positively. Human being is seen as a creature that can survive from any helplessness and maximize its self-potential. Positive psychology also sees human being as a figure capable of defining its way to appreciate life. Positive psychology is centred on the meaning of life, the way a human being interprets everything within, in which the meaning is subjective (Seligman & Peterson, 2005). One of the aspects in positive psychology is happiness, since, basically, happiness is one of human's basic needs. Philosophers like Aristotle and psychologist like William James declares that the purpose of life is to seek for happiness. Then, Western scientists like Seligman and Csikzsentmihalyi (2000) also conducted a study on happiness, focusing on the aspect of happiness, positive affects and individual optimism. Positive psychology has started as an object of study since, recently, studies on psychology are mainly focused on psychoanalysis and intervention studies leading to depression, stress, pessimism and negative experience.

Studies on happiness are essential since happiness is the main objective that every human being wants to achieve. Up to now, there are multiple perspectives to define happiness theoretically, while the meaning of happiness can be very subjective and different to everyone. Commonly, happiness is defined as a positive emotion which is experienced by an individual who has a pleasant and meaningful experience that leads to happiness (Rahardjo, 2007). Snyder & Lopez (2006) defined happiness as a state of positive emotion which is subjectively defined by every individual. Happiness is a bunch of feelings that can be felt in the form of feeling happy, peaceful, and have peace (Rusydi, 2007). Happiness according to Biswas, Diener & Dean (2007) is the quality of the whole human life—what makes life good overall as better health, higher creativity or higher income. Furnham (2008) also states that happiness is part of well-being, contentment, to do your life satisfaction or equally the absence of psychology distress. It adds that the concept of happiness is a synonym of life satisfaction or satisfaction with life (Veenhoven, 2000). Diener (2007) also states that satisfaction with life is a real form of happiness or happiness where happiness is something more than an achievement of purpose because in reality happiness is always associated with better health, higher creativity and a better workplace.

Sumner (in Veenhoven, 2006) describes happiness as "having a kind of positive attitude toward life, which is entirely a form of possession of cognitive and affective components. The cognitive aspect of happiness consists of a positive evaluation of life, measured either by standard or expectation, in terms of affective happiness consisting of what we refer to in general as a sense of well-being, finding a living or favourable wealth or feeling satisfied or fulfilled by these things."

Schimmel (2009) clarified that happiness is individual assessment of quality of life. According to Schimmel (2009), sometimes happiness can be described as subjective well-being. While Diener & Ryan (2009) mentioned that happiness relates to positive emotions, whereas subjective well-being includes both positive and negative emotions. However, both terms refer to individual assessment of quality of life. From these definitions, human being is expected to be more active in making efforts to seek for and gain happiness.

The effort or activity done in achieving happiness can vary from individual to individual, relating to the understanding and concept of the happiness orientation that each individual has. Martin Seligman (2002) in his research on orientation to happiness states that there is a tendency for one to depend on one orientation of happiness over another. In addition, the orientation of happiness can also affect the actions and choices of the activities undertaken by individuals (Peterson, Park, and Seligman, 2005). The so-called happiness orientation by Seligman (2002) is one's preference for achieving happiness.

Myers (2010) suggests four characteristics of happiness, namely self-respect, high optimism, open minded, and self-control. While in study conducted by Diener (Franken, 2002), people who obtained high scores experienced issues like : (1) showing positive emotions; (2) showing less negative emotions; (3) having the tendency to get involved in fun activities; and (4) feeling satisfied with their life. The second thing to notice happiness is by paying attention to diversity in culture (Franken, 2002). Diversity in culture influences the level of happiness of people in their life. Specifically, in the context of Western Culture, happiness tends to relate to personal achievement. In this context, an individual acts based on the motivation to maximize the experience of positive affects. Self-esteem is the best prediction for happiness. On the other hand, in Eastern Asia, happiness is closely related to interpersonal relation achievement. In this context, individual performs actions based on the motivation to maintain the balance of positive and negative affects. For people with this cultural background, like in Indonesia, an individual prefers to have considerations from family and friends as well as other people to evaluate his/her life (Suh, Diener, Oishi & Triandis dalam Franken, 2002).

Based on the research conducted by Frontier Consultant Group in 2007 (Wijayanti & Nurwiyanti, 2010), the result shows that from six provinces in Indonesia, the happiest people settled in Central Java. The index of happiness in Central Java was recorded as 48,17, better than average index of happiness in Indonesia. The next places were North Sulawesi (47,95), West Java (47,85), East Java (47,19), DKI Jakarta (46,20), and North Sumatra (46,12). In fact, if observed from the income level, people in Central Java have less income compared to people living in DKI Jakarta. People living in Central Java have a higher level of happiness because, probably, they do not have a high expectation. Besides that, the attitude of accepting things, which has been the character of Javanese, contributes to their acceptance to life so that they feel more relaxed and enjoy what they already have.

Based on the survey of happiness in Indonesia, the study on the definition of happiness has become more interesting, especially on college students in Semarang which represents the community living in an area of Central Java. Semarang is the Capital City of Central Java which holds the Javanese traditions and ways of life. According to Ismawati, the Javanese, in terms of cultural anthropology, are people who speak in Javanese as well as its various dialects from generation to generation. People living in Semarang are characterized as the Javanese who are known as polite, friendly, respectful, subtle, upholds ethics and manners, and conserve the values of culture and traditions from generation to generation and highlight the principles of harmony as well as apply the sense of kinship in their daily life. According to Achidsti (2009), being friendly, empathetic, generous, unadorned, feeling bad, and other manners that are identical to Javanese.

Furthermore, the aim to analyse the meaning of happiness in college student was based on the consideration that, theoretically, college students are in the stage of early adulthood (transitional stage from late adolescence). They have experienced their first quarter of life and, surely, their characteristics have been developed and still undergo a process to be independent and productive individuals. The statement above refers to the theory defined by Hurlock (2004) that early adulthood is a transitional stage to new patterns of life and new social expectations. People in early adulthood are expected to play new roles like being a husband or wife, parents, or breadwinner as well as developing more mature attitudes, desires, and values according to their new role. The transition has become the crucial and challenging period of one's life span since, as an adult, they are expected to perform individual transition independently. So, happiness can act as the foundation of positive character building of college students.

Differing views on what matters most to one can affect one's own meaning toward happiness, so there is a diversity of things that make a person happy [Jersild (1982) in Oetami & Yuniarti, 2011]. In the academic and social life of the students, it was found that the orientation of happiness has a positive correlation with various aspects such as achievement motivation, student involvement with community and extracurricular activities, and clarity in career planning (Walker, Winn, & Lutjens, 2012). But not all happiness orientations can be positively correlated with aspects of student's academic life. The happiness orientation of meaning and engagement can be a positive predictor of adolescent career development, while orientation towards pleasure has no significant effect on career development (Hirschi, 2011). Some of these results suggest that a tendency towards a certain happiness orientation can be beneficial in a student's academic life. In this study, researchers want to examine the trend of happiness orientation at students of Faculty of Psychology, in a University of Semarang, Central Java, Indonesia.

Method

The research design used in this research is descriptive method, where the research tries to describe a phenomenon, event, or situation. The aim is to systematically, factually and accurately describe the facts under investigation. The data related on happiest moments experienced by respondents were obtained through open-ended questionnaires. The questions were to reveal the moments that make the respondents happy and the characteristics of happy individuals according to the respondents.

Sample

The respondents in the research are college students. College students were considered in the research since they are in the transitional stage between late adolescence and early adulthood (Hurlock, 2004) and they are already in the stage of living the values of life. The number of respondents was 156 psychology college students of a university in Semarang, Central Java, Indonesia. The respondents' age was between 18 to 22 years old.

Analysis

To get an idea of the events that make the college students the happiest, then the respondent is given an open question as follows: "Write the event that makes you happiest! Respondent's answer to this question varies greatly. This can be seen from the large categories of responses shown in Graph 12.1. Based on the data obtained from 156 psychology college students in a state university in Semarang, the overview or happiness orientation on those students is shown in Graph 12.1.

Discussion

This research is a preliminary study and the form of support obtained respondent to the formation of happiness orientation. Nevertheless, preliminary research conducted by indigenous psychology method is at

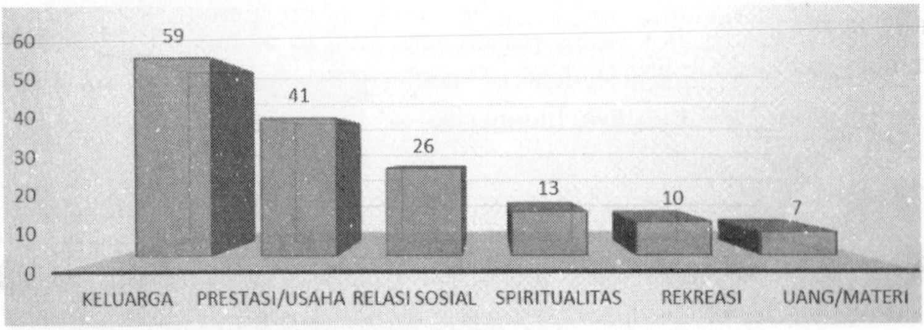

Graph 12.1: Happiness of college students

least able to reveal the typical information of the respondents. Nevertheless, preliminary research conducted by indigenous psychology method is at least able to reveal the typical information of the respondents. It is also hoped that this research can be a trigger for further research which is done more deeply by using indigenous psychology method so that it can contribute to the development of psychology science and also for the benefit of education and social life.

The results of this study indicate that there are six categories of events that make students feel the happiest:

(a) Bond or sense of kinship

Bond or sense of kinship is reflected on material and immaterial supports from family. The sense can be strengthened through harmony or family gathering, which is in line with what was stated by Miranti (2014) who believes that family serves as the foundation for forming happiness. Similar concept was also stated by Fuad (2005) saying that an ideal family of every human being is a family that has healthy mental characteristics: *sakinah* (tranquility), *mawaddah* (love) and *rahmah* (mercy). Family members should practice love and affection to generate a family unity. Happiness experienced from family contributes to college students' positive characters. The statement was based on the theory of Eddington & Shuman (2005) stating that the frequency of positive experiences correlates to positive effects. For example, a person who frequently undergoes some situations which create happiness within him/her tends to possess a high level of happiness. Besides that, Gunarsa (2003) stated that family is the smallest social unit in community which contributes to social development especially at the early stages which becomes the foundation for further personality development. The welfare of the community is highly dependent on the family in the community. If the whole family is prosperous, then the community tends to be prosperous too.

(b) Achievement

The achievement stated in the result of the research is the personal achievement of college students, academically or non-academically. Personal achievement also includes accomplishment or progress to accomplish personal needs in general such as goals, prosperity, or life satisfaction. Achievement-related experience contributes to optimisms as the source of happiness (Seligman, 2005).

(c) Social Relations

Social relations as one of college students' sources of happiness can be described as retaining best friends, acquaintances or supporting environment. Social relations refer to the relation between an individual and others in their social environment. A good social relation is characterized by being adaptive in one's social environment, able to perform social activities, sociable, supported by close friends, having a sense of togetherness and supported by one's social relations. According to a research conducted by Cheng and Furnham (2002), having friends at the same age is essential to a teenager's happiness since they gains benefits such as social support, sharing opportunities, and enjoying similar favourite activities as well as getting positive feedback. During the application, social support functions as: 1. Coping mechanism to reduce the negative effects of stress and conflicts (Calson & Perrewe in Gantari, 2008); 2. Providing satisfaction to the environment that provide social supports (Calson & Perrewe in Gantari, 2008); 3. Supporting individual health, mentally and physically (Argyle in Gantari, 2008).

(d) Free Time

Free time as the source of happiness of college students consists of making jokes, playing games, going on vacations and watching movies.

(e) Money

The ownership of money or certain materials either derived from the work itself or obtained from the provision of others.

(f) Spiritual Needs

Spiritual experience as the source of happiness is when religious orders are obeyed well. It is in line with what was stated by Al-Ghazali (2003) about happiness. Happiness is one's ability to fight over desire and control excessive behaviour. Basically, happiness is closely related to spiritual education since the objective of spiritual education is to obtain happiness, both in the world and in the hereafter. Therefore, for an individual, true happiness includes both physical and spiritual happiness, and then the positive mental and physical attitude will support individuals to achieve success in life.

Conclusion

Based on the study, it can be concluded that:

1. The main source of happiness of college students living in Semarang is family, so family attachment has become the priority to increase happiness of college students. Family attachment could be obtained by applying an open communication pattern and increasing the quality as well as the quantity of family gatherings. Family, especially parents, might start the attachment with college students through simple things, such as arranging a regular family gathering, organize recreational activities or familiarize themselves to share stories of fellow family members.
2. One of the components that generate happiness is positive perception towards the future or the needs of achievement, so, in order to increase happiness of college students, they should be given opportunities to actualize themselves. With the opportunity to actualize their potential, college students will be more self-respecting so that they will have a positive perspective on themselves and their environment.
3. The sources of happiness of college students need to be followed up as a basis for further research by designing a scale or a special measure of happiness for college students and a programme to reinforce the character of happiness for students so that their positive characters can be strengthened.

References

Al-Ghazali, Imam, (2003). *Meraih Kebahagiaan Dunia dan Akherat*. Mutiara Persada, Semarang.

Biswas, M.A., Diener, E.D and Dean, U. (2007). Personality, Culture, and Subjective Well-Being: Emotional and Cognitive Evaluations of Life. *Annual Revision Psychological Journal*. Vol. 54, pp. 403-25.

Cheng dan Furnham (2002). Personality, peer relations, and self-confidence as predictors of happiness and loneliness. *Journal of Adolescence*, *25*, 327-339. doi:10.1006/yjado.475.

Diener, E.D. (2007). Personality, Culture, and Subjective Well-Being: Emotional and Cognitive Evaluations of Life. *Annual Revision Psychological Journal*. Vol. 54; pp. 403-25.

Diener, Ed and Ryan, Katherine (2009). Subjective Well-Being: A General Overview. *South African Journal of Psychology*. Vol. 39 (4), pp. 391-406.

Eddington, Neil. Shuman, Richard. (2008). *Subjective Well-Being (Happiness)*. California: Continuing Psychology Education Inc.

Franken, Robert E. (2002). *Human Motivation*, 5th Edition. USA: Wadsworth Group/Thomson Learning, Inc.

Fuad, N. (2005). *Profil orang tua anak-anak berprestasi*. Yogyakarta: Insania Citra Press.

Furnham (2008). Psychological well-being: Meaning, measurement, and implications for psychotherapy research. *Psychotherapy and Psychosomatics, 65,* 14-23.

Gantari, E., 2008. *Hubungan Antara Perceived Social Support Dengan Subjective Well-Being Pada Ibu Pekerja*. Skripsi. (tidak diterbitkan). Universitas Indonesia.

Gunarsa, S.D. (2003). *Psikologi perkembangan anak, remaja dan keluarga*. Jakarta: Gunung Mulia.

Hurlock, E.B. (2004). Psikologi Perkembangan: Suatu Pendekatan Sepanjang Rentang Kehidupan Edisi Kelima. Jakarta: Erlangga.

Kim, U., Yang, K., Hwang, K. (2006). *Contributions to Indigenous and Cultural Psychology: Understanding People in Context*. Dalam Kim, U., Yang, K., Hwang, K., (Eds.). *Indigenous and Cultural Psychology: Understanding People in Context*. New York: Springer.

Miranti, A., 2014. *Faktor-faktor Pembentuk Kebahagiaan Dalam Keluarga* (*Konteks Budaya Jawa dan Pengaruh Islam*.) Skripsi: Psikologi UMS. Tidak Diterbitkan.

Myers G David, *Psikologi Sosial*, Jakarta: Penerbit Salemba Humanika, 2012, edisi 10.

Rahardjo, Wahyu, 2007. Kebahagiaan Sebagai Suatu Proses Pembelajaran. *Jurnal Penelitian Psikologi*. Volume 12, No. 2.

Rusydi, A.C. (2007). Analisis faktor yang mempengaruhi kebahagiaan. *Artikel ilmiah*. Diambil dari http://www.af.uinsgd.ac.id/wp-content/uploads/2013/05/53-60manusia-dan-kebahagian-dilah.pdf

Schimmel, Jörg. 2009. Development as Happiness: The Subjective Perception of Happiness and UNDP's Analysis of Poverty, Wealth and Development. *Journal of Happiness Studies*, Vol. 10, Issue 1, pp. 19, 93-111.

Seligman, M.E.P. and Csikszentmihalyi, M. (2000). Positive Psychology: an Introduction. *American Psychologist, 55*, pp. 5-14.

Seligman, Martin. E.P., 2002. *Authentic Happiness.* New York: Free Press.

Seligman, M.E.P. (2005). Positive Psychology Progress: Empirical Validation of Interventions. *Psychological Science, 7,* 186-189.

Snyder, C.R., and Lopez, S.J. (2006). Positive Psychology: The Scientific and Practical Explorations of Human Strengths. California, Sage Publications, Inc.

Uchida, C. dan Tor-Anyiin, S.A. (2004). Psychosocial effects of retirement on retirees: Implication for pre-retirement counselling in Nigeria. A paper presented at the *28th Annual National Conference of Counselling Association of Nigeria.* Maiduguri. Diambil pada tgl. 10 Oktoberr 2013 dari: http://www.unilorin.edu.ng/publications/idowuade/Prof.%20Idowu's% 20Paper.pdf

Wijayanti, H., Nurwianti, F. (2010). Kekuatan karakter dan kebahagiaan pada suku jawa. *Jurnal Psikologi*, Vol. 3.

13
Influence of Self-compassion on Procrastination

Priyanka Pathak and *Shobhna Joshi*

The world salutes to rising sun. "Success" the basic and ultimate goal of almost each and every individual is a very precarious position which never stays permanently to any person.

The society's overemphasis on achievement and relating one's self-esteem and confidence with the success is the root cause of all sufferings. From very early years of lives, we all are taught to build ourself esteem by competing successfully. This kind of social comparison leads to many negative effects as considering others obstacles to our way to success, disconnect with people making our territory etc., therefore, looking at this darker side of high esteem, and its undesirable consequences, it seems better to replace it with a more positive and constructive concept, which helps oneself in looking himself in a positive light even in failure and consequent difficult situations. The healthier self-concept is self-compassion (Sharma and Davidson, 2015).

Framed within the religious tradition of Buddhism as well as within current psychology, 'self-compassion' is a topic that has received increasing attention (Krieger *et al.*, 2013). Based on the perspectives of Buddhism and founded in a social psychological framework, Neff (2003a; 2003b) developed a positive self-oriented concept, called 'self-compassion'. After publishing the first two articles on self-compassion by Neff in 2003, more than 200 journal articles and dissertations were published on this topic within a period of ten years (Germer & Neff, 2013). The earliest psychological usage of the term 'compassion' appeared in "A Group Test for the Measurement of Cruelty-Compassion: A Proposed

Means of Recognizing Potential Criminality" (Hawthome, 1932) where the concept is, however, not well defined. Later, Macintyre (1966) elaborated further on the concept and defined compassion as "to put oneself imaginatively in the place of the sufferer and to alter one's actions appropriately either by desisting for what would have caused pain or by devoting oneself to its relief". In this process of compassion, one loses the self completely and focuses on the sufferer. Neff narrowed down the broad perspective of the other-oriented concept of compassion to a more self-oriented concept without losing the benefit of the former aspect. Self-compassion is defined as, being touched by and open to one's own suffering, not avoiding or disconnecting from it, generating the desire to alleviate one's suffering and to heal oneself with kindness. Self-compassion also involves offering non-judgemental understanding to one's pain, inadequacies and failures, so that one's experience is seen as part of the larger human experience (Neff, 2003b).

Similar psychological concepts can be found in the humanistic approach such as Rogers's 'unconditional positive regard' (1961), Maslow's 'B-perception' (1968) and Ellis's 'unconditional self-acceptance' (1973) that concentrate on the individual. Self-compassion encompasses them with its unique focus on a sense of shared humanity without isolating the individual from other human beings and with its notion of mindfulness (Barnard & Curry, 2011; Neff, 2003a).

Traditionally in India, a compassionate individual is normally considered a mentally healthy person because of the inner contentment and being fair to everyone equally (Paranjpe, 2002). To be compassionate with oneself aims to liberate oneself from one's suffering and at the same time acts as a prerequisite for an advanced form of self-compassion — compassion for others (Ladner, 2004). Buddhism describes compassion as "Karuna" an important quality to lead a meaningful and content life (Ladner, 2004). From a Buddhist perspective, an ideal person is the one who is free from any negativity toward any creature and is, instead, filled with positive qualities of compassion, friendliness and selflessness (Paranjpe, 2002).

Christianity is called "the religion of compassion" (Walker, 1979) because of its teaching of compassion as a "homage rendered to the Lord" (Achtemeier, 1962). But it does not mention self-compassion directly. At the same time, the higher level of self-compassion, that is, compassion for others is well explained in Christianity, and it is mainly attributed to the character of God, who is full of compassion. Every Christian is called to follow the example of God's compassion that should not be reserved for friends and neighbours alone, but extended to everyone without exception, even to one's enemies (Walker, 1979). Considering its significance in relationships, compassion is understood on three levels: family, community and dependent people like children, the elderly, the poor, orphans and widows (Achtemeier, 1962).

A short historical overview can explain why self-compassion is significant among Indian Christians. Christianity is a minority group (2.5 per cent of the total population) in India, but with a tradition dating back to the first century. Early Indian Christians, known as St. Thomas Christians, are found in Kerala, one of the southern states of India. Later, from the fourteenth century onwards, European Christian missionaries came to India and baptised many into Christianity in the Latin Catholic tradition. Therefore, three individual Churches of Latin, Syro-Malabar, and Syro-Malankara constitute the Catholic Church in India.

Interestingly, Christians in India have never separated themselves from others except in their strong Christian faith, and they have been following indigenous traditions and incorporating interreligious elements in their religious practices (Brown, 1982; Collins, 2007). During different stages of life, every Catholic in India is religiously trained through different religious programmes. For example, during the school and college years, a Catholic receives religious education through a system of Sunday school classes that take one and a half hour a week (Thurackal, Corveleyn and Dezutter, 2016).

A Catholic seminary is a place for the spiritual, moral, and intellectual formation of priests (O'donohoe *et al.*, 2002). According to the Indian worldview, an individual acquires qualities like compassion in the first stage of human life called *Brahmacharya Ashrama* (student life) in order to lead the other three stages of life (*Grihastha Ashrama* — household stage, *Vanaprastha Ashrama* — retired life, *Sannyasa Ashrama* — renounced life) successfully. For this reason, one has to leave the family and live with the teacher (Bhawuk, 2011). This tradition of student life is incorporated into the Catholic seminary system in India, where candidates leave their family and live in an institution with many scholar priests who specialise in different religious disciplines and serve as examples for the novices.

At different stages of seminary formation, a candidate allows oneself to be formed by the social, cultural and religious realities in which he lives (Padinjarekuttu, 2005). The entire training in a major seminary is intended to the formation of true pastors. Candidates are trained for the ministry of the word of God, which has to be expressed in words and in example. The capacity to relate to others is fundamental for them since they are responsible for a community. Therefore, genuine compassion is considered to be an important quality of a pastor (John Paul II, 1992). Being a shepherd, a Catholic priest continues the work of compassion, incorporating truth, love and life (John Paul II, 1992).

For better understanding about self-compassion, it is important to consider what the meaning of compassion is more generally. From the Buddhist point of view, compassion is given to our own as well as to others' suffering (2003a). Compassion involves sensitivity to the experience of suffering, coupled with a deep desire to alleviate that suffering (Goetz, Keltner, & Simon-Thomas, 2010).

Western psychologists have only recently begun to examine self-compassion, but the construct is central to the 2,500 year old tradition of Buddhist psychology. It indicates the acceptance and adoption of painful and unpleasant aspects of life and also includes caring, understanding and compassionating of self in the difficulties situations and failures.

Self-compassion is simply compassion directed inward, relating to ourselves as the object of care and concern when faced with the experience of suffering (Neff, 2003a). Self-compassion is an open-hearted way of relating to negative aspects of oneself and one's experience that enables greater emotional resilience and psychological well-being (Neff, 2003). Self-compassion is relevant when individuals face personal inadequacies, mistakes, and failures, as well as when struggling with more general life situations that cause us mental, emotional, or physical pain.

Neff (2003b) has operationalised self-compassion as consisting of three main elements: self-kindness, common humanity, and mindfulness. These components combine and mutually interact to create a self-compassionate frame of mind.

Self-kindness refers to being kind and understanding toward oneself in instances of pain or failure rather than being harshly self-critical. Self-compassion entails not being self-critical when one's expectations are not met and being unharmful to an individual's ego in order to make achievements. Instead, self-compassion suggests that the individual should encourage his/her ego gently and patiently to change behaviours (Neff, 2009).

Common humanity, the second dimension of self-compassion, is seeing one's happy or painful experiences as not personal, but as all human being's. The sense of common humanity principal to self-compassion involves recognizing that all humans are imperfect and that they fail and make mistakes (Neff, 2009). Having this kind of awareness, one perceives these experiences as part of the larger human experience rather than feeling isolated and alienated from the society and harshly criticizing oneself for failure and suffering experiences (Neff, 2003a). This awareness also emphasizes one's relatedness to all other humans and to another individual (Kirkpatrick, 2005).

Mindfulness, the third component of self-compassion, is a pre-conceptual awareness that allows individual to accept life's most stressful and painful emotions without being carried away by them (Gunaratana, 1993; Martin, 1997; Neff, 2003a; Nisker, 1998; Rosenberg, 1999). It is a non-judgamental, receptive mind-state in which thoughts and feelings are observed as they are, without suppressing or denying them. It is also a state of balanced awareness that one's feelings and thoughts are observed without avoiding or trying to change them, without exaggeration and prejudice. Individuals accept and tolerate their distress and pain when they are gentle and kind towards themselves and they avoid suppressing their emotions and thoughts. Thus, when they know that distress and pain are something all humans experience, they cannot be trapped by over-identification (Neff, 2003a).

As a whole we can say that self-compassion is a response to personal suffering or failure and can be generally defined as maintaining a kind, understanding attitude towards oneself while accepting one's limitations as a natural part of the human experience.

In recent time one of the variables associated with self-compassion studies is procrastination. In a study Neff *et al.* (2005) suggested that self-compassion may be effective in coping and adaptive behaviour in the field of education which is required to enjoy learning.

Procrastination as a common and serious problem, affect not only on mental health, but also physical health and well-being (Siros, 2007). It is the act of delaying starting or completion of a task that needs to be done in a given time. Procrastination has been defined as the tendency to delay initiation or completion of important tasks (Lay, 1986). Procrastination is generally defined as the intention or the thought of completing a task, but failing to finish the task within the expected time limit (Senecal, Koestner, & Vallerand, 1995) or to delay tasks to the point of discomfort (Solomon and Rothblum, 1984).

At this point it is necessary to make a distinction between procrastination and simple delay. According to Pychyl (2010), when people delay certain tasks due to unforeseen/uncontrollable life circumstances (e.g., a child's illness), they are actually setting priorities, and as this is not a voluntary delay, it is not procrastination. However, when one procrastinates, one needlessly and voluntarily chooses to put off an intended action that needs to be attended to at present. One potential explanation for the individual's tendency to put off tasks could be the negative emotions linked to an activity. In their review of the intra-personal processes underlying procrastination, Sirois and Pychyl (2013) suggested that procrastination may be described as prioritizing of short-term mood regulation at the cost of long-term goals.

Procrastination generally occurs when individuals are perceiving tasks as aversive. In the face of unpleasant feelings and negative mood brought about by aversive tasks, many individuals resort to engaging in avoidant behaviour that temporarily relieves them of the distress associated with the task at hand (Tice & Bratslavsky, 2000). In other words, they focus on short-term mood repair as a strategy to regulate their emotions (Sirois & Pychyl, 2013). Thus, procrastination can be considered as a strategy employed by the individual to deal with distressing emotions such as shame and anxiety experienced when faced with a perceived aversive task.

The procrastination research is generally classified according to four main forms *viz.,* (a) academic procrastination, (b) work-related procrastination, (c) life routine procrastination, (d) decisional procrastination, and (e) compulsive or dysfunctional procrastination.

Researches indicate that procrastination plays a significant role in students' lives. Academic procrastination is found to be related to anxiety, fear of being unsuccessful in a person's action owing to negative perceptions. Despite the fact that there are many types of procrastination *viz.,* academic procrastination is considered to be a widespread serious problem. It involves postponing academic tasks.

It can best be understood as the expression of procrastination in an academic situation. Academic procrastination is fairly common among college students and may negatively impact academic achievement (Clark & Hill, 1994; Ellis & Knaus, 2002; Harriott & Ferrari, 1996; Soloman & Rothblum, 1984; Wesley, 1994). According to Ellis & Knaus (2002) academic procrastination refers to the postponement of academic goals to the point where optimal performance become highly unlikely. Wolters (2003) defined academic procrastination as failing to perform an academic activity within a desired time frame or postponing until the last minute activities one needs to complete.

A large number of college students suffer from academic procrastination and its internal and external negative consequences. External-negative consequences include decreased learning, lost opportunities, increased health risks and strained relationships (Beswick, Rothblum, & Mann, 1988; Tice & Baumeister, 1997) and internal consequences of procrastinator behaviour may include irritation, regret, despair and self-blame (Burka & Yuen, 1983). Internal consequences have a serious influence on a learner's behaviour also. Academic procrastination is highly frequent in students and regarded as detrimental to academic progress and success.

Work-related procrastination is another form of procrastination in work setting. According to Hammer and Ferrari (2002) suggested that work procrastination affects performance of the team and is considered more costly than that of academic procrastination. In a prevalence study carried out with working adults, Ferrari (1992) found that procrastination was a self-perceived problem for many. The level of perceived problem reflected an individual assessment of personal performance related to personal standards (Van Eerde, 2003).

Everyday procrastination (Life Routine Procrastination) is another form of procrastination engaged frequently (Lay, 1986). It has been referred as difficulty in scheduling time of the recruiting life routines and doing them on schedule (Lay & Brokenshire, 1997; Sigall *et al.*, 2000). General procrastination behaviour is described as difficulties in performing daily tasks due to incapability to organize time and management effectively (Ferrari *et al.*, 1995).

Decisional form of procrastination is defined as inability to make timely decision (Effert & Ferrari, 1989) or as repeated postponement of major life decision (Ellis & Knaus, 1977).

Dysfunctional procrastination is defined as "the time past the optimal beginning point for completion of an important task that has a high probability of needing completion and that does not have unreasonable demands of personal costs associated with attempted completion" (Ferrari *et al.*, 1995).

Procrastination is such a widespread phenomenon affecting the lives of so many students as well as individuals. Very few studies have been conducted to investigate the association between self-compassion and procrastination. While past empirical studies on procrastination have tended to focus on the factors that are associated with the motive to procrastinate. More specifically, the study has been designed to investigate the research question of how self-compassion influence procrastination both directly and indirectly.

Self-compassion predicts emotional, behavioural and cognitive reactions to negative events in everyday life. It leads people to acknowledge their role in negative events without feeling overwhelmed with negative emotions (Leary *et al.*, 2005). It allows us to adopt a broader perspective on ourselves and our lives. So, that when faced with difficult life experiences instead of not reaching to pick their ideal angry, they tend to be treated with kindness (Sbarra *et al.*, 2012). It is positively associated with psychological well-being, such as self-acceptance, self-esteem, mindfulness, autonomy, environmental mastery, purpose in life, personal growth, reflective and affective wisdom, curiosity and exploration in life, happiness, and optimism (Kirkpatrick, 2006) positive mental health benefits and adaptive functioning (Neff, 2004), life satisfaction and social connectedness (Neff, 2003a), well-being (Neff *et al.*, 2008), mastery goals and emotion-focused coping strategies (Neff *et al.*, 2005), social supports, academic success (Conway, 2007), positive affects, wisdom, personal initiative, curiosity and exploration, agreeableness, extroversion, and conscientiousness (Neff *et al.*, 2007) and negatively associated with self-criticism, depression, anxiety, rumination, thought suppression, and neurotic perfectionism (Neff, 2003a; Kirkpatrick, 2006), negative affect and neuroticism (Neff *et al.*, 2007), performance goals, avoidance-oriented strategies (Neff *et al.*, 2005). On the other hand, procrastination is positively associated with anxiety, depression, rumination and stress. Based on the research findings, procrastination is increasing widely.

In early reviews many studies dealt with self-compassion and procrastination demonstrated that self-compassion is negatively related to positive correlates of procrastination and reviews have proved it. These evidences show that self-compassion is directly or indirectly related to negative tendencies like procrastination and its correlates. So, self-compassion requires that, when person damage, failure or feel incompetence stopped the suffering endured rather than ignore or criticized, would be kind to him and understand him (Neff, 2010).

In a study conducted with college undergraduates, Williams, Stark and Foster (2008) studied the impact of self-compassion on procrastination. Results indicate that procrastination is largely associated with lower levels of self-compassion. In other study Alexander (2011), reveal that impact of self-compassion on procrastination and the finding showed that self-compassion has a moderator role on procrastination scores.

In another investigation, a component of self-compassion, mindfulness, and its relations with trait procrastination, stress and health was examined in a large sample of undergraduate students (Sirois & Tosti, 2012). Procrastination is associated with stress, low levels of mindfulness and less frequent practice of mindfulness promoting activities such as *yoga* and meditation. More importantly, mindfulness mediated the association between stress and procrastination. Because self-compassion includes not only mindfulness but also self-kindness and common humanity (Neff, 2003b), the lack of which could be considered being self-critical and self-blaming, it is possible that lower levels of self-compassion are linked with trait procrastination. Over time these frequent negative self-evaluations may foster a more generalized tendency towards self-blame, self-criticism, as well as difficulty in disengaging from their ruminative self-judgements (Neff, 2003b). Consistent with this notion, McCown and colleagues (2012) content analysis of trait procrastinators' self-referent cognitions revealed a generalized tendency to be critical and unkind to oneself with statements such as "I'm simply too stupid..." which is akin to having a lack of self-compassion.

Research demonstrating the link between having less self-compassion and fear of failure (Neff *et al.*, 2005) provides further evidence for the possible multidirectional relationship between procrastination and self-compassion, as fear of failure is often known as reason for procrastination (Steel, 2007). Together with recent empirical work on the role of negative self-evaluations for interfering with task persistence (Evans, Baer, & Segerstrom, 2009), a role of low self-compassion in the development of tendency to procrastination seems plausible. Students who had high levels of self-forgiveness for procrastinating on studying for their first midterm examination reported less studying procrastination on their subsequent mid-term examination (Wohl, Pychyl, & Bennett, 2010).

Most studies in the literature are concerned with self-compassion, and procrastination of students, related to studying and behaviour in school or university separately. The performance measures included grades, missing deadlines, the time spent on preparing a task, and completing tasks, such as assignments. However, there was very limited study about related to relation between self-compassion and procrastination. Procrastination is a barrier to academic achievement, as with stress and negative consequences in the lives of students, led to reduce the quality and quantity of educational achievement (Akinsola *et al.*, 2007; Tan *et al.*, 2008). Procrastination is widely serious problem among students and it adversely affected the success of academic achievement. Beswick, Rothblum, and Mann (1988) found a negative relationship between procrastination and academic performance, with students who procrastinate by putting off studying for their exam experiencing greater anxiety during the exam.

For many university students, setting goals and accomplishing tasks that are directly relevant to the achievement of these goals are part-and-parcel of their academic life. However, despite having the best intentions, many students fail to complete their academic tasks in a given time. In other words, for many students, the tendency to procrastinate represents a barrier to the successful completion of their success in academic life or in general life.

In a recent study Hajiazizi & Ho (2015) investigated the direct and indirect influences of self-compassion on academic procrastination among 200 Assumption University students in Thailand. Results from the study indicated that the participants' reported level of self-compassion was negatively associated with their level of academic procrastination, i.e. the higher their level of self-compassion, the lower their reported level of academic procrastination. It was also found that self-compassion had a negative influence on the participants' reported level of anxiety. Finally, neither shame nor anxiety had a significant influence on academic procrastination. The results from the study showed that the participants' reported level of anxiety was significantly and inversely related to their reported level of self-compassion. As such, the higher individuals' level of self-reported self-compassion, the lower their tendency to experience feelings of anxiety. This finding corroborates those obtained from previous studies which indicate that, particularly in the face of hardship, self-compassion can lead to healthier mental functioning such as lower anxiety and depression (Neff *et al.*, 2003a; Leary *et al.*, 2007).

In one of the studies related to self-compassion and academic achievement, Neff *et al.* (2005) examined the relationship between self-compassion, academic achievement goal and coping with academic failure on 222 undergraduates. They found that there was positive relationship between self-compassion and mastery goal, a negative relationship between self-compassion and performance approach goal, and strong relationship between self-compassion and performance avoidance goal. It was found that self-compassion is associated with adaptive academic motivational patterns. Self-compassion was positively related to the adoption of mastery goals in learning contexts, suggesting that self-compassionate individuals are able to see failure as a learning opportunity and focus on accomplishing tasks at hand. Similarly in a recent study, conducted on 251 university students, Iskender (2011) examined the relationship between self-compassion, academic procrastination and dysfunctional attitude and on the basis of his findings, he concluded that there was significant and positive relationship between self-compassion and academic procrastination.

It is also observed that a critical issue has been involved in interpreting the relationship between self-compassion and procrastination. Self-compassion is a positive tendency whereas procrastination is a negative tendency. Researches show substantial controversies regarding the relationship between self-compassion and procrastination because some studies shows positive relationship with self-compassion and academic procrastination while other shows negative.

Most of the attempts have been made by the researchers establish the relationship between self-compassion and related to the psychopathology in context to procrastination such as depression, stress and anxiety etc.

Researches shows that depression with symptoms such as low self-esteem, loss of motivation, difficulty in concentrating and making decisions, fear of failure, humiliation and low scores, has an important role in procrastination. On the other hand, self-compassion is negatively associated with depression. Evidences show that people who have higher self-compassion, experience less depression and rumination challenging tasks (Neff, 2003). Pauley & Pherson (2010) studied experience and sense of compassion and self-compassion in patients with depression, the results of the study showed that participants act with kindness and compassion by having two main features, they reported that self-compassion in relation to their experiences is important and useful. Although participants believed that self-compassion was important in relating to their experiences, it is difficult for them because of their perception of the experience of illness and mental disorder. This has a negative effect on their ability to self-compassion.

Raes (2010), states that self-compassion is predictive for depression, anxiety and rumination. In another study, Raes (2011) studied self-compassion effect on depressive symptoms in a non-clinical sample. The results showed that self-compassion as a potentially important factor for the protection and conservation problems of depression.

Brown *et al.* (2014) studied the role of self-compassion in daily functioning and depressive symptoms of 206 women 40 to 60 years old, who had recently uncomfortable experience. The results showed that self-compassion has a direct effect on depressive symptoms. In another study, Basharpour and Isazadegan (2012) found that self-compassion is negatively correlated with depression.

A study by Breines and Chen (2012) on the effect of self-compassion on self-improvement motivation suggests that self-compassion's bolstering of positive emotion curbs the influence of negative feelings and attitude towards the self and helps individuals see that they are not defined by their shortcomings. In sum, self-compassion allows for recognition of one's suffering and moving beyond that suffering in order to have a more adaptive life by adopting a more balanced awareness and expression of self-kindness (Neff, Rude, & Kirkpatrick, 2007). On the other hand, less self-compassionate individuals are more prone to types of mental states that involve rumination, isolation, and self-criticism (Neff, 2003b).

Review of the literature indicates that evaluating oneself in an unkind, critical, and judgemental manner may be one way that procrastinators contribute to the stress they experience. If we conceptualize less self-compassion as taking a negative evaluative stance towards oneself then having less self-compassion may be one quality that explains the procrastination-stress relationship. Self-compassion is one quality that may provide additional insight into the stress associated with trait procrastination as well as possible ways to reduce procrastination-related stress and perhaps even procrastination tendencies.

In a very recent study Sirois (2014) investigated self-compassion as a mediator of the relationship between trait procrastination and stress on undergraduates and community adults. Trait procrastination was associated with lower levels of self-compassion and higher levels of stress. A meta-analysis of this study revealed a moderate negative association of procrastination with self-compassion. It is found that self-compassion mediated the relationship between stress and procrastination. The findings of the study suggest that lower levels of self-compassion may explain some of the stress experienced by procrastinators and interventions that promote self-compassion could therefore be beneficial for these individuals

Procrastination is a common and pervasive problem that can take a toll on not only psychological, but also physical health and well-being (Flett, Blankstein, & Martin, 1995; Sirois, Melia-Gordon, & Pychyl, 2003; Tice & Baumeister, 1997). Theoretical explanations for the links between chronic procrastination and health implicate stress as an outcome of poor self-regulation that negatively impacts health outcomes through both direct physiological and indirect behavioural routes (Friedman, 2000; Sirois *et al.*, 2003). Although, there is some support for the proposed role of stress in explaining the poor health-related outcomes associated with procrastination (Sirois, 2007; Sirois *et al.*, 2003; Sirois & Tosti, 2012), the ways in which procrastination may be linked to increased stress have not been fully explored. From a behavioural perspective, rushing around at the last minute to complete important and necessary tasks can be stressful as can the consequences of not meeting deadlines on time. Yet, there is emerging evidence that the stress associated with procrastination may also arise from the intra-personal processes linked to the negative self-judgements that procrastinators inflict upon themselves when dealing with difficult tasks as well as during the aftermath of unnecessary delay (Sirois & Stout, 2011; Sirois & Tosti, 2012). Self-compassion — taking a kind and understanding stance toward oneself in instances of pain or failure rather than being harshly self-critical (Neff, 2003b) — is an adaptive quality that may promote effective self-regulation, reduce the stress associated with self-blame, and provide a buffer against negative reactions to self-relevant events (Leary, Tate, Adams, Allen, & Hancock, 2007; Terry & Leary, 2011)

A number of studies have been conducted to see the effect of self-compassion and procrastination with different correlates related to both the variables. In summary, self-compassion play important role to overcome the tendency of procrastination.

Discussion

The findings from this study provide support for the proposed relationship between procrastination and self-compassion. Procrastination is significantly associated with lower levels of self-compassion. This study also reveal that lower levels of self-compassion partially explained the indirect effects of procrastination by different other variables such as depression, stress and academic related tasks, It is also found that strength of the association between procrastination and self-compassion appeared larger in the student samples compared to the adult sample. Studies show that higher levels of stress, depression, anxiety and negative feelings etc. associated with procrastination. Previous work found a role of mindfulness, a component of self-compassion is playing important role to intervene the tendency of procrastination.

It is also found that to becoming over identified with the negative states associated with procrastination, negative self judgements and feeling isolated by one's procrastinating can be a stressful experience that compromises the well-being of those who chronically procrastinate. In this study findings expand on the growing body of research demonstrating the problems associated with lower levels of self-compassion (MacBeth & Gumley, 2012) by highlighting the self-regulation difficulties associated with not being self-compassionate. Self-compassion is known as a quality that can enhance self-regulation through reducing negative states, feeling and self-evaluations. On the other hand, procrastination is a form of self-regulation failure associated with negative self-evaluations and poor psychological well-being and overall well-being. It is noted that lower levels of self-compassion among chronic procrastinators treating themselves harshly, with self-blame, criticism, and a general lack of kindness and acceptance after failure to act on intended actions. It may contribute to the stress associated with procrastinating and further compromise well-being, and potentially physical health.

It is possible that the lack of self-compassion may prepare individual for initial instances of procrastination to become more chronic in nature. Procrastinators not being compassionate to oneself or another person. Procrastination could contribute to the self-blame and overidentification with negative states that arise from this act that could be facilitate ruminatively focused on the unattained goal rather than on the ways to attain the goal. These negative self-evaluations or self-blaming thinking could therefore promote a cycle of procrastination. Together with recent empirical work on the role of negative self-evaluations for interfering with task persistence (Evans, Baer, & Segerstrom, 2009), a role for low self-compassion in the development of a tendency to procrastination seems plausible.

In recent scenario, different interventions exists related to self-compassion and mindfulness which is useful to prevent procrastination. Interventions that focus on increasing self-compassion may be beneficial for reducing the stress and procrastination. There is mounting evidence that interventions such as mindfulness based stress reduction (MBSR) and Mindful Self-compassion programmes (MSC) are effective ways to increase self-compassion (Birnie, Speca, & Carlson, 2010; Lee & Bang, 2010; Rimes & Wingrove, 2011) and therefore may be useful for reducing the stress associated with trait procrastination may be accomplished. Rather than encouraging procrastination by minimizing the consequences of this problematic behaviour, research indicates that interventions that increase self-compassion can help people recognize their part in negative events (such as failure to act in a timely manner) without becoming entangled with the associated negative emotions and the ruminative procrastinators' cognitions that can promote future procrastination (Stainton *et al.*, 2000). For example, one study found that experimentally inducing a self-compassionate perspective helped people become less overwhelmed by their negative emotions in response to a negative event

(Leary *et al.*, 2007). Interventions that increase self-compassion may be beneficial to procrastinators because they reduce the negative states and feelings. Moreover, decreased negative mood explained the link between increased self-forgiveness and reduced procrastination. Although self-forgiveness may only occur after a single act or event, self-compassion can be viewed as a quality that can be cultivated to help reduce overall self-judgement and overidentification with the negative states. Interventions aimed at increasing self-compassion may therefore have more sustained effects for procrastinators.

Conclusion

Self-compassion stands for the quality of the human-being. This makes him kind and understanding towards oneself, even in the face of adverse situations. It suggests the perception of one's experiences as a part of broad human experience. Self-compassion has various implications in academic and professional life. As it provides an intrinsic motivation to an individual, it facilitates a self-initiated behaviour and curiosity and exploratory behaviour (Sharma and Davidson, 2015).

On the basis of deep review of literature, it reveals that self-compassion play important role in procrastination and its effects directly and indirectly on the tendency of procrastination. The present study suggests that self-compassion has a negative influence on procrastination by lowering the participants' tendency to procrastinate in their task. The present study provides some insights into how to overcome some of the stress associated with procrastination, and how to reduce instances of situational procrastination.

Limitations and Future Suggestions: It is also found that there are very limited study showing relationship between self-compassion and procrastination. Some of these limitations are related to the nature of the variables. On the other hand, this study predisposes the way for future research related to variables. These findings are reassuring, there is still much more to be investigated about the positive role that self-compassion plays in decrement of procrastination. Future research will promote the underlying mechanisms through which self-compassion exerts its positive influences on the way individuals live their lives. Furthermore, in line with positive psychology, the study clearly demonstrates that self-compassion is a significant positive psychological attribute that conjures up interconnectedness, feelings of kindness and equanimity, high levels of optimism, motivation, and positive affect in countering life's adversities.

Today, much importance is being given to psychological health because it is found that a poor mental health condition may prevent an individual from doing any progressive activity. Mentally healthy people are able to fulfil their different roles successfully. They enjoy peace of mind, happiness, self-confidence and self-esteem. Students of the country are tomorrow's citizens. So, there is need of good psychological health, good physical health and overall well-being. For that we must be aware of the variables that affect one's psychological health. It can be further concluded that self-compassion and procrastination influence the psychological health of the individual.

References

Achtemeier, E.R. (1962). 'Mercy' in G.A. Buttrick, T.S. Kepler, J. Knox, H.G. May and S. Terrien, eds., *The Interpreter's Dictionary of the Bible* (New York: Abingdon), pp. 352-54.

Akinsola, M.K., Tella, A., and Tella, A. (2007). Correlates of academic procrastination and mathematics achievement of university undergraduate students. *Eurasia Journal of Mathematics, Science and Technology Education, 3*(4), 363-370.

Barnard, L.K., and J.F. Curry. (2011). "Self-Compassion: Conceptualizations, Correlates, and Interventions". *Review of General Psychology, 15*, 289-303.

Basharpour, S., and Isazadegan, A. (2012). Predict personality traits of self-compassion and forgiveness on the severity of predictability of student's depression. *Behavioural Science Research, 10* (6), 452-461.

Beswick, G., Rothblum, E.D., and Mann, L. (1988). Psychological antecedents of student procrastination. *Australian Psychologist, 23*, 207-217.

Bhawuk, D.P.S. (2011). *Spirituality and Indian Psychology: Lessons from the Bhagavad Gita* (New York & London: Springer).

Birnie, K., Speca, M., and Carlson, L.E. (2010). Exploring self-compassion and empathy in the context of Mindfulness-based Stress Reduction (MBSR). *Stress and Health, 26*, 359-371.

Bridges, K.R., and Roig, M. (1997). Academic procrastination and irrational thinking: A re-examination with context controlled. *Personality and Individual Differences, 22*, 941-944.

Breins, J.G., and Chen, S. (2012). Self-compassion increases achievement motivation. *Personality and Social Psychology Bulletin*. DOI: 10.1177/0146167212445599.

Brown, L., Bryant, C., Brown, V.M., Bei, B., and Judd, F.K. (2014). Self-compassion weakens the association between hot flushes and night sweats and daily life functioning and depression. *Maturitas, 78*, 298-303.

Burka, J.B., and Yuen, L.M. (1983). *Procrastination: Why do you do it, what to do about it?* CA: Addison-Wesley Publishing Company.

Clark, J.L., and Hill, Jr.O.W. (1994). Academic procrastination among African-American College students. *Psychological Reports, 75,* 931-936.

Collins, P.M. (2007). *Christian Inculturation in India.* (Hampshire & Burlington: Ashgate).

Conway, D.G. (2007). *The role of internal resources in academic achievement: Exploring the meaning of self-compassion in the adaptive functioning of low income college students.* Unpublished doctoral dissertation study.

De Paola, M., and Scoppa, V. (2014). Procrastination, academic success and the effectiveness of a remedial programme. *Journal of Economic Behaviour and Organization.*

Effert, B.R., and Ferrari, J.R. (1989). Decisional Procrastination — Examining Personality-Correlates. *Journal of Social Behaviour and Personality, 4*(1), 151-156.

Ellis, A. (1973). *Humanistic Psychotherapy: The Rational-Emotive Approach.* (New York: Julian).

Ellis, A., and Knaus, W.J. (1977). *Overcoming Procrastination.* NY: New American Library, Signet Books.

Ellis, A., and Knaus, W.J. (2002). *Overcoming procrastination* (Rev. Ed.). NY: New American Library.

Evans, D.R., Baer, R.A., and Segerstrom, S.C. (2009). The effects of mindfulness and self-consciousness on persistence. *Personality and Individual Differences, 47*(4), 379-382.

Ferrari, J.R. (1992). Procrastination in the workplace: Attributions for failure among individuals with similar behavioural tendencies. *Personality and Individual Differences, 13*(3), 315-319.

Ferrari, J.R., Johnson, J.L., and McCown, W.G. (1995). *Procrastination and task avoidance: Theory, research, and treatment.* New York: Plenum Press.

Ferrari, J.R., and Scher, S. (2002). Toward an understanding of academic and nonacademic tasks procrastinated by students: The use of daily logs. *Psychology in the Schools, 37,* 359-366.

Ferrari, J.R., O'Callaghan, J., and Newbegin, I. (2005). Prevalence of procrastination in the United States, United Kingdom and Australia: Arousal and avoidance delays among adults. *North American Journal of Psychology, 7,* 1-6.

Flett, G.L., Blankstein, K.R., and Martin, T.R. (1995) Procrastination, negative self-evaluation, and stress in depression and anxiety: A review and preliminary model. In J.R. Ferrari and M.B. Shure (Eds.), *Procrastination and Task Avoidance Theory, Research, and Treatment* (pp. 37-167). New York: Plenum.

Friedman, H.S. (2000). Long-term relations of personality and health: Dynamisms, mechanisms, tropisms. *Journal of Personality, 68*(6), 1089-1107.

Germer, C.K., and K.D. Neff. (2013). "Self-Compassion in Clinical Practice", *Journal of Clinical Psychology, 69,* 856-67.

Goetz, J.L., Keltner, D., and Simon-Thomas, E. (2010). Compassion: An evolutionary analysis and empirical review. *Psychological Bulletin, 136*, 351-374.

Gunaratana, V.H. (1993). *Mindfulness in plain English.* Somerville, MA: Wisdom Publications.

Hammer, C.A., and Ferrari, J.R. (2002). Differential incidence of procrastination between blue- and white-collar workers. *Current Psychology: Developmental, Learning, Personality, Social, 21*(4), 333-338.

Hawthorne, J. (1932). "A Group Test for the Measurement of Cruelty-Compassion: A Proposed Means of Recognizing Potential Criminality". *Wyman Journal of Social Psychology, 3*, 189-211.

Harriott, J., and Ferrari, J.R. (1996). Prevalence of procrastination among samples of adults. *Psychological Reports, 78*, 611-616.

Hajiazizi, A., and Ho Robert (2015). The relationship between self-compassion and academic procrastination being mediated by same and anxiety. *The International Journal of Indian Psychology.*

Howell, A.J., Watson, D.C., Powell, R.A., and Buro, K. (2006). Academic procrastination: The pattern and correlates of behavioural postponement. *Personality and Individual Differences, 40*(8), 1519-1530.

Iskender, M. (2011). The influence of self-compassion on academic procrastination and dysfunctional attitudes. *Educational Research and Reviews, 6*(2), 230-234.

John. P. II. (1992). "Post-Synodal Apostolic Exhortation *Pastores dabo vobis*... On the Formation of Priests in the Circumstance of the Present Day", retrieved 25 May, 2015 from http://w2.vatican.va/content/john-paul-ii/en/apost_exhortations/documents/hf_jp-ii_exh_25031992_pastores-dabo-vobis.html.

Kirkpatrick, K.L. (2005). *Enhancing self-compassion using a gestalt two-chair intervention.* Unpublished doctoral dissertation.

Krieger, T., D. Altenstein., I. Baettig., N. Doerig., and M.G. Holtforth. (2013). "Self-Compassion in Depression: Associations with Depressive Symptoms, Rumination, and Avoidance in Depressed Outpatients", *Behaviour Therapy, 44*, 501-13.

Ladner, L. (2004). *The Lost Art of Compassion: Discovering the Practice of Happiness in the Meeting of Buddhism and Psychology* (New York: Harper Collins).

Lay, C.H. (1986). At last, my research article on procrastination. *Journal of Research in Personality, 20*, 474-495.

Lay, C.H:, and Brokenshire, R. (1997). Conscientiousness, procrastination, and person-task characteristics in job searching. *Current Psychology, 16*(1), 83.

Leary, M.R., Tate, E.B., Adams, C.E., Allen, A.B., and Hancock, J. (2007). Self-compassion and reactions to unpleasant self-relevant events: The implications of treating oneself kindly. *Journal of Personality and Social Psychology, 92*, 887-904.

Lee, W.K., and Bang, H.J. (2010). The effects of mindfulness-based group intervention on the mental health of middle-aged Korean women in community. *Stress and Health, 26*(4), 341-348. doi: 10.1002/smi.1303

MacBeth, A., and Gumley, A. (2012). Exploring compassion: A meta-analysis of the association between self-compassion and psychopathology. *Clinical Psychology Review, 32*, 545-552.

MacIntyre, A. (1966). *A Short History of Ethics.* (New York: MacMillan).

Martin, J.R. (1997). Mindfulness: A proposed common factor. *Journal of Psychotherapy Integration, 7,* 291-312.

Maslow, A.H. (1968). *Toward a Psychology of Being* (New York: Nostrand).

McCown, W.G., Blake, I., and Keiser, R. (2012). Content analyses of the beliefs of academic procrastinators. *Journal of Rational-Emotive and Cognitive-Behaviour Therapy*, 1-10. doi: 10.1007/s10942-012-0148-6

Neff, K.D. (2003). Self-compassion: An alternative conceptualization of a healthy attitude toward oneself. *Self and Identity, 2,* 85-102.

Neff, K.D. (2003a). Development and validation of a scale to measure self-compassion. *Self and Identity, 2*, 223-250.

Neff, K.D. (2003b). Self-compassion: An alternative conceptualization of a healthy attitude toward oneself. *Self and Identity, 2*, 85-102.

Neff, K.D., Hseih, Y., and Dejitthirat, K. (2005). Self-compassion, achievement goals, and coping with academic failure. *Self and Identity, 4*, 263-287.

Neff, K.D., Kirkpatrick, K. and Rude, S.S. (2007). Self-compassion and its link to adaptive psychological functioning. *Journal of Research in Personality, 41,* 139-154.

Neff, K.D., Pisitsungkagarn, K., and Hseih, Y. (2008). Self-compassion and self-construal in the United States, Thailand, and Taiwan. *Journal of Cross-Cultural Psychology, 39,* 267-28

Neff, K.D. (2008). Self-compassion: Moving beyond the pitfalls of a separate self-concept. In J. Bauer and H.A. Wayment (Eds.) *Transcending Self-Interest: Psychological Explorations of the Quiet Ego* (95-105). APA Books, Washington DC.

Neff, K.D. (2009). Self-Compassion. In M.R. Leary and R.H. Hoyle (Eds.), *Handbook of Individual Differences in Social Behaviour* (pp. 561-573). Guilford Press.

Neff, K.D., and McGeehee, P. (2010). Self-compassion and psychological resilience among adolescents and young adults. *Self and Identity, 9*, 225-240.

Nisker, W. (1998). Mindfulness: The opposable thumb of consciousness. *In Buddha's nature: A practical guide to discovering your place in the cosmos.* New York: Bantam Books.

O'Donohoe, J.A., W. Baumgaertner., and K. Schuth. (2002). 'Seminary Education' in Th. Carson, ed. *The New Catholic Encyclopedia, 15* (2), 12:893-99.

Onwuegbuzie, A. (2000). Academic procrastination and perfectionist tendencies among graduate students. *Journal of Social Psychology and Personality, 15,* 103-110.

Padinjarekuttu, I. (2005). "What Ails Priestly Formation Today?" *Vidyajyoti, 69*, 904-14.

Paranjpe, A.C. (2002). *Self and Identity in Modern Psychology and Indian Thought*. (New York: Kluwer).

Pauley, G and McPherson, S. (2010). The experience and meaning of compassion and self-compassion for individuals with depression or anxiety. *Psychology and Psychotherapy: Theory, Research and Practice, 83*, 129-143.

Pychyl, T.A., Lee, J.M., Thibodeau, R., and Blunt, A. (2000). Five days of emotion: An experience sampling study of undergraduate student procrastination. *Journal of Social Behaviour and Personality, 15*(5), 239-254.

Pychyl, T.A. (2010). *The procrastinator's digest: A concise guide to solving the procrastination puzzle.* Bloomington, IN: Xlibris Corporation.

Raes, F. (2010). Rumination and worry as mediators of the relationship between self-compassion and depression and anxiety. *Personality and Individual Differences, 48*, 757-761.

Raes, F. (2011). The Effect of Self-Compassion on the Development. *Mindfulness, 2*, 33-36.

Rebetez, Marie M.L., Rochat, L., and Martial, Van der L. (2015). Cognitive, emotional, and motivational factors related to procrastination: A cluster analytic approach. *Personality and Individual Differences, 76*, 1-6.

Rimes, K.A., and Wingrove, J. (2011). Pilot study of Mindfulness-Based Cognitive Therapy for trainee clinical psychologists. *Behavioural and Cognitive Psychotherapy, 39*(2), 235-241.

Rogers, C.R. (1961). *On Becoming a Person: A Therapist's View of Psychotherapy* (Boston: Houghton Mifflin).

Rosenberg, L. (1999). Breathing with the body. In *Breath by Breath: The liberating Practice of Insight Meditation* (pp. 10-39). Boston: Shambala.

Rothblum, E., Solomon, L., and Murakami, J. (1986). Affective, cognitive, and behavioural differences between high and low procrastinators. *Journal of Counselling Psychology, 33*, 387-394.

Salzberg, S. (1997). *Loving kindness: The Revolutionary Art of Happiness.* Boston: Shambala.

Sbarra, D.A., Smith, H.L., and Mehl, M.R. (2012). When leaving your Ex, love yourself: Observational ratings of self-compassion predict the course of emotional recovery following marital separation. *Psychological Science, 23*, 261-269.

Schouwenburg, H.C. (2004). Procrastination in academic settings: General introduction. In H.C. Schouwenburg, C.H. Lay, T.A. Pychyl and J.R. Ferrari (Eds.), *Counselling the procrastinator in academic settings* (pp. 3-17). Washington, DC: American Psychological Association.

Schraw, G., Wadkins, T., and Olafson, L. (2007). Doing the things we do: A grounded theory of academic procrastination. *Journal of Educational Psychology, 99*(1), 12-25.

Senecal, C., Koestner, R., and Vallerand, R. (1995). Self-regulation and Academic procrastination. *The Journal of Social Psychology, 13*(5), 607-619.

Sharma, M., and Davidson, C. (2015). Self-compassion in relation to personal initiativeness, curiosity and exploration among young adults. *Indian Journal of Health and Well-being, 6*(2), 185-187.

Sigall, H., Kruglanski, A., and Fyock, J. (2000). Wishful thinking and procrastination. *Journal of Social Behaviour and Personality, 15,* 283-296.

Sirois, F.M. (2013). Procrastination and stress: Exploring the role of self-compassion. *Self and Identity.*doi:10.1080/15298868. pp. 2-18.

Sirois, F.M., Melia-Gordon, M.L., and Pychyl, T.A. (2003). "I'll look after my health, later": an investigation of procrastination and health. *Personality Individual Differences, 35*(5): 1167-1184.

Sirois, F.M. (2007). "I'll look after my health, later": A replication and extension of the procrastination—health model with community dwelling adults. *Personality Individual Differences., 43*(1): 15-26.

Sirois, F.M., and Stout, D. (2011). *When knowing better doesn't mean doing better: Understanding the roles of procrastination and self-blame in the health and well-being of nurses.* Paper presented at the 7th Biennial Conference on Procrastination, Amsterdam, The Netherlands.

Sirois, F.M., and Tosti, N. (2012). Lost in the moment? An investigation of procrastination, mindfulness, and well-being. *Journal of Rational-Emotive and Cognitive-Behaviour Therapy*, 1-12.

Sirois, F.M., and Pychyl, T. (2013). Procrastination and the priority of short-term mood regulation: Consequences for future self. *Social and Personality Psychology Compass*, *7*(2), 115-127.

Sirois, F.M. (2013). Procrastination and stress: Exploring the role of self-compassion. *Self and Identity.*doi:10.1080/15298868, pp. 2-18.

Sirois, F.M. (2014). Procrastination and stress: Exploring the role of self-compassion. *Self and Identity, 13*(2), 128-145.

Solomon, L.J., and Rothblum, E.D. (1984). Academic procrastination: Frequency and cognitive-behavioural correlates. *Journal of Counselling Psychology, 31,* 503-509.

Stainton, M., Lay, C.H., and Flett, G.L. (2000). Trait procrastinators and behaviour/trait-specific cognitions. *Journal of Social Behaviour and Personality, 15*(5), 297-312.

Steel, P. (2007). The nature of procrastination: A meta-analytic and theoretical review of quintessential self-regulatory failure. *Psychological Bulletin, 133,* 65-94.

Tan, C. R,. Ang, R., Klassen, L., Yeo, I., Wong, V., and Huan, W. Chong. (2008). "Correlates of Academic Procrastination and Students' Grade Goals," *Current Psychology, 27*(2), 135-144.

Terry, M.L., and Leary, M.R. (2011). Self-compassion, self-regulation, and health. *Self and Identity, 10,* 352-362.

Thurackal, J.T., Corveleyn, J., and Dezutter, J. (2016). Personality and self-compassion. *European Journal of Mental Health, 11,* 18-35.

Tice, D., and Baumeister, R. (1997). Longitudinal study of procrastination, performance, stress and health: The costs and benefits of dawdling. *Psychological Science, 8,* 454-458.

Van Eerde, W. (2003). A meta-analytically derived nomological network of procrastination. *Personality and Individual Differences, 35*, 1401-1418.

Walker, W.L. (1979). 'Compassion' in G.W. Bromiley, ed., *The International Standard Bible Encyclopedia* (Grand Rapids, MI: Eerdmans), 755.

Watson, D.C. (2001). Procrastination and the five-factor model: a facet level analysis. *Personality and Individual Differences, 30*(1), 149-158.

Wesley, J. (1994). Effects of ability, high school achievement and procrastinatory behaviour on college performance. *Educational and Psychological Measurement, 54,* 404-408.

Wolters, C.A. (2003). Understanding procrastination from a self-regulated learning perspective. *Journal of Educational Psychology, 95*, 179-187.

Williams, J.G., Stark, S.K., and Foster, E.E. (2008). The relationships among self-compassion, motivation, and procrastination. *American Journal of Psychological Research, 4*(1), 37-44.

Wohl, M.J.A., Pychyl, T.A., and Bennett, S.H. (2010). I forgive myself, now I can study: How self-forgiveness for procrastinating can reduce future procrastination. *Personality and Individual Differences, 48*(7), 803-808.

14

Letting Go Method as Self-Help Alternative Solution to Increase Resilience Ability on People with Lupus

Anggun Resdasari Prasetyo, Erin Ratna Kustanti, and *Dinie Ratri Desiningrum*

Introduction

Health is an important factor for human-beings to be able to develop their life potential well. Health in human-beings can occur if all self-aspects of both physical and psychological are able to adapt to various environmental situations and conditions. But in fact, many people are experiencing disease that affects their physical and psychological condition. One of the most deadly diseases among today is Lupus. However, many people are still odd with the disease so that physical and psychological handling become too late though the danger of Lupus is as deadly as cancer. Lupus is a chronic autoimmune disease in which there is an immune system disorder that causes inflammation in some organs and systems of the body. The mechanism of the immune system cannot distinguish between the body's own tissues and foreign organisms (e.g. bacteria, viruses) because autoantibodies (antibodies that attack the body's own tissues) are produced in large quantities and immune complexes (antigen-bound antibodies) in tissues (Syamsi Dhuha Foundation, in Syafi'i, 2012).

Every year there are about 5 to 100 people affected by Lupus that causes death. Number of people with Lupus in Indonesia, based on data released by Lupus Foundation Indonesia, continues to increase (Zubairi, in Syafi'i, 2012). Lupus is very dangerous because it can cause death. The cause of death in Odapus, is a chronic Lupus that attacks the kidneys, brain, lungs, and heart. The disease is generally vulnerable to attack those aged 15-44 years and people in good health (Agnesa, 2009). However, most people are late realizing Lupus, because Lupus in early symptoms does not show that the person suffers from Lupus. They look normal and usually move as usual. The manifestation of Lupus in each person has a distinctive pattern that changes over time, which sometimes are quickly. In general, people with chronic Lupus, *e.g.* Renal Lupus or central nervous system (CNS), and those who suffer from more than one type of autoantibody disease tend to have serious and persistent symptoms. People with mild symptoms may continue to experience mild symptoms or even develop the more serious one (Agnesa, 2009).

The high risk of death by Lupus and its often late diagnosis, of course, has a psychological impact on people with Lupus. They have to deal with changing physical conditions that continue to increase and require tremendous adaptability in order to survive. In people with Lupus, they will experience physical changes from the face that appear reddish spots, hair loss, sensitive to sunlight, the body began to swell, the skin began to scaly and began to peel, arise sprue around the mouth, pain in the joints of the hands and feet, to the parts of the body that are difficult to move. Physical changes can make people with Lupus feel worried, inferior, anxious and other feelings began to rage, especially when having to mingle and connect with others that led to the feeling of stress. That's why psychological treatment is needed for people with Lupus in order to stay with optimistic feeling to survive and recover. The ability to survive or resilience to threatening situations or conditions such as illness, loss of spouse, disaster or accident is referred to as resilience.

Current resilience is an important theme emerged by academics and researchers to identify and understand the proper psychological constructs of how the human capacity or endurance to survive and develop in adverse conditions and to determine the ability of individuals to return to recovery from the pressure conditions (McCubbin, 2001). Wolin and Wolin (in Chandra, 2009) describe resilience as a coping skill when individuals are faced with the life challenges or individual capacity to stay in wellness and continue to do the self-repair. There are two conditions that are needed in order to explain resilience toward individual's life: (a) the occurrence of adaptation and development on significant adversity or threat; and (b) the function and development continue to run well despite significant adversity. Research on resilience has been done by Ong and associates (2006), which then resulted in the definition of resilience as a bouncing back from negative emotional experiences and the ability to adapt flexibly to changing demands of stress experiences.

McCubbin (2001) explains that researchers recognize that resilience has a wide range of definitions and psychological constructs that still need to be studied more deeply. Even though, from some of the literature that McCubbin has reviewed, the resilience is at least in four different perspectives but remains interconnected as follows: (a) as good outcomes in spite of adversity; (b) as a sustained competence in difficult situations; (c) as recovery from traumatic experience; and (d) as an interaction between protective and risk factor. The first concept that states resilience as a good outcome in spite of adversity focuses on the concept of resilience as outcomes. This concept is like the definition of resilience that Rutter describes (in McCubbin, 2001) which express resilience as a positive outcomes in handling adversity such as poverty (McCubbin, 2001).

Two other perspectives emphasize on the importance of individual competence when facing stress and the ability to recover from a traumatic experience. Both of these concepts emphasize on the resilience as an individual's competence to adapt or bounce back when facing difficult situations (McCubbin, 2001). This concept emphasizes on the study of resilience on the qualities of a resilient individual. The concept is the same as Grotberg's (1995) which defines resilience as human capacity to face and overcome life stress. This concept also has similarities to Garmezy *et al.* (in McCubbin, 2001) which describes resilience as the capacity to produce successful adaptation in facing misery or adversity. Initial studies such as Werner (2005) focus more on this concept that examines the qualities of a resilient individual. A fourth concept that states resilience as an interaction between the protective and risk factor, attempts to conceptualize and tries to measure resilience as a process (Lutar in McCubbin, 2001). The definition proposed by Luthar in the previous section represents this concept which explains resilience as a dynamic process in which there is positive adaptation under significant adversity. However, the basic assumption agreed by researchers in resilience is that all persons are subject to stressors and adversity, and many potential factors that contribute to how an individual overcomes the difficulty (Harvey & Delfabbro, 2004).

One method that can be used to improve resilience is by letting go technique. Corey (2005) uses the term of letting go in the sense of letting go, relating to pain and hatred, and guilt, and self-destructive patterns such as thoughts, feelings, and behaviours. Zimberoff and Hartman (2003) use the term of letting go as a technique to bring back the unconscious to be accessible. Meanwhile, according to Freshwater and Robertson (2002) letting go in therapy is done by releasing expectations that are not realized. Fortunas (2003) conducted a qualitative study to look deeper about the effectiveness of letting go. The conclusion of his research explains that the process of letting go has an analogy with the process of problem solving related to self-changes, which invites clients to free himself from a condition which trap them. Friedman (2002) uses the term of letting go in the sense of releasing judgement and hatred against oneself or others. Bowman (2003) and Lewis (2005) add that the way to let go is by forgiving. While Shepherd (2007) uses the term of letting go related to releasing emotions, feelings, and shadows.

Based on the problems stated above, this research will test the Letting Go Method as an alternative solution of self-help to improve resilience ability in people with Lupus. Letting Go method is expected to help people with Lupus have self-help skills or psychological treatment of the disease.

Method

Subjects used in this study were 8 people. The research method used mix method type of research that is quantitative-qualitative, that is by interviewing, observating, focus group discussing, therapy giving and analysing the result of therapy. Self-monitoring is also given to determine the changing tendency of subject depression during the letting go method. Letting go therapy activities conducted on a group of subjects can be an additional data on the reflection of the resilience tendency. Resilience scale is given to the subject to assist the researcher in knowing the resilience tendency of the subject before and after therapy.

1. Interview: Qualitative interviews are conducted by the researcher in order to gain knowledge of subjective meanings which understood by the individual regarding the studied topic and intend to explore the issue; something that cannot be done through another approach. The type of interview used is semi-structured interview. Question items in interview guidelines on the subject, among others: Respondent's Identity, Respondent's Background, Relationship among family members. History of disease, resilience tendency of Respondent, Respondent's way in overcoming the impact of Lupus, resilience tendency of respondent after doing letting go method, respondent's process in doing letting go activity, and meaning of respondent to letting go activity.

2. Observation: Researchers used non-participant observations in this study. Given the proposition of this research is the tendency of resilience, then the observation will be more focus on self respondents, among others:

(a) Physical profile and respondent's appearance, and
(b) Behaviour and respondent's reaction.

3. Self-Monitoring: Self-monitoring is a record written by a person to observe so as to gain an understanding of themselves, which is particularly about the experience of resilience they experience. The self-monitoring format that will be used in this research is shown in Table 14.1.

Table 14.1: Self-Monitoring Resilience

Situation	*Feeling*	*Mind*	*Resulted Behaviour*
What? How? When? Where? Who?	What is the resulted feelings?	What is the resulted mind?	What behaviour is resulted by, when the method happen.

Source: Greenberger & Padesky (2004).

Self-monitoring is done to find out a psychological state of a person, that is by monitoring, realizing and giving attention to his/her own psychological state which then recording its development for several days.

4. Resilience Scale: This resilience scale is given to the pretest and post-test of letting go therapy. This scale contains 22 items of questions that must be answered by the subject. Scale in this study using The Connor-Davidson Resilience Scale (CD-RISC).

5. Letting Go Therapy: According to Dwoskin (2005), the way to do letting go is by releasing 5 kinds of desires or the main negative emotions that is inside human beings. So that, there will get three top positive emotions (spirit, acceptance, and sincerity). Psychotherapy used in this research is by applying letting go method. This letting go method consists of various healing techniques in Dwoskin psychology (2005), namely: (1) *Depth relaxation* is a breathing activity in the body to enter a unique characteristic signed by low heart rate and breathing, decreased blood pressure, quieter brain activity, and reduced metabolic rate so that one can be in a comfortable and quiet state, (2) *Interoception*, is to explore the feelings and mind of subjects about the body condition or state, which is associated with body image experienced by the subject. (3) *Evaluation and cognitive processing* is toward (a) *time sense*: positive or negative feelings about time or events; and (b) *sense of identity*: perception about identity. (4) *Emotion recognition,* is to know back the negative emotions along with their reactions. (5) *Forgiveness,* is an action or response directed to the positive motivation to decrease negative feeling or emotion.

The letting go method provided through non-randomized pretest post-test in one group design is experimental design done with pretest (before treatment) and post-test (after treatment). Letting go method will be given as much as 2 times of implementation, the pause between implementations will be given assignment (self-monitoring) done by each subject.

Research Findings

Here is an overview of the results of the resilience scale of the subjects before and after the implementation of letting go. All subjects had an increased tendency of resilience after given letting go therapy.

	Subject 1	*Subject 2*	*Subject 3*	*Subject 4*	*Subject 5*	*Subject 6*	*Subject 7*	*Subject 8*
Pretest	58	46	56	48	48	52	54	46
Post-test	64	58	67	62	60	60	68	76

The following is the findings of qualitative analysis on all 8 subjects of people with Lupus.

Reseach Finding on Subject 1: The subject in the interview before the letting go therapy, explained that he was trying to heal and still have belief that one day he can be healed because he still wants to be with his family and beneficial to others. The subject basically already has a fairly good understanding, that when he is in a state of calm or happy then the physical pain also decreased, so he was happy when he could talk or gather with his closest people.

The subject tells that when the time of the letting go process, he imagines all the feelings inside of him. The subject felt that he was feeling very sad and anxious, then the subject was asked to release his negative feelings one by one until relieved.

Research Findings on Subject 2: The subject tells that the current psychological state still not able to calm down. She still cannot really accept her current condition. The subject tells when her body drops, she immediately fears if suddenly she will die. She always wishes that there would be a miracle for her to be healed. However, the more she thought about the healing, the more helpless and exhausted she was. Based on the description of the psychological and physical states experienced by the subject, she still has not achieved optimal resilience. Subject resilience has not been achieved because she is still experiencing self-conflicts that she is still expecting for her wishes can be realized. Some strong desire is to keep the subject to keep thinking about it but what she met was a feeling of disappointment and sad because her desire has not realized as well.

Subject on the implementation of letting go was asked to confess honestly on what things are still desirable. At the time of letting go, the subject told that she identified the desires that are bound to her: want to be better in terms of physical, health, psychological, financial; want to heal a broken heart; want to have a lot of friends; We want to be a more cheerful, optimistic, and easy going and grateful woman.

The subject then in the process of letting go, was asked to further identify what is felt in each of these desires, whether there is any discomfort feelings accompany it. Negative feelings that arise are then released one by one until subject finds a peace. The subject explained that from the letting go therapy, she felt more comfortable and peaceful. She also began to realize to learn to be more calmly to organize her desires and let God set the way of life.

Research Findings on Subject 3: The subject told that his psychological condition is not yet calm now because he still felt the pressure that prop inside of him. The subject felt uncomfortable. The subject has not been able to accept the condition of the disease. This condition is indicated by psychic responses and cognitive distortions. The subject felt as a disgusting, unattractive person. Moreover, the subject is still a teenager, where the opportunity to grow is still wide open, but the subjects felt no longer have a chance. This condition makes the subject feel lonely and regret with his current condition. Moreover, subject feels no support from parents. Parents' attitudes toward his current condition are believed to be subjects as pressure. The accumulation of these pressures leads to the idea that God is evil and encourages subjects to hate God. The emerging response is indicated by aggressive behaviour.

Based on the description of psychological dynamics above, subject still has not achieved optimal resilience. Resilience has not been achieved because the subject is still experiencing self-conflict that is still not able to control the wishes to be realized. His emotional regulation was also not good enough. The subject still showed anger at God because it is him who got this pain, not someone else.

In the implementation of letting go, subject was asked to honestly accept his current condition, then confessed what things are his wishes. The subject then re-identified the things he wants. The wishes are: the subject wants to grow like other teenage friends, to actively participate in various activities; The subject wants the parent not to press and manage his life; Subject wants his parents and people who know the disease not to disseminate information about it because the subject feels uncomfortable and when others know about the disease he suffered; he wants others not to pity him for wanting to show that the subject is a strong person.

The subject was then invited to feel the disease and admit it. This will help him more easily to accept his illness. After that the subjects were invited to believe in God's greatness and mercy by calculating how big the role of each member of his body to help the subject in the activity since he was born until now. This will help him to remain grateful for what God has given to him, so that anger and hatred for God will be eliminated. Subsequently, subject was asked to release negative feelings and to affirm for each of his wishes can be fulfilled. Then after the implementation of letting go subjects, he feels relieved. The subject feels more comfortable, more able to accept his condition.

Research Findings on Subject 4: The subject told that she had not yet felt comfortable with her current condition. The diagnosis of a physician turned her into a people with Lupus raises her fears. The subject feels deformed and fears that something worse will happen. This condition raises anxious, less confident, and loneliness. The reactions that emerge are the subject often cry without cause and easily panic when unable to complete the task.

Based on the description of psychological dynamics above, subjects still has not achieved optimal resilience. Resilience has not been achieved because the subject is still feeling pessimistic. This is indicated by the fears she experienced. The subject also has not been able to show self-efficacy and improve her positive aspects. The subject actually has a strong motivation to go through this process and fight to become a winner. But the fears that arise make the subject weak and feel tired of life.

In the implementation of letting go, the subject was asked to honestly accept her current condition, and then confessed on what things are her fears. The subject then re-identified the things that become her fears, namely: the subject fears of not being able to survive with Lupus, fears of not having a life companion and fears of lack of friends.

The subject was then invited to feel the disease and admit it. This will help her more easily accept herself for her disease. After that the subject was invited to find reasons that can weaken those fears. Moreover, subject was asked to release negative feelings and affirmation to create optimism that the subject is able to survive the pain, the subject can still live her life in the future including getting a life companion and having friends who always support her. After the implementation of letting go, the subject feels relieved, feels more comfortable, and able to accept her condition.

Research Findings on Subject 5: The subject told that since he was diagnosed with Lupus, the subject showed a change in his psychic condition. The subject becomes morose because of the heavy burden he faces. The subject becomes fear of new problems related to the disease. The changing health conditions of subject also make him less confident. There was a feeling that subject was different from his friends. Subjects cannot be free to do various activities like his friends. It also encourages him to limit himself and tend to be reserved. Subjects increasingly depressed because of the condition of this disease resulted in his family becomes not conducive. The disease suffered by the subjects requires regular medical treatment with no small cost. The attention of the parents who later became more intensive to him turned out to cause problems for his brother, because he felt that all the attention focused on his brother. The subject's concern was more on his mother's safety, because his brother changed his attitude to being rude. Based on the description of psychological dynamics above, subject still has not achieved optimal resilience. Resilience has not been achieved because the subject is still feeling pessimistic. This is indicated by the fears he experienced.

In the implementation of letting go, subject was asked to honestly accept his current condition, then acknowledge what things are his fears. The subject then re-identified the things that become his fears, namely: the subject of fear when the pain was getting worse, the fear of financial difficulties due to the cost of expensive treatment and fear of his mother's safety because the condition of his family becomes no longer conducive.

The subject was then invited to feel the disease and admit it. This will help him nore easily accept herself for his disease and reduce his anxiety when the pain gets worse. After that the subject was invited to find reasons that can weaken these fears. Subsequently subject was asked to release negative feelings and affirmation to create optimism that the subject was able to survive the disease, there was still hope to stay on and the family would remain conducive. After the implementation of letting go, subject feels relieved. The subject feels more comfortable, more able to accept his condition.

Research Findings on Subject 6: The subject told that since becoming people with Lupus, he always feels unsteady. Response that appears on the subject is often nervous when considering the disease and become confused with him. The subject feels uncomfortable with himself because he is not ready with the physical changes that may possibly deteriorate his health condition. The subject is scared when his condition would be getting worse. This makes the subject anxious. The changing conditions also make him anxious with other's judgement about his condition.

Based on the description of psychological dynamics above, subject still has not achieved optimal resilience. Resilience has not been achieved because the subject is still feeling pessimistic. This is indicated by the fear of his condition will be getting worse. But the subject has the power to be able to achieve resilience faster because the subject is quite capable of understanding the positive aspects in him. The subject has enough self-confidence so that although suffered from Lupus, the subject believes that the people around him will still receive his condition. His high motivation is useful to others and also as a driving force to be able to get through the healing process well.

At the implementation of letting go, subject was asked to honestly accept his current condition, then admit what things are his fears. The subject then re-identified the things that become his fears, namely: the subject of fear when the pain gets worse, fear of the judgement of others.

The subject is then invited to feel the pain and admit it. This will help him more easily accept his disease and reduce his anxiety when the disease gets worse. After that the subject was invited to find reasons that can weaken these fears. Subsequently subject was asked to release negative feelings and do affirmations to create optimism that the subject is able to get through the healing process well and the people around him can accept his condition. After the implementation of letting go, subject feels relieved. The subject feels more comfortable, more able to accept his condition.

Research Finding on Subject 7: The subject told that she had not felt at ease with her current condition. At first the subject always wondered what the reason God sent this disease to her. The subject is confused whether this is a form of God's punishment to her, warning or test for her to go up on a class. The subject is scared because she is not ready to accept the punishment from God. The subject is also afraid if at any time had to leave her family. The condition of this subject raises the psychic response of stress.

Based on the description of psychological dynamics above, subject still has not achieved optimal resilience. Resilience has not been achieved because the subject is still feeling pessimistic. This is indicated by the fears she experienced.

At the implementation of letting go, subject was asked to honestly accept her current condition, and then admit what things are her fears. The subject then re-identified the things that become her fears, namely: the subject's fear of disease is due to punishment from God, the subject is afraid of not being able to survive with Lupus so the family must lose her.

The subject was then invited to feel the disease and admit it. This will help her more easily accept herself for her disease. After that the subject was invited to find reasons that can weaken these fears. Subsequently subject was asked to release negative feelings and affirmation to cultivate optimism that God sends this pain not as a punishment, the subject is able to withstand the condition, the subject can still accompany her family, can see her children grow up.

After the implementation of letting go, subject feels relieved. She also feels more comfortable, more able to accept her condition.

Research Findings on Subject 8: The subject told that she had not yet fully calm with her current condition. At first the subject was confused by her condition, there was concern about the disease caused by witchcraft. The subject also experienced a shock because since being diagnosed with Lupus, her physical condition has decreased drastically. The condition of this subject raises the psychic response in the form of complaining, stress and even depression. Depression is triggered because the subject has a miscarriage for the second time. The reaction that appears is that the subject always fainted when hearing the baby crying. The family as the main source of support is able to change the thinking of the subject. This makes her more grateful and sincere to live her life.

Based on the description of psychological dynamics above, subject has been able to achieve resilience though not optimal. The subject has been able to show optimism, good emotional regulation and improved positive aspects of her life.

On the implementation of letting go, subject was invited to feel disease and admit it. This will help her more easily accept herself for her disease. After that the subjects are invited to further strengthen positive sources such as family support, the power of gratitude and sincerity as the foundational strength and healing for subject. Subsequently subject was asked to release negative feelings and affirmation to increase optimism that the subjects would survive and recover from the disease. After the implementation of letting go, subject feels relieved, more comfortable and more able to accept her condition.

Cross-Subject Discussion

People with Lupus will react to it strongly because the situation or condition of the disease will bring fear to someone. The high risk of death from Lupus and its often late diagnosis, of course, has a psychological impact on people with Lupus. They have to deal with changing physical conditions that is decreasing continually and require tremendous adaptability in order to survive. The reactions of both psychology, cognition, and behaviour are essentially the reactions of a person to try to adapt to the disease. They try to fit in or survive.

Banaag (in Chandra, 2009) states that resilience is a process of interaction between individual factors and environmental factors. Individual factors serve to resist self-destruction and self-constructing positively, while environmental factors serve to protect individuals and soften the difficulties of individual life. But not everyone who tries to adapt to the disease is able to adapt to positive construction, because anyway Lupus can make someone feels anxious, stressed or even depressed.

The ability of a person to be able to achieve resilience depends on someone's adaptability, personality and family and environmental support. The prominent character in the eighth person is the person who tends to control everything in order to run well, which makes them lose their way when they diagnosed by the disease, so they feel they have nothing left. This character is formed from family background, that is from parenting, childhood experience and close relationship with parents and siblings. They tend to get used to hide negative feelings rather than express it to others because they do not want to burden their problems to others. They do not want to be known to have a particular problem.

Letting go is done to the eight subjects, encouraging the individual to think and express feelings of anger, hurt and disappointment, as well as negative thoughts. After being able to express their feelings and thoughts, the subjects will feel more comfortable and lightweight, so as to better understand their own feelings, then be able to understand their partner and the problem. This understanding causes the subjects to make adjustments and know how to solve the problem. Finally, the ability of resilience can be optimal.

Conclusion

Based on research that has been done on the eight people with Lupus, then the conclusions of this study are as follows:

The state of resilience tendency in people with Lupus, before and after Letting Go

1. People with Lupus tend to be at risk of experiencing negative emotional states such as anxiety, stress or even depression. The reactions actually arise because they are trying to adapt. When they build adaptations with a negative construction, it is risky to experience depression, whereas if the construction of adaptation is positive then they can achieve optimal resilience.
2. Symptoms of psychiatric conditions that appear on people with Lupus, shown among others:
   A. *Emotional symptoms:* feeling guilty, feeling afraid, not feeling confident, feeling depressed, feeling sad and crying often.
   B. *Cognitive symptoms:* feeling pessimistic, feeling no way out, hesitating, feeling life is not useful, feeling like a loser.
   C. *Motivational symptoms:* feeling dependent, feeling not wanting to face tomorrow, and lazy to do activities.
   D. *Behavioural symptoms:* being unproductive, lacking concentration, and little activity.
   E. *Somatic symptoms:* decreased appetite, difficulty sleeping, often sick, tired quickly.

3. After the letting go therapy, the individual feels more relieved, lighter and more comfortable, though the effect has not yet reached optimal resilience, but the individual's negative tendency after letting-go therapy shows a marked reduction in symptoms of real emotional states, such as less sadness, no longer thinking too much of bad experience, seeing the future more optimistic, no longer having sleeping trouble, and more reconciled with his heart. So that, to reach the optimal point, then letting go needs to be applied everyday.

How to Use *Letting Go*

Based on the findings of the research, there are certain similarities made by the subject of research in doing Letting go. How to use Letting go to get maximum result is:

(a) Do Letting go in a quiet, lonely atmosphere and in a fairly private place, so no worries that it will be known by others.
(b) Do Letting go everyday, at least once per day.
(c) The topics to be released are free, but it is more effective to imagine or feel an unpleasant experience accompanied by revealing the deepest feelings and thoughts that have never been told to others.

References

Agnesa, A. (2009). Makalah penyakit Lupus. *Paper Unpiblished*. Purwokerto: Jurusan Ilmu Kesehatan masyarakat, Fakultas Kedokteran dan Ilmu-ilmu Kesehatan.

Bowman, I.G. 2003. Exploring the retrospective experience of self-forgiveness in psychotherapy. *Dissertation*. Pretoria: Department of Psychology, University of Pretoria.

Chandra, S. (2009). Diunduh pada tanggal 30 Januari 2013 dari www. putrassyamsuri-blogspot.com/ 2009/ 02/ resiliensi.html.

Corey, G. (2005). *Theory and Practice of Counselling and Psychotherapy*. Seventh Edition. Velmont: Brooks/Cole— Thompson Learning.

Dwoskin, H. (2005). Sedona Method: How to get Rid of your Emotional Baggage and Life the Life you want. London: Element.

Fortunas, D. (2003). The experience of letting go: A phenomenological study. *Dissertation*. Pretoria: Department of Psychology, University of Pretoria.

Freshwater, D. and Robertson, C. (2002). *Emotion and Needs*. Buckingham: Open University Press.

Gow, K.M. (1999). Letting go: For physical, emotional, and spiritual health, *Journal of Religion and Health*.

Grotberg, E. (1995). *A Guide to Promoting Resilience in Children: Strengthening the Human Spirit*. Benard Van Leer Foundation.

Harvey, J. and Delfabbro, P.H. (2004). Psychological resilience in disadvantaged youth: Critical overview. *Australian Psychologist*, *39* (1), 3-13.

Lewis, J.L. (2005). Forgiveness and psychotherapy: The prepersonal, the personal, and the transpersonal. *The Journal of Transpersonal Psychology*. *37* (2), 124-142.

McCubbin, L. (2001). Challenge to the definition of resilience. *Paper presented at The Annual Meeting of The American Psychological Association in San Francisco.*

Ong, D.A., Bergeman, S.C., Bisconti, T.L., and Walles, K.A. (2006). Psychological resilience, positive emotions, and successful adaptions to stress in later life. *Journal of Personality and Social Psychology, 91*(4), 730-749.

Poerwandari, Kristi (2001). *Pendekatan kualitatif untuk penelitian perilaku manusia*. Fakultas Psikologi, Universitas Indonesia: Lembaga Pengembangan Sarana Pengukuran dan Pendidikan Psikologi (LPSP3)

Reivich, K. and Shatte, A. (2002). *The Resilience Factor*. New York: Broadway Books.

Shepherd, P. (2007). *Heart intelligence: Tools for transformation*. Download at January 31, 2013 from http://www.trans4mind.com.

Syafi'i, M. (2012). Dukungan sosial dala membangun keterampilan resiliensi pada penderita lupus. *Skripsi. Unpublished.* Surabaya: Programme Studi Psikologi, Fakultas Dakwah Institut Agama Islam Negeri Sunan Ampel.

Wartapedia. (2012). LUPUS: Penderita Lupus di Indonesia capai 1,5 juta orang. Download at February 1, 2013 from www. wartapedia.com/ 2012

Zimberoff, D. and Hartman, D. (2003). Transpersonal psychology in heart-centred therapies. *Journal of Heart-Centred Therapy, 6*, 123-144.

15

Empowerment on Resilience and Coping Skills of Frontline Workers of Earthquake Affected Area of Nepal

[1]*Narendra Singh Thagunna*

Introduction

"Most people are exposed to at least one violent or life-threatening situation during the course of their lives. Resilience is common and multiple pathways can lead to it" (Bonanno, 2004).

Resilience is the process of adapting well in the face of adversity, trauma, tragedy, threats or significant sources of stress — such as family and relationship problems, serious health problems or workplace and financial stressors. One example is the response of many Indians to the January 26, 2001 natural disaster earthquake in Bhuj, Gujarat or in June 2013, a multi-day cloudburst centred on the North Indian state of Uttarakhand caused devastating floods and landslides and individuals' efforts to rebuild their lives. In 25th April, 2015, devastating earthquake in Nepal caused many sufferers in 14 districts and individuals' effort to rebuild their lives. Being resilient does not mean that a person does not experience difficulty or distress. Everyone experiences varying degrees of setbacks. Some of these challenges might be relatively minor while others are disastrous on a much larger scale. Resilience does not eliminate stress or erase life's difficulties. Instead, it gives people the strength to tackle problems head on, overcome adversity and move on with their lives.

Resilience is a dynamic process wherein individuals display positive adaptation despite experiences of significant adversity or trauma. This term does not represent a personality trait or an attribute of the individual (Luthar *et al.*, 2000). Researchers focused on that which differentiated children who were well adjusted (despite adversity) from those who were not. Resilience was understood as successful adaptation, positive functioning and competence in the face of severe trauma or chronic stress (Luthar, 1993) (Egeland, Pianta, & O'Brien, 1993). Studies on resilience looked at the personal qualities of resilient children (such as high self-esteem or autonomy) (Masten & Garmezy, 1985 in Luthar *et al.*, 2000), but it was soon recognized that external factors were also relevant when the idea of 'growth' in the face of adversity was introduced (Gordon, 1995).

In South Asian culture practices of meditation (*dhyana*), *yoga*, or worship (*puja*) were said to make the "mind fresh" and foster feelings of "peace" (*shanti*) or "relief" (*ananda*) in the heart-mind. Another strategy was "diverting the heart-mind", or keeping the heart-mind "busy" or "engaged," (*byasta rahana*). In addition, engagement in cultural rituals group activities such as (*Uvouli, Rodi, Deuda, Jhoda Chachari chhapali different Melas*) at the different tribal ethnic groups can generate positive feelings that promote resilience in their own right. In other words, activity heals not only by distracting the mind from unpleasant thoughts, but also by introducing positive feelings such as "relief" (*ananda*), "lightness" (*halka*), and "fun/enjoyment" (*maja*) to the heart-mind.

Relevant psychological literature on resilience hasn't always used the term 'resilience' or 'psychological resilience'. Consider searching for material using synonyms or closely related keywords, such as Adaptive Coping, Adversity Quotient, Emotional Intelligence (Daniel Goleman), Hardiness, Learned Optimism (Martin Seligman), Learned Resourcefulness (Rosenbaum), Life Orientation, Resourcefulness, Self-esteem, Self-concept, Self-confidence, Self-efficacy, Self-healing personality (Howard Friedman), Sense of Coherence (Aaron Antonovsky), Sense of Meaning (Viktor Frankl), Thriving (Al Siebert-Thrivenet.

Stress has been defined as "a demand (environmental and/or internal) made upon the adaptive capacities of the mind and body (Fontana, 1989). If the individual's adaptive capacities can meet the demand, then the situation may be perceived as a challenge with the prospect of successful problem-solving. This may be called emotional excitement or emotional pro stress (D'Zurilla & Nezu, 1989). When demand exceeds or overwhelms capacity, the individual can suffer from physical and mental debilitation that results in burnout, that is, he or she is emotionally spent and deprived of productive energy; stress has turned into distress (Neenan & Palmer, 1996). Stress can have both immediate and long-term psychological, physiological, and behavioural effects.

The task of a therapist is to help stressed individuals to identify, challenge and change those patterns of thinking that produce emotional disturbance and problem-solving interference in the face of environmental stressors; this process of cognitive change enables the individual to develop an enduring emotional and practical problem-solving outlook (Abrams & Ellis, 1994).

However, in those cases when a therapist or other mental health professional is not available, it becomes a concern of any significant other in the individual's environment, who has knowledge and understanding of mental health and stress-related issues, to facilitate such change through available means. Primary prevention attempts to forestall a problem from occurring altogether. With urbanization and industrialization, society today seems colder and harsher. Individuals are less self-reliant and therefore turn to the government and a variety of professionals to meet their needs. However, not everyone with a mental disorder or adjustment problem is able to receive treatment from professionals. Early intervention may therefore be a better measure for preventing mental disorders altogether wherever and whenever possible.

Objectives of the Study

The researcher has been observing during his training experience that a majority of south Asian participants especially Indian and Nepali participants, irrespective of the course of study they are pursuing, are not equipped to cope with the challenges of life. They are prone to stress, burnout and frustration. The scenario is more complex in the case of MHPSS training; Not only are they being fitted for a belief system where many of their idealistic perceptions of the profession are likely to be disturbed; but they will also witness the emotional distress of people who are adversely affected by this system. As counsellor, they are expected to mould healthy human beings. But their own work pressures and professional limit may restrict them from doing so. The commonly-cited causes of such stress are high expectations of parents; an insensitive school system; bullying that focuses exclusively on marks, irrespective of the impacts on mental health; increasing competition for jobs; and breakdown of traditional systems of familial and social support. The consequences can range from emotional disorders to violence and aggression. In such a scenario, training in resilience and coping skills is urgently needed for MHPSS trainees. It is expected that this will facilitate them for handling their own stress as well as that of their clients. The researcher wished to explore how resilience and coping skills training imparted in the training session in an inconspicuous way during the course of facilitation, could equip the trainees with coping strategies for not just the course but for all areas of life functioning.

The Objectives of the present study

- To identify the causes of stress among the frontline workers of Earthquake affected area of Nepal.
- To instruct training in resilience and coping skills to frontline workers of Earthquake affected area of Nepal.
- To facilitate the participants to develop personal and culturally accepted coping strategies and techniques.

Design: This study may call exploratory and "instinctive" rather than quantitative. The researcher was not objectively detached from the participants but rather supportively involved in his role as facilitator and mentor. His approach was broadly humanistic and psychosocial. He was aided in this exploration by the course content which included components psychotherapy supervision, guidance and counselling, mentoring, and counselling approaches.

Sample: The sample consisted of 760 trainees of MHPSS to front-line workers of Earthquake affected area of Nepal: 14 districts of Nepal (*e.g.* Gorkha, Dhading, 3 districts of Kathmandu Valley, Kavre, Sindhupalchok, Sindhuli, Okhaldhunda, Ramechhap, Dolakha, Makwanpur and Nuwakot Tanhau), both male and female, employees of different INGO/NGO/ Government staffs. The trainees, both male (280) and female (480), were aged between 18 and 49. Some were fresh graduates while others had considerable work experience. Many of them were married and had children. While none initially appeared to be suffering from significant psychological distress, the investigator was concerned about the possible impact of stressors on the long-term mental health of the trainees.

Tools: The researcher integrated within the training hall setting, several therapeutic exercises and practices bound for towards self-exploration of the trainees. The purpose of these exercises was to—

- Lower defenses
- Overcome from traumatic events and burnout while working in emergency situation.
- Encourage questioning
- Develop insight
- Achieve catharsis

The following methods were used for promoting resilience and coping skills toward life stress events:

1. **Gratitude letter:** Participants were instructed to write a letter to anyone whom they wished. The letter could be grateful towards their success; in short, they were to express their feelings towards any person, force or situation in their lives and put their positive names at the end. Once all the letters were collected, each participant had to choose one randomly and reply aloud as if it was addressed to them. (2 sessions of 50 minutes each).

   Investigator's Observation: Some addressed their letters to their parents, some to friends and some to themselves. A few even addressed them to God. A significant emotional expression of satisfaction was observed, along with gratitude, forgiveness and expectation. Overall, this exercise was seen to be energizing and leading to better group cohesion.
2. **The Unsent Letter:** Participants were instructed to write a letter to anyone whom they wished. The letter could be angry, regretful, joyous or grateful; in short, they were to express their feelings towards any person, force or situation in their lives. The participants did not put their names at the end. Once all the letters were collected in one place, each participant had to choose one randomly and reply aloud as if it was addressed to them, (2 sessions 50 minutes each).

   Investigator's Observation: Some addressed their letters to their parents, some to friends and some to themselves. A few even addressed them to God. A considerable emotional expression of resentment and dissatisfaction was observed, along with an outflow of gratitude, forgiveness and expectation. Overall, this exercise was seen to be cathartic and leading to better group cohesion.
3. **Narrative Exposure Techniques:** The word 'narrative' refers to the stories of people's lives. Narrative approaches to

counselling accept people as the experts in their own lives. They assume that people have many skills, beliefs, values, and abilities that will assist them to reduce the influence of problems in their lives. By telling their story, people can find meaning in contradictory events, accept alternate truths, and shape happy endings. Participants in the narrative Exposure Therapy exercise were asked to draw lifeline with the help of rope and put flowers for happiest movements of life and stones for sad traumatic events of life. It was symbolic for hot and cold memory of individuals. The narration writes down their lives, or particular phases of their lives. After initial reluctance, some participants were able to relate incidents from their lives that they thought formed a complete story. Participants in the narrative exercise were asked to write down their lives, or particular phases of their lives, as stories in the third person. After initial reluctance, some participants were able to relate incidents from their lives that they thought formed a complete story. The task was now to thread the entire life into one story with purpose and 'Personification' as a narrative device was adopted, wherein conflicts were to be depicted as characters in the story, enabling the participant to externalize the problem (8 sessions 50 minutes each).

Researcher's Observations: There was a defensive attitude in the participants about sharing their personal stories in session, which gradually reduced as researcher explained the significance of the narrative approach. Gradually, they were able to plunge into the exercise with enthusiasm. Most found this exercise challenging, but by the end of the session they were willing to re-write their life stories to find meaning.

4. **Dream Disclosure:** The researcher asked to trainees to write down their unfulfilled dreams secretly on a piece of paper. The papers were then collected and in turn, each participant was to pick up one randomly, read out the contents, and then speak aloud how they would have responded had this been their dream. Participants were instructed to respond immediately, with not more than a minute allowed for thinking about their response. This was done to encourage spontaneity and discourage psychological defenses. Emphasis was laid on possible courses of action they would have adopted.

   Researcher's Observation: A common unfulfilled dream that

emerged was not being able to pursue one's chosen vocation. Since the participants were all teacher trainees, it raised the question of what constraints inhibited them from pursuing their chosen goal, and their motives in pursuing their present course.

5. **Me Map:** The researcher asked to trainees to draw their own me map to explore their support system on a piece of paper. There were four different circles, these circles denotes support system on stressed situation. When he/she is in problematic situation, used to share with whom are in first circle and last one is least preferred.

   Researcher's Observation: Very useful for the remembrance of the past events and support systems of trainees.

6. **Positive Emotions Exercise:** Participants were asked to collect the different magazines and cut out the colourful pictures they like to. They had to attach those pictures in one drawing chart paper. Each participant had to express their emotions, feeling through those cut out pictures relating about their dreamed life and they had to keep particular heading.

   Researcher's Observations: During the presentation, all participants were excited and happy to express their emotions about their dreamed life. They express their desire and future which they want in their life. A considerable happiness and positive hope towards their future can be seen on the participants during the presentation which was quite effective to release their happiness and sadness both aspect.

7. **Colour breathing:** In this activity, first of all trainee were asked to deep breath and become aware of incoming and outgoing respiration. Then they had to imagine that the incoming air is of golden colour and outgoing breath is of brown air. Then they are asked to imagine with each golden colour incoming breath, positive energy is entering into their body making them peaceful and comfortable while with each outgoing brown colour breathing negative energy from their body such as tension and stresses are going outside of their body. For about five minutes trainee had to do this activity and slowly open their eyes with observing nearest objects first then looking away farther and be aware.

8. **Blindfold painting:** It was proposed that playing with different colours would stimulate trainees' brain especially when they are affected by trauma and disaster. Hence in this activity children

had to fold an A4 size paper and put some drops of water colour from colour tube. After doing this they had to spread the colour smoothly in the blindfolded paper. When they open the blindfolded paper then there is a beautiful drawing with multiple colour and shades just like ink blot.

9. **Cross and crawl activity:** Hand body coordination especially left and right part of body is supposed to stimulate left and right hemisphere of brain that is supposed to do good with traumatized children and adult. For this activity trainees' had to touch their right thigh with left hand, left thigh with right hand ten times. Then they had to touch with left elbow to right thigh, right elbow to left thigh ten times. Lastly, they would touch their left toe with right hand and right toe with left hand ten times.
10. **Lazy eight:** In this activity trainees' had to continuously look at their thumb while making an infinitive sign on air. This would increase their ability to concentrate.
11. **Playing with a balloon:** In this activity trainees had to blow a balloon and write their current emotions on it with a colour pen. In a group they would play with the balloons for some time. Then they find a pair and put the balloon back to back and without dropping it they had to sit down and stand up.
12. **Play dough activities:** Trainees had made different objects with play dough of various colours. After some free play they had to make an animal for each of their family members and place them on a A3 size paper. This activity could be used for both assessment and therapy.

Results and Discussion

Based on the investigator's observations during the above programme of resilience and coping skills training, the causes of stress among the trainees were found to be:

Duel role training and job responsibility pressures: During the training time they felt refreshed but they were worried about job responsibility put a lot of pressure on the trainees.

Family and Marital conflicts: In some cases arising from or aggravated by the study pressures of the trainees: As stated earlier, many of the trainees were married with children. An interesting anomaly was that many trainees' families (in-laws) wanted them to pursue the training course so that the family income could be enhanced; but at the same time shied away from providing help in household duties to ease the pressure on the trainee. Balancing family responsibilities with study was proving to be a cumulative burden. In some cases, there was no role conflict but still there were underlying family issues adding to their stress.

Unrealistically high expectations from oneself: Some trainees had been scoring consistently well throughout their academic career. Others had been performing in the average to low range before joining the course, but were eager to take training to enhance their professional opportunities.

Lack of fluency in the language of study: English was the medium of instruction for the course. As most of the trainees were native Nepali speakers, and many had carried out their entire education in the Nepali medium, they faced a major problem in understanding basic concepts and expressing themselves adequately.

Lack of job security: Many trainees had been employed prior to joining the course. The training programme was a step to enhance their professional qualifications. They were concerned that the time invested in the programme may not lead to continuation employment after completion of the course.

Daily long commutes: The workplaces were remote areas located in the outskirts of the city and worked with the vulnerable population in earthquake affected areas which increased level of stress.

Dissatisfaction with one's career choice: The investigator found that some trainees had been forced to receive the higher education according to family pressure, financial needs, confusion about their own career options. They had not received any career counselling in their entire academic career. This pointed to a dire need for providing career assessment and counselling at the secondary and higher education levels.

One notable finding that emerged was that the participants, who held belief in a higher Power, were able to cope better under stress. They found it beneficial to recall incidents in their life when this Power had sustained them under difficult circumstances. Moreover, the more such instances they recalled, the more responsive they were to the coping skills training. The investigator therefore suggests that a transpersonal perspective may be useful while working with stress-related problems. The central concept in Transpersonal Psychology is a sense of self-identity which is deeper or higher, broader, and more unified with the Whole. The root of the term, transpersonal or literally "beyond the mask", refers to this self-transcendence. Faith in a Higher Entity that is a source of power and strength has been an inseparable part of the Indian ethos. With Indian students, therefore, this approach may even work with those individuals who are otherwise feeling too "hemmed in" by circumstances, to re-appraise their life situations in a more positive manner.

Implications for Mental Health and Community Empowerment

The American Psychological Association suggests ways to Build Resilience are: **Make good connections and relationships** with close family members, friends or others are important. Accepting help and support from those who care about you and will listen to you strengthens resilience. **Avoid seeing crises as insurmountable problems**. You cannot change the fact that highly stressful events happen, but you can change how you interpret and respond to these events. Try looking beyond the present to how future circumstances may be a little better. Note any subtle ways in which you might already feel somewhat better as you deal with difficult situations. **Accept that change is a part of living**. Certain goals may no longer be attainable as a result of adverse situations. Accepting circumstances that cannot be changed can help you focus on circumstances that you can alter. **Move toward your goals**. Develop some realistic goals. Do something regularly — even if it seems like a small accomplishment — that enables you to move toward your goals. Instead of focusing on tasks that seem unachievable, ask yourself, "What's one thing I know I can accomplish today that helps me move in the direction I want to go?" **Take decisive actions**. Act on adverse situations as much as you can. Take decisive actions, rather than detaching completely from problems and stresses and wishing they would just go away. **Look for opportunities for self-discovery**. People often learn something about themselves and may find that they have grown in some respect as a result of their struggle with loss. Many people who have experienced tragedies and hardship have reported better relationships, greater sense of strength even while feeling vulnerable, increased sense of self-worth, a more developed spirituality and heightened appreciation for life. **Nurture a positive view of yourself**. Developing confidence in your ability to solve problems and trusting your instincts helps build resilience. **Keep things in perspective**. Even when facing very painful events, try to consider the stressful situation in a broader context and keep a long-term perspective. Avoid blowing the event out of proportion. **Maintain a hopeful outlook**. An optimistic outlook enables you to expect that good things will happen in your life. Try visualizing what you want, rather than worrying about what you fear. **Take care of yourself**. Pay attention to your own needs and feelings. Engage in activities that you enjoy and find relaxing. Exercise regularly. Taking care of yourself helps to keep your mind and body primed to deal with situations that require resilience.

Mutual respect emerges when participants gather the courage to share their painful emotions and experiences in front of their classmates and accept the solutions emerging from the process. Critical reflection skills develop when expression of feelings leads to an understanding of the causes wherein those feelings sprung from. Caring and group participation stem from the realization that many others are in the same predicament and that by simply sharing one's experiences, a more closely-knit class community can develop. One can view above mentioned exercises as a means of empowerment within the community. Empowerment can be defined as "an intentional, ongoing process centred in the local community, involving mutual respect, critical reflection, caring, and group participation, through which people lacking an equal share of resources gain greater access to and control over those resources" (Zimmerman, 2000). The "resources" in this context refer to opportunities that have been denied to many participants. Even though the majority comes from the average to above average socio-economic classes; conservative family backgrounds and gender restrictions have inhibited many of them from realizing their potential as fully functional individuals. Stereotyped notions of women being suited only for certain professions (such as teaching); the role conflict arising from the demands of the study course and family life; lack of awareness about career choices; and a process of socialization that encourages denial of feelings, have all contributed to self-defeating habits and low motivation to change. Self-expression ranges from fluent and creative in some members to rigid and conformist in others. Resources here also refer to access to mental health services. Not a single trainee from the sample had ever visited a mental health professional in their lives, even though many of them reported intense feelings of depression, despair, anger and even suicidal impulses.

Self-disclosure of emotional imbalances in a group setting lowered the barriers of doubt or shame that restricted individuals from taking professional help. Accepting that one had missed opportunities due to social conformity, helped group members to shed defenses and identify means of self-expression.

References

Abrams, M. and Ellis, A. (1994). Rational emotive behaviour therapy in the treatment of stress. *British Journal of Guidance and Counselling, 22* (1), 39-50

D'Zurilla, T.J. and Nezu, A.M. (1989). Clinical stress management. In A.M. Nezu and C.M. Nezu (Eds.), *Clinical Decision-making in Behaviour Therapy: A Problem-solving Perspective.* Champaign, IL: Research Press.

Duffy, K.G. (1998). Community psychology. In S. Cullari (Ed.), *Foundations of Clinical Psychology*, pp. 348-365, Allyn and Bacon.

Gilgun, J. (1996). Human Development and Adversity in Ecological Perspective. *Families in Society: The Journal of Comtemporary Human Services,* 77.

Gordon. (1995). *Children Remember the Holocaust.* Egeland, P., Pianta, R.C., and O. Brien, M.A. (1993). Maternal intrusiveness in infancy and child maladaptation in early school years. *Development and Psychopathology, 5* (3), 359-370.

Fontana, D. (1989). *Managing Stress.* London: Routledge Publications.

Luthar, S.S. (1993). Annotation: Methodological and conceptual issues in the study of resilience. *Journal of Child Psychology and Psychiatry, 34*, 441-445.

Luther, S., Cicchetti, D., and Becker, B. (2000). The Construct of Resilience: A Critical Evaluation and Guidelines for Future Work. *Child Development, 71* (3), 543-562.

Neenan, M. and Palmer, S. (1996). Stress counselling: A cognitive-behavioural perspective. *Journal of the International Stress Management Association (UK Branch), 8* (4), 5-8.

16
Inner Self Integration: Theory and Therapy

Kamal Khurana and *Aradhana Shukla*

This theory argues for a Inner Self Integration theory on the grounds that it provides a better form of therapy in psychology and cognitive science. In this theory, grounds for evaluating competing models of psychotherapy are presented and several recent accounts of psychological explanation are analysed and evaluated. It is an inclusive model, which incorporates transpersonal psychology, Western psychological therapy models and ancient eastern wisdom is also developed. This is a pursuit of psychotherapy with improved effectiveness drives the entire psychology research community as well as large parts of the well-being research communities.

The concept of self was defined by the Western schools of thought in psychology. At the same time the self was also defined in the eastern psychology at a very deeper level. The eastern concept of 'self' transcends the idea of 'personal self', while responding to the situations in the environment and being functional at the same time. The Inner Self Integration theory attempts at explaining the inter link between cognition, behaviour and transpersonal self, thereby developing the capability to handling life situations in a much effective way.

Inner Self Integration is a collection of theories and techniques that form one of the leading edge approaches to therapy. Most therapies are designed not on composite model, but either on a transpersonal model or on the Western non-directive cognitive behaviour therapy, hence these therapies often do not perform well on all the clients and their impact is sometimes unstable. Because Inner Self Integration Therapy is based on transpersonal psychology, ancient eastern wisdom and cognitive behaviour therapy, it offers some distinct advantages for improving efficiency.

In this theory, we develop a stable model of psychotherapy by synthesizing a blend of transpersonal psychology, ancient eastern wisdom and cognitive behaviour therapy (CBT). Using a mix of directive and non-directive therapy, the Inner Self Integration techniques are applied to guarantee the stability of the clients. This therapy provides stability and functionality not only for a life-long period, but also for making the client capable of handling all the situations of life. We included the discussions on several limitations and problems that we encounter and have identified potential avenues of future research.

Objectives of the Theory and Therapy

The objectives of the theory and therapy are as follows:

- To facilitate the people in a way that may help them to sustain their happiness and functionality in contrast to common myths and misconceptions.
- To improve the quality of thinking that affects functioning, physical health and well-being of an individual in particular and in the society.
- To promote healthy acceptance of the perpetual problems which change over time, but never go away even in the case of happy people move over.

This theory provides tool to the therapist that helps in assessing the pattern of self in following ways:

- Inculcation of Quality Life Enhancing Postulates—This facilitates the basis for –
    - logical thinking,
    - identify and address solvable problems,
    - understand and manage unnecessary confusions by creating a 'sense of unimpactedness'.
- It provides foundation for living a free and functional life.
- It develops the concept of 'living objectively'—i.e. the existential foundation of life that helps people to discover the purpose for living a life with justification of the feelings and circumstances.

No doubt, by various methods and techniques, it will provide a chance to the therapists to cure the clients. It will assure the people in terms of:

- Strategies and tools to successfully manage the irrational thinking in the mind.
- Skills to deal with long stuck issues by uncovering their underlying beliefs, emotional baggage, and imaginations.
- Methods to process situations in their life and heal their life.
- Techniques and effective interventions to help understand their struggles.

This theory is named as "Inner Self Integrations theory" because it focuses on the integration of self and tries to remove all the hazards (termed as *Sapt Badhak* / Seven Interruptions) that block the self situated activities. It is a process which helps in modification of cognitions which lead to dysfunctional behaviours. In present day, each and every person of the society is facing ample problems which block his/her common and acceptable behaviour. In this process his/her self becomes injured yet he/ she is expected to be normal and produce desirable behaviours. This theory will provide a sense of positivity and suggest self to overcome the behavioural hazards and act normally and in an integrated way. Thus, Inner Self Integration therapy goes well beyond the problem context, into the everyday aspect of life. Moreover, it represents a systematic approach to build functionality and a general sense of satisfaction and happiness in the clients, by enabling them to understand the nature and helplessness of fellow humans who co-exist with them. Clients learn to search new ways to deal with their problems, in a selectively healthier way while forgiving those whom they feel hurt from. This theory is the combination of cognitive, behavioural, affective and existential theories and thus, it is based on sequential, time sense and mathematical modelling approaches. In addition, this theory is embedded with simple executives, diagnostic and intervention devices which not only empowers the client but also well-equips the clinicians.

Rationale of the Theory: How the Idea Occurred?

In this world of glamour and show-offness peop00le are deprived of from inner peace and as a consequence, they search it outside of them, i.e. they search it in the outer curtain of religion, *yoga* and yogic exercises. In search of peace, either they focus their attention in these parallel modes of life or they indulge themselves in worldly affair. Prior to doing something in this area, many people had put across following questions. We are thankful to them that their questions enabled us to go further to construct this theory and therapy. Those questions were:

1. How do people become happy?
2. What is the thing that makes the people happy?
3. How do people gain proper functionality in life ?

The base of Inner Self Integration started taking shape in the year 2016 when *Khurana and Shukla (2016)* found that individuals in distress were caught in a dreadful dance of negative thinking and limited identity, that kept them stuck and unable to deal with their challenges. Using the '*Advaita*' philosophy and other psychotherapies he developed a treatment to help these people in distress. It has been found that people practicing Inner Self Integration regularly move from distress to recovery, and they show significant improvements. These results appear to bless susceptible to relapse than those from other approaches. The therapeutic treatment is also correlated with psychological measures of life, depression, personality academic motivation and marriage relation. Through Test-retest design it was found that the participants got recovered (*details are presented in the section of psychological implications).*

Insight to the questions which gave ground to the theory—

1. ***How do people become happy?:*** This query was focused on the notion that it is the duty of the therapist as well as of the clients to reason the happiness evoking actions, while acting out to share the same with the others.
2. ***What is the thing that makes the people happy?:*** There are a lot of events that facilitate the feelings—sense of happiness amongst people. Such events evoke many types of feelings resulting to which a person expresses the same. Happiness of a person depends on the personal attributes as well as the existing circumstances. Inner Self Integration aids in searching the essence of such things and helps in making the person happy.
3. ***How do people gain functionality in life?:*** It is a common fact that human beings are always active in nature. At all the times, either he thinks or acts. This functionality is based on his characteristics, the existing situations, external forces that intervene etc. All these components jointly influence his actions

and enable him to be functional in response to any stimulus, event or goal.

The Inner Self Integration theory is scientifically-based and represents a systematic approach to the following three goals for producing lasting effects in therapy.

- Clients are empowered to meet their internal demands and also understand the external world with a positive attitude.
- Reducing negativity during issue resolution –

  Reducing negativity during issue resolution is the second thing and this aim deals with the reduction or atleast minimization of the negative thought and attitudes so that the person will inset positivity in him and spread it in the society. It is event based but useful for every situation.
- Increasing positivity during issue resolution.

Increasing positivity during issue resolution: This aim is also situations based and facilitates the client to change his negativity into positivity. It is also event based.

In this way this theory teaches the client, how to deal with common and difficult presenting life problems and *(sapt badhakas)* solve them on their own.

Therapeutic Tasks in Inner Self Integration for Individuals: Psychological Perspective and Validation

The therapeutic task is an immediate problem that a client needs to resolve in a session. Inner Self Integration therapeutic tasks are empathy-based, relational, experiential, reprocessing, and response oriented. Inner Self Integration therapeutic intervention process is a sequence of action carried out by the therapist and the client in working on the presenting concern—the immediate problem. The client expects the desired resolution of the immediate problem. To fulfil the client's expectation the therapist works in a way such that the client understands and accepts his/her mistakes and limitations before the therapist while formulating the resolution tasks and leaves the place satisfactory. The therapy also reduces and eliminates the blocking feelings of guilt, self-rejection, self victimization and self-blame in the given the problem (s) and by promoting new thoughts around client's incapacity region in the past, resilience is established.

Inner Self Integration is based on the concept that negative emotion and behaviours result from limited sense of identity; and that it is possible for people to modify thinking so as to establish positive ways of feeling, behaving and living. And this is done by integrating with the Inner Self.

In 2005, we came in touch with various schools of spiritual practices and *Advaita*. We observed that using a mix of spiritual concepts with psychotherapy based psychological intervention, clients tended to feel better more quickly. Post therapy, clients were able to change their outlook towards themselves, their life situations and the world. We reasoned that integrating the clients with their Inner Self (as he refers the true self-concept) directly helps the client's beliefs and behaviour. Thus was founded the new technique known as Inner Self Integration.

Inner Self Integration as Theory of Existence

Inner Self Integration is not only a set of techniques—it is also a comprehensive theory of existence. Inner Self Integration proposes a 'psycho-spiritual' explanation of existence, i.e. a combination of psychological, and spiritual factors that govern the way people feel and behave. The most basic premise of Inner Self Integration theory, which it shares with other cognitive behavioural theories, is that almost all human feelings and behaviours are the consequence of what people think, assume or believe (about themselves, other people, and the world in general). Also, it focus on what people believe about situations they face, and not the situations themselves that determines how they feel and behave. However Inner Self Integration, also argues that a person's social learning affects their feelings and behaviours, as it is a reminder to the practitioner that there are limitations for the change of the mindset of the client.

Inner Self Integration as Theory of Change

The main premise of Inner Self Integration is change. Change is a very obvious part of every moment of an individual's life. An individual becomes anxious on witnessing a change. The change makes the mind think about the future. Fear is a prime emotion which an individual experiences when thoughts about unexpectedness of life appears in mind. Before trying to change the situation, one needs to come in total acceptance of the change. This certainly reduces the level of anxiety. The Inner Self Integration technique involves modification of the underlying beliefs that make a person react for self-preservation in challenging situations. The

Inner Self Integration therapist uses a structured process of therapy which includes cognitive, emotive and behavioural strategy.

Unique Features of Inner Self Integration

Inner Self Integration has a number of characteristics that are original to the approach. They are as follows:

Sense of Unimpactedness

Inner Self Integration has a unique approach to the common therapeutic problem of 'low self-esteem'. Many therapists try to help people with low self-esteem, by encouraging them to regard themselves as 'worthy' human beings. Inner Self Integration practitioners take a different approach by encouraging the client to throw out the limited identity *(doer-ship)* and drop the habit of perceiving life events and good or bad entirely! This involves giving up the practice of trying to judge life events as good (a notion, incidentally, that implies that "if life events are favourable, then life is good")!; and getting rid of the idea of doer-ship, that implies that "people do things".

The client is, instead, urged to (1) aim for operating from sense of "inner self" irrespective of how people see them; (2) acknowledge that they simply exist as the "self" and choose to stay unimpacted, experience peace within, and avoid expectation; and (3) instead of judging themselves and judging life, to concentrate on living free and experiencing life fully, the way it happens and as an effect of this living peacefully, responding righteously to the problem *(challenge)* at hand.

Willingness to Live Fully

Inner Self Integration points out that people frequently get obsessed with their problems due to challenging situations in life. By letting these 'obsessions' form, they complicate their emotional and behavioural difficulties. Expecting life to continue in a particular way, is a common obstruction to living fully. People who experience anger issues, chronic anxiety, low self-esteem, fear and hysteria, frequently find themselves on hazards of a peaceful life. Clients who want to experience change through Inner Self Integration, must be open to the concept and have willingness to live fully. If they are not open and are unwilling to have peace as their objective, then they will not overcome their problems, as quickly as they think they 'should' be able to. Sometimes, for therapy to be effective, the willingness issues need to be addressed before addressing and resolving the primary problem.

Obsessive Thinking of the Mind

Inner Self Integration suggests that obsession with the limited concept of 'Self'—the limited identity or ego often leads to emotional disturbance. 'The Limited Identity'—a concept that gets formed right from childhood because of social learning and because of practical purpose ιo exist in the world with others. Inner Self Integration, however, uniquely argues that there is another critical factor—"Resilience", i.e. is ability to recover readily from adversity or any challenging life situation. Inner Self Integration facilitates increase in the level of resilience in the client.

Leaning to Use Inner Self Integration

To practice Inner Self Integration, it is important to have a good understanding of concept of Self. This can be obtained by a critical reading of the substantial literature available. The most effective ways of learning, i.e. how to help clients uncover and dispute their irrational beliefs is by practicing Inner Self Integration on ownself first. Inner Self Integration is just not a momentary therapeutic process, rather it is a way of living. It is a healthy preventive measure that one can get benefitted from, in everyday life. The therapist has to be a believer of this way of living. Otherwise, the therapist may find it difficult to implement the technique. This technique is just not a symptomatic resolution method. It is more of a culture and a life philosophy.

Premise of Inner Self Integration?

The theme of Inner Self Integration is to facilitate a seamless transition from the state of 'Neediness' to 'Unimpactedness'. Neediness here is referred as a continued dependency on specific things and situation, so as to gain momentary satisfaction and sense of peace. This is a constant loop of anxious thinking and behaving, so as to attain the objects of desire or desired situations.

The final outcome of the Inner Self Integration theory is a state of relative 'Unimpactedness'. Unimpactedness is an ability to stay balanced and composed in the middle of challenges, both emotionally and functionally.

Peace is a basic nature of all existence, but there are interruptions to this sense of peace. Peace comes from the state of rest, calm and 'no war'. This theory of Inner Self Integration holds on the premise that there are these seven interruptions which disturb the state of peace. The aim of the Inner Self Integration therapist is to help the client gain the ability to become aware of these interruptions, handle these interruptions and become resilient to them.

Hazards of Self Integrations: Seven Interruption – *Sapt Badhaka*

1. Sense of limited identity
2. Unawareness of limited bodily existence
3. Compulsive longing for things expected occurrence of life
4. Hurt proneness of the mind
5. Obsessive thinking
6. Limited sense of control over life events
7. Purpose of existence.

1. Sense of Limited Identity

Inner Self Integration theory mentions about 'Sense of Limited Identity' that a person carries throughout life. The concept of Limited Identity starts from the time when the child **(age 2 and 3 onwards)** understands that he has a name and a gender. Slowly there are additions to the person's attributes. The self concept gets continuously formed through constant feedbacks (positive or negative) with the social environment. The opinions and judgements about the individual are provided in the intimate relations with family, couple and friends. Even the media has a major influence on the development of this concept of 'Self'. Perhaps the most impact is from the body image. A person relates Self with the body and that is how the body image is also a critical factor. Since decades, the advertisers of beauty products and garment companies have been creating a gap between ideal body image and the real image. This all has lead to anxiety and depression.

Marsh and Seeshing (1997) have stated that fundamentally within the field of Educational Psychology, there has been a constant preoccupation regarding the links between self-concept and academic performance. However, there is a lack of evidence indicating the precise nature of the relationship between both variables. Right from childhood, an individual starts identifying the materialism with the concept of Self. And this happens because of a frequent search for external factors, tangible and intangible, to use as determinants of the concept of self. An individual relates to these factors as Self. The theory of Inner Self Integration considers these components of Self as 'limited'. Although materialistic factors cannot be denied or rejected, yet they can bc used for positive and creative somas and means. It leads to the fact that concepts of matter and energy are both important.

Whereas transpersonal psychology extends the concept of Self, much beyond the 'reality' of the physical world. They postulate a psychological or psychical reality, just as real and more real than physical reality. Physicists study only the "outside" physical world. Rowan (1976) mentioned about the experience of ecstasy as studied in humanistic (or transpersonal) psychology. Maslow also researched the peak experiences in the highest state—Self Actualisation.

Gordon Allport Presented the theory of functional autonomy (1937) in which the concept of self is not referred as self, but he calls it 'proprium'

Morgan and King (1956) refers to two distinct set of meaning of self psychology. One set refers to people's attitude about themselves, their picture of the way they look and act, the impact they make on others, their traits and abilities their foibles and weaknesses. The second set of meanings relates to the psychological processes which are the 'executive functions', the process by which the individual manages and copes, thinks, remembers, perceives and plans. Now the big question is—where are the these experiences happening?. This second set of Self is beyond.

Also according to Roger's Self Theory, the organism, as psychologically conceived, is the locus of all experience. Experience includes everything potentially available to awareness, that is going on within the organism at any given moment. Rogerian self is a process self—a fluid process. It is capable of growth, change, and personal development.

Inner Self Integration theory helps an individual to experience and become aware of this complete Sense of Self, which in Inner Self Integration theory, is referred to the awareness of true identity, i.e. 'Inner Self'.

2. Unawareness of Limited Bodily Existence

Most people do not realize that death is in-evitable. Mortality is not at all considered as a not-negative process. Rather mortality is viewed as something negative. Thoughts of someone else's death, obviously generate the emotion of sadness, but this emotion prevails only for a limited period. Inner Self Integration theory proposes, that to live a fully functional life, to be in a state of peace, and to experience the larger purpose of life, it is important to become aware of limited bodily existence. People live their lives as a pursuit of fulfilling aspirations and desires. This excessive obsession of the desire fulfillment disturbs the state of peace in a person and creates a sense of vacuum in life.

Dr. Viktor Frankl (1946) the founder of logotherapy, also coined a term in the same regards called 'Noogenic Neurosis', denoting a form of neurosis stemming from "existential frustration" or 'existential vacuum'. Noogenic neurosis in itself is not a psychopathology, but it may progress into psychopathology. Noogenic neurosis has a sociological origin arising out of consumerism and materialism which fails to satisfy core human need for meaning. This finally leads to noogenic depression and anxiety. Inner Self Integration theory stresses that the noogenic neurosis happens because a person does not appreciate the value of life, which can happen when there is awareness of death. Studies by Taylor, (1983) and Emmons, (2007) have found that people who have been confronted with life-threatening diseases report that their appreciation for life itself has increased. It was also that very grateful people have often gone through very difficult—if not life threatening-circumstances.

Only when one is aware of limited bodily existence, which means that death can happen any time and it has to finally happen, one can appreciate life. Frijda, (1988, 2007) stated that "because of the emotional law of habituation, we tend to become accustomed to beneficial situations that are relatively unchanging. Certainly, life itself is one of those benefits that we enjoy constantly (at least while we are alive), and thus we often fail to notice the basic advantages of life and may even take this benefit for granted. When one is confronted, however, with a situation where their life is in jeopardy, appreciation for this benefit may result because they have become more aware of what 'might not be' – which in this case is life itself. The study by Janoff-Bulman and Berger (2000) also argued that appreciation is simply the cognitive process of appraising something with increased value.

Studies by Cozzolino, (2006) and Cozzolino *et al.* (2004) add the concept that not all mortality salience induction result in undesirable consequences; death reflection has now been shown to increase intrinsic motivation, decrease greed, and increase gratitude. This concept of limited body existence can clearly be seen in the Hindu concepts of "*Kshana Bhangura*" or "*Nashwar*".

3. Compulsive Longing for Things/Expected Occurrence of Life

Inner Self Integration theory also states, that the compulsive longing for things (materials) and expectations of life, also obstructs the state of peace. Seligman and Maier (1967) also explained this as "The phenomenon of learned helplessness". Expectations lead to the obsession to success and finally results in anxiety and sadness. Studies have revealed that, if a child believes failure to be a result of his lack of ability or a result of external factors beyond his control, he is unlikely to persist in his efforts. On the other hand, if a child believes failure to be a result of his lack of motivation, he is likely to escalate his effort in an attempt to obtain the goal. Dweck and Reppucci, (1973) also studied that those children who are characterized as learned helpless tent to regard failure in the former way, while those who are characterized as persistent tend toward the latter view.

Inner Self Integration theory goes a step behind. The obsession of working towards a goal itself, is a cause of such a phenomenon of learned helplessness. Rationalizing failure as an outcome of lesser effort has come much later as a symptomatic therapy. Attributing life as a flow of events, helps in the development of peace much before. A person living such a life will be more peacefully living while acting on the goals at the same time, but does not feel the resistance within when the results of action are not as expected. Bell (1985) defined that disappointment is a psychological reaction to an outcome that does not match up against prior expectations. Basically, an individual disappointment is assumed to be indirect proportion to the difference between what (s) he expected and what (s) he got Van Dijk and Van der Pligt (1996).

4. Hurt Proneness of the Mind: 'Over Sentimentalism'

Most individuals experience the feeling of hurt. This feeling is so easy to come, because of so many factors. And it also disturbs the state of peace. Inner Self Integration theory promotes emotional intelligence. Salovey and Mayer (1990) conceptualized emotional intelligence as a mental ability consisting of three abilities, that is, "ability to monitor one's and others' feelings and emotions, to discriminate among them and to use this information to guide one's thinking and actions". Mostly people are unable to monitor feelings of their own and end up reacting accordingly, without having any control of their response, which further adds to their feeling of hurt.

Taylor, Bagby and Parker (1991) defined Alexithymia and stated that it comprises of four dimensions — (a) difficulty in identifying feelings and distinguishing between feelings and the bodily sensations of emotional arousal; (b) difficulty in describing feelings to others; (c) constricted imaginal processes; and (d) externally-oriented cognitive style. As per Costa and McCrae (1992) Neuroticism refers to the tendency of experiencing anger, anxiety sadness, guilt, embarrassment, and disgust Mayer and Salovey (1997) stated that a frequent experience of such emotional states could be probably attributed to the low emotion regulation ability skill that is considered as an important dimension of ability model of emotional intelligence.

Damasio (1999) stated that Emotions involve a series of internal changes that result in external actions that have balance proven advantageous for humans over the long sweep of evolutionary history. As per Gross (1998b, 2001, 2002) emotions are generated in a series of stages that include attending to a situation, giving it a balanced meaning, and producing a loosely coupled set of experiential, behavioural, and physiological responses.

5. Obsessive Thinking

Thinking is a function of mind. It is impossible to stop the thought process. Inner Self Integration theory suggests that thinking too much is an obstruction to the state of peace and hampers functionality. Also, it is important to identify, what is being thought. Thinking needs to be objective. However, a person may try stop thinking repeatedly, he/she will always think, till he/she is alive. Important is to be in Wilson, Dunn, Kraft, and Lisle (1989) and Millar and Tesser (1986a) suggested that analysing reasons is most likely to change attitudes that have a large affective component, because people are less likely to know the actual causes of these attitudes and analyzing reasons is likely to emphasize cognitions and obscure the affect (Millar & Tesser (1986a), the explanation.

Wilson (1990) Wilson, Dunn, Kraft and Lisle (1989) in their studies, have suggested that thinking about why we feel the way we do could change our attitudes. Still it is unclear whether the direction of this change is advantageous, negative, or neutral, Wilson et al. (1990) studied that analysing reasons reduces people's satisfaction with their choices, also they suggested that it may not always be a good idea to analyse the reason for our preferences too carefully. It is also not wise to analyse the effects of every attribute of every alternative. Evaluating multiple attributes may lead to non-optimal preferences.

6. Limited Sense of Control Over Life Events

People mostly live in an illusion that they have full control over situations and outcomes and their and other people's behaviours. Newton studied and concluded that the universe lived in an infinite and featureless space. There was no boundary, and no possibility of conceiving anything outside of it. Newton referred to the infinity of space was then a necessary reflection of the infinite possibilities of events. Einstein described the same concept through his new general theory of relatively that universe was finite, but closed, exactly like the surface of a globe that has finite area but no boundary. Hoyle an eminent scientist also stated the fact that carbon is essential for life, but why carbon is here. He had assumed that since there is a lot of carbon in the world it must somehow have been made in stars. In simple terms everything and every event in the universe is interdependent and inter-related. So, nobody can singularly take claim over any event in the universe. In psychology this is described as Multi-levelness which is a psychological equivalent to the theory of relativity. Multi-levelness analysis helps in understanding the fact that psychological frames relate relativistically. An individual projects self out from the centre, to the horizon, the functional perceptual limit of the boundary of the self. An individual is an integral part of others in particular of the whole in general.

In attribution theory (Kelly) it is stated that people tend to make to explain that cause of success or failure may be internal or external. People may succeed or fail because of factors that they believe have their origin within them or because of factors that originate in the environment. Also, the cause of the success or failure may be either stable or unstable. If the cause of success and failure is unstable, the outcome is likely to be different on another occasion. The most critical fact is that the cause of the success or failure may be either controllable or uncontrollable. The uncontrollable factors cannot be can easily altered.

Attribution theory (Weiner, 1980, 1992) suggests that people attribute their successes or failures to factors that will enable them to feel as good as possible about themselves. Weiner (1992) stated that when learners succeed at an academic task, they are likely to want to attribute this success to their own efforts or abilities; but when they fail, they will want to attribute their failure to factors over which they have no control, such as bad teaching or bad luck.

A major concept in the study of attribution theory is locus of control i.e. whether one interprets events as being caused by one's own behaviour or by outside circumstances. A person with an internal locus of control, an "internal,". Locus of control determines the degree to which an individual believes that he or she is in control of life events. Naila (2000) suggested that the term 'locus of control' refers to the sense that one can affect the course of one's life, also called "Can-ness". Julian Rotter was first psychologist who paid more attention to this issue of locus of control. Locus of control describes the degree to which individuals perceive that outcomes result from their own behaviours or from forces that are external to themselves.

Rotter (1966) states that locus of control can be generalized into a basic dichotomy: internal and external. Individuals with an internal locus of control believe that future outcomes depend primarily on personal actions, whereas individuals with an external locus of control ascribe actions of factors outside of their control, such as fate or chance. The balance needs to be arrived at. Inner Self Integration theory focuses more on the balance between the internal and the internal locus of control.

7. Purpose of Existence

Eminent figures in Psychology like Frankyl (1978), Klinger (1977), Ruffin (1984) and Tillich (1952) have identified that meaninglessness of life and of existence is a malifise of the present times. If it remains unresolved, this vacuum can lead to symptoms of anxiety, depression, hopelessness, or physical decline.

Frankyl's (1978) theory and his book on the search for meaning, or "Will to meaning" suggests that "Will to meaning" is not as primary need as a need for physical survival, yet it is very critical. Meaning here refers to making sense, order or coherence out of one's existence. The term 'purpose' refers to intention, some function to be fulfilled or goals to be achieved.

Buhler (1959), Erikson (1963) and Jung (1971) also stated that the perceived meaning and purpose in life play an important role in coping with development crisis. Erikson (1963) linked societal values with developmental tasks to be accomplished. Buhler (1959) described four developmental phases that emphasizes changes in goal setting. The early phases involve evaluation of the successes and failures in life and new directions for the course of life are contemplated. During the later phase integration become the primary goal. Jung (1971) observed that the meaning from the first half of life is examined from the "inner" part of life, by the processes of self reflection and reevaluation.

Positive feelings of mental and physical health are contributed to, by the meaning and purpose in life whereas lack of meaning and purpose predicts perceived psychological and physical discomforts. Shupe's (1985) also concluded that having a sense of control of one's life was a strong predictor of physical and psychological well-being.

Helping People Change

The following steps help people to change the course of their lives:

- The first task of the Inner Self Integration therapist is to help the client know clearly, the thoughts that lead to specific emotions and behaviours.
- The second task is to dwell the deeper unknown reasons behind such dysfunctional thoughts and behaviours. This involves uncovering of the relevant beliefs. The ABC format is invaluable here. Using an episode from the client's own recent experience, the therapist notes the 'C', then the 'A'. The client is asked to consider (as 'B'): 'What was I telling myself about 'A', to feel and behave the way I did at 'C'? As the client develops understanding of the nature of irrational thinking, this process of 'filling in the gap', will become easier. Such education may be achieved by reading, direct explanation, and by self-analysis with the therapist's help and as homework sessions.
- Teach the client how to dispute and change the irrational beliefs, replacing them with more rational alternatives. Again, education will aid this. The ABC format is extended to include 'D' (Disputing irrational beliefs), 'E' *(the new Effect the client wishes to achieve, i.e. new ways of feeling and behaving),* and 'F' *(Further Action for the client to take).*
- Help the client get into action. Action against irrational beliefs—for example, disputing the belief that disapproval is intolerable by deliberately doing something to attract it, then discovering that one survives, is an essential component of REBT. Its

emphasis on both rethinking and action makes it a powerful tool for change. Such activities are usually referred to as 'homework'.

The Seven Means of Life: The Main Task of Inner Self Integration Therapy

The aim of the Inner Self Integration therapy is to facilitate the client to deal with the seven interruptions. One part of the therapy includes psycho-educating the client on the antidotes of the seven interruptions to peace. The antidotes include making the client aware about seven means to peaceful life. They are as follows:

1. Awareness of true identity—Inner Self
2. Awareness of limited bodily existence
3. Relishing the existing abundance
4. State of Unimpactedness
5. Acting effortlessly
6. Enjoying life with complete experience.
7. Meaningful Existence

1. **Awareness of true identity:** It is the first means. Here the client will be taught to get in touch with ownself and understand—"Who is he/she"?. That is to say, that the client will be taught to sense the own identity *(here referred as 'Inner Self')* and while in connection with the 'Inner Self' try to evaluate his/her experiences throughout life.
2. **Awareness of limited body existence:** This means of Inner Self Integration theory unveils that one should have a knowledge and/or awakens of the morality of the body. According to Indian concept it is the "Kshana bhangurata" or "Nashwarata". It deals that human has a limited time and existence, but the soul is immortal. Therefore, we should try to develop our self and souls, not the body.
3. **Relishing existing abundance:** This notion deals with the concept of life satisfaction. We are living in such a world which is full of many privileges. Achieving all of them are impossible for a person. But people do not understand this and always try to get something more and are never satisfied with the existing conditions. This results in terms of depression, prostrations and failure. Through the process of Inner Self Integration, one can learn to live in existing munities and relish them.

4. **State of unimpactedness:** This notion leads to emotional balance/control and mediates the process of relishing existing abundance. Impactedness is the outcome of selectedness, deprivation and tendency to acquire everything, whether useful or not. Unimpactedness, leads to satisfaction and balance. It is partially related with the Indian concept of "*Aparigraha*", which is the virtue of non-possessiveness, non-grasping and non-greediness steming from being self-restraint.
5. **Acting Effortlessly:** It is unconditional desolation to the work. It means to say that without thinking pros and cans, if a person is engaged in any work. If a client will see the problem in such way, he/she can never be influenced by it.
6. **Enjoying life with complete experience:** This deals the fact that life cannot be evaluated. It is given by the God to us, it should be loved and valued

   All experiences should be enjoy perceived as facilitators and motivators for new learning.
7. **Meaningful experience:** The aim of meaningful experiences is to explore "good" from all experiences whether they are of any type. It deals the fact that a person should always be happy and seek positivity in each and every event. Following there seven means (Sapvidhi) therapist treats the client by:

The basic aims of the theory:

- The basic aim of Inner Self Integration is to leave clients at the completion of therapy, with freedom to choose their emotions, behaviours and lifestyle.
- Emotions are seen as dys-functional until they are accepted and understood. Inner-Self Integration aims at accepting (while not approving) the thoughts, emotions and behaviours so as to finally modify them as per the situation and personal capability.
- Inner Self Integration aims at borrowing techniques and strategies from other approaches and allows therapists to use their imagination.
- Inner Self Integration aims at facilitating the clients to learn and use the technique on their own. So, it is a collaborative and psycho-educative approach.
- Inner Self Integration aims to being brief so that the client gains functionality immediately, so, a minimum time is spent on acquiring historical information.

- Inner Self Integration aims to be task-oriented and focuses on problem-solving considering the present.

Psychological Significance of Inner Self Integration Theory

As it is apparent that the concept of self is highly regarded in the world of Psychology and many psychologists like Rogers and Kelly have deeply emphasized in this regard. In the process of the formation of this theory cum therapy an endeavour was made to correlate the experience of clients with psychological processes like, depression, anxiety and stress. We had a lot of data and it was not possible to correlate with psychological process. Therefore some important demographical variables were taken and 200 participants were taken in each study. The demographic variables were age, gender, marital status and employment status. It was not possible to compile all studies under one roof therefore, some sub studies were made. The basic aim of these studies, was to find out the relative impact of Inner Self Integration therapy on the psychological behaviour of client. For the implementation of this process a study programme was made in which three sub-studies had been taken. Their description is as follows:

Study I: The Inner Self Integration Therapy as a Facilitator of Depression in Adolescents

The aim of this study was to find out the impact of Inner Self Integration exercises on the participants having severe depression. It was confined that the exercises based on Inner Self Integration would reduce the magnitude of depression. Two hundred participants of the age range 18-26 years were studied. They had many adjustment problems and they were suffering from depression as well. Findings were analysed by 3 way analysis of variance and it was found that age $(F, 1, 199=5.91\ P<.01)$ and gender $(F, 1, 199=4.76\ P<.05)$ yielded their impact revealing the fact that variation in age and gender caused variation in the magnitude of depression. Moreover, it was noted that variation in therapeutic exercises also caused variation $(F, 1, 199=6.68\ P<.01)$ in the magnitude of depression.

The ages x gender $(F, 1, 199=6.59\ P<.01)$ interaction was significant and it was followed by significant age and therapeutic conditions interaction $(F, 1, 199=5.78\ P<.01)$. The age and therapeutic interaction was also significant $(F, 1, 199=5.78\ P<.01)$. It was also followed by the three way interaction of age, gender and therapeutic exercise $(F, 1,$

199=5.19 P<.01), which showed that all variables laid their impact on depression.

Study II: Impact of Age, Marital Status and Inner Self Integration Exercises on Anxiety

This piece of work deals with the annoyance of married people and explains their pre- and post-therapeutic status of anxiety as a function of their age. People of various age groups were studied but only two age groups namely, 25-35 and 45-60 years were taken and they were arranged according to the requirements of 4 way factors design *(with repeated measure on the last factor)* with two age levels *(25-30 and 45-60 years)*, two marital status (married and unmarried), two gender *(male and female)* and two types of therapeutic condition *(pre-therapeutic condition and post-therapeutics condition)*, i.e. 15 participants per cell. There were 120 participants in total, but, they were presented as 240 for therapeutic conditions because each participant was tested twice. Four way analysis of variance revealed that the difference between the magnitude of anxiety *(F, 1, 119= 5.99 P<.01)* showing high anxiety in old age group than their younger participants. The next main effect showed that married participants were in more anxiety than unmarried participants *(F, 1,119=6.01 P<.01)*. The main effect of gender was also significant *(F, 1,119=4.11 P<.01)*. The fourth main effect of therapeutic conditions was also significant (*F, 1,239=4.86 P<.05)* and it was noted that the magnitude of anxiety decreased after therapeutic exercises.

The two way interaction of age and gender was significant *(F,1,119=5.01 P<.01)*. It was followed by the interaction of age and marital status *(F,1,119=6.61 P<.01)* and age therapeutic conditions *(F,1,239=5.11 P<.01)*.

The gender and marital interaction was also significant *(F,1,119=4.71 P<.01)*. It was also followed by the interaction of gender and therapeutic conditions *(F,1,239=5.48 P<.01)*. The marital status and therapeutic conditions interaction was also significant *(F,1,239=5.94 P<.01)*.

The three way interactions of age, marital status and gender was significant (*F,1,119=6.64 P<.01)*. It was followed by the interactions among age, marital status and therapeutic conditions *(F,1,239=5.90 P<.01)*. The age, gender therapeutic condition interaction was also significant *(F,1,239=6.61 P<.01)* and it was followed by the interaction of age, gender and therapeutic conditions *(F,1,239=6.67 P<.01)* and gender, marital status and therapeutic conditions *(F,1,239=6.98 P<.01)*.

The four way interaction of age, gender, mental status and therapeutic condition was significant *(F,1,399=8.72 P<.01)* and it showed that all variables laid their impact on anxiety.

Study III: A Study of Stress as Affected by Age, Gender and Therapeutic Conditions in Adolescents

The aim of this study was to find out the pattern of stress in adolescents as affected by their age, gender and therapeutic condition. The participants, taken in study one were taken and the measure of stress was administered on them. Data were analyzed by three way analysis of variance with repeated measure on the last factor and it was found that the main effect of age was significant *(F,1,119=6.12 P<.01)*. The next main of gender was also significance *(F,1, 119=5.19 P<.01)*. The third main effect of therapeutic conditions was significant *(F,1,239=5.41 P<.01)*.

The two way interaction of age and gender was significant *(F, 1, 199=4.48 P<.05)*. The age and therapeutic conditions significant interaction was significant *(F, 1, 239=4.06 P<.05)*. It was also followed by gender and therapeutic condition which was highly significant *(F, 1, 239=4.86 P<.05)*.

The three way interaction of age, gender and testing condition was also significant *(F, 1, 239=6.74 P<.01)* and it revealed the tact that all variables laid their impact on the magnitude of the stress of the participants.

Psychological Justification of Inner Self Integration Theory

Hjelli and Ziegler (1987) have proposed nine assumptions on the basis of which they have evaluated so many theories of personality. Their assumptions assess one's nature and place him/her at an extent on the particular assumption.

Each assumptions is depicted as continuum with a pole or an extreme position at its opposite end. As the theory of Inner Self Integration is directly linked with the personality of people. So, an attempt has been made here to justify this on the basis of the following assumption:

1. **Freedom-Determinism:** One of the most basic question is that—"Up to what extent is a person is internally true and able to implement his/her internal feeling in action. In other words, we can say that whether a person actually possesses direction and

control in his/her daily behaviour *(freedom)*. His/her behaviour is directly controlled by the external environmental factors is called 'Determinism'. In this regard we can say, that the Inner Self Integrations theory is highly able to provide strength in a person to organize and control his/her behaviour according to his/her own willingness because once a person goes through this theory cum therapy practice, he/she becomes capable (after regular exercise and winning the hazards of life) and act on the basis of his/her 'Inner Self'.

2. **Rationally-irrationality:** The basic issue underlying the rationality-irrationality dimension, is the degree to which the reasoning powers are capable of influencing our every day behaviour. It means to say that "Are humans directed by their primary and pure rational thoughts or they are directly governed by secondary and impure irrational thoughts. In this course, it can be claimed that the Inner Self Integration theory is purely rational, because when a person *(after going through the therapeutic process)* meets his/her personal as well as external circumstances, he/she uses his/her rationality and intellectual thoughts to get over the negative circumstances. Therefore, it is right to say that rationality has paramount impact in human behaviour.
3. **Holism-Elementalism:** The holistic assumption is that human nature is such that behaviour can be explained only by studying person in totality. Elementalism deals that human nature in such that behaviour can be explained only by investigating each specific, fundamental aspect of it independent of the rest. The Inner Self Integration theory is holistic in the some way, that it motives a person to study the complete situation at first, before acting on it.
4. **Constitutionalism-Environmentalism:** Constitutionalism refers to seeing human nature more as a product of internal physical forces than external environmental agents. Environmental forces deal with the importance of external forces in order to shape the behaviour. The Inner Self Integration theory is purely constitutional because it deals with internal forces and motivations.
5. **Changeability-unchangeability:** The basic issue involved in this assumption is that the degree to which an individual sees himself/herself as capable of fundamental change throughout

the life. It is a basic step of human evolution. Contrarily, the unchangeability deals with the conformation or sometimes rigid nature of the individual. It is true that change is the law of nature and it helps a person to deal with the environmental demands and actualize the inherited potentials. This theory of Inner Self Integrations is highly changeable because it helps people to retrospect their life and make a change in their action, behaviour and thought.

6. **Subjectivity-objectivity:** Do human beings live in a high personal, subjective world of experience that lays a major influence on the behaviour ? Or the human integration theory can better be explained by following the path of subjectively. The inner world of the individual appears to have more significant influence upon his behaviour than does the external environmental stimuli.
7. **Proactivity-Retroactivity:** The proactivity – retroactivity issue is essentially concerned with focus of causality in exploring human behaviour, i.e., When are the real causes of human actions to be found? The concept of proactively leads the fact that human beings act rather than react. Maslow (1961) has stated that "Man has his future within him. He is dynamically active at this present movement". On the other hand, reactive react for the external environment. He believes in stimulus-response and/or behaviour-environment relationship.

   The Inner Self Integration theory is proactive in structure because people generate their own behaviour internally.
8. **Homeostasis–Heterostasis:** This dimension is purely and fundamentally concerned with human motivation. Individual are motivated primarily and maintain their inner state of equilibrium *(Homeostasis).* The other pole deals with goal direction. Stimulus seeking and self-actualization (*Heterostasis*). The Inner Self Integration theory leads the homeostasis aspects and it helps a person to maintain the state of equilibrium.
9. **Knowability–Unknowability:** This dimension of Know ability-Unknowability deals with the concepts of determines–objectivity ie, an inner knowledge and awareness and objective knowledge of external world. The Inner Self Integration theory is knowable because it deals with the knowledge of one's internal world.

The Application of Inner Self Integration Therapy

Inner Self Integration therapy is being successfully used in psycho-traumatic perspective and has already been testes upon many set of participants. This therapy is efficient in curing the client of temporal depression, chronic depression, Anxiety, phobia in particular and in general and post-traumatic stress. It also deals with the management of anger, pain and general stress management. So, many attempts have been made to deal with the academic, personal and familial problems and we got lots of success. Therefore, it is suitable for these problems also. Some reports have made is terms of research papers and it has been clearly described earlier.

R & D Effect: As already been stated that there are several dimensions and aspects of Inner Self Integration. These theories have been analysed here and their practical implication have also been discussed. Not only this chapter assimilates the concept of self and related concepts, but also they are discussed as the facilitator of Inner Self in particular and positive mental health in general. The concepts are well and they deal the structure and function of Inner Self Integration. Moreover, therapeutic perspective is also discussed and surely they are beneficial for society. Therefore, it is surely fair to say that the significance of Inner Self Integration in theory while therapeutic perspective cannot be denied.

References

Bell, D.E. (1985). Disappointment in decision-making under uncertainty. *Operations Research*. 30, 961-981

Buhler, C. (1959). Theoritical observations about life's basic tendencies. *American Journal of Psychotherapy, 13,* 561-581.

Costa, P.T., and McCrae, R.R. (1992). Revised NEO Personality Inventory (NEO PI-R) and NEO Five Factor Inventory (NEO-FFI): Professional Manual. Odessa, F.L.: Psychological Assessment Resources, Inc.

Cozzolino, P.J. (2006). Death contemplation, growth, and defense: Converging evidence of dual-existential systems? *Psychological Inquiry*, 17, 278–287.

Cozzolino, P.H., Staples, A.D., Meyers, L.S., and Samboceti, J. (2004). Greed, death, and values: From terror management to "transcendence management" theory. *Personality and Social Psychology Bulletin*, 30, 278–292.

Damasio AR. 1999. The feeling of what happens: Body and emotion in the making of consciousness. New York: Harcourt Brace.

Dweck, C.S., and Reppucci, N.D. (1973). Learned helplessness and reinforcement responsibility in children. *Journal of Personality and Social Psychology*, 25, 109-116.

Emmons, R.A. (2007). Thanks!: How the new science of gratitude can make you happier. New York: Houghton Mifflin.

Erikson, E.H. (1963), *Childhood and Society*, Norton, New York.

Frankyl, V.E. (1978). The unheard cry for meaning: *Psychotherapy and Humanism*, Simon & Schuster, New York.

Frijda, N. (1988). The laws of emotion. *American Psychologist*, 43, 349–358.

Frijda, N. (2007). The laws of emotion. Mahwah, NJ: Lawrence Erlbaum.

Gross, J.J. (1998b). Antecedent- and Response-focused emotion regulation: divergent consequences for experience, expression and physiology. *J. Personal. Soc. Psychol.* 74:224-37.

Heider, F. (1958). *The Psychology of Interpersonal Relations*. New York: John Wiley and Sons. ISBN 0-471-36833-4. Retrieved March 14, 2009, from en.wikipedia.org/wiki/Attribution_theory

Janoff-Bulman, R., and Berger, A.R. (2000). The other side of trauma: Towards a psychology of appreciation. In J.H.

Jung, C.G. (1971). *The Stages of Life*. In J. Campbell, The Portable Jung, Viking Press, New York.

Khurana, K. and Shukla, A. (2016). Thinking about inner self integration Personal Communication.

Khurana, K. and Shukla, A. The Inner self integration therapy as a facilitators of depression in adolescents, *Paper in preparation.*

Khurna, K. and Shukla, A, Impact of age, marital status and inner self integration exercise on anxiety. *Paper in Preparation.*

Khurana, K. and Shukla, A., A study of stress as affected by age, gender and therapeutic conditions in adolescents. *Paper in Preparation.*

Klinger, E. (1977). *Meaning and Void*. University of Minnesota Press, Minneapolis.

Maddi, S.R. (1970). The search for meaning, *Nebrasska Symposium on Motivation*, 134-183.

Marsh, H. W., and Seeshing, A. (1997). Causal effects of academic self-concept on academic achievement: Structural equation of longitudinal data. *Journal of Educational Psychology, 86,* 439-456.

Mayer, J.D., Salavey, P. (1993). The intelligence of emotional intelligence *Intelligence*, 17, 433-442.

Millar, M.G., Tesser, A. (1986a), Effects of affective and cognitive focus on the attitude behaviour relationship. *Journal of Personality and Social Psychology*. 51. 270-276.

Rotter, J. B. (1966). Generalized expectancies for internal versus external control of reinforcement. Psychological Monographs, 80, (1 Whole No. 609). Retrieved April 24, 2007, from www.questia.com/PM.qst?a=o&se=gglsc&d=5000224082

Ruffin, J.E. (1984). The anxiety of meaninglessness, *Journal of Counseiing and Development*, 63, 40-42.

Seligman, M., and Maier, S. (1967). Failure to escape traumatic shock. *Journal of Experimental Psychology*, 74, 1-9.

Shupe, D.R. (1985). Perceived control, helplessness and choice. In J.E. Birren and Livingston (Eds). *Cognition, Stress, and Aging* (pp. 174-199), Prentice Hall, Englewood Cliffs.

Taylor, S.E. (1973). Adjustment to threatening events: A theory of cognitive adaptation. *American Psychologist*, 38, 1161-1173.

Taylor, G.J., Bagby, R.M., and Parker, J.D.A. (1997). *Disorders of affect regulation: Alexithymia in Medical and Psychiatric Illness*. Cambridge, England: Cambridge University Press.

Tillich, P. (1952). The courage to be. Yale University Press, New Haven, CT.

Van Dijk, W.W., van der Pligt, J., and Zeelenberg, M., (1999). Effort invested in vain: The impact on effort on the intensity of disappointment and regret. *Motivation and Emotion*. 23, 203-220.

Weiner, B. (1992). An attributional theory of emotion and motivation, New York: Springer-Verlag. Retiieved Dec 12, 2009, from http://education.calumet.purdue.edu/vockell/EdpsyBook/Edpsy5/edpsy5_attribution.htm

Wilson, T.D. (1990), Self-persuasion *vs* self-reflection. In J.M. Olson and M.P. Zanna (Eds). *Self inference processes: The Ontario symposium* (Vol. 6. pp. 43-67). Hillsdale, NJ: Erlbaum.

Wilson, T.D., Dunn, D.S., Kraft, D., Lisle, D.J. (1989). Introspection, attitude change, and attitude behaviour consistencey: The disruptive effects of explaining why we feel the way we do. In L. Berkowitz (Ed). *Advances in Experimental Social Psychology* (Vol. 19, pp. 123-205). San Diego, CA: Academic Press.

17

Review on "The Dialectical Behavioural Therapy (DBT) with Mindfulness Technique for the Prevention of the Suicide and its Applicability in Nepali Context"

Yubaraj Adhikari

Introduction

Befrienders Worldwide (2015) outlined that over one million people die globally by suicide every year. Nepal does not go far from this burden. The overall figures says that 6840 people die by suicide annually, which is 24·90 suicides per 1,00,000 people (Cousins, 2016). Nepal lacks a systematic data collection and there is not yet any prevalence study on suicide in Nepal (Pradhan, Poudel, Thomas and Barnett, 2011), however, WHO claimed that Nepal has second highest suicide per capita in south Asia (WHO, 2014). Women from reproductive age were found severely affected, with 16 per cent of the total death toll (leading cause of death), due to various socio-cultural and economic factors (Simkhada, Van Teijlingen, Winter, Fanning, Dhungel and Marahatta, 2015; Pradhan, Poudel, Thomas & Barnett, 2011). Children are suffered a lot due to the loss of their mothers. Nepal equally lacks systematic dealing with the suicide problem (Pradhan, Poudel, Thomas & Barnett, 2011).

Studies explored that clinical interventions have limited outcomes on reducing the suicide burden (Yip, 2015). However, community driven mindfulness based cognitive behavioural therapy and dialectical behaviour therapy (DBT) have demonstrated effectiveness to prevent the suicide (Williams, Duggan, Crane & Fennell, 2006, Stanley, Brodsky, Nelson & Dulit, 2007; Klonsky & Muehlenkamp, 2007). The DBT has developed and tested the concept for the survivors of self-harm or the people with a rigorous desire of self-injuries (Linehan, 1987). The DBT also found effective to maintain the treatment outcomes and higher retention rates as compared to alternative treatments (Yip & Law, 2010). Nevertheless, DBT has yet explored and used in few cultures and mainly with the client's suicidal thoughts diagnosed with borderline personality disorders. DBT has not been exclusively implemented in diverse populations across the culture, though the inclusion of DBT with various CBT techniques including mindfulness and acceptance-based treatments has proved as evidence-based approach for suicide prevention (Le & Gobert, 2013; Ward-Ciesielski, 2013). DBT, though its partial roots were found in eastern cultures (Boehnlein, 2006), have been not widely implemented, tested and applied in low and middle-income countries (LMIC) for the suicide prevention (Aggarwal & Berk, 2015) as it has been done in the West. The religious and cultural factors in relation to the suicide were also found correlated (Bertolote & Fleischmann, 2002), therefore, contextual adaptation and culturally blend DBT not only remained a challenge but equally provide an opportunity to explore and prevent the suicide burden. Nevertheless, few efforts for the contextualization and application of the DBT with the Nepali-speaking Bhutanese refugees and small groups of women with suicidal ideation from remote areas of Nepal has initiated (Robkin, 2012; Kohrt, Maharjan, Timsina & Griffith, 2012; Ramaiya, 2015).

This study aims to understand the applicability, adaptation and use of the DBT and mindfulness techniques to the Nepali women, which face severe mental health complications and suicide burden. Despite few literatures available in this topic, this analysis will open an avenue to revisit the efforts of contextualization and paves a way forward while applying and adapting the DBT techniques in to the Nepali women living in remote locations. This review hypothesized that "DBT along with mindfulness techniques are applicable with Nepali women population to mitigate the impact of suicide with contextual and cultural adaptations".

Method

The chosen method for this work follows a systematic review through applying aqualitative understanding of the adaptation process and utilization of the DBT and mindfulness techniques in Nepali context. A review of the literature allows summarizing available literature on the subject matter with a specific focus on strengths and limitations of the practice sand equally allows developing new insights while applying into the practice (Cook & West, 2012). A descriptive review focuses on the qualitative process related outcomes rather than a quantitative analysis and is emphasized by a systematic review (Pautasso, 2013). DBT and mindfulness techniques in relation to the suicide prevention in Nepalese and south Asian contexts outside of the personality disorder do have limited resources to carry out a systematic quantitative analysis of efficacy and effectiveness of DBT in wide ranges of Nepali populations. This review focuses more on process of adaptation and use of the DBT and mindfulness to the cultural context. Nevertheless, effectiveness and efficacy of the DBT to wider populations across the globe remained a systematic analysis in the literature review section.

Procedure

The procedure applied for the search and selection of the published and unpublished resources, which were focused on population, intervention, comparison with other approaches and outcomes of the interventions (Cook & West, 2012). Furthermore, process and methods on the adaptations were reviewed to accelerate future use of the similar tools and techniques across the culture.

The search criteria of the resources followed mainly published scientific journals, reports of the credible health institutions, dissertations used for the academic purposes, and media reports for the prevalence of the mental health difficulties such as depression and suicide across the populations. During the search process, keywords 'Dialectical Behavioural Therapy', 'Mindfulness', 'Depression', 'Suicide', 'Suicide Prevention', 'women', 'Asia', 'South Asia' and 'Nepal' were used for the initial search. The search process was further reduced after reviewing the abstract and keywords of the articles. The resources for this review were mainly based on the freely available online resources with the keywords and abstract on the subject matter, which includes, Google scholar, the university of Liverpool online library, PubMed, PMC, researchgate, and science direct. Out of the available resources, the use of DBT with mindfulness techniques were found mostly applied in Western contexts with the populations diagnosed with personalitydisorders. Only a few resources in relation to the cross-cultural adaptations of the DBT were outlined which are described in detail in the literature review section. The available literature has explored the possibility for future research and implementation of the tools with a limited scope of generalizability across the population due to unavailability of literatures with the controlled trials or clinical interventions with efficacious results in low and middle-income countries. The inclusion criteria include the "DBT, women, suicide and suicide prevention" as keywords in the abstract sections. Whereas, keywords only including "depression, women and mindfulness" or 'DBT', 'Depression' and 'women' were excluded from the analysis.

Results and Discussion

Depression and Suicide—A Global Issue

World Health Organization (WHO)'s recent report on global health outlines that the mental disorders along with the dementias cover 6.2 per cent of the global disease burden as calculated through the disability-adjusted life year (DALY). Most importantly, approximately 45 per cent of the burden in terms of years life lived with disability (YLD) comes from the mental disorders where neurotic difficulties mainly anxiety and depression among the economically active age (16-59) people have a significant impact (WHO, 2015). Prince and associates (2007) believed that the burden of death and disability might be higher than the projected as suicide has been categorized as an intentional injury rather than a mental health issue. Maternal depression especially in low income countries not only affects the mother but equally hampers the both physical and psychological health of the children due to inadequate care, malnutrition and incomplete or no immunizations (Parsons, Young, Rochat, Kringelbach & Stein, 2012). The burden of depression and suicide are directly associated with the economic situation, gender role and familial factors (Qin, Agerbo & Mortensen, 2003). Prince *et al.* (2007) highlighted that the mental health burden of mothers, mainly due to depression, has widely affected the overall development of the children that ultimately affects the psychological and mental health situation of the children when they grow older. WHO (2015) outlined that the substance abuse has become now a mental health burden, which not only carries the burden of depression and deliberate self-harm but equally impacts the situation of intimate partner violence and domestic violence (Ellsberg, Jansen, Heise, Watts & Garcia-Moreno, 2008; Tolman & Rosen, 2001). The effect of domestic violence is directly associated with the depression and suicide of the women particularly in low and middle-income countries (Devries *et al.*, 2011). The male suicide rate is found three times higher than female due to unavailability to express emotions, loss of income or employment and maladaptive coping behaviours including substance abuse in high-income countries (Möller-Leimkühler, 2003; Vijayakumar, John, Pirkis & Whiteford, 2005). Economic crisis, unemployment, and scarcity of job remained a key factor for depression and suicide not only in high income countries but the economic migration equallyimpacted the burden in low-income countries (Chang, Stuckler, Yip & Gunnell, 2013; Uutela, 2010; Reeves, Stuckler, McKee, Gunnell, Chang & Basu, 2012; Otsu, Araki, Sakai, Yokoyama & Voorhees, 2004; Missinne & Bracke, 2012).

The ratio of male to female is low in low and middle-income countries (WHO, 2015). Sexual minorities, LGBTI, people with chronic illnesses and people with HIV/AIDS have more suicidal thoughts (Manetta & Cox, 2014; Juurlink, Herrmann, Szalai, Kopp & Redelmeier, 2004). Suicide attempt and depression among the women and children with HIV/AIDS were found extremely high (Cooperman & Simoni, 2005); however, it was found equally prevalent among the pregnant women populations who were equally prone to the Human Immuno-deficiency Virus (HIV; Rochat, Bland, Tomlinson, & Stein, 2013). Old age people are not only prone to depression and suicide due to economic vulnerabilities and poor health conditions co-morbid with chronic illnesses; the population of old age people with depression will be doubled by 2030, which further worsen the situations in low and middle-income countries (Reynolds III *et al.*, 2012). People with mental disorders have twice the rate of premature deaths as compared with the people without any mental disorder; where, over 1.8 per cent global death are by suicide yearly (Suicide.org, 2015). The unavailability of effective treatment of depression in low and middle-income countries could not reduce the suicide burden as compared to the high-income countries. Two third people with depression lack treatment facility in low and middle-income countries (WHO, 2015). The main cause of treatment gap is not only an evidence-based practice and cultural adaptation of treatment and lack of access to a treatment facility, but equally an unavailability of trained human resources in low and middle-income countries (Bruckner *et al.*, 2011).

Depression and Suicide in South Asia

Depression is generally viewed as a widely predictable problem in the south Asian population, which generally comes through real life problems such as family conflict, intra-family disputes, marital complications, loneliness, loss of bread earner and economic loss due to various unpredictable life situations. South Asian people generally conceptualize loneliness, hopelessness, and helplessness related difficulties in social terms and do not seek medical help as the people in Western communities do. Therefore, depression is not seen as a medical concern and prevalence of depression is not widely studied (Karasz, Patel, Kabita & Shimu, 2013). Prevalence of depression in three major cities of Pakistan was found 46 per cent across the population in community sample; whereas, the sample of an outpatient psychiatric clinic in the cities were equally 47 per cent of cases of depression. The figures of Pakistan shows that depression is a general phenomenon across the population but understudied. In India, a large study covering more than 24,000 sample in south Indian state with a comparison of the prevalence rate in rural and urban setting revealed that the prevalence of depression is 15.9 per cent of the population (Poongothai, Pradeepa, Ganesan & Mohan, 2009). As Indian urban population is emerging, the prevalence of depression among the urban centres with outpatient psychiatric facilities is even more than 20 per cent of the total population (Nambi, Prasad, Singh, Abraham, Kuruvilla & Jacob, 2002; Pattanayak & Sagar, 2014). Economically and socially unprivileged strata of the population; and elderly and women from reproductive age were found more depressed as compared to the other strata of the population in India (Grover, Dutt & Avasthi, 2010).

In Bangladesh, a recent review of Newman (2013) outlined that 6.6 per cent to 97 per cent of the people depending upon the various sub-target population and strata have been found affected by the depression. Despite a collective and nationwide study, the actual prevalence could not define, nevertheless, people affected by violence, poverty, inequality and socially marginalized including women, elderly and adolescents were found highly affected. Depression is found highly co-morbid with chronic illness among the Bangladeshi population and highly affected the women and elderly (Mohit, Maruf, Ahmed & Alam, 2011). Due to the prolonged civil war and debilitating consequences of the natural disaster in Sri Lanka, the prevalence of depression and PTSD was found common among the general population. A study of Catani, Jacob, Schauer, Kohila & Neuner (2008) in a northern province of Sri Lanka outlined 19.6 per cent depression among the children. In another study at Colombo district, the prevalence of depression was found 10.6 per cent in men and 14.9 per cent of the female population (Ball, Siribaddana, Kovas, Glozier,

McGuffin, Sumathipala & Hotopf, 2010). Perera, Torabi, Jayawardana & Pallethanna (2006) explored 57.7 per cent of adolescents were found depressed in their study. A national survey on depression on old age people outlined that 24.0 per cent old male and 30.8 per cent old aged female were found above the threshold of depression symptoms (Ball, Siribaddana, Kovas, Glozier, McGuffin, Sumathipala & Hotopf, 2010). Conclusively, the depression burden in Sri Lanka is equally high and women, adolescents and elderly were among the largely suffered; in which war, natural disaster and increasing violence within the family remained major factors (Catani, Jacob, Schauer, Kohila & Neuner, 2008). In Bhutan, except the Bhutanese refugees, the prevalence of depression is 9.2 per cent among the adults (Pelzanga, 2012). The burden of depression and suicide among the Bhutanese refugees resettled in the US was found alarming, where 16 people committed suicide within three years of their stay in the US. 67 cases of suicide and 64 cases of suicide attempt were recorded in the refugee camp of Nepal from 2004 to 2010 (Ao, Taylor, Lankau, Sivilli, Blanton, Shetty & Lopes-Cardozo, 2012). The overall depression prevalence among the Bhutanese refugees was 16 per cent among the male and 26 per cent among the female (Vonnahme, Lankau, Ao, Shetty & Cardozo, 2015).

The prevalence of depression and suicide among the Bhutanese refugees found higher than the Nepali population and their counterpart US population where the refugees were resettled (Hagaman, Sivilli, Ao, Blanton, Ellis, Cardozo & Shetty, 2016). Prevalence of depression and suicide study is found limited in Afghanistan. A national representative survey on Mental Health, Social Functioning, and Disability with 799 adult in: household members (699 non-disabled and 100 disabled respondents) in 2004 revealed that 67.7 per cent ($p=.05$) respondents were found with above the cut-off of depression symptoms followed by the co-morbidity of PTSD. Women were found extremely suffered as compared to the male (Cardozo *et al.,* 2004). A separate study equally highlighted the higher prevalence of depression and PTSD among the Afghanistan people in post-war situations, where, 38 per cent respondents were revealed with high level of depression co-morbid with the anxiety and the PTSD (Scholte *et al.*, 2004). Over the years, hopefully due to the war on terror on Afghanistan, recent studies were only found focused on the military and veterans deployed in Afghanistan with limited interventions and research on the mental health and depression study. Not only the people living in south Asia, the migrant population from south Asia to developed countries were equally outlined with higher level of depression and suicide associated with the depression (Ratkowska & De Leo, 2013). In the UK, South Asian women were three times higher affected by the depression and suicide (Ineichen, 2008), where the causes of depression are family disputes, acculturation and adjustment difficulties and high expectations from the women by their family members (Hicks & Bhugra, 2003; Baldwin & Griffiths, 2009). Arrange marriages, marital conflicts, in-laws pressure and higher workloads at homes apart from the workplaces as compared to the men are additional factors (Bhugra & Gupta, 2010). South Asian women are perceived as 'bearers of blame' as cited the work of (Bhugra & Gupta, 2004) by Ineichen (2008).

The migrant workers' situation in the gulf from the south Asia is equally found terrible. The rates of suicide and prevalence of mental illnesses including depression among the migrant workers have been reported and studied extremely high. In Dubai only, one case of suicide is reported in every four days among the Asian migrant workers, out of which majority come from south Asia (Adhikary, Keen & Van Teijlingen, 2011). In a separate study, Al-Maskari and associates (2011) revealed that 25.1 per cent of the migrant workers (N=239) were above the cut-off of the depression score, out of which, 6.3 per cent reported recurrent suicidal ideation and 2.5 per cent attempted suicide. Suicide in south Asia, not only limited to depression but in relation to the causes of depression such as poverty, inequality, gender role, maternal depression, substance abuse, political violence, conflict natural disaster, migration of males and many more, has been increased across the continent (Manoranjitham, Rajkumar, Thangadurai, Prasad, Jayakaran & Jacob, 2010; Gajalakshmi & Peto, 2007; Jordans, Kaufman, Brenman, Adhikari, Luitel, Tol & Komproe, 2014, Patel, Rahman, Jacob & Hughes, 2004; Ball *et al.*, 2010; Selim, 2010). A recent review by Jordans and colleagues (2014) on suicide in south Asia outlined that south Asian rates of suicide are studied higher as compared to the word average. The review included, 114 different studies (84% published literature) comprising the findings from six countries (Afghanistan, Pakistan, Sri Lanka, India, Nepal, and Bangladesh) and explored that the average suicide rate is 25.2 (SD =28.60) per 1,00,000 persons; which is more than double of the global average suicide rate (11.2 per 1,00,000 in 2012) (World Health Organization, 2014). Nevertheless, the figure does not account the official reported suicide rates because most of the countries in south Asia do not have systematic tracking of suicide related deaths and incidences (Jordans *et al.*, 2014).

Depression and Suicide in Nepal

Depression in Nepal equally perceived as large public health burden. The Director of National Mental Health outlined that "people suffering from severe depression and mental illness can be a major cause of suicide if people of ten ignored and depreciated" (Xinhuanet, 2012). In post-conflict and political unstable situation, the prevalence of depression in Nepal has been increased from 30.9 to 40.6 per cent (Kohrt *et al.*, 2012). The ethnic minorities and women from low socio-economic class have been examined the most suffer. Among the population heavily affected by depression, the women from reproductive age and following the post-partum period are worst affected. Women living in rural areas with low caste representation are further at risk of the depression. A study from a remote village in Nepal revealed that 42.2 per cent respondent were found with high level of depression out of the 326 studied (Kohrt, *et al.*, 2009). The situation of pregnant women is even distressing, Shakya, Sitaula & Shyangwa (2008) revealed that out of the surveyed pregnant women during their hospital visit, 50 per cent did have some form of depression (N=44). Giri, Khatri, Mishra, Khanal, Sharma & Gartoula (2015) explored that 30 per cent post-partum mothers face the burden of depression. In another study, the depression among the post-partum women was ranging from 19.4 to 22.22 between the 6th week and 10th week of the delivery period; where bad communication with husband, intra-family dispute, and violence of intimate partners was studied mainly related to the increment of the depression (Budhathoki, Bhusal, Ojha & Basnet, 2013). Prevalence of depression among the psychiatric patients was found nearly 16 per cent (N=240)(Banerjee, Roy, Banerjee, Sathian, Mondal & Saha, 2011). High level of monthly income (USD 1000 per month) and diagnosis of type-2 diabetes mellitus were found highly correlated with the depression in urban centres of Nepal. 40.3 per cent prevalence of depression with type-2 diabetes and without a prior history of mental illnesses respondents (N = 365) were studied in Kathmandu valley. In a separate study, 54 per cent patients of diabetics were observed above the cut off score of depression (Mishra, Sharma, Bhandari, Bhochhibhoya & Thapa, 2015). People with older age have also a high level of depression in Nepal. A study among the Old age Rai population, the prevalence of depression was found 29.7 per cent (N=165). A separate study in hospital care setting outiined that 52.2 per cent (N=100) old aged patients were diagnosed with depression, out of which 83.3 per cent patients were explored with high level of depression in both the measuring scales (Geriatric Depression

Scale (GDS-30 items) and ICD-10 Classification of Mental and Behavioural Disorders—Diagnostic Criteria for Research (ICD-10 DCR) (Khattri, 2006). A comparative study of the elderly living in old-age homes and community settings outlined that the prevalence of depression in old age centres is more than two times higher as compared with their community-dwelling counterparts. 52.7 per cent (N=44) of old age people in residential care were found depressed as compared to 25.43 per cent (N=44) of old age people living in community settings (Ghimire, Pokharel, Shyangwa, Baral, Aryal & Mishra, 2012). The cause of the high level of depression among the elderly was revealed to be associated with chronic illness, lack of financial security, worries about the future, insecurity of care, and dissatisfaction with their living environment (Timalsina, R., Sherpa, P.D., & Dhakal, 2014). The effect of ten-years long (1996-2006) war has affected the mental health and psychological situations of the women and children. In an internal survey of International Committee of the Red Cross to respond the needs of the wives of disappeared persons in rural areas of Bardiya district in 2010 explored that 43 per cent wives (N=263) were facing a moderate and severe level of depression co-morbid with 37 per cent anxiety. The study had included 80 per cent of Tharu women who were among the highest worst affected by the disappearance, sexual violence, and torture during the conflict. A separate study outlined 27.5 per cent (N=720 adults) of the prevalence of depression among the war survivors; however, the differences between women and men having depression was found large (Women= 33.1 per cent and Male: 21.5%). Both the studies explore that the mental health and depression impact among the women is large among the Nepali post-conflict survivors.

Children's mental health situation and prevalence study on depression in Nepal are rare. A compared study on the prevalence of depression among the children associated with armed conflict and armed forces with the community children outlined that the prevalence of depression among the child soldier was 53.2 per cent (N=141) as compared 24.1 per cent (N=141) to non-associated children with armed forces and armed groups (Kohrt *et al.,* 2008). Mental health and depression impact of the mega Earthquake 2015 has yet to be studied, nevertheless, some studies have indicated the increased case loads of depression among the earthquake survivors in Nepal (Simkhada, van Teijlingen, Pant, Sathian & Tuladhar, 2015; Cousins, 2016). Conclusively, the prevalence of depression among the elderly, children, people with diabetics and people with psychiatric illnesses were examined higher. The impact of women, especially in rural women from low caste and socio-economically vulnerable populations, conflict-affected women and women from reproductive age (pregnant and post-partum) were outlined as severely affected by the depression. Suicide is a global public health burden; Nepal itself cannot be an exception. As claimed by NASPAR (2013), around 4000 people commit suicide in Nepal every year, which has been increased by 6840 suicides annually, or 24·9 suicides per 1,00,000 (Cousins, 2016 : 16). Women from reproductive age were found severely affected due to various socio-cultural and economic factors (Simkhada, Van Teijlingen, Winter, Fanning, Dhungel & Marahatta, 2015; Pradhan, Poudel, Thomas & Barnett, 2011), where children suffered a lot due to the loss of their mothers. A recent editorial report in Lancet written by Cousins (2016) outlines that Nepal falls among the few countries, where suicide remains the leading cause of death among the women from child-bearing age. Furthermore, "Nepal has the seventh highest suicide rate in the world, according to the latest data available from WHO in 2012" (Cousins, 2016 : 16). WHO (2014) claimed that Nepal has second highest suicide per capita in south Asia followed by Sri Lanka. Nepal lacks a systematic data collection and prevalence study on suicide in Nepal (Pradhan, Poudel, Thomas & Barnett, 2011). Nevertheless, a recent police data shows that there is 41 per cent increase in suicide after the earthquake within three months period of 2015 (Cousins, 2016). The ten year long conflict, political instability, migration of young and married male to the gulf and first world countries, domestic violence, intra-family disputes, pressure of in-laws to the newly married and pregnant women, recent mega-earthquake, and unavailability of mental health services were found behind the high prevalence of suicide in Nepal (Cousins, 2016; Pradhan *et al.,* 2011; Karki, 2012). Nevertheless, a true number of incidences and root causes of suicide are yet to be formally studied by the Governmental sources, which were lack due to social stigma, a culture of impunity and lack of political willpower (Cousins, 2016; Pradhan, Poudel, Thomas & Barnett, 2011).

Suicide Prevention Efforts and Dialectical Behavioural Therapy

Suicide is a complex but preventable public health concern; which generally resulted through complex socio-cultural, economic, political, biological and environmental factors. Prevention of suicide is even more complex and cannot be an easy task which requires not only an understanding of prevailing factors, addressing the pushing factors and enhancing treatment facilities with regular availability of trained staff (Hendin *et al.*, 2008). Few promising outcomes in suicide prevention across the developed countries are observed (Hendin *et al.*, 2008). However, Nepal in particular lacks efforts to systematically understand the cause, address underlying socio-economic, gender and class-based concerns, and treatment facilities for substance abuse, mental illness and finally, depression which is the leading cause of suicide neither at community settings nor at clinical facilities (Cousins, 2016; Pradhan *et al.*, 2011). Phillips & Cheng (2012) outlines that most of the suicide prevention programmes are not targeted to change the psychological aspects of the people. WHO led MHGap and other interventions are either focused on awareness raising and/or developing the capacity of health professionals to address the suicide-related cases at clinical settings with biomedical aspects are focused. People with depression and rigorous suicidal ideation in Nepal often seek medical advice for their somatic complaints and are often not addressed the root causes of somatic complaints, or seek the services of traditional healers (Kohrt *et al.*, 2009). Whereas, advanced clinical interventions cannot much reduce the burden of suicide (Yip, 2015). Panos, Jackson, Hasan & Panos (2013) explored that DBT was an efficacious treatment as compared to treatment as usual for the prevention of the suicide, which was explored through five different randomized controlled trials. Crane & Williams (2010) revealed the effectiveness of the mindfulness-based approach to the treatment of suicidal ideation and preventing suicide to the depressed individuals. Similar findings were outlined through the previous research (Williams, Duggan, Crane & Fennell, 2006). Marsa Linehan, the innovator of the DBT, developed and tested the concept for the survivors of self-harm or the people with a rigorous desire of self-injuries (Linehan, 1987). DBT is a form of cognitive behavioural therapy (CBT), which moreover focuses on educating the acceptance of emotions, thoughts, behaviours, self and the world. The DBT comes from the foundation of dialectical philosophy, in which, the therapist try to make balance while creating acceptance and applying change related approaches of the client (Chapman, 2006). The concept of dialectical approach outlines that individual's emotional dysregulation is the product of sensitive biological vulnerability intersecting with the invalidating environmental factors, where individual's needs to address the emotional regulation difficulties through acceptance and commitment for the change. DBT primarily focuses on the reduction of ineffective behaviours associated with the dysregulated emotions (Lynch, Trost, Salsman & Linehan, 2007). With mindfulness techniques, "heart lies the search for synthesis and balance, a task that has proven effective in replacing the rigid, often extreme and dichotomous responses characteristic of self-destructive individuals" (Ramaiya, 2015 : 11). Linehan (2007) outlines that the DBT treatment follows responsibility, commitment, acceptance and enough energy to accept and validate the ongoing distresses and challenges of the client. Simultaneously, the clients can learn skills to regulate their emotions and equally observe and understand the behaviours. The treatment approach follows individualized therapy, group based skills enhancement, telephone follow-up and consultation group of health service providers to manage the consistency of the support to the client. The clients are assigned to homeworks and requested to maintain a diary of thoughts, emotions, behaviours and arousals in relation to their life. DBT provides value, respects the emotions of the client, and equally motivate to reveal inner expressions and learn skills to manage or change the problematic behaviours. Over the last years, DBT has proven efficacious and effective therapy for the women with deliberate self-harm and people with personality disorders (Robins & Chapman, 2004). DBT found effective suicide prevention therapy (Stanley, Brodsky, Nelson & Dulit, 2007; Klonsky & Muehlenkamp, 2007). Research on DBT as a suicide prevention strategy has found that after a year of care, 23.1 per cent of DBT patients reported suicide attempts, compared with 46.7 per cent of recipients of alternative expert treatments (Yip & Law, 2010 : 24). The DBT also found effective to maintain the treatment outcomes longer with higher retention rates as compared to alternative treatments (Yip & Law, 2010). Nevertheless, DBT has not been exclusively implemented in diverse populations across the culture, though the inclusion of DBT with various CBT techniques including mindfulness and acceptance-based treatments for suicide prevention has found effective and evidence-based approach for the suicide prevention (Le & Gobert, 2013; Ward-Ciesielski, 2013; Luoma & Villatte, 2012). The use of DBT with an inclusion of mindfulness techniques served as an effective treatment of choice for suicide prevention to different socio-economic, cultural and treatment settings across the globe (O Donohue & Fisher, 2009; Dimeff & Koerner, 2007).

Suicide Prevention Efforts and Dialectical Behavioural Therapy in Nepal

DBT, though its partial roots were found in eastern cultures (Boehnlein, 2006), have been not widely implemented, tested and applied in low and middle-income countries (LMIC) for the suicide prevention (Aggarwal & Berk, 2015) as it has been done in the West. The religious and cultural factors in relation to the suicide were also found correlated (Bertolote & Fleischmann, 2002), therefore, contextual adaptation and culturally blend DBT not only remained a challenge but equally provide an opportunity to explore and prevent the suicide burden. Use of DBT in Nepali context for the prevention of the suicide is relatively rare, nevertheless, few efforts for the contextualization and application of the DBT with the Nepali-speaking Bhutanese refugees and small women with suicidal ideation from remote areas of Nepal has initiated (Robkin, 2012; Kohrt, Maharjan, Timsina & Griffith, 2012; Ramaiya, 2015). Kohrt *et al.* (2012) initiated the concept of Nepali ethno psychology to be considered while adopting and using the DBT and mindfulness techniques in suicide prevention. As DBT follows the historical use of Hindu and Buddhist practices of mindfulness and applies connection between the acceptance and change, the application of DBT in Nepali context is useful not only to enhance awareness of the individual distresses individual face and the interconnection of the distresses through their interpersonal experiences (Kohrt et *al.*, 2012). Nepali ethno-psychology, which not only separate the brain and heart into heart-mind and brain-mind to understand the psychological and mental illnesses, but equally considers, body (as physical entity to express the emotions and distress) along with spirits, social status and family/community relationships as factors affecting the psychosocial and mental health situation of the individuals (Kohrt *et al.*, 2012). DBT not only focuses on the emotions, thoughts and physical reactions (behaviours) of an individual but eventually considers the wider experiences of interpersonal relationships, impacts of culture and society into shaping and affecting individual's psychological health; and focuses to address such interactions along with the techniques and skills transferring to manage the individual arousals of the distresses. Conclusively, Nepali ethno psychological perspective is found corroborative to the DBT and mindfulness techniques dealing with the individual distresses and deliberate self-harm behaviours (Kohrt *et al.*, 2012). Despite the lack of much applied research of the DBT and mindfulness approach to prevent the suicide in Nepali context. Ramaiya (2015) carried out a process, piloted cross-cultural validation and application of DBT along with mindfulness techniques under the third generation CBT, and applied to the rural women from a Midwestern mountainous district of Nepal. The study as a Ph.D. dissertation paper not published yet as a journal article, presents that DBT is found flexible and applicable to Nepali women both in individualized and group format. Training to the counsellors on DBT for suicide prevention provided a cultural and sociological understanding of the difficulties, terminology, and perception of the problem of the client. Buddhist philosophy, under the mindfulness techniques, were found aligned with the Nepali society as most of the Hindu people in Nepal are also found familiar with the Buddhism and share common values of both the traditions. The DBT techniques were conceived and applied techniques from the Zen Buddhist principle, also found applicable to apply both mindfulness practice and acceptance to reduce the self-destructive thoughts among the Nepali women (Ramaiya, 2015). The cross-cultural adaptation of the DBT in Nepali context followed, an ethno-psychological understanding of the depression and suicide, training and translation of the standard DBT manual on managing self-harm into Nepali language. 8-10 group therapy sessions with women (N=10) were provided, and modifications of diary cards and pictorial aids on the distress monitoring, developing acceptance and monitoring the positive behaviours (Ramaiya, 2015). Despite the various challenges with excellent exercise on cultural adaptation of the DBT, a large sample size study is required to further prove the effectiveness of the DBT and mindfulness techniques for the suicide prevention to the Nepali women. The effort of cultural validation of the DBT has opened the applicability of DBT in Nepali content and proven that DBT is applicable to Nepali population too for the prevention of suicide.

Conclusion

This review concludes that depression and suicide is a global burden affecting many people despite their age, sex, economic status and cultures. Elderly, adolescents, people with chronic illnesses, women from childbearing age, sexual minorities, and people diagnosed with mental illness were outlined at more risk. Culture-specific and context-specific severity and prevalence of suicide were found, which includes, more male from developed world were affected as compared to the women from reproductive age from the south Asian context. Women in south Asia face debilitating consequences of depression and suicide due to the socio-cultural legal and familial factors where discrimination, stigma, and marginalization is huge with limited empowerment and economic opportunities to the women. Advancement of the clinical care and treatment facilities for institutional care cannot prevent the suicide burden, which needs to be dealt with the ecological and ethno psychological perspectives because the root causes of the problem are interconnected with the gender role, exclusion, marginalization, exploitations and socio-cultural violence. The root causes of the problem also affected the burden of post-partum depression, suicidal behaviours and aggravating situations of stigma and discrimination due to the suicide. Eventually, stand alone clinical care cannot address the suicide burden. Different approaches such as individualized therapy, group therapy, and family-based psycho-education have initiated and applied in beyond the institutionalized medication and therapy support to the individuals with depression, suicidal ideation and self-harm behaviours in the developed countries. Such efforts have found effective and outlined efficacious results to mitigate the impact of suicide and preventing the suicidal ideation to the individuals. Out of many psychotherapeutic approaches, CBT-based DBT and mindfulness techniques were observed efficacious, which were applied to the wide range of populations including individuals diagnosed with the depression and personality disorders. Despite the effective use of DBT and mindfulness techniques for suicide prevention in developed countries, the applicability of such techniques was restricted in low and middle-income countries due to various limitations including unavailability of trained human resources, lack of funding, inadequate willpower to change the biomedical approach to health etc. Most importantly, the rich cultural diversity and collective societies mainly in Asia, Latin America, and Africa, did not allow to immediately replicate the DBT and mindfulness techniques across the populations and demanded cultural adaptation of such techniques before initiating the applications.

Nepal did not remain out of the scenario, where the burden of suicide across the population in general and women of childbearing age are studied highly affected by depression and suicide. Nevertheless, accessible, quality and culturally blend or suitable approaches of the DBT and mindfulness techniques were found limited not only in terms of validation and adaptation of the tools but equally piloting its implementation for the scientific and rigorous outcomes to be validated and applied to the wider strata of the population. This review revealed that the DBT and mindfulness techniques for the suicide prevention are in line with the cultural origin of Nepali population and equally the techniques and approaches follow the Nepali ethno-psychological understanding of the mental health and psychological health. Furthermore, application of DBT in Nepali society in general and women from rural areas and refugee populations with high level of distresses needs to be understood first through the socio-cultural and ecological perspectives, develop the training and application toolkits which represents the socio-cultural aspects of the mental health and validate this through applying the techniques in wide ranges of populations. This review explored that adaptation and validation process of the DBT to rural women groups and refugee populations were applied. The study findings provided avenues to apply the DBT across the populations. Certain amendments on the techniques, tools and practical settings for the therapy implementation were explored and provided handy tools to the practitioners and future researchers to effectively apply the DBT and mindfulness therapy techniques to the population. However, this review could not find evidence that DBT and mindfulness approach for suicide prevention is efficacious across the populations, in principle, Nepal needs more application and scientific research to generalize the outcomes and claim that these approaches do have reliability and validity to apply to the wider strata of the populations and the survivors. Nevertheless, it is concluded that Ramaiya (2015) and Brandon *et al.* (2012) provided a validated tool with certain recommendations to the future users and researchers, so that, the DBT and mindfulness approach for suicide prevention can be applied to the Nepali population in general. Eventually, the cultural gap between the use of CBT based therapies in Nepali context are narrowed and provided an avenue to explore future training and use of contextualized tools and techniques. The outcomes equally helped to establish an evidence-based approach for suicide prevention in Nepali context, which is absolutely a need to mental health and psychosocial practitioners, health care authorities and social workers.

References

Adhikary, P., Keen, S., and Van Teijlingen, E. (2011). Health Issues among Nepalese migrant workers in the Middle East. *Health Science Journal*, *5*(3), 169-175.

Aggarwal, S., and Berk, M. (2015). Non-suicidal self-injury in Indian adolescents: Non-existent or unacknowledged? *International Journal of Social Psychiatry*, *61*(5), 516-517.

Ahmed, S.M., Chowdhury, M., and Bhuiya, A. (2001). Micro-credit and emotional well-being: experience of poor rural women from Matlab, Bangladesh. *World Development*, *29*(11), 1957-1966.

Al-Maskari, F., Shah, S.M., Al-Sharhan, R., Al-Haj, E., Al-Kaabi, K., Khonji, D. and Bernsen, R. M. (2011). Prevalence of depression and suicidal behaviours among male migrant workers in United Arab Emirates. *Journal of Immigrant and Minoriy Health*, *13*(6), 1027-1032.

Ao, T., Taylor, E., Lankau, E., Sivilli, T.I., Blanton, C., Shetty, S., and Lopes-Cardozo, B. (2012). An investigation into suicides among Bhutanese refugees in the US 2009-2012 stakeholders report. *Centre for Disease Control and Prevention.* Retrieved from http://www.refugeehealthta.org/files/2011/06/.

Ball, H.A., Siribaddana, S.H., Kovas, Y., Glozier, N., Mcguffin, P., Sumathipala, A., and Hotopf, M. (2010). Epidemiology and symptomatology of depression in Sri Lanka: a cross-sectional population-based survey in Colombo District. *Journal of Affective Disorders, 123*(1), 188-196.

Banerjee, I., Roy, B., Banerjee, I., Sathian, B., Mondal, M., and Saha, A. (2011). Depression and its cure: A drug utilization study from a tertiary care centre of Western Nepal. *Nepal Journal of Epidemiology, 1*(5), 144-152.

Bertolote, J.M., and Fleischmann, A. (2002). A global perspective in the epidemiology of suicide. *Suicidologi, 7*(2), 6-8.

Bhugra, D., and Gupta, S. (Eds.). (2010). *Migration and Mental Health.* Cambridge, U.K.: Cambridge University Press.

Boehnlein, J.K. (2006). Religion and spirituality in psychiatric care: looking back, looking ahead. *Transcultural psychiatry, 43*(4), 634-651.

Bruckner, T.A., Scheffler, R.M., Shen, G., Yoon, J., Chisholm, D., Morris, J. and Saxena, S. (2011). The mental health workforce gap in low-and middle-income countries: a needs based approach. *Bulletin of the World Health Organization, 89*(3), 184-194.

Cardozo, B.L., Bilukha, O.O., Crawford, C.A.G., Shaikh, I., Wolfe, M.I., Gerber, M.L., and Anderson, M. (2004). Mental health, social functioning, and disability in postwar Afghanistan. *Jama, 292*(5), 575-584.

Catani, C., Jacob, N., Schauer, E., Kohila, M., and Neuner, F. (2008). Family violence, war, and natural disasters: A study of the effect of extreme stress on children's mental health in Sri Lanka. *BMC Psychiatry, 8*(1), 33-43.

Chang, S.S., Stuckler, D., Yip, P., and Gunnell, D. (2013). Impact of 2008 global economic crisis on suicide: time trend study in 54 countries. *BMJ,* 347:f5239.

Chapman, A.L. (2006). Dialectical behaviour therapy: current indications and unique elements. *Psychiatry (Edgmont), 3*(9), 62-68.

Cook, D.A., and West, C.P. (2012). Conducting systematic reviews in medical education: a stepwise approach. *Medical Education, 46*(10), 943-952.

Cooperman, N.A., and Simoni, J.M. (2005). Suicidal ideation and attempted suicide among women living with HIV/AIDS. *Journal of Behavioural Medicine, 28*(2), 149-156.

Cousins, S. (2016). Nepal's silent epidemic of suicide. *The Lancet, 387*(10013), 16-17.

Crane, C., and Williams, J.M.G. (2010). Factors associated with attrition from mindfulness based cognitive therapy in patients with a history of suicidal depression. *Mindfulness, 1*(1), 10-20.

Devries, K., Watts, C., Yoshihama, M., Kiss, L., Schraiber, L.B., Deyessa, N., and Berhane, Y. (2011). Violence against women is strongly associated with suicide attempts: Evidence from the WHO multi-country study on women's health and domestic violence against women. *Social Science and Medicine*, *73*(1), 79-86.

D'Augelli, A.R., Grossman, A.H., Salter, N.P., Vasey, J.J., Starks, M.T., and Sinclair, K.O. (2005). Predicting the suicide attempts of lesbian, gay, and bisexual youth. *Suicide and Life-Threatening Behaviour*, *35*(6), 646-660.

Dimeff, L.A., and Koerner, K.E. (2007). *Dialectical Behaviour Therapy in Clinical Practice: Applications across Disorders and Settings*. New York, USA, Guilford Publication.

Ellsberg, M., Jansen, H.A., Heise, L., Watts, C.H., and Garcia-Moreno, C. (2008). Intimate partner violence and women's physical and mental health in the WHO multi-country study on women's health and domestic violence: An observational study. *The Lancet*, *371*(9619), 1165-1172.

Fuchs, C., Lee, J.K., Roemer, L., and Orsillo, S.M. (2013). Using mindfulnessand acceptance based treatments with clients from non-dominant cultural and/or marginalized backgrounds: Clinical considerations, meta-analysis findings, and introduction to the special series: Clinical considerations in using acceptance and mindfulness-based treatments with diverse populations. *Cognitive and Behavioural Practice*, *20*(1), 1-12.

Gadit, A.A.M., and Mugford, G. (2007). Prevalence of depression among households in three capital cities of Pakistan: Need to revise the mental health policy. *Plos One*, *2*(2), e209.

Gajalakshmi, V., and Peto, R. (2007). Suicide rates in rural Tamil Nadu, South India: verbal autopsy of 39,000 deaths in 1997-98. *International Journal of Epidemiology*, *36*(1), 203-207.

Ghimire, H.; Pokharel, P.K.; Shyangwa, P.M.; Baral, D.D.; Aryal, A., and Mishra, A.K. (2012). Are elderly people living in old-age home, less depressed than those of community? Findings from a comparative study. *Journal of Chitwan Medical College*, *1*(2), 5-8.

Giri, R.K., Khatri, R.B., Mishra, S.R., Khanal, V., Sharma, V.D., and Gartoula, R.P. (2015). Prevalence and factors associated with depressive symptoms among post-partum mothers in Nepal. *BMC Research Notes*, *8*(1), 111.

Grover, S., Dutt, A., and Avasthi, A. (2010). An overview of Indian research in depression. *Indian Journal of Psychiatry*, *52*(7), 178-188.

Hagaman, A.K., Sivilli, T.I., Ao, T., Blanton, C., Ellis, H., Cardozo, B.L., and Shetty, S. (2016). An Investigation into Suicides Among Bhutanese Refugees Resettled in the United States Between 2008 and 2011. *Journal of Immigrant and Minority Health*, *18*(1), 819-827.

Hendin, H., Phillips, M.R., Vijayakumar, L., Pirkis, J., Wang, H., Yip, P. and Fleischmann, A. (2008). Suicide and suicide prevention in Asia. *Mental Health and Substance Abuse*, World Health Organization.

Hicks, M.H.R., and Bhugra, D. (2003). Perceived causes of suicide attempts by UK South Asian women. *American Journal of Orthopsychiatry*, *73*(4), 455-462.

Ineichen, B. (2008). Suicide and attempted suicide among South Asians in England: Who is at risk? *Mental Health in Family Medicine*, *5*(3), 135-138.

Jordans, M.J., Kaufman, A., Brenman, N.F., Adhikari, R.P., Luitel, N.P., Tol, W.A., and Komproe, I. (2014). Suicide in South Asia: A scoping review. *BMC Psychiatry, 14*(1), 385-394.

Juurlink, D.N., Herrmann, N., Szalai, J.P., Kopp, A., and Redelmeier, D.A. (2004). Medical illness and the risk of suicide in the elderly. *Archives of Internal Medicine, 164*(11), 1179-1184.

Karasz, A., Patel, V., Kabita, M., and Shimu, P. (2013). Tension in South Asian Women: Developing a measure of common mental disorder using participatory methods. *Progress in Community Health Partnerships: Research, Education, and Action, 7*(4), 429-441.

Karki, C. (2012). Suicide: Leading cause of death among women in Nepal. *Kathmandu University Medical Journal, 9*(3), 157-158.

Khattri, J.B. (2006). Study of depression among geriatric population in Nepal. *Nepal Medical College Journal, 8*(4), 1-4.

Klonsky, E.D., and Muehlenkamp, J.J. (2007). Self-injury: A research review for the practitioner. *Journal of Clinical Psychology, 63*(11), 1045-1056.

Kohrt, B.A., Hruschka, D.J., Worthman, C.M., Kunz, R.D., Baldwin, J.L., Upadhyaya, N. and Jordans, M.J. (2012). Political violence and mental health in Nepal: prospective study. *The British Journal of Psychiatry, 201*(4), 268-275.

Kohrt, B.A., Jordans, M.J., Tol, W.A., Speckman, R.A., Maharjan, S.M., Worthman, C.M., and Komproe, I.H. (2008). Comparison of mental health between former child soldiers and children never conscripted by armed groups in Nepal. *JAMA, 300*(6), 691-702.

Kohrt, B.A., Maharjan, S.M., Timsina, D., and Griffith, J.L. (2012). Applying Nepali Ethno-psychology to psychotherapy for the treatment of mental illness and prevention of suicide among Bhutanese refugees. *Annals of Anthropological Practice, 36*(1), 88-112.

Kohrt, B.A., Speckman, R.A., Kunz, R.D., Baldwin, J.L., Upadhyaya, N., Acharya, N.R., and Worthman, C.M. (2009). Culture in psychiatric epidemiology: using ethnography and multiple mediator models to assess the relationship of caste with depression and anxiety in Nepal. *Annals of Human Biology, 36*(3), 261-280.

Le, T.N., and Gobert, J.M. (2013). Translating and implementing a mindfulness-based youth suicide prevention intervention in a native American community. *Journal of Child and Family Studies*, 24(1), 12-23.

Linehan, M.M. (1987). Dialectical behavioural therapy: A cognitive behavioural approach to parasuicide. *Journal of Personality Disorders, 1*(4), 328-333.

Linehan, M.M. (2007). *Dialectical Behaviour Therapy in Clinical Practice: Applications across Disorders and Settings. L.A.* Dimeff, and K. Koerner (Eds.). New York, NY, US: Guilford Press.

Luoma, J.B., and Villatte, J.L. (2012). Mindfulness in the treatment of suicidal individuals. *Cognitive and Behavioural Practice, 19*(2), 265-276.

Lynch, T.R., Trost, W.T., Salsman, N., and Linehan, M.M. (2007). Dialectical behaviour therapy for borderline personality disorder. *Annual Review of Clinical Psychology, 3*, 181-205.

Manetta, A.A., and Cox, L.E. (2014). Suicidal behaviour and HIV/AIDS: A partial test of Joiner's theory of why people die by suicide. *Social Work in Mental Health, 12*(1), 20-35.

Manoranjitham, S.D., Rajkumar, A.P., Thangadurai, P., Prasad, J., Jayakaran, R., and Jacob, K.S. (2010). Risk factors for suicide in rural south India. *The British Journal of Psychiatry, 196*(1), 26-30.

Mishra, S.R., Sharma, A., Bhandari, P.M., Bhochhibhoya, S., and Thapa, K. (2015). Depression and Health-Related quality of life among patients with type 2 diabetes mellitus: A cross-sectional study in Nepal. *PloS one, 10*(11).

Missinne, S., and Bracke, P. (2012). Depressive symptoms among immigrants and ethnic minorities: a population based study in 23 European countries. *Social Psychiatry and Psychiatric Epidemiology, 47*(1), 97-109.

Mohit, M.A., Maruf, M.M., Ahmed, H., and Alam, M.T. (2011). Depression and physical illnesses: An update. *Bangladesh Medical Journal, 40*(1), 53-58.

Möller-Leimkühler, A.M. (2003). The gender gap in suicide and premature death or: Why are men so vulnerable? *European Archives of Psychiatry and Clinical Neuroscience, 253*(1), 1-8.

Nambi, S.K., Prasad, J., Singh, D., Abraham, V., Kuruvilla, A., and Jacob, K.S. (2002). Explanatory models and common mental disorders among patients with unexplained somatic symptoms attending a primary care facility in Tamil Nadu. *National Medical Journal of India, 15*(6), 331-335.

NASPAR (2013). Event Report: World Suicide Prevention day. Retrieved from https://www.iasp.info/wspd/ pdf/2013/2013_wspd_nepal.pdf. [Online]

Newman, M.S. (2013). Review of studies of mental health in Bangladesh, with a focus on depression. *International Journal of Mental Health*, 42(4), 48-77.

Niraula, K., Kohrt, B.A., Flora, M.S., Thapa, N., Mumu, S.J., Pathak, R., and Shrestha, R. (2013). Prevalence of depression and associated risk factors among persons with type-2 diabetes mellitus without a prior psychiatric history: a cross-sectional study in clinical settings in urban Nepal. *BMC Psychiatry, 13*(1), 1-11.

O' Donohue, W.T., and Fisher, J.E. (Eds.). (2009). *General Principles and Empirically Supported Techniques of Cognitive Behaviour Therapy*. New Jersey, Canada: John Wiley & Sons.

Otsu, A., Araki, S., Sakai, R., Yokoyama, K., and Voorhees, A.S. (2004). Effects of urbanization, economic development, and migration of workers on suicide mortality in Japan. *Social Science and Medicine, 58*(6), 1137-1146.

Panos, P.T., Jackson, J.W., Hasan, O., and Panos, A. (2013). Meta-analysis and systematic review assessing the efficacy of dialectical behaviour therapy (DBT). *Research on Social Work Practice*, e1049731513503047.

Parsons, C.E., Young, K.S., Rochat, T.J., Kringelbach, M.L., and Stein, A. (2012). Post-natal depression and its effects on child development: a review of evidence from low-and middle-income countries. *British Medical Bulletin, 101*(1), 57-64.

Patel, V., Rahman, A., Jacob, K.S., and Hughes, M. (2004). Effect of maternal mental health on infant growth in low-income countries: new evidence from South Asia. *BMJ, 328*(7443), 820-823.

Pattanayak, R.D., and Sagar, R. (2014). Depressive disorders in Indian context: a review and clinical update for physicians. *Journal of the Association of Physicians of India, 62*(9), 827-32.

Pautasso, M. (2013). Ten simple rules for writing a literature review. *PLOS Computational Biology*, 9(7), e1003149.

Pelzanga, R. (2012). The pattern of psychiatric admissions in a referral hospital, Bhutan. *WHO South-East Asia Journal of Public Health, 1*(1), 52-58.

Perera, B., Torabi, M.R., Jayawardana, G., and Pallethanna, N. (2006). Depressive symptoms among adolescents in Sri Lanka: prevalence and behavioural correlates. *Journal of Adolescent Health, 39*(1), 144-146.

Phillips, M.R., and Cheng, H.G. (2012). The changing global face of suicide. *The Lancet, 379*(9834), 2318-2319.

Poongothai, S., Pradeepa, R., Ganesan, A., and Mohan, V. (2009). Prevalence of depression in a large urban South Indian population—The Chennai Urban Rural Epidemiology study (CURES-70). *Plos One, 4*(9), e7185.

Pradhan, A., Poudel, P., Thomas, D., and Barnett, S. (2011). *A Review of the Evidence: Suicide among Women in Nepal.*

Prince, M., Patel, V., Saxena, S., Maj, M., Maselko, J., Phillips, M.R., and Rahman, A. (2007). No health without mental health. *The Lancet, 370*(9590), 859-877.

Qin, P., Agerbo, E., and Mortensen, P.B. (2003). Suicide risk in relation to socio-economic, demographic, psychiatric, and familial factors: a national register-based study of all suicides in Denmark, 1981-1997. *American Journal of Psychiatry, 160*(4), 765-772.

Ramaiya, M.K. (2015). *Suicide Prevention in Rural Nepal: A Cultural Adaptation of Dialectical Behaviour Therapy* (Doctoral dissertation).

Ratkowska, K.A., and De Leo, D. (2013). Suicide in Immigrants: An Overview. *Open Journal of Medical Psychology, 2*(3), 1-10.

Reeves, A., Stuckler, D., Mckee, M., Gunnell, D., Chang, S.S., and Basu, S. (2012). Increase in state suicide rates in the USA during economic recession. *The Lancet, 380*(9856), 1813-1814.

Reynolds III, C.F., Cuijpers, P., Patel, V., Cohen, A., Dias, A., Chowdhary, N. and Lotrich, F. (2012). Early intervention to reduce the global health and economic burden of major depression in older adults. *Annual Review of Public Health, 33* (1), 123-135.

Robins, C.J., and Chapman, A.L. (2004). Dialectical behaviour therapy: Current status, recent developments, and future directions. *Journal of Personality Disorders, 18*(1), 73-89.

Robkin, N.T. (2012). *Mental Health and Suicide Among Women in Jumla, Nepal: A Qualitative Exploration* (Doctoral dissertation, Emory University).

Rochat, T.J., Bland, R.M., Tomlinson, M., and Stein, A. (2013). Suicide ideation, depression and HIV among pregnant women in rural South Africa. *Scientific Research 5*(3), 1-12.

Scholte, W.F., Olff, M., Ventevogel, P., de Vries, G.J., Jansveld, E., Cardozo, B.L., and Crawford, C.A.G. (2004). Mental health symptoms following war and repression in eastern Afghanistan. *JAMA*, *292*(5), 585-593.

Selim, N. (2010). Cultural dimensions of depression in Bangladesh: a qualitative study in two villages of Matlab. *Journal of Health, Population and Nutrition, 28*(1), 95-106.

Shakya, R., Sitaula, S., and Shyangwa, P.M. (2008). Depression during pregnancy in a tertiary care centre of eastern Nepal. *Journal of Nepal Medical Association*, *47*(171), 128-131.

Simkhada, P., van Teijlingen, E., Pant, P. R., Sathian, B., and Tuladhar, G. (2015). Public health, prevention and health promotion in post-earthquake Nepal. *Nepal Journal of Epidemiology*, *5*(2), 462-464.

Stanley, B., Brodsky, B., Nelson, J.D., and Dulit, R. (2007). Brief dialectical behaviour therapy (DBT-B) for suicidal behaviour and non-suicidal self-injury. *Archives of Suicide Research, 11*(4), 337-341.

Suicide.org (2015). *International Suicide Statistics*.

Timalsina, R., Sherpa, P.D., and Dhakal, D. (2014). Factors associated with depression among elderly living in old age homes in Kathmandu Valley. *Journal of Institute of Medicine*, *36*(1), 90-96.

Tolman, R.M., and Rosen, D. (2001). Domestic violence in the lives of women receiving welfare mental health, substance dependence, and economic well-being. *Violence against Women*, *7*(2), 141-158.

University of Liverpool. (2012). *Code of Ethics*. Retrieved from https://www.liverpool.ac.uk/research-integrity/ policies-guidance/

Uutela, A. (2010). Economic crisis and mental health. *Current Opinion in Psychiatry*, *23*(2), 127-130.

Vijayakumar, L., John, S., Pirkis, J., and Whiteford, H. (2005). Suicide in developing countries (2) Risk Factors. *The Journal of Crisis Intervention and Suicide Prevention*, *26*(3), 112-119.

Vonnahme, L.A., Lankau, E.W., Ao, T., Shetty, S., and Cardozo, B.L. (2015). Factors associated with symptoms of depression among Bhutanese Refugees in the United States. *Journal of Immigrant and Minority Health*, *17*(6), 1705-1714.

SECTION V
Psychological Hazards of Mental Health in Asia

18

Psychological Health of Informal Caregivers of Cancer Patients

The Population at Risk

Purnima Awasthi and *Kuhu*

Introduction

The latest figures published in the *British Medical Journal*, The Lancet show that around one million new cancer cases are being diagnosed in India each year, projected to nearly double to 1.7 million new cases in 2035. More than 5,75,000 people die of cancer, and more than 1.5 million people are diagnosed with cancer per year. According to the World Health Organization, the number of new cancer cases is expected to rise by about 70 per cent over the next 20 years. Around 7,00,000 people are dying from cancer in India annually projected to rise to around 1.2 million deaths in 2035 (WHO, 2015).

This drastic disease has a ripple effect on the family members and informal caregivers of the cancer patients. Its impact has been compared to the dropping of a stone in the pond. Once you drop a stone in the pond, it causes some changes. Similarly, once a family member is diagnosed with cancer, the family members are directly confronted with the illness experience. The members of the family provide the context of adjustment in which the person diagnosed with cancer responds to her/ his disease. Although the disease dwells in the body of the patient only, but it causes a huge psychological effect on the informal caregivers of the patient, i.e. the family members or friends.

It has been observed that caregiving is a life changing and consuming task, leaving the caregivers stressed out and depressed. Around 15 per cent of family caregivers report high level of stress as a result of caring for an older family member, close friends or loved ones with long term care needs. However, the experience of caregiving does not always come with negative experiences only, the role of caregiving can also render positive and rewarding experiences. Some caregivers deal with their caregiving role in a very positive way by handling the stress well by turning to friends, family and prayers as a coping mechanism. Historically, caregiving has not been a topic of much concern and focus for the research. With the decline in healthcare resources and rising healthcare costs, informal caregiving is gathering attention by the researchers. Numerous studies have been reviewed and some studies, which investigated the psychological effects of cancer care on mental health of informal caregivers of cancer patients, are presented in Table 18.1.

Brouwer, Berg, Bos, Exel, and Koopmanschap (2005) found out that the process of caregiving does not always lead to negative psychological effects on the caregivers but also has a positive effect on the psychology of caregivers. This study was based on the fact that utility is not always derived from the outcome but also from the process involved in reaching to the outcome. The empirical evidence of process utility was presented on the basis of a large sample of 950 Dutch caregivers. The process utility was measured as the difference in happiness between the current situation in which the patient is cared for by the caregiver and the hypothetical situation that someone else takes over the care tasks, all other things equal. The caregivers were given questionnaires to probe into the background information, the objective burden was assessed and the subjective burden of caregiving was assessed using the Caregiver Strain Index and a Self-Rated Burden Scale. The process utility was measured by comparing the two situations mentioned above in terms of happiness. The results indicated that the influence of process utility on total happiness can be substantial. It was found that some caregivers would lose a major part of their happiness if asked to give up their caregiving role. The process utility was affected by the caregiver characteristics and the subjective burden of caregiving too. However, it seems as though focusing only on the negative side of the informal care does not do justice with the value of informal care. So on an average, the happiness would decline when the caregiving tasks were handed to someone else.

Cotrim and Pereira (2007) identified and assessed the impact of colorectal cancer and colorectal cancer patients and their families. The study included 96 informal caregivers. A cross-sectional study with a correlation design was done. Patients completed a set of questionnaires

Table 18.1: Presentation of review of studies investigating the psychological effects of cancer care on the mental health of informal caregivers of cancer patients

Citation/author/ year/country	*Method and Design/ LR/MA*	*Sample characteristics*	*Measures*	*Main findings*
Brouwer, *et al.* (2004) Netherlands	Multivariate regression analysis	Dutch caregivers (n = 950)	Caregiver Strain Index and a Self-Rated Burden Scale.	Caregivers derive positive utility from informal care and on average happiness would decline if informal care tasks were handed to someone else.
Cotrim and Pereira *et al.* (2008) Portugal	Descriptive cross-sectional study	96 informal caregivers	Burden assessment scale, Beck depression inventory, State trait anxiety inventory	Patient's depression and anxiety level were related to the caregiver's burden. The stoma patient's caregivers also suffer from high levels of anxiety and depression.
Stenbeg, *et al.* (2010) Norway	Review of literature	192 articles	Many measures were used in the literature review.	Caregivers experience many difficult problems and responsibilities during and after the patient is undergoing treatment and rehabilitation of cancer.
Sorensen, *et al.*, (2003) Germany	Meta-analysis	84 articles	Perceived Stress scale, Hamiltan depression rating scale, Beck depression inventory and other scales like positive affect scales and self-efficacy scales were also used.	The largest differences were found between the caregivers and non-caregivers with regard to depression, stress, self-efficacy and subjective well-being.
Grov, Dahl, and Fossa (2005) Norway	Structured questionnaire	49 primary caregivers of women and 47 primary caregivers of men	Hospital anxiety and depression scale and the quality of life was assessed by SF-36.	Mental quality of life was significantly lower in male primary caregivers. The level of anxiety was higher than in norm in both Genders.

(*Contd.*)

Citation/author/ year/country	*Method and Design/ LR/MA*	*Sample characteristics*	*Measures*	*Main findings*
(Nijboer, Triemstra, Tempeelar, Sanderman and Bos, 1998) Netherlands	Assessment scales were used	148 caregivers	Caregivers reaction assessment scale	Negative caregiver experiences were associated with different factors. Caregivers with low education level and caregivers of patients of stoma were able to derive more self-esteem from caregiving. Caregivers may sustain their quality of life by deriving self-esteem from caregiving.
Dumont, *et al.* (2006) Canada	Interview method	212 family primary caregivers	ECOGPS (Eastern Collaborative Oncology Group Performance Scale)	Family caregivers of patients with advanced stages of cancer experience high level of psychological distress, which significantly increases as the patient loses autonomy.
Grunfeld *et al.* (2004)	Longitudinal study, Questionnaire method	89 caregivers of women with advanced breast cancer	Karnofsky Performance Status index, SF-36, Hospital Anxiety and Depression Scale, the Zarit Burden Inventory, FAMCARE, Medical Outcomes Study Social Support Survey.	Caregiver's depression and perceived burden increase as the patient's functional status declines.
LL Northhouse *et. al.* (2012)	Literature review	Different studies included different sample size	Various measures were used	There is a significant reciprocal relationship between caregiver and patient emotional distress. Cancer can affect the quality of life of family caregivers particularly in the psychological domain.

Goldzweig *et al.* (2013) Israel	3 way MANOVA	216 partners who were primary caregivers	Brief Symptom Inventory, Brief Cope, and Social support.	Cancer caregivers reported high levels of distress, low levels of social support and coping capabilities which are negatively correlated to distress.
Braun *et al.* (2007) Israel	Hierarchical regression	101 spouse caregivers	BDI-II, Caregiving Burden Scale, Experiences in close relationships scale and Enrich marital Satisfaction Scale	Spouse caregivers of patients with advanced cancer are a high risk population for depression.
Cameron *et al.* (2002) Canada	Structured quantitative interview, regression analysis, Pearson and partial correlations	44 family caregivers	Caregiving Impact Scale, Caregiving Assistance Scale, Profile of mood states	Caregivers experience increased emotional distress regardless of the amount of care provided when limited in their ability to participate in valued activities and interests. Also caregivers with less than a high school education level experience more emotional distress.
Song, *et al.* (2011) Korea	Survey method using questionnaires	33 inpatient palliative care services participated in the study	The EQ-5D was used to assess health related quality of life using an index score and a visual analogy scale. The Caregiver Assessment Scale was also used.	Family caregivers of patients with terminal Cancer experience mental health problems and deterioration of health related QOL.
Papastavrou, *et al.* (2009) Cyprus	One way Anova and independent sample t-tests were used. Questionnaires were used.	130 primary caregivers	BI, CES-D and the ways of coping questionnaire.	Caregivers reported high levels of burden and depression.

6-8 months after the surgery of the colorectal cancer. The measures used for the caregivers included the Beck depression inventory, state trait anxiety inventory and the burden assessment scale. It was found that the colorectal cancer has a major impact at the level of psychological morbidity. It also showed that high levels of burden related to the care of patients with cancer. This would probably lead to more stress resulting into depression. Also significant levels of differences were also found between the depression and state anxiety of the stoma and the non-stoma patients.

Miaskowski, Ruland and Stenbeg (2009) did a review of literature on the effects of caring for a patient with cancer. A number of emotional problems related to the caregiving of these family caregivers were identified. Of the 192 studies, 164 articles were research based studies, 12 were systematic reviews and 6 were more general reviews and 10 were expert opinions. Among the emotional problems of the family caregivers, studies have found that the family caregivers experience more depression and anxiety than non-caregivers. The other emotional problems included stress, uncertainty, hopelessness, sad feelings, frustration, guilt and many other emotional problems and reactions.

Pinquart and Sorensen (2003) conducted a meta-analysis on the differences between the caregivers and the non caregivers in psychological and physical health. Studies were identified from the developmental and gerontological literature through electronic databases (PsycINFO, Medline, Psyndex), browsing through library shelves and looking up references found in the other articles. The inclusion criteria included a sample of informal caregivers of older adults compared to a sample of non-caregivers with regard to perceived stress, depression, general subjective well-being, physical health or self-efficacy and the differences between the caregivers and the non-caregivers can be converted into standard deviation units. Perceived stress was measured with Perceived Stress scale, depression with Hamiltan depression rating scale, Beck depression inventory and other scales like positive affect scales and self-efficacy scales were also used. Two common groups of statistical procedures were used in the Meta-analysis-fixed and random effect models. The effect of caregiver status was tested on the psychological and physical health. It was found that the caregivers had higher levels of stress and depression and lower levels of subjective well-being, physical health and self-efficacy than the non-caregivers. On a whole, the meta-analysis suggested that the caregivers fare worse than the non-caregivers as they are more stressed, depressed and have lower levels of subjective well-being and self-efficacy than the non-caregivers.

Dahl, Grov, and Fossa (2005) performed a study on anxiety, depression and quality of life in caregivers of patients with cancer in late palliative phase. The sample included 49 primary caregivers of women with breast cancer and 47 primary caregivers of men with prostate cancer. Levels of anxiety and depression were assessed by Hospital anxiety and depression scale (HADS) and the quality of life were assessed by SF-36. The results indicated an increased level of anxiety symptoms and prevalence of HADS-defined anxiety disorders in primary caregivers of both the genders compared with the norms. Women had a significantly higher prevalence of HADS-defined depression compared with the norms. Thus the findings confirmed the impaired mental health and QOL in many primary caregivers compared to age and gender adjusted norm samples.

Bos, Sanderman, Nijboer, Triemstra and Tempeelar (1998) conducted a longitudinal study in Netherlands on the determinants of caregiving experiences and mental health of partners of cancer patients. It included both negative and positive dimensions of caregiving outcomes. It also examined the caregivers' mental health 6 months after the hospital discharge. The sample consisted of 148 patients newly diagnosed with colorectal carcinoma and their partners. The caregiver's experiences were assessed by Caregiver Reaction Assessment Scale which consisted of four negative sub-scales and one positive sub-scale. The mental health of the caregivers was assessed in terms of depression and quality of life. The level of depression of caregiver was measured by CES-D (Centre for Epidemiologic Studies Depression Scale). The caregiver's initial quality of life was measured with a one item linear visual analogue self-assessment scale. The results indicated that although caregiving may lead to depression, especially in those experiencing loss of physical strength, caregivers may sustain their quality of life by deriving self-esteem from caregiving. A unique finding derived in this study was that the caregivers with a high level of education derived low self-esteem during the course of caregiving than with the caregivers with a low level of education. Thus, for the caregivers with low level of education the task of caregiving would lead to the positive outcome of a higher level of self-esteem.

Allard, Charbonneau, Dumont, Gagnon, Turgeon and Vezina (2006) accomplished a study and found out those family caregivers of the patients in the advanced stages of cancer experience a high level of psychological distress which further increases as the patient loses autonomy. A total of 212 primary caregivers were interviewed. The family caregivers were divided into three cohorts according to the patient's performance status, as measured by the ECOGS (Eastern Collaborative Oncology Group

Functional Scale). The results indicated that the caregiver's distress is strongly associated with the patients' terminal disease progress and the declined functioning. Moreover, the percentage of caregivers with a high level of psychological distress varies from 41 per cent to 62 per cent while the percentage is estimated at 19.2 per cent in general population.

Clinch *et al.* (2004) carried out a longitudinal study of breast cancer patients and their principal caregivers. Out of 89 caregivers, around half were males. The psychological distress was measured by the Hospital Anxiety and Depression scale. The other measures used were Zarit burden inventory, satisfaction with care was measured using FAMCARE (a scale to measure family satisfaction with advanced cancer care) instrument and "Medical Outcome Study Social Support Survey" was used to measure the patients' social support. The psychological impact of caregiving experience showed that the similar proportions of caregivers were anxious at the start of the terminal period as at the start of the palliative period. (39% v. 9%, p=0.18). More of these caregivers were found to be depressed (30% v. 9% p=0.02) at the start of the terminal period than at the start of the palliative period. However, caregiver burden was found to be the most important predictor of anxiety and depression.

Katapodi, Northhouse, Schafenacker, and Weiss, (2012) accomplished a review of research on the impact of caregiving on the psychological well-being of family caregivers and cancer patients. This review of literature confirmed that cancer can affect the quality of life of family caregivers in many ways, but particularly in the psychological domain. It was also indicated that the patient and the caregiver distress is evident in each phase of illness but is found to be greater in some phases like diagnosis phase and the survivorship phase.

Altman, Baider, Ganon, Goldzweig and Merims, (2013) carried out a study on 216 partners (96 men, 120 women) who were primary caregivers of cancer patient aged 60+ and compared them with 76 partners of healthy people aged 60+ and diagnosed with any terminal illness. Partners were interviewed by the psychologists. Each cohort was divided into two age groups—Younger (age 60-70) and Older (age 70+). The measures utilized for the study were background variables, Brief symptom inventory, Brief cope and Social Support. A two-way MANOVA (Group × Patient's Age) compared levels of psychological distress reported by older and younger participants within the research and control groups. Levels of distress measured among the research group were significantly higher and about triple the distress measures reported by the control group participants. Moreover, within the research group, but not within the control group, caregivers to older patients with cancer reported distress levels doubling the distress levels reported by caregivers to younger cancer patients' interaction effect. Thus, caregivers to cancer patients reported high levels of distress, low levels of social support and low levels of coping abilities which are negatively correlated to distress. Also increased patient age was found to accentuate these processes. However further researches need to focus on the variables that make the patients' age an important factor in contributing to caregivers illness.

Braun, Mikulincer, Rodin, Rydall and Walsh (2007) accomplished a study to assess psychological distress among advanced cancer patients and their spouse caregivers, while examining the contribution of caregiving burden and relational variables (attachment orientation and marital satisfaction) to depressive symptoms in the spouse caregivers. The sample (n=101) spouse caregivers were recruited for the study. The measures used were BDI-II, Caregiving Burden Scale, and Experiences in Close Relationships Scale and ENRICH Marital Satisfaction Scale. Hierarchical regression was used to examine the main predictions. Hierarchical regression was used to determine to what extent subjective caregiving burden, attachment scores and marital satisfaction contribute to the prediction of spouse caregiver's depression, beyond the contribution of objective caregiving burden. Overall, this model explained a total of 37 per cent of variance of spouse caregiver's depression scores, with subjective caregiving burden, caregiver's anxiety and avoidance attachment orientations and marital satisfaction remaining as the significant predictors. The study is unique in providing information about the contribution of relational variables about the caregiver's depression. Higher caregiver's attachment anxiety and avoidance were associated with more depression. Overall, the findings from this study suggested high prevalence of depression in spouse caregivers of patients with advanced cancer.

Cameron, Cheung, Franche and Stewart (2002) completed a study in Canada which indicated that caregivers experience increased emotional distress, regardless of the amount of care provided, when limited in their ability to participate in valued activities and interests. Also it was found that the caregivers with less than a high school education experience more emotional distress. The sample (n=44) family caregivers were made to participate in a structured quantitative interview. The measures that were used included: Caregiving impact scale, Caregiver assistance Scale and Profile of Mood states. Pearson and partial correlation were used to test whether lifestyle interference mediated the relationship between caregiving assistance and emotional distress. Regression analyses determined overall correlates of emotional distress. An overall regression model identified education level and lifestyle interference to be significant and unique correlates of emotional distress. So the results of this study and the findings by Nijboer, Triemstra, Tempeelar, Sanderman, and Bos (1998) both suggest that the level of education is an important factor which determines the positive or negative psychological affects that are experienced by the caregivers.

Song, Shin, and Choi (2011) conducted a study in Korea to study the quality of life and mental health in family caregivers of patients with terminal cancer. The family caregivers of terminal cancer patients who received palliative care services in Korea were surveyed. Control individuals were selected from the participants in the first round of fourth Korea National Health and Nutrition Examination Survey and were matched with family caregivers using the propensity score method to optimize the comparative analysis. The EQ-5D was used to assess health related quality of life using an index score and a visual analog scale. The Caregiver Assessment Scale was also used. The results revealed that the health related quality of life is significantly lower than that of the general population. Also the caregiver's level of anxiety and depression were found to be significantly different from that of the general population.

Charalambous, Papastavrou and Tsangari (Cyprus) executed a study to identify the caregiver outcomes among the relatives caring for the patients with cancer and also to examine the patient caregiver variables that predicted the caregiver depression and burden. The sample (n=131) caregivers completed the BI, the CES-D and the ways of coping questionnaire. One way ANOVA was used for the statistical analysis. One way ANOVA showed that there are significant differences among the various educational levels ($p<0.001$) and the income ($p=0.005$) of the caregiver in terms of the overall burden. 66.4 per cent of the caregivers had depression above the usual cut-off point for the depression. In regression analysis, it was found that only the caregivers' income and patients' age are statistically significant in predicting the caregivers' depression and burden. So, the overall findings suggested that the caregivers reported high levels of burden and depression. These outcomes of care-giving are related to several variables, but the caregiver's income and patient's age are predictive of depression and burden.

One of the serious psychological impacts of caregiving of cancer patients includes depression. It leads to health deterioration and early death in caregivers. Caregiving involves a lot of stress toll on the caregivers of cancer patients. Depression emerges as a result of specific emotional reaction to the stress of caregiving role. It has been found that 32 to 50 per cent of the cancer caregivers suffered from depressive symptoms at a level suggesting clinical depression (Covinsky *et al.*, 2003; Butler, Turner, Kaye, Ruffin, & Downey, 2005). The identification of the depressive symptoms among the caregivers is highly important not only for the purpose of evaluation but also for further interventions (Haley, LaMonde, Han, Narramore, & Schonwetter, 2001). Also there has been found a direct relation between caregiver depression and patient depression in many of the studies (Bambauer *et al.*, 2006; Fleming *et al.*, 2006; Land, Hudson, & Stiefel, 2003). Individuals who are suffering from dysfunctional grief pattern can also be identified through assessment of individuals with depressive symptoms and hence interventions can be made to prevent them from reaching to higher levels of depression (Grassi, 2007). When the caregivers remain depressed, their experience of depressive symptoms may include insomnia, excessive sleep, fatigue, inability to concentrate and indecisiveness (American Psychiatric Association, 2000) which may hinder the caregivers from meeting the needs of cancer patients. As a result, the physical and mental energy that is required for the caregiving function may overwhelm the depressed caregivers (Scanlan *et al.*, 2001; Schulz & Beach, 1999). One example of depression effecting the caregivers' decision caused due to the experience of depression is seen in the cases where the caregivers decide to remove the patient from familiar home environment to long-term care facility. Besides depression, factors like patients' age and the stage of the illness have been found to be exerting great effect on the caregivers' psychological health. Also the caregivers' level of education and income seems to be a determining factor affecting the psychological health of the caregivers either in a positive or a negative way.

Theoretical Framework

Some psychological theories have been found to be quite useful in dealing with preventive aspects of health of caregivers of cancer patients. According to the attachment theory by Bowlby (1969-1982), the real role of attachment system is the protection of a person from danger. This can be done by making sure that the person ensures proximity to supportive and caring people who provide security, protection and relief in times of need. This attachment system continues lifelong but is most evident during the infancy days. During evolution, the chances of survival, reproduction and successful parental care were enhanced due to the emotional attachment to caregivers like parents or being the caregiver oneself, by helping the injured, needy or dependent, like—children, ill parents, injured family members. The innate parameter of the attachment system keeps on altering with the societal experiences and interactions with the attachment figures resulting into different forms of attachment styles (Gillath, Mikulinser, Nitzberg & Shaver, 2005).

Theory of reasoned action by Ajzen and Fishbein (1980) shows the relationship between attitude and behaviour. It aids in predicting as to how an individual will behave based on their behavioural intentions and pre-existing attitudes and behaviours. This theory states that an individual undertakes a particular action based on the expectations of the outcomes of a particular behaviour that is expected to follow a particular course of action. Also people decide their behavioural intentions before hand and this in turn predicts their later behaviour. These intentions are further based on — attitudes regarding the behaviour and attitudes regarding the subjective norms. The attitudes regarding the behaviours weigh the possible outcomes of the behaviours and evaluate them as to how good these behaviours are. The attitudes regarding the subjective norms are based on the acceptability, acceptance by the others and the beliefs regarding the behaviour (Mishra & Awasthi, 2004).

This innate parametre of attachment system founds support in a study described above by Braun, Mikulincer, Rodin, Rydall & Walsh (2007) where attachment orientation was found to be a strong predictor of caregiver's (spouse) depression. Higher caregiver's attachment anxiety and avoidance were associated with more depression in the caregivers.

The theory of reasoned action also provides a strong base for supporting the caregivers' role in caring for the patient. This is because every caregiver undertakes the responsibility of care-giving based on the expectations of the outcome (better health of the patient). Any caregiver weighs the outcome of his behaviour (better health of the patient) and weighs them as to how good these behaviours (caregiving role) are in getting the expected outcome.

Agenda for action

Studies described in this chapter clearly indicate that the informal caregivers of cancer patients are a high risk population for various psychological problems like depression, anxiety, psychological burden due to caregiving role and some other negative effects of caregiving function too. The reasons behind all this is that the caregivers perform their functions of caregiving without any sufficient knowledge of the skills that they need to master to efficiently take-up the caregiving task. Although, researches have started to focus on the skills that the caregivers need, however, little attention has been paid regarding the interventions provided by the clinicians for the same.

A formal skill assessment programme should be conducted by the health care providers in order to assess the overall skills that a caregiver needs. It is very necessary to identify the extent to which a caregiver possesses the skills that are needed to manage her/his care-giving role and to provide her/him with the needed assistance. It is very mandatory for the improvement of patient care and to reduce the negative psychological effects on the caregivers. Certain points that need to be focused here are reducing the uncertainty regarding the caregiving role which would further help the caregivers to take decisions and solve their problems more efficiently. The plans of care should take into account both the recipients' need and the caregivers' capacity (Given, 2008).

Community and educational programmes should run at the educational and community level in order to enhance the skills, knowledge and strategies of the caregivers. So, the health care professionals and the informal caregivers should come forward together to provide optimum care to the patient along with maintaining a positive outlook on the part of the caregiver.

Given, Given, Jeon, Sherwood, Shikoskii, and Rahbar (2006) developed a cognitive behavioural intervention programme to help the caregivers of cancer patients with symptom management as a result of which the caregivers would themselves be free of such a high levels of distress due to patients' elevated symptoms.

Interventions that include the definition of problems, generating their alternatives, implementing strategies should increase a caregiver's sense of effectiveness. One such intervention technique was developed by Blanchard, Toseland, and McCallion (1996). These intervention techniques should be implemented and adopted by the health care professionals and should be monitored at the community level.

Psycho-educational interventions should be facilitated at the community level where the caregivers can be provided emotional support and educational knowledge. As a study by Northhouse, Mood, Templin, Mellon, and George (2000) reported that the caregivers felt more positive after the home visits (emotional support) and phone calls by the nurses or health care professionals.

Psycho-educational telephone based interventions developed by Jepson, McCorkle, Adler, Nuamah, and Lusk (1999) can be adopted in countries like India in order to coordinate resources and improve the well-being of the caregivers of cancer patients. Also it should be kept in mind that the psycho-educational interventions that involve active participation by the caregivers should always be the main concern because these report to be having the broadest effects as stated in a meta-analysis study by Pinquart and Sorenson (2006).

Thus, various interventions and programmes for the caregivers need to run at the level of health care departments and also at the community level. These would further aid the informal caregivers of cancer patients to take optimum care of the patients along with maintaining their own psychological health.

Recommendations and Implications for Future Research

Cancer is the leading cause of morbidity and mortality worldwide. As the cases of cancer are expected to raise manifold in the coming times, so is the need for informal caregivers for the cancer patients. The research on the physical and psychological effects on the informal caregivers of cancer patients has gained a good pace in the recent years but still there is a great deal of work that needs to be done in this regard. Of the various studies that have been done so far, the majority of the studies focused on the negative psychological effects of care giving.

A study by Brouwer and associates (2005) came-up with the findings of positive process utility derived from caregiving. However, more researches in the choice process of becoming a caregiver needs to be done preferably from different perspectives. More studies are needed to better understand the relationship between the care provided by the health professionals and patients' well-being, especially qualitative data. In this regard, it becomes important to know what kind of information the caregivers and the patients prefer, which will further reduce the stress and anxiety caused by the unpredictability during the course of the disease. Health care providers should be supportive of family caregivers and should help them to gain knowledge and skills in order to maximise their quality care. The task of converting this knowledge into skills requires a great hand at practice. The unfortunate part is that our mode of helping only provides the information but not the skills that are needed which further hamper the quality care. Research on how interventions affect patient outcomes needs further evaluation. Very limited researches have been done on how the caregiver's problems change as the stage of patient's illness alters. Little has been explored on how various variables change during the course of caregivers experience like the social support, role strain and employment. More researches are recommended to probe into the comparison between the caregivers and the non-caregivers in relation to certain outcome variables like social integration which will further enable more tailored interventions.

Given the fact that health care systems depend heavily on the efforts of informal caregivers, it is important for the policy-makers to realize that it stands crucial to assist the informal caregivers who are in need of support to retain the benefits of informal care. Programme planners, providers and policy-makers must show cohesiveness in order to render the support services needed by the informal caregivers. In a country like India, financial care to alleviate the economic stress of informal caregivers, caregivers' education and support programmes along with the primary care interventions need to be addressed urgently. This would surely benefit the informal caregivers of chronic illness like cancer.

There is an urgent need to cater to the need of the informal caregivers in India because the burden of caring for a loved one is real and can have debilitating effects on the psychological health of the family caregivers. We cannot expect the traditional family network to take-up the whole burden of caring as they are not capable of absorbing such high amount of stress. So, the caregiving responsibility should be shared among the individuals, families and the government. In order to sustain the long term care that is provided by the informal caregivers, it stands mandatory for the government and society at large to come forward and join hands together. It will help in fostering the well-being of the informal caregivers and enhance their support system and psychological health. A public health framework will assist in strengthening the care given by the informal caregivers. Also in a developing country like India, it is warranted to provide specific attention to those caregivers who live only with the patient, with a low income, those with a distressed relationship and with a high level of patient dependency and care involvement.

In the same regard, there is a need to explore the number of caregivers in a particular population along with their characteristics, the arrangements for their care and support, do they get the full information that they deserve in order to perform their caregiving role. Also we need to explore the kind of support the caregivers get from the health services.

In Indian context, a number of areas in the field of informal care giving need to be explored. We need to focus on the predictors of caregiving strain; we can probe into the cultural factors that promote interdependence and compassion. All these factors sum up to produce a healthy caregiving scenario. In the Indian context, we need to put efforts in order to mitigate the caregiving burden and improve the level of caregiving provided by the informal caregivers. This will greatly help the family unit (Avasthi, 2010). Efforts to preserve and strengthen the family through counselling and various interventions should be promoted in order to promote psychological health of informal caregivers of Cancer patients.

References

Adams, I., Fleming, D.A., Ingham, J., Mangan, P.A., Sheppard, V.B., Tallarico, M., Taylor, K.L. (2006). Caregiving at the end of life: Perceptions of health care quality and quality of life among patients and caregivers. *Journal of Pain Symptom Management, 31*(5), 407-420.

Allard, P., Dumont, S., Charbonneau, C., Gagnon, P., Turgeon, J., and Vézina, L. (2006). Caring for a Loved One with Advanced Cancer: Determinants of Psychological Distress in Family Caregivers. *Journal of Palliative Medicine, 9*(4), 912-921.

Altman, A., Baider, L., Goldsweig, G, Ganon, R., Merims, S. and Peretz, T. (2013). Informal caregiving to older cancer patients: preliminary research outcomes and implications. *Annals of Oncology,* pp. 1-6.

American Psychiatric Association. (2000). Practice guidelines for the treatment of patients with major depressive disorder (2nd ed.). Retrieved January 27, 2008, from http://www.psychiatryonline.com/pracGuide/pracGuide ChapToc_7.aspx.

Avasthi, A. (2010). Preserve and strengthen family to promote mental health. *Indian Journal of Psychiatry, 52*, 113-126. Ajzen, I., and Fishbein, M. (1980). *Understanding Attitudes and Predicting Social Behaviour.* Englewood Cliffs, NJ: Prentice-Hall.

Bambauer, K., Block, S.D., Maciejewski, P.K., Pirl, W.F., Prigerson, H.G., Sahay, N., and Zhnag, B. (2006). Mutuality and specificity of mental disorders in advanced cancer patients and caregivers. *Social Psychiatry and Psychiatric Epidemiology, 41*(10), 819-824.

Baik, K., Choi, S., Choi, J., Kang, J., Kim, E., Kwak, J., Mo, H., Park, M., Shin, D. and Song, J. (2016). Quality of life and mental health in family caregivers of patients with terminal cancer. *Springer,* 1-15.

Blanchard, C.G., Toseland, R.W., and McCallion, P. (1996). The effects of a problem-solving intervention with spouses ofcancer patients. *Journal of Psychosocial Oncology, 14*(2),1-21.

Bowlby, J. (1969/1982). *Attachment and Loss: Attachment.* New York: Basic Books.

Bos, G., Nijboer, C., Sanderman, R., Tempeelar, R., and Triemstra, M., (1998). Determinants of Care-giving Experiences and Mental Health of Partners of Cancer Patients. *Cancer,* 86, 84.

Braun, M., Mikulincer, M., Rodin, G., Rydall, A., and Walsh, A. (2007). Hidden Morbidity in Cancer Spouse Caregivers. *Journal of Clinical Oncology, 25, (30),* 4829-4834.

Brouwer, B.F., Berg, B., Bos, G., Exel, N., and Koopmanschap, M. (2004). Process utility from providing informal care: The benefit of caring. *Health Policy, 74,* 85-99.

Butler, S.B., Downey, R., Kaye, L.W., Ruffin, L., Turner, W. (2005). Depression and caregiver burden among rural elder caregivers. *Journal of Gerontological Social Work, 46*(1), 56.

Burton, L., Hirsch, C., and Jackson, S., Mittlemark, M., Newsom, J., and Schulz, R. (1997). Health effects of caregiving: The Caregiver Health Effects Study: An ancillary study of the Cardiovascular Health Study.: *Annals of Behavioural Medicine, 19*(2), 110-116.

Cameron, J., Franche, R., Cheung, A., and Stewart, D. (2002). Lifestyle Interference and Emotional Distress in Family Caregivers of Advanced Cancer Patients. *Cancer, 94*(2), 21-527.

Charalambous, A., Papastavrou, E., and Tsangari, H. (2009). Exploring the other side of cancer care: The informal caregiver. *European Journal of Oncology Nursing, 13*, 128-136.

Clinch, J., Coristine, M., Coyle, D., Earle, C.C., Glossop, R., Grunfeld, E., Janz, T., Reyno, L., Viola, R., Willan, A., and Whelan, T. (2004). Family caregiver Burden: Results of a longitudinal study of breast cancer patients and their principal caregivers. *Canadian Medical Association Journal,* 1795-1801.

Cotrim, H., and Pereira, G. (2008). Impact of colorectal cancer on patient and family: Implications for care. *European Journal of Oncology Nursing, 12,* 217-226.

Covinsky, K.E., Newcomer, R., Fox, P., Wood, J., Sands, L., Dane, K., *et al.* (2003). Patient and caregiver characteristics associated with depression in caregivers of patients with dementia. *Journal of General Internal Medicine, 18*(12), 1006-1014.

Dahl, A.A., Fossa, S.D., Grov, E.K., and Moum, T. (2005). Anxiety, depression, and quality of life in caregivers of patients with cancer in late palliative phase. *Annals of Oncology, 16,* 1185-1191.

Ferlay, J., Franceschi, S., and Martel, C. (2012). Global burden of cancers attributable to infections in 2008: A review and synthetic analysis. *The Lancet Oncology, 13,* 607-615.

Fleming, D.A., Sheppard, V.B., Mangan, P.A., Taylor, K.L., Tallarico, M., Adams, I., *et al.* (2006). Caregiving at the end of life: Perceptions of health care quality and quality of life among patients and caregivers. *Journal of Pain Symptom Management, 31*(5), 407-420.

Gillath, O., Mikulincer, M., Nitzberg, R., and Shaver, P. (2005). Attachment, Caregiving, and Altruism: Boosting Attachment Security Increases

Compassion and Helping. *Journal of Personality and Social Psychology, 89*(5), 817-839.

Given, B., Given, C., Sherwood, P. (2008). What Knowledge and skills do caregivers need? *American Journal of Nursing, 108*(9), 28-34.

Given, B., Given, C., Jeon, S., Sherwood, P., Shikoskii, A., and Rahbar, M. (2006). The impact of providing symptom management assistance on caregiver reaction: results of a randomized trial. *Journal of Pain and Symptom Management, 32*(5), 433-443.

Grassi, L. (2007). Bereavement in families with relatives dying of cancer. *Current Opinion in Supportive and Palliative Care, 2007*(1), 43-49.

Haley, W.E., Han, B., LaMonde, L.A., Narramore, S., Schonwetter, R., (2001). Family caregiving in hospice: Effects on psychological and health functioning among spousal caregivers of hospice patients with lung cancer of dementia. *Hospice Journal, 15*(4), 1-18.

Jepson C. McCorkle R., Adler D., Nuamah I., Lusk E. (1999). Effects of home care on caregivers' psychosocial status. *Image the Journal of Nursing Scholarship 31*, 115-120.

Jepson, C., *et al.* (1999). Effects of home care on caregivers' psychosocial status. *Journal of Nursing Scholarship, 31*(2), 115-20.

Katapodi, M.C., Northhouse, L.L., Schafenacker, A.N., and Weiss, D. (2012). The impact of caregiving on the psychological well-being of family caregivers and cancer patients. *Seminars in Oncology Nursing, 28*(4), 236-245.

Land, H., Hudson, S.M., and Stiefel, B. (2003). Stress and depression among HIV-positive and HIV-negative gay and bisexual AIDS caregivers. *AIDS and Behaviour, 7*(1), 41-53.

Miaskowski, C., Ruland, C.M., and Stenberg, U. (2014). Review of the literature on the effects of caring for a patient with cancer. *Psycho-Oncology, 19*, 1013-1025.

Mishra, R.C. and Awasthi, P. (2004). Health Psychology and Community Development. *Indian Journal of Community Psychology, 1*, 156-170.

National Centre on Caregiving. (2014). *Family Caregiver Alliance*. San Francisco: California.

Nijboer, C., Triemstra, M., Tempelaar, R., Sanderman, R. and Bos, Van den G., A.M. (1999). Determinants of caregiving experiences and mental health of partners of cancer patients. *Cancer, 4* (86), 577-588.

Northouse, L.L., Mood, D., Templin, T., Mellon, S., George, T. (2000). Couples' patterns of adjustment to colon cancer. *Social Science Medicine, 50*(2), 271-84.

Ochs, H.D., Savage, M., Scanlan, J.M., Vitaliano, P.P., and Zhang, J. (2001). Lymphocyte proliferation is associated with gender, caregiving, and psychosocial variables in olderadults. *Journal of Behavioural Medicine, 24*(6), 537-559.

Pinquart, M., and Sorenson, S. (2003). Differences between Caregivers and Non-Caregivers in Psychological Health and Physical Health: A Meta-Analysis. *Psychology and Aging, 18*(2), 250-267.

Pinquart, M., Sörensen, S., (2006). Helping caregivers of persons with dementia: which interventions work and how large are their effects? *International Psychogeriatrics, 18*(4), 577-95.

Rivera, J.R.H. (2009). Depression Symptoms in Cancer Caregivers. *Clinical Journal of Oncology Nursing, 13*(2), 195-202.

Scanlan, J.M., Vitaliano, P.P., Zhang, J., Savage, M., and Ochs, H.D. (2001). Lymphocyte proliferation is associated with gender, caregiving, and psychosocial variables in older adults. *Journal of Behavioural Medicine, 24*(6), 537-559.

Schulz, R., and Beach, S. (1999). Caregiving as a risk factor for mortality: The caregiver health effects study. *Journal of the American Medical Association, 282*(23), 2215-2219.

Song, J.I., Shin D.W., Choi J.Y., *et al.*, (2011). *Quality of life and mental health in family.*

The Times of India. (2014, April 12). (Sinha, K. TOI). 1 million new cancer cases being diagnosed in India each year: Study.

World Health Organization. (2015). *World Cancer Report 2014*. Geneva: Switzerland.

19

Evaluation of the FRIENDS Intervention for Childhood Anxiety in Hong Kong

Parul Batra Sabey, Diane C. Zelman and
Christopher D. Tori

Introduction

Anxiety is a common childhood problem affecting as many as 10 per cent to 20 per cent of children (Cartwright-Hatton, McNicol, and Doubleday, 2006; Essau, Conradt, Sasagawa, and Ollendick, 2012). Characterized by persistent inaccurate perception of danger or threat and avoidance of feared stimuli, childhood anxiety problems include phobias, separation anxiety, generalized anxiety, social anxiety, panic and agoraphobia. They are distinguished from fears that are developmentally normal by their chronicity, their severity, and the extent to which they interfere with everyday functioning (Essau, 2007). Despite their interest in friendship, children with anxiety problems are more likely to face difficulties in peer relationships, including being less likely to initiate social interaction, being less able to respond when others extend interest in interaction, and being more prone to peer rejection (Coplan & Ooi, 2013; Knitzer, 2003). Childhood anxiety also adversely influences educational achievement (Barrett, Lock, & Farrell, 2005; National Scientific Council on the Developing Child, 2010). Untreated anxiety can increase the risk of later affective disorder, substance abuse and unemployment (Skryabina, Morris, Byrne, Harkin & Rook, 2016).

A number of psychotherapeutic interventions have established efficacy for childhood anxiety, with cognitive behaviour therapy showing particularly robust effects among both children and adolescents in randomized controlled trials and other research (David-Ferdon & Kaslow, 2008; Reynolds, Wilson, Austin & Hooper, 2012; Seligman & Ollendick, 2011; Silverman, Pina & Viswesvaram, 2008). Cognitive behavioural interventions typically utilize problem-solving to challenge mental schemas that give rise to inaccurate perceptions of threat, as well as psychoeducation, collaborative problem-solving, skills training, and homework assignments to help new skills generalize to everyday life (Beck, 1995).

Schools can be an ideal venue for the delivery of prevention and intervention programmes for anxiety and depression. A recent meta-analysis of school-based CBT programmes for youth, reviewing 63 studies, noted that school-based interventions can reduce stigma when school screenings and programmes are universally available to students, that such interventions increase access to mental health care, and that they provide helpful liaison in school settings in which the impact of anxiety or depression may be greatest (Mychailyzn, Brodman, Read & Kendall, 2012). Both interventions provided on a school-wide basis and those targeted at children with depression and anxiety have shown efficacy; targeted interventions may be more cost-effective and associated with larger effect sizes (Ahlen, Breitholtz, Barrett, & Gallegos, 2012; Silverstone, Bercov, Suen, Allen, Cribben, Goodrick, *et al.*, 2017).

FRIENDS is a cognitive behavioural therapy-based programme developed to reduce anxiety and enhance resiliency in children, that has demonstrated efficacy in several countries (Skryabina *et al.*, 2016). Developed by Paula Barrett (1995), a leading psychologist in the area of prevention and treatment of childhood anxiety in Australia, the FRIENDS programme was designed as an intervention for childhood anxiety and depression, as a preventive intervention that can be useful regardless of individuals' risk status, and as part of general school curriculum (Farrell & Barrett, 2007; Pahl & Barrett, 2001). This resilience-building programme was designed to enable children to better cope with stress and thereby reduce symptoms of anxiety and depression; helping them to be resilient in the face of adversity.

The FRIENDS programme is geared to children's changing developmental needs, and includes three separate forms of the programme: one for preschool children (Fun FRIENDS; ages 4-6), another for school age children (FRIENDS for Life; ages 6-10) and the last for older youth

(FRIENDS for Youth; ages 10-16 years). The primary goals of the group format are positive modelling of approaches to manage anxiety, normalizing the experience of anxiety, and reinforcing successes. The cognitive behavioural therapy components include identifying thoughts and feelings, relaxation strategies, cognitive restructuring, problem solving, self-reward, and relapse prevention. The social skills components include the establishment of a social support network, managing conflict, and helping others. Children receive weekly experiential homework assignments to provide them the opportunity for practice of newly learned skills and generalization to coping with real-life situations. The family skills component can be accomplished through parenting workshops.

FRIENDS utilizes evidence-based intervention and has been acknowledged as an effective means of treating anxiety in children by the World Health Organization. Barrett's research team and other researchers have continued to publish outcome and cross-cultural research. Preliminary evidence for the effectiveness of the cognitive behavioural therapy *Coping Koala* programme, the manualized treatment guide for FRIENDS, was provided by Barrett, Dadds, and Rapee (1996), who found that 73 per cent of the children in the cognitive behavioural therapy groups and 95.6 per cent of the children in the cognitive behavioural therapy + family intervention group no longer fulfilled the diagnostic criteria for anxiety at 6- and 12-month follow-ups. Lowry-Webster, Barrett, and Dadds (2001) further examined its effectiveness in children aged 10-13, revealing significant decrements in anxiety and depression for subjects in the treatment condition. At a 12-month follow-up prevention effects were maintained for 85 per cent of children. Barrett and Turner (2001) evaluated the effects of the FRIENDS as a preventive measure for internalizing symptoms in children (ages 9-10) in 10 schools in Brisbane; the FRIENDS programme tested favourably for children and youth, and was implemented as part of the standard curriculum during class time (Barrett, Lowry-Webster, and Turner, 1999). Skryabina and colleagues (2016) recently utilized qualitative research methodology to ascertain the acceptance of the FRIENDS programme among children and classroom teachers in England, reporting that both children and teachers felt the programme inculcates useful skills and that teachers felt the programmes was well-structured in its presentation of the cognitive behavioural model.

In sum, there has been a great deal of support for the efficacy of the FRIENDS programme as a universal treatment and prevention approach, which has been successfully extended to several versions in different languages, and has been associated with successful trials in the United

States, the United Kingdom, Canada, the Netherlands, Germany, Norway, Finland, and Mexico. Research indicates that up to 80 per cent of children showing anxiety symptoms no longer exhibited these upon completion, and its long-term effectiveness has been confirmed at 6 years post-treatment (Barrett, Duffy, Dadds, and Rapee, 2001; Fisak, Richard, & Mann, 2011).

The aim of this study was to evaluate the effectiveness of the FRIENDS programme in the treatment of anxiety and socio-emotional problems among Hong Kong, Chinese and Western-expatriate children. Although the majority of the empirical evidence studied internationally shows that the FRIENDS programme has benefits for young people from culturally diverse populations, whether the efficacy of FRIENDS interventions extends to Chinese, expatriate and multicultural population within Hong Kong has received relatively little attention.

Previously a British colony, Hong Kong has been influenced by Western ideas and practices. However, Hong Kong still retains a largely Chinese socio-cultural emphasis (*via,* for example, encouragement of Confucian values such as obedience, social conformity, and high academic performance). Wong and Tsoi's (1999) review emphasizes the very high value placed on educational accomplishment by Hong Kong parents, values that can engender academic anxiety. Given the large emphasis on emotional restraint in Asian cultures, personal distress is likely modulated through internalizing behavioural patterns (Chen and Swartzman, 2001), wherein individuals in distress may attempt to control emotions and direct their negative feelings towards themselves; leading to withdrawal, depression and anxiety. Research has indicated that higher levels of anxiety exist among Chinese children compared with their Western counterparts and has attributed this in part to academic pressure (Tsoi and Pryde, 1999). Data from the Hong Kong Hospital Authority indicated that adolescent use of their outpatient clinics had increased greater than 30 per cent between the years of 2001/2002 and 2006/2007 (Choi and Hung, 2011). A study of 500 secondary school students in Hong Kong presented a 16.4 per cent prevalence of psychiatric disorders, with anxiety disorders demonstrating the highest prevalence (6.9%) across all disorders (Leung, Hung, Ho, Lee, Liu, *et al.*, 2008).

There is a need to explore interventions such as FRIENDS that might help children in Hong Kong who may be especially prone to internalizing problems. The efficacy of FRIENDS in reducing internalizing symptoms in children aged 8-10 was investigated by Siu (2007), indicating significantly higher self-esteem and fewer internalizing symptoms among children with anxiety enrolled in the programme. A subsequent study also supported the premise that the FRIENDS programme is suitable for a Hong Kong based child population (Siu, 2008).

Additionally, to establish the validity of FRIENDS in a multicultural society such as Hong Kong, more research addressing the expatriate community of Hong Kong is needed. The term "Third Culture Kids" has been coined to describe children, generally of privileged classes, whose upbringing has been characterized by growing up in a society other than that of their birth or their parents' birth and culture (Cockburn, 2002). They have often experienced frequent international moves to accommodate parents' professional assignments, and they often attend international schools with similar children of many national origins, including the host country. Their psychological identities often represent a complicated blend of their culture of origin, their adopted culture, and the culture of peers with similar international experiences. The emotional impact of such upbringing includes both positive and negative features. Negative adjustment reactions include stress responses from the need to frequently adapt to new communities, peers and schools, confused identity, and unresolved grief, leading to a high prevalence of depressive and anxiety symptoms (Bell-Villada, Sichel, Eidse, & Orr, 2011; Cockburn, 2002; Pollock & Van Reken, 2009). Positive responses may include the internalization of multiple identities, stronger multicultural competence and confidence in intercultural communication (Moore and Barker, 2012).

In sum, childhood anxiety remains a pressing mental health issue today. FRIENDS is one of few programmes in Hong Kong that directly address childhood anxiety. As the FRIENDS programme can be implemented as both a group therapy and within a general school curriculum, it could be adapted to reach many children in Hong Kong. Considerable data has confirmed the effectiveness of FRIENDS when provided in a range of settings (e.g., schools, clinic) and across cultures.

The present research aimed to investigate first, the extent to which children with anxiety problems who participated in FRIENDS showed greater reduction in anxiety and socio-emotional problems relative to a benchmark comparison sample of children in the same community with anxiety who did not participate. The second research question was whether treatment effects, if any, were more pronounced among preschool/ elementary age (Fun FRIENDS) or primary school age children (FRIENDS for Life). The final research question was whether the percentage of children who meet criteria for anxiety disorders would diminish after participation in the FRIENDS programme.

Method

Study Design

This study compared a sample of participants in the FRIENDS intervention condition to a benchmark comparison group. The FRIENDS programme groups were adapted to accommodate different developmental stages and age groups: Fun FRIENDS for children of 4-6 years of age, FRIENDS for Life for children of 7-9 years of age, and My Youth for children 10-14 years of age. Due to the small number of participants in the My Youth age group (n = 3), this group was removed from further analysis.

Participants

Participants (N=48, 28 boys and 20 girls) were students between 4 and 9 years of age in Hong Kong who were enrolled in local international schools, 78 per cent Western/expatriate, 22 per cent ethnic Chinese, mean age of 7.2 (SD = 2.22). All children were deemed to have sufficient English proficiency to participate. The FRIENDS intervention sample (n=33) consisted of 16 children enrolled in Fun FRIENDS (ages 4 to 6) and 17 children enrolled in FRIENDS for Life (ages 7 to 9). Participants were recruited via advertisementat local international schools in Hong Kong and included in the programme if they reported anxiety symptoms with related socio-emotional difficulties (e.g. difficulties with sleep or peer relationships), based on interview by the programme director, by study measures (described below), or by teacher/parent report.

The benchmark comparison group (n=15: Fun FRIENDS, n = 7, FRIENDS for Life, n = 8) consisted of children who resided in a neighbourhood inhabited by both English-speaking expatriate and ethnic Chinese children. The students attended international schools but did not participate in the FRIENDS programme. After an initial assessment, children's' data were retained for the present analysis if they demonstrated a Clinician Severity Rating of 4 on at least one diagnosis on the Anxiety Disorders Interview Schedule for DSM-IV Child and Parent Versions (ADIS-IV, Brown, Di Nardo & Barlow, 1994) or if they had scores above recommended clinical cut-off scores on Spence's Children's Anxiety Scale (SCAS, Spence, 1997) or the Preschool Anxiety Scale (PAS, Spence, Rapee, McDonald & Ingram, 2001).

All procedures were approved by the Institutional Research Board of Alliant International University.

Measures

The Anxiety Disorders Interview Schedule for DSM-IV. The Anxiety Disorders Interview Schedule for DSM-IV Child and Parent versions (ADIS-C/P; Brown, Di Nardo, and Barlow, 1994) is a commonly used diagnostic and research interview to establish the presence, type and severity of anxiety and mood or psychotic disorders in children. Each anxiety disorder assessment yields a score on an 8-point Clinician's Rating Scale (CSR; 1 = low or little risk to 8 = high risk). A CSR score of 4 or greater for an anxiety disorder is defined as representing a clinically significant diagnosis. In the present study, the ADIS Parent version was used, and two scales, Generalized Anxiety Disorder and Social Phobia were scored. The ADIS-IV has received research support and has demonstrated sensitivity to treatment effects (Barrett *et al.*, 1996; Broeren & Muris, 2008; Spence, Donovan, & Brechman-Toussaint, 2000). The ADIS-IV possesses sound psychometric properties (Rapee, Barrett, Dadds, & Evans, 1994). It has demonstrated acceptable to excellent test-retest reliability in assessing DSM-IV anxiety disorder symptoms and diagnoses in children (Silverman, Saavedra, & Pina, 2001), and has acceptable interrater agreement when examining both principal diagnoses (*kappa* = 0.92) and individual anxiety disorders (*kappas* = 0.8 – 1.0; Lyneham, Abbott, & Rapee, 2007).

Spence's Children's Anxiety Scale (SCAS). The SCAS (Spence, 1997) evaluates symptoms related to Social Phobia, Separation Anxiety, Generalised Anxiety, Obsessive-Compulsive Disorder, Panic-Agoraphobia, and fears and phobias related to physical injury, in children between the ages of 8 and 12 years. It contains 45 items that are rated by participants on a 4-point Likert scale, which correspond with the frequency to which specified symptoms are experienced, ranging from "Never" (Score=0) to "Always" (Score=3). Mean SCAS-C total scores of 32.20 are reported for clinically anxious children (Barrett and Turner, 2003). Higher scores are indicative of a greater severity of anxiety symptoms.

High internal consistency has been reported for total Anxiety scores in a community child sample (Cronbach's α =.92; Spence, 1997) and an adolescent sample (Cronbach's α =.92; Spence, 2003), with a 6-month test-retest reliability of .60 and .63 respectively (Spence, 1997). In this study, internal consistency reliability (Cronbach's α) was obtained for both the pre-test and post-test administration of the SCAS. Cronbach's α's were as follows for pre-and post-tests: (a) Overall Anxiety (.65 and .90), (b) Generalized Anxiety Disorder (.42 and .58), (c) Social Phobia

(.60 and .51), (d) Separation Anxiety Disorder (.75 and .68), (e) Obsessive Compulsive Disorder (.73 and .85), (f) Panic and Agoraphobia (.75 and .70), and (g) Personal Injury Fears (.40 and .68).

The Preschool Anxiety Scale (PAS). The PAS is a 34-item preschool form adapted from the SCAS, for children between the ages of 2.5 and 6.5 years (Spence, Rapee, McDonald & Ingram, 2001). The instrument has 28 anxiety-based items, and 6 post-traumatic stress disorder items (non-scored). Like the SCAS, the parent indicates the frequency of occurrence on a 4-point scale from "Not at all" to "Very often true."The PAS yields five sub-scale scores of Separation Anxiety, Physical Injury Fears, Social Phobia, Obsessive Compulsive Disorder and Generalized Anxiety Disorder, and a composite measure of anxiety can be calculated. High scores are indicative of anxiety symptoms. The authors reported adequate psychometric properties (Spence, Barrett, & Turner, 2003). In the present study, internal consistency coefficients (Cronbach's α) were computed at both the pre-test and post-test administration of the PAS. Cronbach's α's were as follows: (a) Overall Anxiety (.64 and .90), (b) Generalized Anxiety Disorder (.42 and .40), (c) Social Phobia (.75 and .85), (d) Separation Anxiety Disorder (.64 and .54), (e) Obsessive Compulsive Disorder (.80 and .86), and (f) Physical Injury Fears (.40 and .68).

The Strengths and Difficulties Questionnaire (SDQ). The SDQ is an internationally used adult-completed 25-item behavioural screening measure of children and adolescent's (between 4 and 16 years of age) strengths and problems (Goodman, 1997). Items are rated on a 3-point scale (from 1=Not True to 3=Certainly True), that yield scores on scales assessing Emotional Symptoms, Conduct Problems, Hyperactivity, Peer Relationship Problems, and Prosocial Behaviour. The aggregate sum represents the "Overall Stress" score, and a score pertaining to the impact of the child's behaviour. SDQ scores are highly correlated with corresponding scales on the well-established Rutter questionnaires (Elander & Rutter, 1996), and the scale developer reports sound psychometric properties of the informant-rated SDQ (Goodman, 1997). High internal reliability of parent-completed SDQ scales was found in a Swedish population sample (Cronbach's α =.76; Smedje, Broman, Hetta, & von Knorring, 1999). Smedje *et al.* (1999) reported a test-retest reliability of .96 for total scores over a 2-week period. Goodman (2001) found support for the internal consistency of the scale (Cronbach's α = .73), the test-retest reliability after between 4 and 6 months (mean = .62), and the validity of the SDQ in measuring the adjustment and psychopathology of children and youth on a nationwide epidemiological British sample. In this study, internal consistency reliability coefficients (Cronbach's α) for the pre-and post-test administration of the SDQ test were as follows: (a) Stress (.65 and .57), (b) Emotional Symptoms (.66 and .70), (c) Peer Problems (.60 and .59), (d) Conduct Problems (.51 and .53), (e) Hyperactivity and Attention Difficulties had high reliability (.76 and .73), and (f) Prosocial Behaviour (.78 and .73).

Procedure

Groups were co-led by a registered psychologist and a clinical psychology intern, who conducted the groups according to the Coping Koala FRIENDS manualised treatment guide. The treatment consisted of twelve 1.5-hour sessions, and two parent workshops. The programme engages students in small and large group activities, games and discussions, with interventions including identifying feelings and their links with thoughts, relaxation strategies, cognitive restructuring, self-reward, home practice, and relapse prevention; the interpersonal components include establishing a social support network, managing conflict, and helping others (Albano, Marten, Holt, & Barlow, 1995; Siu, 2008). Skills and strategies were taught in accordance with the FRIENDS acronym which directs a specific order for teaching of skills (*F*eelings, *R*emember to *R*elax, *I*nnermost thoughts, *I* can do it, *I* can do my best!, *E*xplore solutions and coping step plans, *N*ow reward yourself/*N*urture, *D*on't forget to practice!, and *S*mile! *S*tay calm! And talk to your *S*upport Networks!).

The two parent workshops were conducted at the outset of the programme and at a 3-month interval. They consisted of discussion and role-play to encourage family communication, address children's anxiety and inculcate positive thoughts. The family skills component focused on helping their children recognize bodily clues and feelings, the importance of relaxation and quiet time everyday, encouraging their child to focus on the positive (e.g., by sharing "happy things" as a family). Parents were taught the key components of the programme through the use of role-play and discussions of anxiety and threatening experiences. These were: (a) recognizing and dealing with their own anxiety, (b) reinforcement strategies to strengthen their child's positive behaviour, for example, praise and social or tangible rewards (there is an emphasis on the effort, rather than on being perfect), and "planned ignoring" was also taught as a means to deal with excessive complaining, (c) cognitive techniques to challenge unhelpful "red" thoughts and replace them with positive "green" thoughts, and family resilience-building techniques to encourage participants to break coercive cycles (Rombouts, 2010), and (d) lastly, parents were trained briefly to accommodate the needs of their children through effective communication, partner support, and problem solving skills (Shortt *et al.*, 2001). Measurements were collected prior to and following the 12-week intervention and at the beginning and end of a 12-week interval for the benchmark group.

Pre-assessment for the benchmark comparison group involved the administration of the same instruments as for the treatment group. All children whose data were retained for the purposes of the present study demonstrated symptoms of anxiety, as determined by a Clinician Severity Rating (CSR) of 4 on at least one of the stated anxiety diagnoses on the ADIS-IV, and/or a recommended cut-off score of 42 on the SCAS. The participants were assessed again after a 12-week interval.

Results

Preliminary chi-square and t-test analyses found no significant differences in the gender or ethnicity ratio or age between FRIENDS and benchmark comparison samples. Table 19.1 provides means and standard deviations for pre- and post-intervention measures and results of a 2 × 2 mixed ANOVA (Group = intervention versus benchmark; Time = pre-versus post-) performed for dependent measures for the Fun FRIENDS group (ages 4-6). Table 19.2 provides the same data for the FRIENDS for Life group (ages 7-9). Intervention effects were interpreted based on significant Group × Time interactions. To protect for Type 1 error, alpha level was set at .01 for interpretation of significant findings.

Anxiety Symptoms. In the Fun FRIENDS group, there was a significant Group × Time interaction in Overall Anxiety and in subscales for separation anxiety, social phobia and physical injury fear on the PAS, $F(1, 21) = 33.67, 29.98, 15.44$ and 11.68, all $p < .01$. Greater reduction in symptoms was found in all four subscales relative to the benchmark group. In the FRIENDS for Life group, there were significant Group x Time interactions on the SCAS for Overall Anxiety and the Generalized Anxiety Disorder subscale, $F(1, 23) = 21.32$ and 11.47, both $p < .01$, with scores decreasing to a greater extent in the intervention group.

Socio-Emotional Difficulties. In the Fun FRIENDS group, there was a significant Group x Time interaction for the Overall Stress Score, and the Emotional Symptoms, Conduct Problems and Hyperactivity subscales of the SDQ, $F(1,21) = 21.32, 15.74, 33.57$ and 12.56, all $p < .01$. Symptom

Table 19.1: Pre- and Post-Means, and Group × Time Interaction ANOVA for Fun FRIENDS Group (Ages 4-6) and Benchmark Comparison Group

Variables	*Fun FRIENDS Ages 4-6 (n=16)*		*Benchmark Ages 4-6 (n = 7)*		*Interaction Effect (Group × Time)*
	Pretest Mean (SD)	*Post-test Mean (SD)*	*Pretest Mean (SD)*	*Post-test Mean (SD)*	
Anxiety (PAS)					
Overall Anxiety	65.50(*6.99*)	51.06(*5.56*)	59.57(*8.50*)	58.43(*7.68*)	*F* (1, 21) =33.67*, ηρ²=.62
Separation Anxiety Disorder	63.69(*9.54*)	50.44(*6.18*)	60.71(*13.09*)	63.71(*10.59*)	*F* (1, 21) =29.98*, ηρ²=.56
Social Phobia	71.75(*11.36*)	54.31(*8.44*)	61.57(*11.30*)	58.00(*8.15*)	*F* (1, 21) = 15.44*, ηρ²=.42
Generalised Anxiety	59.28(*11.69*)	48.75(*7.46*)	59.33(*9.10*)	59.80(*8.83*)	*F* (1, 21) = 4.04, n.s, ηρ² =.24
Disorder	56.00(*9.55*)	49.44(*7.99*)	52.86(*12.92*)	53.43(*12.67*)	*F* (1, 21) = 11.68*, ηρ² =.36
Personal Injury Fears					
Socio-emotional (SDQ)	18.00 (5.22)	9.50 (2.58)	16.14 (3.07)	14.71 (3.25)	*F* (1, 21) = 13.26*, ηρ² =.39
Overall Stress	5.25 (2.52)	2.19 (1.64)	5.29 (1.80)	5.29 (1.89)	*F* (1, 21) = 15.74*, ηρ² =.43
Emotional Symptoms	3.44 (3.44)	1.50 (1.51)	2.29 (1.38)	3.14 (1.68)	*F* (1, 21) = 33.57*, ηρ² =.62
Conduct Problems	3.38 (3.38)	1.06 (1.06)	2.00 (.82)	2.43 (1.51)	*F* (1, 21) = 12.56*, ηρ² =.37
Hyperactivity	4.06 (4.06)	2.31 (1.54)	3.71 (2.29)	3.14 (2.12)	*F* (1, 21) = 2.27, n.s., ηρ² =.1
Peer Problems	5.75 (1.77)	7.00 (1.67)	6.71 (2.29)	6.86 (2.27)	*F* (1, 21) = 2.98 n.s., ηρ² =.20
Prosocial Behaviour					
Anxiety Diagnoses (ADIS)					
Generalised Anxiety	2.19 (2.99)	0.63 (1.75)	1.00 (2.65)	1.00 (2.65)	*F* (1, 21) = 2.08, n.s., ηρ² =.09
Disorder Social Phobia	5.00 (2.25)	1.31 (2.02)	4.86 (2.34)	5.00 (2.45)	*F* (1, 21) = 24.08*, ηρ² =.53

Note: PAS = The Preschool Anxiety Scale; SDQ = Strengths and Difficulties Questionnaire; ADIS = The Anxiety Disorders Interview Schedule for DSM-IV, *SD* = standard deviation. *p <.01

Table 19.2: Pre- and Post-Means, and Group × Time Interaction ANOVA for FRIENDS for Life Group (Ages 7-9) and Benchmark Comparison Group

	FRIENDS for Life Ages 7-9 (n=17)		*Benchmark Ages 7-9 (n = 8)*		*Interaction Effect (Groupx Time)*
	Pretest Mean (SD)	*Post-test (SD) Mean*	*Pretest Mean (SD)*	*Post-test (SD) Mean*	
Anxiety (SCAS)					
Overall Anxiety	52.94 (6.65)	42.82 (7.34)	54.38 (4.21)	52.88 (4.70)	F (1, 23) = 21.32*, n.s., $\eta\rho^2$ =.48
Social Phobia	56.00 (11.65)	49.06 (6.56)	54.63 (5.85)	54.88 (5.79)	F (1, 23) = 3.44, n.s., $\eta\rho^2$ =.13
Panic Disorder/Agoraphobia	46.77 (6.67)	43.47 (4.82)	51.75 (12.3)	51.13 (11.70)	F (1, 23) = 3.37, n.s., $\eta\rho^2$ =.04
Separation Anxiety Disorder	55.77 (8.30)	49.71 (9.31)	58.25 (11.61)	60.63 (9.55)	F (1, 23) = 3.75, n.s., $\eta\rho^2$ =.14
Generalised Anxiety Disorder	54.47 (8.45)	45.77 (5.83)	56.13 (7.70)	58.38 (6.82)	F (1, 23) = 11.47*, $\eta\rho^2$ =.33
Personal Injury Fears	56.23 (8.67)	50.06 (9.63)	52.38 (11.61)	53.75 (12.62)	F (1, 23) = 4.81, n.s., $\eta\rho^2$ =.17
Socio-emotional (SDQ)					
Overall Stress	16.88 (3.57)	10.12 (5.65)	11.88 (4.61)	10.50 (3.67)	F (1, 23) = 11.12*, $\eta\rho^2$ =.33
Emotional Symptoms	4.12 (2.18)	2.41 (1.91)	3.25 (1.39)	2.88 (1.81)	F (1, 23) = 1.99, n.s., $\eta\rho^2$ =.08
Conduct Problems	2.47 (1.55)	1.94 (1.44)	2.25 (1.91	1.75 (1.83)	F (1, 23) =.00, n.s., $\eta\rho^2$ =.00
Hyperactivity	2.76 (1.95)	1.71 (1.90)	2.00 (2.56)	1.88 (2.64)	F (1, 23) = 1.09, n.s, $\eta\rho^2$ =.05
Peer Problems	3.59 (1.91)	1.71 (1.45)	2.00 (1.85)	2.00 (1.77)	F (1, 23) = 6.54, n.s., $\eta\rho^2$ =.22
Prosocial Behaviour	5.77 (2.97)	6.82 (3.03)	7.88 (1.96)	7.88 (1.96)	F (1, 23) = 1.39, n.s., $\eta\rho^2$ =.06
Anxiety Diagnoses (ADIS)					
Generalised Anxiety Disorder	3.47 (3.48)	1.06 (1.98)	2.13 (3.04)	2.25 (3.24)	F (1, 23) = 6.66, n.s. $\eta\rho^2$ =.22
Social Phobia	4.83 (2.92)	1.76 (2.19)	2.00 (2.88)	2.13 (3.04)	F (1, 23) = 15.89*, $\eta\rho^2$ =.41

Note: SCAS= The Preschool Anxiety Scale; SDQ = Strengths and Difficulties Questionnaire; ADIS = The Anxiety Disorders Interview Schedule for DSM-IV, *SD* = Standard deviation. *p <.01

scores decreased to a greater extent for the intervention group. For the FRIENDS for Life group, there was a significant Group × Time interaction only for the Overall Stress score of the SDQ, $F(1, 23) = 11.12, p = .003$, with scores decreasing more for the intervention group.

Anxiety Diagnoses. For ADIS-IV Social Phobia scores in the Fun FRIENDS group, there was a significant Group × Time interaction, $F(1, 21) = 24.08, p < .001$, with scores decreasing only for the intervention group. For ADIS-IV Social Phobia scores in the FRIENDS for Life group, there was also a significant Group × Time interaction, $F(1, 23) = 15.89$, $p < .01$, and scores decreased only for the intervention sample. For Generalized Anxiety Disorder scores of the ADIS-IV, the Group × Time intervention was not significant for either the older or younger sample, although the intervention approached significance for the older group, $F(1, 23) = 6.66, p = .02$.

The frequency of clinically significant scores on the ADIS-IV Social Phobia evaluation decreased before and after the group by 39 per cent for the younger group (86.8% to 47.8%) and 26 per cent for the older group (64% to 38%).

Discussion

Anxiety is a problem for children and adolescents worldwide. Cognitive behavioural-based interventions such as the FRIENDS programme has provided over twenty years of successful results, but the programme has received only limited research attention in Hong Kong and among an expatriate and international school community. Clinical writings and research have suggested that prevailing cultural values in Hong Kong emphasizing high achievement can engender anxiety (Tsoi and Pryde, 1999), and that Third Culture Kids in Hong Kong may be prone to social anxiety related to frequent international transitions and changes in peer groups and schools (Cockburn, 2002). Research has shown that school-based interventions can be efficacious when applied both universally (for prevention and resilience) and in a targeted manner (for children and adolescents with anxiety or depression), indicating a need for greater research evaluation of the FRIENDS programme, which is designed to be applied either in schools or clinics.

Together, the current results support the effectiveness of FRIENDS for both younger and older children in a culturally diverse population in Hong Kong, showing its potential to buffer some of the pathogenic effects of stress and anxiety. Evaluation of anxiety scores on the SCAS and its younger child version, the PAS, showed that Fun FRIENDS programme (ages 4-6) yielded reduction in anxiety symptoms (overall symptoms, separation anxiety, social phobia and physical injury fear) relative to the benchmark sample, and that the FRIENDS for Life group (ages 7-9) yielded reduction in overall anxiety and generalised anxiety symptoms relative to the benchmark sample. Degree of severity of social anxiety diagnoses (ADIS-IV) also decreased relative to the benchmark sample for both younger and older groups. FRIENDS was associated with reduction in socio-emotional and behavioural problems in the domains of overall stress, emotional symptoms, conduct problems and hyperactivity for the younger group, and overall stress for the older group.

Evaluation of differences between the age groups in the FRIENDS intervention outcomes reveal that children in the younger Fun FRIENDS (ages 4-6) compared to the older FRIENDS for Life age groups (ages 7-9) benefited most from the intervention, demonstrating greater effect sizes and significant reductions in more domains of anxiety. These results corroborate previous findings that report an inverse correlation between age and degree of anxiety reduction after intervention (e.g., Barrett and Turner, 2001; Lowry-Webster, Barrett and Dadds, 2001; Lowry-Webster, Barrett and Lock, 2003). This suggests that prevention and intervention efforts are most effective when targeted earlier in the developmental phases of the child (Lock and Turner, 2003), and that in prior research, anxiety and socio-emotional symptoms decreased to a greater extent among younger age groups (Lock and Barrett, 2003; Dadds, Spence, Holland, Barrett, and Laurens, 1997).

It is notable that although FRIENDS primary addresses internalizing problems such as depression and anxiety, the programme also yielded reduction in externalizing problems (conduct problems and hyperactivity), although only in the younger sample. This may be because anxiety symptoms among the younger group might present to a greater extent in visible manifestations such as behavioural misconduct, inattention, hyperactivity, restlessness, and irritability.

A number of limitations in the present research should be noted. First, further research should utilize a randomised controlled design. Second, several domains of change reached significance at the $p <.05$, but not the more conservative $p <.01$ level in the present study (e.g., Generalized Anxiety Disorder diagnoses in the older group), suggesting the need to gather larger samples for further research. At the time of this study, the FRIENDS programme in Hong Kong was promoted as a prevention programme building psychological resilience in all children.

Although the programme was quite popular in the international schools, parents of potential participants in this research expressed concerns regarding research measures pertaining to psychological symptoms, showing particular sensitivity to personal and intrusive questions relating to psychological problems or diagnoses. It was noted that predominantly the Chinese families in the international schools showed reluctance to engage in the research study, while being otherwise open to the FRIENDS programme. In addition, the socio-cultural emphasis on emotional restraint, moderation and control of one's feelings, may have reduced openness to disclosure for participants in this Asian setting, particularly for parents of Chinese origin (Williams, Foo and Haarghoff, 2006). Therefore, although interest in the FRIENDS programme was strong in the schools providing the programme, and although recent research has established that the programme is supported both by children and teachers (Skryabina *et al.*, 2016), parents' willingness to participate in the research assessments was lower than expected. In light of cultural stigma related to diagnosis, future FRIENDS research in Hong Kong should utilize more strength-based assessment.

References

Albano, A.M., Marten, P.A., Holt, C.S., Heimberg, R.G., and Barlow, D.H. (1995). Cognitive-behavioural group treatment for social phobia in adolescents: A preliminary study. *Journal of Nervous and Mental Disease, 183,* 685-692. doi:10.1097/00005053-199510000-00006

Ahlen, J., Breitholtz, E., Barrett, P.M. and Gallegos, J. (2012). School-based prevention of anxiety and depression: a pilot study in Sweden. *Advances in School Mental Health Promotion, 5,* 245-257.http://dx.doi.org/10.1080/1754730X.2012.730352

Barrett, P.M. (1995). Group coping koala workbook. Unpublished manuscript, *School of Applied Psychology*, Griffith University, Australia.

Barrett, P.M., Dadds, M.R., and Rapee, R.M. (1996). Family treatment of childhood anxiety: A controlled trial. *Journal of Consulting and Clinical Psychology, 64*, 333-342. doi:10.1037/0022-006X.64.2.333

Barrett, P.M., Duffy, A.L., Dadds, M.R., and Rapee, R.M. (2001). Cognitive-behavioural treatment of anxiety disorders in children: Long-term (6-Year) follow-up. *Journal of Consulting and Clinical Psychology, 69,* 135-141. doi:10.1037/0022-006X.69.1.135

Barrett, P.M., Lock, S., and Farrell, L. (2005). Developmental differences in universal preventive intervention for child anxiety. *Clinical Child Psychology and Psychiatry, 10*, 539-555.

Barrett, P.M., Lowry-Webster, H.M., and Turner, C.M. (1999). *Friends Programme Social Validity and Treatment Integrity Scales*. Brisbane: Australian Academic Press.

Barrett, P.M., and Turner, C.M. (2001). Prevention of anxiety symptoms in primary school children: Preliminary results from a universal trial. *British Journal of Clinical Psychology, 40*, 399-410. doi:10.1348/014466501163887

Barrett, P.M., and Turner, C.M. (2003). Psychometric properties of the Spence Children's Anxiety Scale with young adolescents. *Anxiety Disorders, 17,* 605-625. doi:10.1016/S0887-6185(02)00236-0

Beck, J.S. (1995). *Cognitive Therapy: Basics and Beyond.* New York, NY: The Guilford Press.

Bell-Villada, G.H., Sichel, N., Eidse, F., and Orr, E.N. (2011). Writing out of limbo: International childhoods, global nomads, and third culture kids. Newcastle upon Tyne: Cambridge Scholars.

Broeren, S., and Muris, P. (2008). Psychometric evaluation of two new parent-rating scales for measuring anxiety symptoms in young Dutch children. *Journal of Anxiety Disorders*, 22, 949-958. doi:10.1007/s10578-009-0162-9.

Brown, T.A., DiNardo, P.A., and Barlow, D.H. (1994). *Anxiety disorders interview schedule for DSM-IV (ADIS-IV)*. New York, NY: Graywind.

Cartwright-Hatton, S., McNicol, K., and Doubleday, E. (2006). Anxiety in a neglected population: prevalence of anxiety in pre-adolescent children. *Clinical Psychology Review, 26,* 817-833. doi:10.1016/j.cpr.2005.12.002

Chen, X., and Swartzman, L. (2001). Health beliefs, attitudes and experiences in Asian cultures. In S.S. Kazarian and D.R. Evans (Eds.), *Handbook of Cultural Health Psychology*, pp. 389-410). NY: The Academic Press.

Choi, P.E. and Hung, S.F. (2011). Overview of adolescent mental health problems in Hong Kong. *Journal of Youth Studies, 14*, 3-8.

Cockburn, L. (2002). Children and Young People Living in Changing Worlds: The Process of Assessing and Understanding the 'Third Culture Kid.' *School Psychology International, 23,* 475-485. doi:10.1177/0143034302234008

Coplan, R.J. and Ooi, L. (2013). Young Children's Peer Relations: Links with Early Developing Anxiety and Depression. In: Tremblay RE, Boivin M, Peters RDeV, (eds). Rapee RM, topic (ed). *Encyclopedia on Early Childhood Development* [online]. http://www.child-encyclopedia.com/anxiety-and-depression/according-experts/young-childrens-peer-relations-links-early-developing. Published March 2013. Accessed August 10, 2017.

Dadds, M.R., Spence, S.H., Holland, D.E., Barrett, P.M., and Laurens, K.R. (1997). Prevention and early intervention for anxiety disorders: A controlled trial. *Journal of Consulting and Clinical Psychology, 65*, 627-635. doi:10.1037/0022-006X.65.4.627

David-Ferdon, C., and Kaslow, N.J. (2008). Evidence-based psychosocial treatments for child and adolescent depression. *Journal of Clinical Child and Adolescent Psychology*, *37*, 62-104. doi:10.1080/15374410701817865

Essau, C.A. (2007). Anxiety in children: When is it classed as adisorder that should bc treated? Expert Review of Neurotherapeutics, 7, 909-911. doi:10.1586/14737175.7.8.909.

Essau, C.A., Conradt, J., Sasagawa, S., and Ollendick, T.H. (2012). Prevention of anxiety symptoms in children: Results from a universal school-based trial. *Behaviour Therapy, 43*, 450-464.

Farrell, L., and Barrett, P. (2007). Prevention of childhood emotional disorders: Reducing the burden of suffering associated with anxiety and depression. *Child and Adolescent Mental Health, 12*, 58-65.

Fisak, B.J., Jr, Richard, D., and Mann, A. (2011). The prevention of child and adolescent anxiety: A meta-analytic review. *Prevention Science, 12*, 255-268. doi:10.1007/s11121-011-0210-0.

Goodman, R. (2001). Psychometric properties of the Strengths and Difficulties Questionnaire (SDQ). *Journal of the American Academy of Child and Adolescent Psychiatry, 40,* 1337-1345. doi:10.1097/00004583-200111000-00015

Goodman, R. (1997). The Strengths and Difficulties Questionnaire: A research note. *Journal of Child Psychology and Psychiatry, 38,* 581-586. doi:10.1111/j.1469-7610.1997.tb01545.x

Knitzer, J. (2003). Social and emotional development in young low-income children: What research tells us and why it matters for early school success. *Testimony presented at the Mailman School of Mental Health,* Columbia University, New York.

Leung, P.W.L., Hung, S.F., Ho, T.P., Lee, C.C., Liu, W.S., Tang, C.P., and Kwong, S.L. (2008). Prevalence of DSM-IV disorders in Chinese adolescents and the effects of an impairment criterion: A pilot community study in Hong Kong. *European Child and Adolescent Psychiatry, 17*, 452-461. doi:10.1007/s00787-008-0687-7

Lock, S., and Barrett, P.M. (2003). A longitudinal study of developmental differences in universal preventive intervention for child anxiety. *Behaviour Change, 20,* 183-199. doi:10.1375/bech.20.4.183.29383

Lowry-Webster, H.M., Barrett, P.M., and Dadds, M.R. (2001). A universal prevention trial of anxiety and depressive symptomatology in childhood: Preliminary data from an Australian study. *Behaviour Change, 18*, 36-50. doi:10.1375/bech.18.1.36

Lowry-Webster, H., Barrett, P., and Lock, S. (2003). A universal prevention trial of anxiety symptomatology during childhood: Results at one-year follow-up. *Behaviour Change, 20*, 25-43. doi:10.1375/bech.20.1.25.24843

Lyneham, H.J., Abbott, M.J., and Rapee, R.M. (2007). Interrater reliability of the anxiety disorders interview schedule for DSM-IV: Child and parent version. *Journal of American Academy of Child and Adolescent Psychiatry, 46,* 731-736. doi:10.1097/chi.0b013e3180465a09

Moore, A.M., and Barker, G.G. (2012) Confused or multicultural: Third culture individuals' cultural identity. *International Journal of Intercultural Relations, 36,* 553-562.doi: 10.1016/j.ijintrel.2011.11.002

Mychailyszyn, M.P., Brodman, D.M., Read, K.L., and Kendall, P.C. (2012). Cognitive-behavioural school-based interventions for anxious and depressed youth: a meta-analysis of outcomes. *Clinical Psychology: Science and Practice, 19*, 129-153. doi:10.1111/j.1468-2850.2012.01279.x

National Scientific Council on the Developing Child (2010). *Persistent Fear and Anxiety Can Affect Young Children's Learning and Development: Working Paper No. 9*. February 2010, National Scientific Council on the Developing Child, Centre on the Developing Child at Harvard University. http://www.developingchild.net

Pahl, K.M., and Barrett, P.M. (2007). The development of social-emotional competence in preschool aged children: An introduction of the Fun FRIENDS programme. *Australian Journal of Guidance and Counselling, 17,* 81-90. doi:10.1375/ajgc.17.1.81

Pollock, D.C. and Van Reken, R.E. (2009). *Third Culture Kids. Growing Up Among Worlds*. Boston, MA: Nicolas Brealey Publishing.

Rapee, R.M., Barrett, P.M., Dadds, M.R., and Evans, L. (1994). Reliability of the DSM-III-K childhood anxiety disorders using structured interview: Interrater and parent-child agreement. *Journal of the American Academy of Child and Adolescent Psychiatry, 33*, 984-992.

Reynolds, S., Wilson, C., Austin, J. and Hooper, L. (2012), Effects of psychotherapy for anxiety in children and adolescents: A meta-analytic review. *Clinical Psychology Review, 32*, 251-62, doi: 10.1016/j.cpr.2012.01.005

Rombouts, S. (2010, May). *FRIENDS Professional Training Programme*. Presented at the Blurton Family Development Centre, Hong Kong.

Seligman, L.D. and Ollendick, T.H. (2011). Cognitive behavioural therapy for anxiety disorders in youth. *Child Adolescent Psychiatric Clinics of North America, 20*, 217-238. doi:10.1016/j.chc.2011.01.003.

Shortt, A., Barrett, P., and Fox, T. (2001). Evaluating the FRIENDS programme: A cognitive behavioural group treatment of childhood anxiety disorders. An evaluation of the FRIENDS programme. *Journal of Clinical Child Psychology, 30*, 523-533. doi:10.1207/S15374424JCCP3004_09

Silverman, W.K., Pina, A.A., and Viswesvaran, C. (2008). Evidence-based psychosocial treatments for phobic and anxiety disorders in children and adolescents. *Journal of Clinical Child and Adolescent Psychology, 37*, 105-130. doi:10.1080/15374410701817907

Silverman, W.K., Saavedra, L.M., and Pina, A.A. (2001). Test-Retest reliability of anxiety symptoms and diagnoses with the anxiety disorders interview schedule for DSM-IV: child and parent versions. *Journal of American Academic Child and Adolescent Psychiatry, 40,* 937-944. doi:10.1097/00004583-200108000-00016

Silverstone, P.H., Bercov, M., Suen, V.Y.M. Allen, A., Cribben, I., Goodrick, J., Henry, S. Pryce, C., Langstraat, P., Rittenbach, K., Chakraborty, S. Engles, R.C., and McCabe, C. (2017). Long-term results from the Empowering a Multimodal Pathway Toward Healthy Youth Programme, a multimodal school-based approach, show marked reductions in suicidality, depression and anxiety in 6,227 students in grades 6-12 (aged 11-18). *Front Psychiatry, 8,* 81. doi: 10.3389/fpsyt.2017.00081.

Siu, A.F.Y. (2007). Using FRIENDS to combat internalizing problems among primary school children in Hong Kong. *Journal of Cognitive and Behavioural Psychotherapies, 7,* 11-26. Retrieved from http://jcbp.psychotherapy.ro/vol7no1/using-friends-to-combat-internalizing-problems-among-primary-school-children-in-hong-kong/

Siu, A.F.Y. (2008). A prevalence study on internalizing problems among primary school children in Hong Kong. *Journal of Child and Family Studies, 17,* 779-791. doi:10.1007/s10826-008-9189-y

Skryabina, E., Morris, J., Byrne, D., Harkin, N., Rook, S., and Stallard, P. (2016). Child, teacher and parent perceptions of the FRIENDS classroom-based universal anxiety prevention programme: A qualitative study. *School Mental Health, 8,* 486-498 doi: 10.1007/s12310-016-9187-y

Smedje, H., Broman, J.E., Hetta, and J., von Knorring, A.L. (1999). Psychometric properties of a Swedish version of the "Strengths and Difficulties Questionnaire". *European Child and Adolescent Psychiatry, 8,* 63-70. doi:10.1007/s007870050086

Spence, S.H. (1997). A measure of anxiety symptoms among children. *Behaviour Research and Therapy, 36,* 545-566.

Spence, S.H., Barrett, P.M., and Turner, C.M. (2003). Psychometric properties of the Spence Children's Anxiety Scale with young adolescents. *Anxiety Disorders, 17,* 605-625. doi:10.1016/S0887-6185(02)00236-0

Spence, S.H., Rapee, R., McDonald, C., and Ingram, M. (2001). The structure of anxiety symptoms among pre-schoolers. *Behaviour Research and Therapy, 39,* 1293-1316.

Tsoi, M.M., Pryde, N.A. (1999). Hong Kong's children: overview and conclusion. In N.A. Pryde and M.M. Tsoi (Eds.), *Hong Kong's children: Our past, their future* (pp. 13-20). Hong Kong: Centre of Asian Studies Occasional Papers and Monographs no. 137, University of Hong Kong.

Williams, M.M., Foo, K.H., and Haarhoff, B.A. (2006). Cultural considerations for Chinese people: Implications for CBT. In *29th Australian Association for Cognitive and Behaviour Therapy National Conference* (pp. 33).

Wong, C.K. and Tsoi, M.M. (1999). Mental health of Hong Kong Children. In *Hong Kong's Children: our past, their future* (pp. 153-220). In N.A. Pryde and M.M. Tsoi (Eds.), Centre of Asian Studies Occasional Papers and Monographs no. 137, University of Hong Kong.

20

The Structural Equation Modeling Approach

Future Time Perspective, Un-integrated Personality and Depression of Elderly People in Nursing Home

Dinie Ratri Desiningrum, N. Fauziah, Erin Ratna Kustanti, and *Anggun Resdasari Prasetyo*

Introduction

Being elderly is not a disease, but it is an advanced stage of a process of life characterized by a decreased ability of the body to adapt to stressors. In general, signs of aging process begin to appear since the age of 45 years and will cause problems at the age of about 60 years (Santrock, 2006). The elderly people are part of a growing number of family members and community members in line with increasing life expectancy.

Increasing the number of elderly people will have an impact on socio-economic status both in families, communities, and within the government. An important economic implication of increasing population is an increase in the old age ratio and their dependency. This dependence is due to the condition of many elderly people experiencing physical and psychological impediment, although these hindrance occur in the old age are natural thing (Kuntjoro, 2002). Some of the declines in the elderly can be cognitive problems (Harmand, *et al.* 2014), dementia disorders (Kooten, Smalbrugge, Wouden, Stek, & Hertogh, 2017), sleepiness disorder and depression (Chen, Huang, Cheng, Li, & Chang, 2015), as well as the risk of falling and resulting in broken bones difficult to be cured (Cox, *et al.*, 2016).

Cross-sectional studies of 400 elderly patients admitted to general hospitals or nursing homes were diagnosed with 20 per cent with delirium, 19.3 per cent had subsyndromal delirium (SSD), and 29.8 per cent had only dementia (Sepulveda, *et al.,* 2017). In another study, it was mentioned that physical health status is the most important factor affecting depression (Li, *et al.,* 2016).

Structured physical activity has a positive effect on decreasing anxiety, stress and depression, maintaining mental health and improving psychological vitality. It depends on the individual concerned, whether they choose to stay at home enjoying their days without any activity or busy themselves with exercising, doing activities, and dealing with others (Syamsuddin, 2008). A study of 80 elderly people (40 in experimental group and 40 in control group) looked at the impact of the "Physical Activity Programme" (10 minutes of warming up, 20 minutes of rhythmic exercise, 10 minute cold exercise and 30 minutes of leisurely stroll for four days a week) for the elderly in nursing homes can actually reduce the symptoms of depression and improve their quality of life (Lok, Lok, & Canbaz, 2017).

The family is an important source of support for the elderly, but the increasing number of elderly, the difficult economic life, the busy lifes of family members to take care of the elderly and various other reasons causes the elderly to no longer live with their families, and they live in nursing homes. For the elderly living in the nursing home, they can still do activities and socialize with the nurses and other inhabitants of the nursing home.

The existence of elderly in the nursing home has a positive side, that is the nursing home environment can provide its own pleasure because of socialization in an environment with peer (Syamsuddin, 2008). But this condition is not fully working all the time. Many times the conditions of nursing homes are not conducive and can cause stress. Prolonged stress can trigger anxiety and result in depression. The physical and psychological effects of nursing home institutions can affect the condition of the elderly (Harmand, *et al.,* 2014). Another study with a cross-sectional design of eight nursing homes was performed on 102 elderly people. And the results obtained that the empowerment of care can affect the quality of life (QOL) of elderly in the nursing home, it means the social support of the nursing home to improve the quality of life of the elderly is needed (Tu, Wang, & Yeh, 2006).

Stress and anxiety that occur in the elderly can create a negative defense mechanism so that the depression appears; especially women have more frequent incidents (Supriani, 2011). At an advanced age, different stressors often cause depression, while the elderly adaptability skills have been decreased, resulting the recovery of depression in elderly often not as good as younger age (Van der Carmmen quoted Austrian, 2002), while depression is risky and potentially crippling conditions for the elderly (Chen, *et al.,* 2015). In a study of 250 elderly people in a nursing home in rural China, it was found that 19.5 per cent of elderly have suicidal tendencies where impartiality and depression have a significant direct impact on suicide intention (Zhang, *et al.,* 2017).

Depression is not a condition caused by a single pathology but is a multi-factorial (Carstensen & Charles, 2002). The occurrence of depression in the elderly is the interaction of biological, psychological and social factors. One of the psychological factors is the elderly perception of life, evaluation of the life and perception of the elderly against the rest of their life. The chronological age of a person is related to one's perception of how much time is left in the future or known as the future time perspective, either expansive (open-ended or limited) or time-constrained, and generally getting older, getting more limited someone sees the future (Lockenhoff & Carstensen, 2004). In the late adult age most people are more likely to view the future as limited (Carstensen, Isaacowitz, & Charles, 2003).

Research on socio-emotional selectivity found that the majority of research subjects who were classified as active elderly and joined in a retired community with various activities turned out to have a limited future time perspective. The rest of the time perceived by the late adult tends to be narrow, this is due to some things such as the feeling of having entered the old age, already have no job responsibilities and taking care of the child, and prepare to face the death, so the elderly use more leisure time to worship (Desiningrum, 2011). Furthermore, in this study which specifically took the elderly subjects in the nursing home with symptoms of depression, the more obvious the relationship; that is the depressed elderly should have a limited perspective of the future, but from the results of preliminary interview on November 26, 2013, stated that 5 of 12 subjects just do not know and do not care about their future and 5 others stated that the future is still long so they choose to stay in the nursing home because no longer know where to live, so there is no definitive reflection about the future time perspective of elderly people in the nursing home

There are other psychological factors that play a role in the emergence of depression that is personality type (Indriana, 2003). In a research finding, it was stated that self-esteem and loneliness can influence suicide intention through mediation of depression and despair. The frequency of child visits, the number of physical illnesses and social activities can also affect the SI through mediation of loneliness or self-esteem (Zhang, *et al.,* 2017). Self-esteem is one type of the individual's personality.

The elderly personality has a distinctive type, unlike other ages. Experts classify the basic personality traits of the elderly, among them Neugarten, Havighurst, and Tobin (1996) divide the elderly personality into four personality types, namely (1) integrated personality, (2) Armored/ Defended Personality, (3) passive dependent personality, and (4) Un-integrated personality.

In the elderly, un-integrated personality type is the worst type of personality, characterized by the elderly having a lot of setbacks and even damage to his psychic function, weak emotional control and many setbacks in his cognitive function. They show disorganized patterns in the process of getting old. They can sustain life in society, but with low activity and low satisfaction (Austrian, 2013). Elderly with an un-integrated personality classified as elderly with low self-control level, difficult to adapt to change, easy to stress so tend to immature. Elderly with an un-integrated personality is considered an extremely unproductive and troubling elderly, its existence even considered the community as an individual who is the burden of the family (Hamilton, 2006). On the other hand, the family remains an important social component for the existence of the elderly. Individual depression and resilience is a mediator of the relationship between family function and quality of life in the elderly (Lu, *et al.,* 2017). Then the existence of elderly in the nursing home affects the condition of the elderly. The social needs of elderly people with dementia in nursing hone are often ignored even though they are able to express their emotions and respond to social interactions. This is related to low quality of life, health, and functional decreasing in the elderly (Kang, 2012).

The purpose of this study is to determine the conditions of future time perspective, un-integrated personality and depression in the elderly, found a model of the relationship between future time perspective, un-integrated personality and depression in the elderly. Furthermore, the study aims to know the relationship of future time perspective and depression in the elderly, and whether un-integrated personality has a role or not mediating variable.

Method

The subjects of this study were the elderly people living in the nursing home "X", 60 to 85 years old (Santrock, 2006), not suffering from chronic and non-senile illness, with consideration to be able to communicate and be mentored in the psychological scale. Subject selection was done by using purposive sampling method. With the subject of study amounted to 155 people, who came from two nursing homes in Semarang, Indonesia. Here is an overview of the elderly demographic data—

Demographic Data	*Elderly Percentage*
60-75/76 years or more	64/36
Female/Male	52/48
Less-educated/ SD/SMP/SMA/PT	39/39/12/8/2
Semarang/Outside Semarang	42/58

Inferential statistical method is used to test the research hypotheses in the form of statistical calculations called Structural Equation Modeling (SEM) using the help of Lisrel 8.80 programme in the process of calculation. In SEM two types of measurement models are known: Measurement model or factor model, and Structural Equation Model (SEM) model (Jöreskog, Karl & Sörbom, 1996). The measurement model test is done by Confirmatory Factor Analysis (CFA) Method. The psychological scale used is—

1. Future time perspective scale, as many as 10 items (Carstensen, & Lang, 2001).
2. Un-integrated personality scale, as many as 22 items (Austrian, 2002).
3. Depression scale, as many as 21 items (Beck, Steer, & Brown, 1996).

Result and Discussion

Majority of research subjects when viewed from the Future Time Perspective are in the Limited category (73%), while only 27 per cent have an expansive view on future time perspective. This is quite in tune with theoretical concepts through various studies in the USA and mainland Asia, which find that the final adult age will generally have a limited view. The rest of the time perceived by the elderly tends to be narrower, this is due to some things like the elderly who feel old, have no job responsibilities and have the boredom of staying in the nursing home, even some feel lonely. So the absence of life responsibilities makes the elderly think that there is nothing more to be expected in life, and be prepared to face the death (Desiningrum, 2011).

Majority of research subjects when viewed from the type of un-integrated personality are in high degree (65%), the remaining 35 per cent have low degrees. The elderly living in the nursing home has an un-integrated personality which means that they have a lot of setbacks and even the damage to their psychic functions, the emotional control of the elderly in this institution is weak and there are many setbacks in its cognitive function. This is seen in daily life, the elderly do much daydreaming, crying regretting life, difficult in controlling emotions, and tend to want to get out of the nursing home even though the subject does not know where to live. This behaviour shows a disorganized pattern in the process of getting old. According to Austrian (2013) elderly with this type can maintain life in society, but with low activity and low satisfaction as well. It was found in the study that there was a decrease in cognitive function and quality of life of elderly people in nursing homes (Harmand, *et al.,* 2014; Tu, Wang, & Yeh, 2006).

Research subjects when viewed from depression, quite a lot of the majority which are in the positive category (58%), and 42 per cent in the negative category. This suggests that in general, the elderly living in the nursing home is depressed enough, saddened by their feelings of helplessness, decreased appetite and sleeping patterns (Chen, *et al.,* 2015). This is felt by the elderly because their existence in the nursing home usually starts from the rejection of the family or children who do not want to take care of the elderly, some elderly no longer have family or friends as residence (Desiningrum, 2010). The family functioned to increase individual resilience and affect the quality of life among the elderly, thus affecting the condition of depression in the elderly (Lu, *et al.,* 2017). In addition, the background of elderly past lives that contain failure and disappointment, can stimulate depression. It can be seen from demographic data which shows the low level of elderly education. This is as one indicator of the low economic conditions of the elderly in youth.

Here are the results of Confirmatory Factor Analysis of two variables (future time perspective and un-integrated personality).

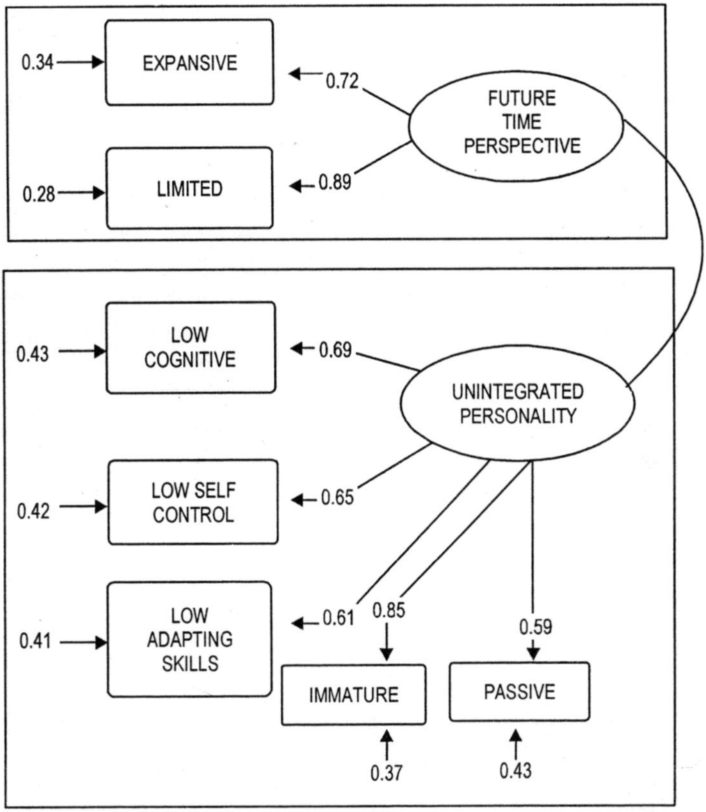

chi-square = 0,00; df = 0; dan *p*-value = 1.00

Fig. 20.1: Results of Future Time Perspective and Un-integrated Personality Equation Models.

The model test results show that the model is fit perfect with empirical data with chi-square value = 0.00; df = 0; And *p*-value = 1.00. This acquired result suggests that the measurement model of Future Time Perspective and Un-integrated Personality Variables matches the research data.

Based on Table 20.1, the limited aspects are relatively dominant in measuring future time perspective than expansive and immature aspects which are relatively dominant in measuring un-integrated personality compared to other aspects.

Table 20.1: Factor Capacity and Significance Value of Variable Equation Model Testing

Variable	*Aspect*	*Factor Capacity*	*t-value*	*p-value*	*Note*
Future Time Perspective	Expansive	0.72	9.07	<.005	Significant
	Limited	0.89	9.44	<.005	Significant
Unintegrated Personality	Low cognitive	0.69	7.88	<.005	Significant
	Low self-control	0.65	7.70	<.005	Significant
	Low adaptation skill	0.61	7.66	<.005	Significant
	Immature	0.85	8.22	<.005	Significant
	Passive	0.59	7.89	<.005	Significant

Here are the results of Confirmatory Factor Analysis of depression variables (Fig. 20.2).

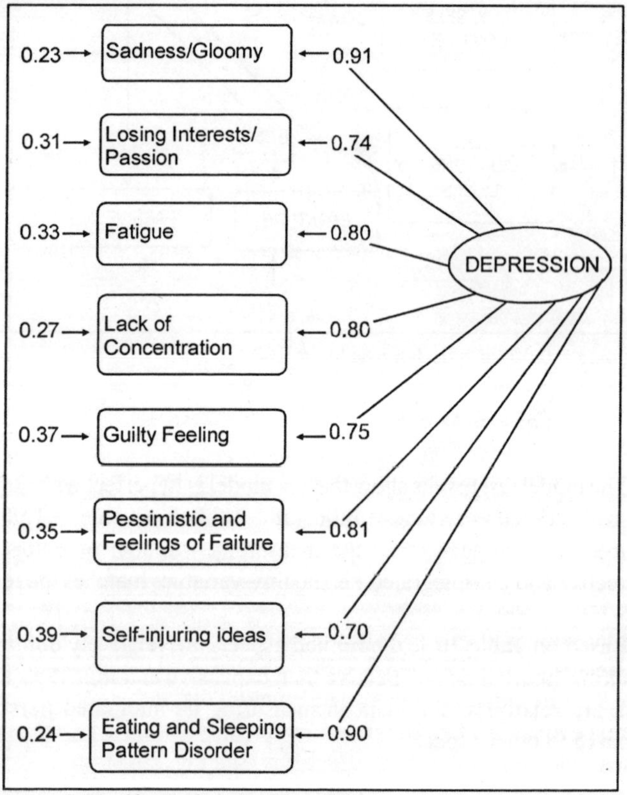

chi-square = 0,00; df = 0; dan *p*-value = 0.99.

Fig. 20.2: The Result of Equation Modeling of Depression Variables

The model test results show that the fit perfect model with empirical data with chi-square value = 0.00; df = 0; and *p*-value = 0.99.

The results of this suggest that the Structural Equation Model of Depression with 8 aspects match the research data.

Table 20.2: Factor Capacity and Significance Value of Equation Model Testing of Depression Variable

Variable	*Aspect*	*Factor Capacity*	*t-value*	*p-value*	*Note*
Depression	Sadness/Sorrow	0.91	13.03	<.005	Significant
	Lost passion	0.74	12.71	<.005	Significant
	Fatigue	0.80	12.36	<.005	Significant
	Lack of Concentration	0.80	12.99	<.005	Significant
	Guilty feeling	0.75	12.06	<.005	Significant
	Pessimistic and Feelings of Failure	0.81	12.22	<.005	Significant
	Self-harming ideas	0.70	12.01	<.005	Significant
	Sleeping and Eating Disorders	0.90	13.01	<.005	Significant

Based on Table 20.2, the aspect of Sadness/Sorrow Attitude and Sleeping and Appetite Disorders is relatively more dominant in measuring depression level than other aspects.

The following explanation is the result of Model of Future Time Perspective and Un-integrated Personality Effect on Depression to test the formulated hypothesis:

H_0 : The result of Model of Future Time Perspective and Un-integrated Personality Effect on Depression matches the empirical data

H_1 : The result of Model of Future Time Perspective and Un-integrated Personality Effect on Depression does not match the empirical data

The test conducted on model provides the evidence that the model matches the empirical data showing the value of chi-square=10,21; df=6; and *p*-value=0,12; RMSEA=0,09; CFI=1,00; RMR=0,02; GFI=0,97; dan AGFI=0,91. The result provides an affirmation that the Model of Future Time Perspective and Un-integrated Personality Effect on Depression agrees with the data of the study (good fit) (*see* Fig. 20.3).

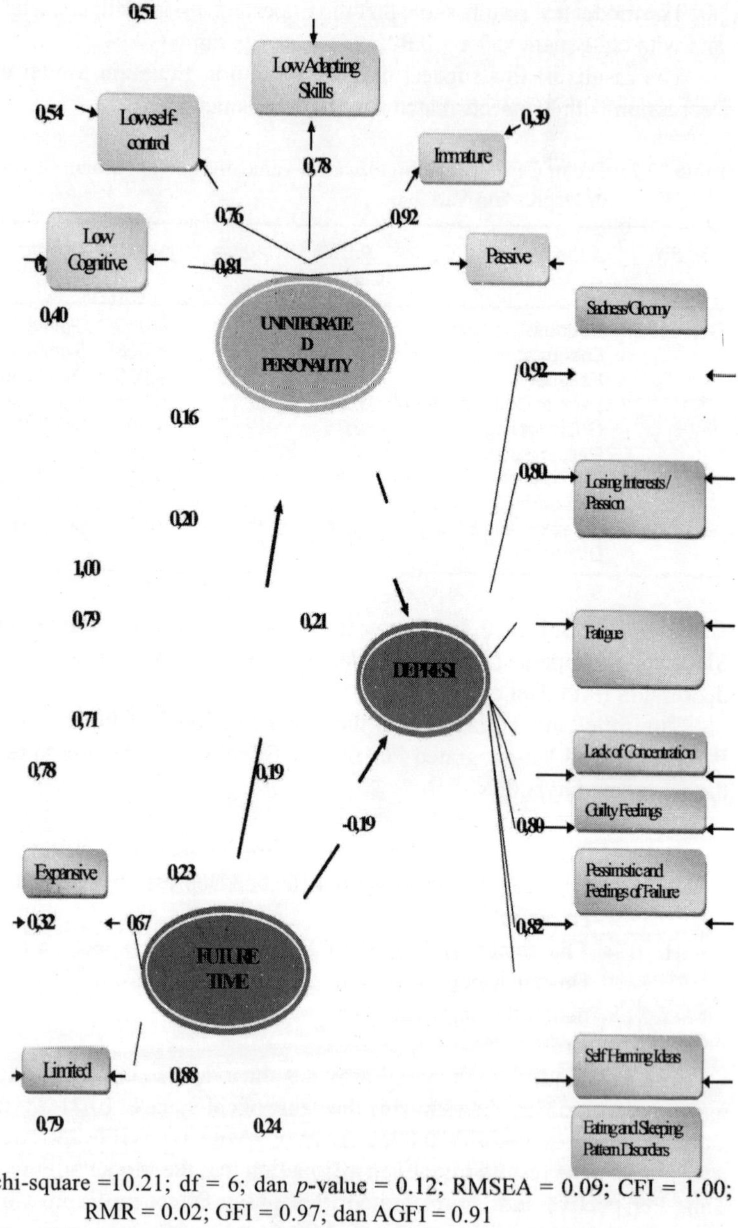

chi-square =10.21; df = 6; dan *p*-value = 0.12; RMSEA = 0.09; CFI = 1.00; RMR = 0.02; GFI = 0.97; dan AGFI = 0.91

Fig. 20.3: The result of Model of Future Time Perspective and Un-integrated Personality Effect on Depression

Table 20.3: Load Factor and Significance Level Testing of Model of Future Time Perspective and Un-integrated Personality Effect on Depression

Variable	*Aspect*	*Load Factor*	*t-value*	*p-value*	*Remark*
Future Time Perspective	Expansive	0.67	8.89	<.005	Significant
	Limited	0.88	10.02	<.005	Significant
Unintegrated Personality	Low Cognitive	0.81	7.88	<.005	Significant
	Low Self-control	0.76	7.70	<.005	Significant
	Lack of Adapting Skills	0.78	7.66	<.005	Significant
	Immature	0.92	8.22	<.005	Significant
	Passive	0.82	7.89	<.005	Significant
Depression	Sadness	0.92	13.03	<.005	Significant
	Lost of Appetite	0.80	12.71	<.005	Significant
	Fatigue	0.79	12.36	<.005	Significant
	Lack of Concentration	0.78	12.99	<.005	Significant
	Guilty Feelings	0.80	12.06	<.005	Significant
	Pessimistic and Feelings of Failure	0.82	12.22	<.005	Significant
	Self-harming ideas	0.79	12.01	<.005	Significant
	Sleeping and Eating Disorders	0.91	13.01	<.005	Significant

Based on the table, limited aspect is more dominant than expansive aspect for future time perspective variables, immature is more dominant than the other aspects for un-integrated personality variables, and sadness is more dominant than the other aspects for depression variables.

Table 20.4: Path Coefficient and Significance of Model of Future Time Perspective and Un-integrated Personality Effect on Depression

Path	*Correlation Coefficient*	*t-value*	*p-value*	*Remark*
Future Time Perspective-Un-integrated Personality	0.71	6.72	<.005	Significant
Future Time Perspective-Depression	–0.19	–0.98	0.34	Not Significant
Un-integrated Personality-Depression	1.00	5.87	<.005	Significant

Table 20.4 presents the results of path coefficient test or correlation between latent or structural variables. The test was intended to test the following sub-hypothesis:

Sub-Hypothesis 1

Sub-hypothesis 1 was aimed to test the level of significance of the correlation between future time perspectives with un-integrated personality using the following hypothesis:

H_0: Future Time Perspective has no correlation with Un-integrated Personality.
H_1: Future Time Perspective correlates with Un-integrated Personality.

Based on the table, future time perspective significantly correlates with un-integrated personality based on measured coefficient 0.71.

Sub-Hypothesis 2

Sub-hypothesis 2 tests the level of significance of the correlation between future time perspectives with depression using the following hypothesis:

H_0: Future Time Perspective has no correlation with Depression.
H_1: Future Time Perspective correlates with Depression.

Based on the table, future time perspective insignificantly correlates to depression.

Sub-Hypothesis 3

Sub-hypothesis 3 was aimed to test the correlation between un-integrated personality with depression using the following hypothesis:

H_0: Un-integrated Personality has no correlation with Depression.
H_1: Un-integrated Personality correlates with Depression.

Based on the table, un-integrated personality significantly correlates with depression measured by correlation coefficient 1.00. The correlation coefficient shows that un-integrated personality strongly correlates with depression.

The test on sub-hypothesis 2 observed that future time perspective does not directly correlate with depression, yet related to un-integrated personality.

Based on the data of subjects through model analysis, the model in Fig. 20.1 fits perfectly and possesses empirical data with chi-square=0.00; df=0; and *p*-value=1,00. It means that structural equation modelling approach of future time perspective matches the data obtained from elderly people as the participants of the study, in which the scale measures the perspectives of elderly people of their life expectation, namely expansive perspective and limited perspective. The figure also presents structural modelling of un-integrated personality which matches the data of the study, meaning that the structure is reliable in measuring un-integrated personality of elderly people in nursing home as the participants in the research.

Based on Table 20.1, limited aspect is relatively dominant in assessing future time perspective compared to expansive aspect. It means that, as described in the profile of the subjects, the subjects tend to have limited perspective on for theif future, yet based on similar load, they also have expansive perspective towards their future, and based on the interview during filling out the scales, they believe that they are old enough and has no more activities to do in the future. Expansive perspective, although less dominant, also contributed to future time perspective, and from the interview, individuals consider their future as expansive since they have the opinion that future is in God's hand so that their purpose is entering the heaven. In the same table, un-integrated personality is relatively dominant, measured from immature aspect. It means that the immature load dominantly illustrates the un-integrated personality of elderly people in nursing home. Aldert (in Hamilton, 2006) stated that immature personality during the elderly is measured from three indicators namely, imbalance mind, anxiety, and lack of confidence. The study found that anxiety disorder and depression in elderly people can be characterized by chronic headache. Elderly patients suffer from chronic headache have high prevalence of mental disorder (Peluso, Quintana, & Ganança, 2016).

Based on Fig. 20.2, the result of model test shows that model fits perfectly with empiric data with chi-square=0.00; df=0; and *p*-value=0.99, and Table 20.2 shows that sadness and sleeping and eating pattern disorder are relatively more dominant in measuring depression compared to other aspects. Depression in elderly people living in nursing home is characterized by sadness and sleeping and eating disorder. During a research, it was found that elderly people are prone to sleeping disorder, nightmare, depression, anxiety reactions, as the neuropsychiatric effect of their medication (Ahmed, Mierlo, & Jansen, 2010).

Based on Fig. 20.2, the result of model test shows that model fits the empiric data with chi-square=10.21; df=6; and *p*-value=0.12; RMSEA=0.09; CFI=1.00; RMR=0.02; GFI=0.97; and AGFI=0.91. The results that Model of Future Time Perspective and Un-integrated Personality Effect on Depression fits (good fit) the study data through the group of elderly people living in nursing home as the subjects of the study. The match shows that the model perfectly measures the correlation between future time perspective and un-integrated personality with depression, from the way variables of future time perspective influence depression on elderly people. It describes the elderly people as participants perceiving future time perspective, and then describes un-integrated personality of elderly people when they live in nursing home, in this case, elderly people having future time perspectives and certain personality types are closely related to psychological conditions of elderly people with their depression level.

Table 20.3 provides the load factor of each indicator to measure the variable and it can be seen that future time perspective is dominantly influenced by limited perspective. It goes in line with the theory that generally, elderly people have limited future time perspective (Carstensen, 2003).

From the same table, it can be seen that un-integrated personality was dominantly constructed from immature, in which fits the result of profile analysis and structural model of un-integrated personality. Dominant immature is characterized by disappointment, anxiety, and lack of interest to interact with other people. It was observed from the elderly people who constantly stating their sadness and disappointment towards themselves and surroundings because of past failure, then the emergence of anxiety when they showed the unwillingness when offered the options to move to different nursing home or return home with their family, then their unwillingness to gather in the hall for exercise or join the lecture. The anxiety in elderly people can be categorized in general anxiety. Generalized Anxiety Disorder (GAD) is commonly observed on elderly people. GAD is one of the characters of severe depression (Zhang, *et al.*, 2015).

Table 20.4 presents the test result of path coefficient or the correlation of variables. It answers the sub-hypothesis. The test on sub-hypothesis 1 shows that future time perspective significantly correlates with un-integrated personality with the coefficient 0.71 which means that future time perspective of the elderly people affects their un-integrated personality when living in nursing home. Those elderly people, when socializing with their peers, see future as limited and their perspective affects them in socializing and participating in many activities in the nursing home which in turn forms the un-integrated personality. On the contrary, the test on sub-hypothesis 2 shows that future time perspective insignificantly correlates with depression which means that depression experienced by the subjects are not influenced by their future time perspective. While the test on sub-hypothesis 3 shows that depression experienced by the subjects are influenced by un-integrated personality with the perfect coefficient 1.00 which means that depression on elderly people are defined by un-integrated personality which means that elderly people with un-integrated personality tend to be depressed in the nursing home if they have limited future time perspective.

The result of test on sub-hypothesis 2 shows that future time perspective does not significantly correlate with depression. It provides the evidence that future time perspective has no direct correlation with depression in elderly people, but it deals with un-integrated personality as the mediating variable.

Based on the description above, un-integrated personality was determined an intervening or mediating variable. It can be concluded that un-integrated personality as an intervening variable has the role to provide the explanation for the elderly people as the participants who have limited future time perspective with un-integrated personality such as immature, passive and low cognitive and adaptive skills, which results in depression which can be seen from the sadness, lack of appetite and sleeping pattern disorder, lack of interest, concentration and energy as well as guilty feelings, and self-harm tendency.

The limitation of the study is the limited number of elderly people which live in two nursing homes that represents a small scale of elderly people in Central Java. The elderly people involved in the research experienced difficulties in filling out the questionnaire and the check-list which represents the psychological conditions of elderly people. The solution was assisting those elderly people in filling out the questionnaire by reading the questions one by one and translating those questions into Javanese to be more easily understood.

Conclusion

Most of the elderly people in nursing home participating in the study have a limited future perspective, un-integrated personality and suffer from depression. The study tested the structural equation modelling approach of future time perspective (which was dominantly measured from limited aspects) and un-integrated personality (which was dominantly measured from immature aspect), model equation approach of depression (which was dominantly measured from sadness and sleeping and eating disorder aspects) and model of future time perspective and un-integrated personality correlation with depression in which the three models fit the subjects of the study. The analysis conducted on model of future time perspective and un-integrated personality correlation with depression shows that future time perspective slightly corresponds to depression, while un-integrated personality exclusively correlates with depression. Another finding affirms that un-integrated personality was an intervening/ mediating variable which means that elderly people in nursing home with limited future time perspective tend to be depressed if they have un-integrated personality.

References

Ahmed, A.I.A., Mierlo, P.V., and Jansen, P., 2010. Sleep disorders, nightmares, depression and anxiety in an elderly patient treated with low-dose metoprolol. *General Hospital Psychiatry. 32* (6): 646.e5-646.e7.

Austrian, S.G., (2002). *Developmental Theories Through the Life Cycle*. New York: Columbia University Press.

Beck, A.T., Steer, R.A., and Brown, G.K. (1996). *Manual for the Beck Depression Inventory-II.* San Antonio, TX: Psychological Corporation.

Carstensen, L.L., and Lang, F. (2001). Future orientation scale. *Unpublished Manuscript*, Stanford University.

Carstensen, L.L., and Charles, S.T. (2002). The salience of emotion across the adult life span. *Journal of Psychology and Aging*, *9*, 259-264.

Carstensen, L.L. (2003). *Growing Old or Longevity*. Stanford University.

Chen, K.M., Huang, H.T., Cheng, Y.Y., Li, C.H., and Chang, Y.H. (2015). Sleep quality and depression of nursing home older adults in wheelchairs after exercises. *Nursing Outlook. 63*(3): 357-365.

Cox, C.A., Jaarsveld, H.J.V., Houterman, S., Stegen, J.C.G.H., Wasylewicz, A.T.M., and Grouls, R.J.E. (2016). Psychotropic drug prescription and the risk of falls in nursing home residents. *Journal of the American Medical Directors Association. 17*(12): 1089-1093.

Desiningrum, D.R. (2010). Family's social support and psychological well-being of the elderly in Tembalang. *ANIMA Indonesian Psychological Journal. 26* (1), 61-68.

Desiningrum, D.R. (2011). The Padjadjaran International Conference on Psychology: Future time perspective, goal orientation and subjective well-being in elderly. *Proceeding.* ISBN: 978-602-19851-1-3, Jilid 1.

Hamilton, I.S. (2006). *The Psychology of Ageing: An Introduction 4th edition.* London and Philadelphia: Jessica Kingsley Publishers.

Harmand, M.G.C., Meillon, C., Rullier, L., Funes, J.A.A., Bergua, V., and Dartigues, J.F. (2014). Cognitive decline after entering a nursing home: A 22-year follow-up study of institutionalized and non-institutionalized elderly people. *Journal of the American Medical Directors Association. 15*(7): 504-508.

Indriana, Y. (2011). *Gerontologi dan progeria.* Semarang: Universitas Diponegoro Press.

Jöreskog, K. and Sörbom, D. (1996). *Lisrel 8: User's Reference Guide*, Scientific Software International.

Kang, H., 2012. Correlates of social engagement in nursing home residents with dementia. *Asian Nursing Research. 6*(2): 75-81.

Kooten, J.V., Smalbrugge, M., Wouden, J.C., Stek, M.L., and Hertogh, C.M.P.M. (2017). Prevalence of pain in nursing home residents: The role of dementia stage and dementia subtypes. *Journal of the American Medical Directors Association.* Available online 22 February 2017.

Kuntjoro, Z.S. (2002). *Dukungan sosial pada lansia.* (Online). (http://www.e-psikologi.com_160802.htm, accessed at November 2013).

Li, N., Chen, G., Zeng, P., Pang, J., Gong, H., Han, Y., Zhang, Y., Zhang, E., Zhang, T., and Zheng, X. (2016). Prevalence of depression and its associated factors among Chinese elderly people: A comparison study between community-based population and hospitalized population. *Psychiatry Research. 243*: 87-91.

Lockenhoff, Corinna E., and Carstensen, L.L. (2004). Socio-emotional selectivity theory, aging, and health: The increasingly delicate balance between regulating emotions and making tough choices. *Journal of Personality.72* (6), 1395-1424.

Lok, N., Lok, S., and Canbaz, M. (2017). The effect of physical activity on depressive symptoms and quality of life among elderly nursing home residents: Randomized controlled trial. *Archives of Gerontology and Geriatrics.70*: 92-98.

Lu, C., Yuan, L., Lin, W., Zhou, Y., and Pan, S. (2017). Depression and resilience mediates the effect of family function on quality of life of the elderly. *Archives of Gerontology and Geriatrics.71*: 34-42.

Neugarten, B.L., Havighurst, R.J., and Tobin, S.S. (1996). Personality and patterns of aging. *The Meanings of Age.* Chicago [ua]: University of Chicago Press, pp. 264-269.

Peluso, E.T.P., Quintana, M.I., and Ganança, F.F. (2016). Anxiety and depressive disorders in elderly with chronic dizziness of vestibular origin. *Brazilian Journal of Otorhinolaryngology. 82* (2): 209-214.

Santrock, J.W. (2006). *Life Span Development.* Tenth Edition. McGraw-Hill Companies.

Sepulveda, E., Leonard, M., Franco, J.G., Adamis, D., McCarthy, G., Dunne, C., Trzepacz, P.T., Gaviria, A.M., Pablo, J.D., and Vilella, E. (2017).

Subsyndromal delirium compared with delirium, dementia, and subjects without delirium or dementia in elderly general hospital admissions and nursing home residents. *Alzheimer and Dementia: Diagnosis, Assessment and Disease Monitoring*. *7*, 1-10.

Supriani, A. (2011). Tingkat depresi pada lansia ditinjau dari tipe kepribadian dan dukungan sosial. *Tesis*. Program Pascasarjana Universitas Sebelas Maret Surakarta. Unpublished.

Syamsuddin (2008). *Penguatan eksistensi panti werdha di tengah pergeseran budaya dan keluarga.* (Online). (http://www.depsos.go.id/modules.php ? name =News & file= article & sid= 704, diakses January 2014)

Tu, Y.C., Wang, R.H., and Yeh, S.H., 2006. Relationship between perceived empowerment care and quality of life among elderly residents within nursing homes in Taiwan: A questionnaire survey. *International Journal of Nursing Studies*. 43(6): 673-680. http://doi.org/10.1016/j.ijnurstu.2005.10.003

Zhang, D., Yang, Y., Sun, Y., Wu, M., Xie, H., Wang, K., Zhang, J., and Jia, J., 2017. Characteristics of the Chinese rural elderly living in nursing homes who have suicidal ideation: A multiple regression model. *Geriatric Nursing*. Available online 25 March 2017. http://doi.org/10.1016/j.gerinurse.2017.02.005

Zhang, X., Norton, J., Carrière, I., Ritchie, K., Chaudieu, I., and Ancelin, M.L., 2015. Generalized anxiety in community-dwelling elderly: Prevalence and clinical characteristics. *Journal of Affective Disorders*. *172*: 24-29. http://doi.org/10.1016/j.jad.2014.09.036

SECTION VI
Parenting Behaviour

21

Parenting Style of the Working and Non-working Mothers

Implications for Cognitive-Emotional Functioning in Offspring

Prativa Sanchary Naima Nigar and
A.K.M. Rezea Karem

Introduction

In our social and cultural structure we see the mothers in different roles and in contemporary world in a major criterion; they are working outside home or simply home-makers, i.e. non-working. Hence, the pertinent question of research may be the professional status of mothers does have any impact on the cognitive emotion regulation of their children and does their working status makes any difference in the parenting style of the children? In a traditional society like most part of Bangladesh, a non-working home-maker mother is mostly awaited and cherished by the elderly members of the family. They think motherhood can only be maintained and obeyed by being 100 per cent involved into family and child. Mothers should stay at home and raise the children without doing any work outside. It makes the life simple and only this can build the future of the child. A homemaker mother can focus on the rearing of the child without any tension of being working outside. This should be the only way of living for a mother as considered by most of the people of such traditional societies like, Bangladesh. On top of all these considerations, a mother who does not work out of home, always takes care of the children, children are the only "work" of them. The potential behaviour of the children builds-up in the family being under the guidance and regulations of the parents and the major role is played by mothers. Mother keeps the foremost impact on the cognitive and emotional functioning of a child such as—how the child will solve a problem, how he/she will handle the emotional situations, how the memory helps him/her to do any mental exercise etc.

Parenting or child rearing is the process of promoting or supporting the physical, emotional, social, and intellectual development of a child from infancy to adulthood (Davies, 2000). Parenting is a complex activity that includes many specific behaviours that work individually and together to influence child outcomes. The most popular ideas about parenting style stem from the work of Diana Baumrind.

During the 1960s, psychologist Diana Baumrind conducted a study on more than 100 pre-school age children (Baumrind, 1967) by using naturalistic observation, parental interviews and other research method and identified four important dimensions of parenting—(1) Disciplinary strategies, (2) Warmth and Nurturance, (3) Communication styles and (4) Expectations of maturity and control. Based on these dimensions, Baumrind suggested that the majority of parents display one of the three different parenting styles—(1) Authoritarian Parenting Style, (2) Authoritative Parenting Style, and (3) Permissive Parenting Style. Further research also suggested the addition of a fourth parenting style (Maccoby & Martin, 1983) that is known as Uninvolved Parenting Style.

Parenting style captures two important elements of parenting: parental responsiveness and parental demandingness (Maccoby & Martin, 1983). Parental responsiveness (also referred to as parental warmth or supportiveness) refers to the extent to which parents intentionally foster individuality, self-regulation, and self-assertion by being attuned, supportive, and acquiescent to children's special needs and demands (Baumrind, 1991). Parental demandingness (also referred to as behavioural control) refers to the claims parents make on children to become integrated into the family whole, by their maturity demands, supervision, disciplinary efforts and willingness to confront the child who disobeys (Baumrind, 1991)

Many researches have been conducted on parental warmth. Parental warmth, expressed in both physical and verbal ways has been found to be a universal phenomenon (Rohner, 1986). It also seems to have a universal association with positive psychological outcomes like psychological well-being, self-esteem and academic achievement. Lack of parental warmth appears to have a universal association with negative psychological outcomes like aggression, school misconduct, emotional unresponsiveness and depressive symptoms.

Beginning in early childhood, authoritative style of parenting has been shown to produce higher levels of social competence (Baumrind, 1978), a greater ability to regulate emotions, high social skills, and self-regulation (Baumrind & Black, 1967). During the years of middle childhood, Baumrind (1993) found that children reared by authoritative parents excel in areas of independence, creativity, persistence, social skills, academic competence, leadership skills, social-perspective taking, and self-control. Adolescents of authoritative parents have higher self-esteem, are socially confident and competent (Baumrind, 1978), are self-reliant, have greater respect for their parents (Baumrind, 1991), display increased academic performance, possess higher levels of self-esteem, engage in fewer acts of deviant behaviour and more pro-social behaviour (Dornbusch, Ritter, Leiderman, Roberts, & Fraleigh, 1987).

Authoritarian parenting in contrast is associated with a myriad of negative outcomes throughout development (Peterson & Hann, 1999; Stafford & Bayer, 1993). Preschool age children exposed to authoritarian parenting have been found to be unhappy, dissatisfied, apprehensive, fearful, socially inhibited, and aggressive and experience difficulty in regulating emotions (Baumrind, 1967; Baumrind & Black, 1967; Hart, Nelson, Robinson, Olsen & McNeily-Choque, 1998; Nix *et al.,* 1999). During adolescence, low self-esteem, low sociability, moodiness, obedience, and apprehensiveness were reported in adolescents of authoritarian parents (Darling & Steinberg, 1993).

Permissive parents have little behavioural control and authoritarian parents exercise extreme levels of control. Permissive parents have little control and few expectations for their children. As a result, preschool children of permissive parents tend to experience difficulty in regulating emotions, have low self-control, and be very immature (Baumrind, 1967). Permissive parenting has been linked to bossy, dependent, impulsive behaviour in children, with low levels of self-control and achievement; these children do not learn persistence, emotional control, or limitation (Baumrind, 1967). The present study was conducted to find out the impact of parenting style on cognitive-emotional functioning in offspring.

Cognitive emotion regulation refers to the conscious, cognitive way of handling the intake of emotionally arousing information (Garnefski, Kraaij, & Spinhoven, 2001) and can be considered part of the broader concept of emotion regulation defined as "all the extrinsic and intrinsic processes responsible for monitoring, evaluating, and modifying emotional reactions, especially their intensive and temporal features" (Gross, 1999; Thompson, 1994). People regulate their emotions or feelings through cognitions or cognitive processes so that they would not be influenced by the power of these emotions, especially during or after they are under pressure (Garnefski, Kraaij, & Spinhoven, 2001).

A detailed review of past researches indicate that better emotion regulation is associated with less depression, anxiety, cultural shock, and homesickness, and high levels of happiness, well-being, marital satisfaction, language proficiency, and income (Matsumoto, 2003). A variety of factors may contribute to the development of cognitive distortion and maladaptive emotion regulation. One of the contributing factors may be parenting.

Rationale of the study

Very few empirical investigations are available from Bangladeshi context to highlight the relationship between mother's working state and their parenting style and children's cognitive-emotional functioning. Adulthood is a period of adjustment and people have to face new life pattern, play new role and form new identity in this new stage of life. Healthy parenting style helps them to handle these situations effectively through better cognitive-emotional functioning in offspring. A person passes more time with his/her mother than father. So, whether mother's working state has any impact on parenting style is yet to explore. Therefore, the present study is an attempt to explore the relationship between mother's working state and their parenting style in order to find out the impact of parenting style in children's cognitive-emotional functioning.

Purposes of the Present Study

The primary purposes of the present study were to investigate—

- The differences in parenting style between working and non-working mothers.
- The association among mother's parenting style on child's cognitive emotion regulation and cognitive distortion.

Hypotheses: The study tested two specific hypotheses:

- There are no significant differences in parenting styles of working and non-working mother.

- There is no significant effect of parenting style on child's cognitive emotion regulation and cognitive distortion.

Method

The survey research design was used in the present study.

Study 1

The purpose of this study was to investigate whether there are any differences in parenting style of working and non-working mothers. In order to attain this end, the following methodology was followed:

Participants: 250 students of 11th and 12th grade participated in this study. They were selected in purposive manner from the Dhaka Commerce College and Dhaka City College, Viqarunnisa Noon College and Saint Joseph College. Their age ranged from 15 to 18 with a mean of (17.26 years) and standard deviation of (0.87). Among the mothers of the participants 74.3 per cent were non-working and 25.7 per cent were working women.

Instruments of Measurement: The following instrument was used to measure parenting style of the selected mothers.

- *Parental Authority Questionnaire (PAQ).* The PAQ originally developed by Buri (1991) is a 30-item questionnaire that measures different parenting styles. It is a 5-point Likert type scale ranging from 1 (disagree) to 5 (agree). The original scale has three subscales namely, Authoritative Parenting, Authoritarian Parenting and Permissive Parenting. Each sub-scale includes 10 items. The internal consistency (Cronbach's α) of the English version PAQ ranges from 0.74 to 0.87 (Buri, 1991).

Procedure

Data acquisition—After getting verbal consent from the participants, the paper-based survey was administered to the participants in a classroom of the respective college. The survey components included an informed consent statement, socio-demographic section, and the PAQ. The PAQ was administered to children. Participants were asked to record their socio-demographic information such as socio-economic status, family type, religion, gender etc. They were asked to read carefully the standard instructions of how to respond before going through the items or questions of the questionnaires. After completion of their task, participants were thanked for their sincere cooperation. Thus, the survey was administered and data were collected over a 12-week period from all the participants.

Data Analyses—Each participant's responses were scored according to the scoring principles of the PAQ. After getting data for 250 mothers in this way they were fed into computer for analyzing in IBM SPSS Statistics 20. The data analysis was done in phase, as below.

Phase I: In order to examine the relationship of the mother's occupation with their parenting style, data were analyzed in a one-way MANOVA using permissive parenting style, authoritarian parenting style and authoritative parenting style as the dependent variables and mother's occupation as the independent variable. Before this analyses were done to test the major assumptions of MANOVA such as absence of multicollinearity among dependent variables, homogeneity of covariance, homogeneity of error variance and multivariate normality. The multicollinearity was tested by Pearson's correlation coefficients, the multivariate normality was approximated by normal P-P plot of the residuals, the homogeneity of covariance was tested by Box's test and the homogeneity of variance was tested by Levene's test.

Study 2

The purpose of this study was to investigate the impacts of parenting style of mothers on their children's cognitive distortion and cognitive emotion regulation. In order to attain this end, the following methodology was followed:

Participants: 250 students of 11th grade and 12th grade who participated in the first study also participated in this study, and gave their valuable data about their cognitive distortion and cognitive emotion regulation. Data about their mother's parenting style were also used in this study in order to achieve the above purpose.

Instruments of Measurement: The following instruments were used to measure children's cognitive distortion and cognitive emotion regulation of the selected participants.

Cognitive Emotion Regulation Questionnaire (CERQ)—The CERQ (Cognitive Emotion Regulation Questionnaire) is a multidimensional questionnaire constructed in order to identify the cognitive coping strategies someone uses after having experienced negative events or situations. It has been constructed both on a theoretical and empirical basis. The original scale was developed by Garnefski, Kraaij, and Spinhoven (2002), Bangla version of the CERQ (Udzzaman & Karim, 2011), is a 36 item Likert type scale with five response alternatives ranging from 'almost never' (1) to 'almost always' (5). The scale has 9 sub-scales, each subscale consisting of 4 items, each item referring to what someone thinks after the experience of threatening or stressful life events. The 9 subscales are grouped broadly as adaptive and less adapted emotion regulation strategies. Adaptive strategies include 5 subscales such as acceptance, positive refocusing, refocus on planning, positive reappraisal, and putting into perspective whereas less adaptive strategies include 4 subscales such as self-blame, rumination, catastrophizing and blaming others. Individual subscale scores are obtained by summing the scores belonging to the particular subscale (a subscale score may range from 4 to 20). Adaptive score is obtained by summing all the items' scores under the adaptive subscale while less adaptive score is obtained by summing all the items' scores under the less adaptive subscale. The scale has high internal consistency (Garnefski *et al.*, 2002). All sub-scales have good internal consistencies ranging from 0.68 to 0.86. Internal consistency ranges from 0.68 to 0.81 for early adolescents from 0.68 to 0.79 for late adolescents, and from 0.75 to 0.85 for adults. The test-retest reliability of the CERQ ranges from 0.48 to 0.65.

The CERQ scale is almost invariant with respect to age and gender. The original CERQ has been shown to have good factorial validity, discriminant validity and construct validity (Garnefski *et al.*, 2002).

How I Think Questionnaire (HIT). The HIT was developed to provide a reliable and valid measure of self-serving cognitive distortion in adolescents (Barriga, *et al.,* 1996, 2001). It contains 54.6-points Likert items varying from totally agree to totally disagree. 39 of these items can be clustered in four types of cognitive distortions: Self-centred, Blaming others, Mislabelling/Minimizing, and Assuming the worst. In addition, each of the 39 items refers to one of the four antisocial behavioural categories of the DSM-IV (American Psychiatric Association, 1994). The categories are opposition-defiance; physical aggression; lying; and stealing. The sum of the opposition defiance and the physical aggression scales forms the overt scale, which refers to direct confrontation with the victim in contrast to the covert scale, which is the sum of the lying and stealing scales. Of the remaining 15 items, 8 are anomalous-responding items and 7 positive filler items to camouflage the 39 main questions. HIT exhibits high test-retest reliability, good internal consistency, and generally good construct validity (Barriga & Gibbs, 1996). The English version has been evaluated on four validation samples and exhibited generally good validity on every validity measure (Barriga *et al.*, 2001).

Convergent validity of the Bangla version HIT was examined by estimating inter-factor correlations and the factor-HIT total correlations. The inter-factor correlations (Pearson's r) were all significant, the coefficient ranging from 0.19 to 0.50. Discriminant validity of the Bangla version HIT was examined by correlating the HIT and HIT factors with the 'Care' dimension of the Bangla version PBI. Negative or non-significant correlations were hypothesized between the measures in order for them to have discriminant validity.

Data acquisition--In order to collect data about the children's cognitive emotion regulation and cognitive distortion, the Bangla version CERQ and the Bangla version HIT were administered to the participants following the same procedure as in study 1.

Data Analyses—Each participant's responses were scored according to the scoring principles of the CERQ and HIT Questionnaire. After getting data for 250 children in this way they were fed into computer for analyzing in IBM SPSS Statistics 20. The data analysis was done in the following phase, as below:

Phase I: In order to examine the relationship among parenting style, cognitive distortion and emotion regulation, data were analyzed in multivariate multiple regression using parenting style as the predictor variables and HIT and two dimensions of CERQ (adaptive and less adaptive) as the criterion variables. Before doing this analysis, the major assumptions of multivariate multiple regression were tested. Specifically, the assumption of multivariate normality of the residuals was approximated by normal P-P plot, the assumption of the linearity of criterion-predictor relationship was examined by partial regression plots, the assumption of homogenous of variances by scatter plots, and the assumption of multi-collinearity of the predictors was examined by tolerance variance inflation factor (VIF).

Results

Study 1

To investigate the relation between mother's occupation and parenting style, data were analysed in one-way MANOVA using mother's occupation as a predictor and three parenting styles: permissive, authoritarian and authoritative as the dependent variables. The MANOVA test results of multivariate (Pillai's trace) statistics (F=1.426, p=.24) illustrated that the effect of mother's occupation on a linear combination of the three dependant variables are non-significant and from there univariate test results it was found that there is no significant effect of mother's occupation on parenting styles (permissive: F = 2.393, p = .123, authoritarian: F = 1.820, p = .179, authoritative: F = 2.436, p = .120).

Study 2

Main Analysis

The results of the present study are illustrated below showing that there is a joint linear effect of parenting styles on cognitive distortion, less adaptive emotion regulation and adaptive emotion regulation in adolescents.

Table 21.1: Multivariate Test Results

	Value	*F*	*Hypothesis df*	*Error df*	*p*
Pillai's Trace	.353	10.621	9.000	717.000	.000
Wilks' Lambda (λ)	.68	11.125	9.000	576.946	.000
Hotelling's Trace	.432	11.308	9.000	707.000	.000
Roy's Largest Root	.28	22.217	3.000	239.000	.000

Predictor: Parenting styles
Criterion Variables: Cognitive distortion, less adaptive emotion regulation and adaptive emotion regulation.

Table 21.1 illustrates the values of different statistical tests showing the significance of multivariate analysis. Among the four tests Wilks' λ 'exact statistic', is the most commonly used test to examine the joint linear effect of the predictors on the criterion variables. The smaller the value of λ the greater is the difference. The value of the λ ranges from 0 to 1. Here, the value of λ is 0.68 which indicates that the joint effect of the predictors contributed to the model. Thus, the overall multivariate model was statistically significant. The univariate test results (Table 21.2) show that with the dependent variables cognitive distortion, adaptive emotion regulation and less adaptive emotion regulation the overall model is statistically significant.

Table 21.2: Univariate Test Results

Source		*SS*	*df*	*MS*	*F*	*p*
Corrected Model	HIT total	17243.110	3	5747.703	19.610	.000
	Cerq_adaptive	4495.201	3	1498.400	11.451	.000
	Cerq_less adaptive	2408.055	4	602.014	5.423	.000
Error	HIT total	70051.071	239	293.101		
	Cerq_adaptive	31274.239	239	130.855		
	Cerq_less adaptive	12755.242	239	53.369		
Corrected Total	HIT total	87294.181	242			
	Cerq_adaptive	35769.440	242			
	Cerq_less adaptive	14290.428	242			

The table of parameter estimates (Table 21.3) shows that with the dependent variable cognitive distortion all the predictors were significant. Similarly with the dependent variable adaptive emotion regulation all the predictors were significant. However, for less adaptive emotion regulation all the parenting styles were significant except authoritative parenting style.

The unstandardized regression coefficients (*B*) indicates that for one raw unit increment of permissive parenting style, the adolescent's cognitive distortion would increase by 1.126 raw units, for one raw unit increment of authoritarian parenting style, the adolescent's cognitive distortion would increase by 1.286 raw units and for one raw unit increment of authoritative parenting style, the adolescent's cognitive distortion would decrease by 0.644 raw units. On the other hand, for one raw unit increment of permissive parenting style, the adolescent's adaptive emotion regulation would increase by 0.569 raw units, for one raw unit increment of authoritarian parenting style, the adolescent's adaptive emotion regulation would decrease by 0.401 raw units and for one raw unit increment of authoritative parenting style, the adolescent's adaptive emotion regulation would increase by 0.331 raw units. Similarly, for one raw unit increment of permissive parenting style, the adolescent's less adaptive emotion regulation would increase by 0.415 raw units, and for one raw unit increment of authoritarian parenting style, the adolescent's less adaptive emotion regulation would increase by 0.055 raw units.

Partial η^2 in Table 21.3 indicates that the contribution of authoritarian parenting style to the variance in cognitive distortion was highest (14%) followed by the contributions of authoritative parenting style (9.3%) and permissive parenting style (3.7%). Similarly, contribution of authoritative parenting style to the variance in adaptive emotion regulation was highest

Table 21.3: Parameter Estimates

Dependent Variable		*B*	*SE*	*t*	*P*	*Partial Eta² Squared (η2)*
(a) HIT total	Intercept	88.537	6.064	14.601	.000	.471
	Paq_permissive	1.126	.370	3.044	.003	.037
	Paq_authoritarian	1.286	.206	6.235	.000	.140
	Paq_authoritative	–.644	.130	–4.956	.000	.093
(b) Cerq_adaptive	Intercept	24.398	4.052	6.022	.000	.132
	Paq_permissive	.569	.247	2.302	.022	.022
	Paq_authoritarian	–.401	.138	–2.907	.004	.034
	Paq_authoritative	.331	.087	3.815	.000	.057
(c) Cerq_less adaptive	Intercept	18.562	2.587	7.174	.000	.177
	Paq_permissive	.415	.158	2.629	.009	.028
	Paq_authoritarian	.055	.088	.619	.536	.002
	Paq_authoritative	.157	.055	2.826	.005	.032

a. Adjusted R^2 =.187, b. Adjusted R^2 =.115, c. Adjusted R^2 =.096.

(5.7%) followed by the contribution of authoritarian parenting style (3.4%) and permissive parenting style (2.2%). The contribution of authoritative parenting style to the variance in less adaptive emotion regulation was highest (3.2%) followed by the contributions of permissive parenting style (2.8%) and authoritarian parenting style (0.2%).

Discussion

The primary purpose of the present study was to investigate whether children's cognitive-emotional functioning varies as a function of mother's occupation and parenting style. It was hypothesized that there is no significant difference in parenting styles of working and non-working mothers and there is no significant effect of parenting style on cognitive-emotional functioning in offspring. The main focus of this study was to see the impact of parenting style on the cognitive-emotional functioning in offspring. At first the effect of mother's working state on their parenting style was investigated to test the first hypothesis.

Results demonstrated in MANOVA indicate no significant differences in parenting style (F = 1.426, p <.24). No relevant study was found regarding working state of mother and their parenting styles. Thus, the result supported our first hypothesis that there is no significant difference of mother's working state with their parenting styles.

However, the effect of family type and mother's occupation were then investigated for the purpose of separating their impacts (if any) from the impact of parenting style. This would help to confirm the impact of parenting style on (if any) the variables of our interest.

Results presented in Table 21.2 indicate parenting styles are significant predictor of cognitive distortion. The result of Table 21.3 indicate that the unstandardized regression coefficients (B) for one raw unit increment of permissive parenting style, the adolescent's cognitive distortion would increase by 1.126 raw units, for one raw unit increment of authoritarian parenting style, the adolescent's cognitive distortion would increase by 1.286 raw units and for one raw unit incrcment of authoritative parenting style, the adolescent's cognitive distortion would decrease by .644 raw units. Partial η^2 in Table 14 indicates that the contribution of authoritarian parenting style to the variance in cognitive distortion was highest (14%) followed by the contributions of authoritative parenting style (9.3%) and permissive parenting style (3.7%). The result of correlation coefficients also indicates that authoritarian parenting style is significantly associated with cognitive distortion and there is a positive correlation with authoritarian parenting style and cognitive distortion. As authoritative parents have high control with lower levels of warmth to their children, this parenting style allows for strong parental command over their child, leaving minimal input of the child in decisions or rationales (Baumrind, 1991). Further, in this form of one-way communication, the child is not permitted to express views or opinions. They have very strict rules for their children that they expect to be followed unconditionally. These parents often utilize punishment, but are not willing or able to explain the reasoning behind their rules. Thus authoritarian parenting encourages compliance, not communication, and it may encourage untruthful communication. As a result, children of these parents may not develop good communication skills. In addition they may not understand the reason behind other people's action. For this misunderstanding they blame other people. Similarly, an authoritative parent sends an unconscious message to the child telling him that the world is not a safe place. Thus, they adopt assuming the worst cognitive distortion.

Permissive parenting style also has a positive correlation with cognitive distortion (Table 21.3). As noted earlier, permissive parents exhibit high levels of warmth and low levels of control (Baumrind & Black, 1967). Permissive parents are the loving ones, but they do not set their children any limits. Such children grow understanding that whatever they do not there is going to be no punishment. It may happen that permissive parenting styles result in children who are disorganized, lack independence and do not accept any authority. Among other possible effects on children are selfishness, aggression and fear of taking responsibility. That is why it will be difficult for him to realize the fact that other people do not owe him anything, so he must exert himself and do something to achieve the desirable. So, the cognitive distortion may develop in the child of permissive parents.

The result of Table 21.1 indicates that the authoritative parenting style has a negative correlation with cognitive distortion. As we mentioned earlier that authoritative parents tend to display both high control and high responsiveness and warmth to their children. This parenting style offers a balance between high nurturance and high control, in addition to clear communication about expectations for the child (Baumrind & Black, 1967). This method is called balanced parenting. This style is based on mutual respect between parents and children. So, it can be easily reasoned that children of authoritative parents tend to develop better cognitive-emotional functioning on their children.

Result of Table 21.3 indicate that for one raw unit increment of permissive parenting style, the adolescent's adaptive emotion regulation would increase by 0.569 raw units, for one raw unit increment of authoritarian parenting style, the adolescent's adaptive emotion regulation would decrease by 0.401 raw units and for one raw unit increment of authoritative parenting style, the adolescent's adaptive emotion regulation would increase by 0.331 raw units. The contribution of authoritative parenting style to the variance in adaptive emotion regulation was highest (5.7%) followed by the contribution of authoritarian parenting style (3.4%) and permissive parenting style (2.2%). However, authoritative parenting contributed much better (5.7%) than authoritarian parenting (3.4%) and permissive parenting (2.2%). These findings are consistent with the previous findings (Baumrind, 1978, 1993; Isley *et al.,* 1996; Baumrind & Black, 1967). These researchers found that authoritative parenting produces higher levels of social competence (Baumrind, 1978), a greater ability to regulate emotions, high social skills (Isley *et al.,* 1996) and self-regulation (Baumrind & Black, 1967). Baumrind (1993) reported that children reared by authoritative parents excel in areas of independence, creativity, persistence, social skills, academic competence, leadership skills, social perspective control and self-control. This means authoritative parenting is best for children to develop positive, happy and pleasant thoughts instead of thinking about threatening and stressful events (Garnefski *et al.*, 2001). Authoritative parenting helps children much more to think in a rational way and positive way (Garnefski *et al.*, 2001). As a result, children reared by authoritative parents excel in social perspective taking, emotion regulation and self-regulation (Baumrind, 1991, 1993; Baumrind & Black, 1967).

Secondly, permissive parenting style has a positive correlation with adaptive emotion regulation. As mentioned earlier, the overall idea of permissive parenting is to allow the child extensive autonomy, corroborated by high parental support, in the hopes of any, is inconsistent and confusing (Baumrind & Black, 1967) and these parents often surrender to the demands of their child. As a result children of permissive parenting might be happy and joyful always which contribute in developing adaptive emotion regulation strategies.

Authoritarian parenting was negatively associated with less adaptive emotion regulation, this finding is consistent with previous studies (Peterson & Hann, 1993; Stafford & Bayer, 1993). Studies have reported low self-esteem, low sociability, moodiness, obedience, and apprehensiveness in adolescents of *authoritarian* parents (Darling &

Steinberg, 1993). So, it might happen that because of authoritarian parenting, adolescent may experience difficulty in regulating emotions in an adaptive way. (Fergusson & Horwood, 1994).

As demonstrated in the present study (Table 21.3), for one raw unit increment of permissive parenting style, the adolescent's less adaptive emotion regulation would increase by 0.415 raw units, and for one raw unit increment of authoritarian parenting style, the adolescent's less adaptive emotion regulation would increase by 0.055 raw units. The contribution of authoritative parenting style to the variance in less adaptive emotion regulation was highest (3.2%) followed by the contributions of permissive parenting style (2.8%) and authoritarian parenting style (0.2%).

Permissive parents tend to be non-demanding and avoidant of controlling behaviour or outlining boundaries in the children's environment (Baumrind & Black, 1967). Bad behaviour of the child is seldom acknowledged or corrected by parents, and rules are either not enforced or not clearly communicated and are therefore inconsistent and confusing. In this style of parenting, children are often left to regulate their own activities, behaviour, and emotions at a young age. As a result, children may develop maladaptive cognitive emotion regulation strategies.

On the other hand, results demonstrated that authoritative parenting has a significant positive correlation and authoritarian parenting has non-significant correlation with less adaptive cognitive emotion regulation. These findings are unusual. One reason could be behind this a typical findings is that authoritative and authoritarian parenting styles are not the only factors to measure less adaptive cognitive emotion regulation in adolescents. Other factors besides parenting style might also contribute in developing adolescents less adaptive emotion regulation.

Implications

The present research was the first to investigate the impact parenting style on cognitive-emotional functioning in offspring. As parents play a major role for child development; a better understanding of the antecedents of adolescents' cognitive distortion and cognitive emotion regulation would benefit researchers, child psychologist, counsellors, clinical psychologist and mental health professionals working in the field of child and adolescence development. The findings of this study will help both the counsellors and policy-makers to understand parent's appropriate behaviours which are necessary for better cognitive and emotional development of their children. Furthermore, the understanding of how parenting styles are related to child's cognitive-emotional functioning might help us to formulate positive parenting strategies to promote healthy mental life of children.

Since prevention is better than remedy, cognitive distortion of children should be prevented by imposing better parenting styles. In a consequence we will be able to contribute to the future national development process by reducing crime from Bangladesh. These results will make social awareness among the people of Bangladesh through the dissemination of findings (e.g., publication, conference presentation etc.). The findings not only inform the general people but also the authority in charge (e.g., parents, government officials) to understand the impact of parenting style on cognitive-emotional development in children. Thus, the findings would help to take proper measures for guiding the vulnerable young age to become further resources of the society.

Limitations and Suggestions

This study has some limitations. First, it was conducted with small number of participants (η=250). Secondly, the sample was chosen only from four colleges in a convenient manner. This makes it difficult to assure how much these findings can be generalized to the whole adolescent population of the country. Due to shortage of time and other support data were collected from only Dhaka city. Thus, it cannot be claimed that the sample was representative. Further, the study could not control some of the extraneous variables like socio-economic condition, number of siblings, family type and others which could affect the result of the study.

The findings of the present study are really fruitful for further research. So, in future a large survey may be conducted with a large number of participants from different areas of Bangladesh. The future research should be designed as to find out more variables such as school influences, socio-economic factors, parental marital relationship, stress, sibling relationships, maternal depression, creativity and locus of control.

Conclusion

The present study advances the understanding that family type and mother's working state are not important for cognitive-emotional functioning in offspring. However, parenting style is a very crucial factor for developing children's adaptive cognitive emotion regulation. Parents provide the most immediate and important environment where an offspring can develop to their full capacities in these domains. The parents have key responsibilities to ensure children's fundamental rights. It can be concluded that proper parenting pattern, parental acceptance and readiness for childhood changes are very important factors in making effective cognitive emotional-functioning at adolescence period and to handle the problems skillfully. It can be argued that the problem of researching children's cognitive-emotional functioning in relation to parenting style and mother's working state is too vast to be dealt with in such a short research. However, it throws light into the area, which needs further studies and exploration.

References

American Psychiatric Association. (2001). Washington, DC: American Psychiatric Association; 1994. *Diagnostic and Statistical Manual of Mental Disorders, 4.*

Barriga, A.Q. and Gibbs, J.C. (1996). Measuring cognitive distortion in antisocial youth: development of "How I Think" Questionnaire. *Aggressive Behaviour, 22,* 333-343.

Barriga, A.Q. and Gibbs, J.C., Potter, G.B., and Liau, A.K. (2001). *How I Think (HIT) Questionnaire Manual,* Champaign, IL: Research Press.

Baumrind, D. (1967). Child care practice anteceding three patterns of preschool behaviour. *Genetic Psychology Monographs, 75* (1), 43-88.

Baumrind, D. (1978). Reciprocal rights and responsibilities in parent-child relations. *Journal of Social Issues, 34*(2), 179-196.

Baumrind, D. (1991). The influence of parenting style on adolescent competence and substance use. *Journal of Early Adolescence, 11,* 56-95.

Baumrind, D. (1993). The average expectable environment is not good enough: A response to Scarr. *Child Development, 64*(5), 1299-1317.

Baumrind, D., and Black, A.E. (1967). Socialization practices associated with dimensions of competence in preschool boys and girls. *Child Development, 38* (2), 291-327.

Buri, J.R. (1991). Parental authority questionnaire. *Journal of Personality and Social Assessment, 57,* 110-119.

Darling, N. and Steinberg, L. (1993). Parenting style as context: An integrative model. *Psychological Bulletin, 113*(3), 487-496.

Davies, M. (2000). *The Blackwell Encyclopedia of Social Work,* Wiley-Blackwell. p. 245.

Dornbusch, S.M., Ritter, P.L., Leiderman, P.H., Roberts, D.F., and Fraleigh, M.J. (1987). The relation of parenting style to adolescent performance. *Child Development, 58,* 1244-1257.

Fergusson, D.M., Horwood, L.J., and Lynskey, M.T. (1994). Parental separation, adolescent psychopathology, and problem behaviours. *Journal of the American of Child and Adolescent Psychiatry, 33* (8), 1122-1131.

Garnefski, N., Kraaij, V., and Spinhoven, P. (2001). Negative life events, cognitive emotion regulation and emotional problems. *Personality and Individual Differences, 30*(8), 1311-1327.

Gross, J.J. (1999b). Emotion regulation: Past, present, future. *Cognition and Emotion, 13*, 551-573.

Hart, C.H., Nelson, D.A., Robinson, C.C., Olsen, S.F. and McNeilly-Choque, M.K. (1998). Overt and relation aggression in Russian nursery-school-age children: Parenting style and marital linkages. *Developmental Psychopathology, 34,* 687-697.

Isley, S., O'Neil, R., and Parke, R.D. (1996). The relation of parental affect and control behaviours to children's classroom acceptance: A concurrent and predictive analysis. *Early Education and Development*, *7*(1), 7-23.

Maccoby, E.E. and Martin, J.A. (1983). Socialization in the context of the family: Parent-child interaction. In P.H. Mussen (ed.) and E.M. Hetherington (vol. ed.), *Handbook of Child Psychology*: Vol. 4. *Socialization, Personality, and Social Development* (4th ed., pp. 1-101).

Nix, R.L., Pinderhughes, E.E., Dodge, K.A., Bates, J.E., Pettit, G.S., and McFadyen Ketchum, S.A. (1999). The relation between mothers' hostile attribution tendencies and children's externalizing behaviour problems: The mediating role of mothers' harsh discipline practices. *Child Development*, *70*(4), 896-909.

Peterson, G.W., and Hann, D. (1999). Socializing children and parents in families. In *Handbook of Marriage and the Family* (pp. 327-370). Springer US.

Rohner, R.P. (1986). *The Warmth Dimension: Foundations of Parental Acceptance-rejection Theory*. Sage Publications, Inc.

Stafford, L., and Bayer, C.L. (1993). *Interaction Between Parents and Children.* Sage Publications, Inc.

Thompson, R.A. (1994). Emotional regulation: A theme in search for definition. *monographs of the Society for Research in Child Development, 59*, 25-52.

Uzzaman, M.A., and Karim, A.R. (2017). Emotional Intelligence Scale: Assessing its Psychometric Characteristics in Bangladeshi Culture. *The International Journal of Indian Psychology*, Volume 4, Issue 2, No. 86, 87.

22

Exclusive Breastfeeding and Motor Development of Children Under Five

Comparative Studies in Toddlers in the Region of Central Java, Indonesia

Dinie Ratri Desiningrum, Narendra Singh Thagunna and *Anggun Resdasari Prasetyo*

Introduction

Children are the most valuable asset to any nation as they are the future. If children are not in good health (both physical and mental), it is certain that the nation will suffer. It is, therefore, important to pay attention to and prioritize the child's developmental needs. Many children experience disturbance in their development process for some reason or other. For example, children might experience speech delay, motor skills disturbance or in establishing social relations. All these phenomena show the need for a comprehensive understanding of the child's development (Pusponegoro, 2006).

Child's development is any changes that happen at the time of: infancy toddlerhood (age 0-3 years), early childhood (ages 3-6 years) and middle childhood (ages 6-11 years) (Santrock, 2011). The development of early childhood (ages 3-6 years) is different from the other ages. At this developmental period, the children are in the active mode with high exploration tendency, and a lot of movement, hence it needs to give the most appropriate stimulation. At this time, the closest environment is very important in determining the optimization of child's development (Soetjiningsih, 2001).

Early childhood is a time when children begin to be sensitive/ insensitive to receive a variety of stimuli (Arya, 2008). Sensitive period for each child is different, along with the rate of growth and development of child individually. Sensitive period is a period in which both the physical and psychological maturity functions are ready to respond to the stimulation provided by the environment. This period is also the time of the foundational basis to develop cognitive, motor, language, socio-emotional, religious and moral skills. The first year of a childhood is a crucial time that will affect the subsequent development phase (Berk, 2005).

Children aged less than five years endlessly explore the house, the surrounding yard, as well as schools and public facilities. Such activities that seem tireless make toddlers prone to accidents; that are still in the early growth and development stage. There are risk factors, such as burns, commonly happen to children under five, if the parents off guard, and it should be worried (Stewart *et al.,* 2016).

Children carry their parents' genetic make-up, so, that quite a lot of children have developmental disturbances due to lack of nutritional factors and in many cases children might also suffer from the disease and obesity due to genetic factor (Capelle *et al.,* 2017). Motor skills of children are also supported by nutritional factors. Motor skills are essential components of the various daily activities such as dressing, eating or playing. Lack of fine motor skills can cause the difficulties in academic achievement, the increasing of anxiety and the lowness of self-esteem in children (Gaul, & Issartel, 2016). Children's motor skills are associated with writing skills and reading ability speed (Julius, Rivka Meir, Nissim, & Japha, 2016). Physical ability, motor and intellectual development of preschool children are correlated (Dordić, Tubić, & Jakšić, 2016), that is why it is important to consider the children's motor condition in general.

Community, including parents, need to know the child's development and the factors that influence children to achieve optimization of the development. Such development is integrally powered by various factors, including biological factors, like genetic and nutrition influences, as well as psychological factors such as upbringing and playing environment (Maslihah, 2005). One of the factors that influence a child's development is nutrients obtained, including breastfeeding.

Breast milk is the best food for babies that should be specially given minimum until 6 months old. World Health Organization (WHO) conducted a study of a group of respondents in breastfeeding, and issued recommendations on the advice of breastfeeding (exclusive or partial) to exclusive age (infants are only given breast milk without given any other fluids over 6 months). With the largest number of respondents, breastfeeding and medication for medical needs are done until the exclusive age of infants and continued breastfeeding up to 2 years (Habicht, & WHO Expert Consultation, 2004).

Breastfeeding is a multidimensional health behaviours influenced by the interaction of demographic, biological, psychological, and social factors. In the current social climate, breastfeeding is considered as the "golden standard" of infants' nutrition and optimal motherhood. This makes the most of the contemporary women begin to breastfeed after give birth (Peleg, Dardikman, Hermoni, & Ginzburg, 2015). Not all mothers are willing and able to breastfeed; the majority of post-birth mother had difficulty in providing breast milk to children, and decided to give formula milk or food additives since birth. It is influenced by many things.

There are internal factors that influence the behaviour of breastfeeding mothers; those are determination and motivation, self-prosperity, self-efficacy, anxiety and maternal affection formed (Peleg *et al.,* 2015; Charlick, Fielder, Pincombe, & McKellar, 2017; Pinto, Chaves, Duarte, Nelas, & Coutinho, 2016). Other internal factors are mother's age, parity (number of children) as adjusted by the body mass in pre-pregnancy index, body mass of pregnancy, complications of pregnancy, illness, smoking and alcohol drinking habits, the process of giving birth, and gender of the child (Kitano *et al.,* 2016; Pinto, *et al.*, 2016; Thet, Khaing, Smith, Sudhinaraset, Oo & Aung, 2016). Maternal health problems, both physical and psychological health, can influence the willingness of mothers to breastfeed. To illustrate, a mother in a state of postpartum depression can contribute to reduce the practice of exclusive breastfeeding (Silva, 2016).

In addition, there are also the external factors that influence the behaviour of breastfeeding mothers, including the support of inpatient and outpatient agencies after they gave birth and support from family members at home, especially their husband and mother (Gu Zhu, Zhang, & Wan, 2016; Thet *et al.,* 2016). Husband provides a support in nursing baby as well as facilitating the needs of mothers, including the giving of affection, so that, the mother is able to provide exclusive breastfeeding optimally. Individuals who live in the area are surely influenced by social demographic, including social and religion norms which are understood. Understood norms also affect the behaviour of breastfeeding mothers, so, they can motivate mothers to breastfeed exclusively (Charlick *et al.,* 2017; Pinto *et al.*, 2016).

In Islam, Allah commands in the *Qur'an*, Surah al-Baqarah: 233, mentions that a mother should breastfeed their babies until the age of two years, and there are virtue and goodness in it (*Qur'an*, 2010), namely optimal growth and development in children both in terms of physical, psychological and spiritual. The World Health Organization and other health organizations also recommend that mothers breastfeed their babies until the age of two years (World Health Organization, 2012) and motivate mothers to try paying attention to the time and duration of breastfeeding (United States Department of Health and Human Services, Centre for Disease Control and Prevention, 2014). Exclusive breastfeeding is important for neurological development of infants and overall (Lucas, & Judge, 2015). Exclusive breastfeeding is giving only breast milk, without formula milk or food additives, except for medical needs such as re-dehydration infants' liquid, vitamins, minerals and medications (American Academy of Pediatrics, 2012).

The duration of breastfeeding is influenced by many factors. Self-efficacy, psychological adjustment, body image, motivation and self-confidence are the important psychosocial factors involved in a woman's ability to maintain the duration of exclusive breastfeeding (Jager & Broadbent, 2015). A study of 133 healthy children aged 10 months to 4 years, with the first group of at least 3 months old of exclusive breastfeeding babies; the second group was given the formula milk; the third group received a mixture of breast milk and formula milk. It was then found that the exclusively breastfed children experience the increasing development of white matter of frontal brain functions, which are anatomically consistent in cognitive and behaviour performances. Constituents of breast milk boost the healthy nerve growth and development of white matter in the brain (Deoni *et al.*, 2013). In addition to cognitive abilities, the duration of breastfeeding also affects motor development of children aged 2-3 years. Moreover, it is advisable to pay attention to the amount of breast milk given during breastfeeding so that it meets the infants need, as well as the mother-child response (communication) because breastfeeding establishes the mother-baby attachment (Bernard *et al.*, 2012).

Big and small cities environment has a variety of different influences on child's development. Central Java is one of the major provinces in Indonesia. There is quite a lot of progress in terms of education, economy, technology and culture from external influence on society. In Central Java, particularly in big cities, people including the parents are knowledgeable enough about better ways to stimulate a child's development, including knowledge about the importance of exclusive breastfeeding. According to the Semarang City Health Office in 2004-2008, the coverage of early detection of toddlers and pre-school development in Central Java Province amounted to 1.5583 million (56.31%) of the number of children under five, in which there are as many as 27,67,378 children under five. It appears that the data obtained only reflects a small portion of the total number of children under five in Central Java (Early Detection of Child's Development, 10 April, 2012).

The purpose of this study was to find out more about the relationship between exclusive breastfeeding and motor skills of children under five. The study was conducted to determine the gross and fine motor development of children, associated with given and not-given exclusive breastfeeding.

Physical Development Aspects

Physical development pattern on children (Desiningrum, 2012) consist of:

(i) *Cephalocaudal* or *head to tail direction* (from head to toe), e.g., lifting head first, then chest and lower extremity.
(ii) *Proximodistal* or *near to far direction* (moving the closest body parts from the centre to further ones), e.g., to move arms is easier for infants than to move fingers.
(iii) *Mass to specific* or *simple to complex* (from the easiest to more difficult movement), e.g., infants move shoulder first, then move fingers or wave hands, finally play with their fingers.

Motor Development Aspects

Motor development is the development of control to body movement through central nerve activities, nerve cords, and coordinated muscles (Hurlock, 2004). Infants' motor skills consist of gross motor skill and fine motor skill. Motor skills on 4-5 years old children grow mostly on gross motor skill, fine motor skill grows more on children older than 5 years old. According to Papalia (Papalia & Olds, 2008), bones and muscles of preschool children grow stronger, and their lungs' capacity get bigger thus enable them to run, jump and climb faster and further. Children develop simple movements such as jump-up and down and run back and forth. For those simple movements, children take the risks. Children are able to climb a ladder with one feet quickly yet they just started learning to descent with the same way (Santrock, 2011).

Children psychomotor development is the most recognizable development by parents. Yet, most parents recognize psychomotor development is only about gross motor skill. Children's psychomotor skills are not only determined by gross motor skill but also fine motor skill. Gross motor skill usually recognized by muscle and body movements. On the other hand, fine motor skills are more about coordinated movements done by children.

Motor development on preschool (2-5 years old) (Desiningrum, 2012):

(i) Gross motor skill on children develops rapidly in this age, e.g., running and jumping which require large muscles capacity.
(ii) Fine motor skill such as buttoning shirt and drawing require coordination between smaller muscles and hand-eye coordination is also developed in preschool age. With the developments of those two motor skills children are able to be responsible to their personal needs.
(iii) On age of 3, children are able to do *handedness* (do things with one hand).

Research Methodology

This research used descriptive-comparative research design, a research using comparison method by comparing similarities and differences between two or more phenomena in order to find out factors causing those phenomena. According to the research objective, this research used cross sectional approach, a research design using measurements and observations at the same time between indicators of each variable (Hidayat, 2007).

This research was conducted in 6 months period, with 3 days effective observation time for each subject. This research was conducted to 3-4 years old children, 165 children who had exclusive breastfeeding and 135 children who never had exclusive breastfeeding (formula milk and additional food), they are from Semarang, Kendal, Jepara and Solo. This research used snowball sampling after obtaining informed consent from their mothers. The data were collected using observation sheet with observation guidance from Clark and McDowel (2008) adjusted to the observed motor development.

Variables in this research are: motor development as dependent variable and exclusive breastfeeding as independent variable. Data were collected using observation sheet. The observation results are tabulated and adjusted according to children' motor development and then analysed using descriptive statistics method by finding proportion and frequencies of subject's characteristics. To determine the size of data centre, the research used the following formula:

Formula for calculating Mean:

$$\text{Mean} = \frac{\Sigma X_1}{n} \quad \text{... (1)}$$

Formula for calculating Standard Deviation:

$$\text{Std. Dev.} = \frac{\Sigma\left(X_i - \bar{X}\right)^2}{n-1} \quad \text{... (2)}$$

The research used SPSS software (*statistical package for social sciences*) version 21.0.

Results

Tables 22.1 and 22.2 show the differences of motor skill on observed children, where gross motor development shows more often than fine motor development.

Table 22.3 shows that child's motor skill shows more often in children who had exclusive breastfeeding than children who did not have it.

Table 22.4 shows that Semarang and Solo region have higher average motor skill appearance than Kendal and Jepara region.

According to Mann Whitney test as shown in Table 22.5, calculated $Z = -2{,}694$ with p-value =.02. Due to p-value (0.02) < α (0.05), it is confirmed that there is a significant difference between exclusive breastfeeding and formula milk toward 7-12 months old infants' nutritional status in Central Java. This difference is shown in the result of univariate analysis in Table 22.3, where children with motor skill appear more frequently on infants who had exclusive breastfeeding (62.18%) than infants who never had exclusive breastfeeding (50.84%).

Discussion

Breast milk is the best food for infants which should be exclusively given to them exclusively for the first 6 months, without any supplementary

Table 22.1: Percentage of frequency of gross motor development on 3-4 years old children

No.	Indicators of behaviour	With Exclusive Breastfeeding	Without Exclusive Breastfeeding
1.	Running	94%	77%
2.	Going upstairs by Walking	54%	56%
3.	Riding 3 or 4-wheeled bicycle	75%	42%
4.	Catching a ball	67%	49%
5.	Tipping	86%	58%
6.	Jumping forward (±0.5 m)	69%	70%
7.	Performing hopscotch	60%	40%
	Mean	**72.14%**	**56%**

Table 22.2: Percentage of frequency of fine motor development on 3-4 years old children

No.	Indicators of behaviour	With Exclusive Breastfeeding	Without Exclusive Breastfeeding
1.	Having meal	58%	39%
2.	Arranging things	39%	33%
3.	Gluing	60%	62%
4.	Cutting	47%	49%
5.	Folding paper	53%	50%
6.	Applying soap	61%	48%
7.	Holding pencil correctly	54%	40%
8.	Colouring	39%	30%
9.	Buttoning clothes	59%	60%
	Mean	**52.2%**	**45.7%**

Table 22.3: Mean and Standard Deviation of Children's Motor Skill

Motor Skills	With Exclusive Breastfeeding	Without Exclusive Breastfeeding
M	62.18	50.84
SD	1.40856	0.73044

Table 22.4: Comparison of Children's Motor Skills according to Region

Criteria	Semarang	Kendal	Jepara	Solo
With Exclusive Breastfeeding	M: 65.13 SD: 1.5098	M: 55.39 SD: 1.0071	M: 57.11 SD: 1.1059	M: 62.19 SD: 1.3096
Without Exclusive Breastfeeding	M: 54.81 SD: 0.9138	M: 35.09 SD: 0.6098	M: 48.22 SD: 0.7954	M: 51.39 SD: 0.8945

Table 22.5: Differences between Exclusive Breastfeeding group and No exclusive Breastfeeding group children

Group	*N*	*Mean Rank*	*Z*	*P-Value*
With Exclusive Breastfeeding	165	13.53	–2,694	0,020
Without Exclusive Breastfeeding	135	21.47		

food or formula milk (WHO, 2012). After that, before they are two years old, breast milk is given with supplementary food (Quran, 2010). Breast milk contains essential nutrition for infants' growth and development and it is composed based on infants' daily need. Infants, who are exclusively breastfeed, tend to have better nutrition status since breast milk provides adequate nutrition needed (Atika, Susanti, & Setyowati, 2014).

Development is the pattern of progress or transformations during one's life. Development is considered as a progressive transformation process which is functionally qualitative and can be observed in both physical and psychological aspects. One of developmental tasks related to physical and motor developments in toddlers are: balanced body proportion, gaining height proximodistally, bone and mass development according to more complex fine-gross motor, and natural fat distribution on parts of the body (Desiningrum, 2012).

Adequate nutrition status enhances children development in general (Santrock, 2011), including motor development in toddlers. In Table 22.3, it is presented that the motor development of toddlers in Central Java is clearly observed who were exclusively breastfeed, which shows M=62.18 with SD=1.408, compared to those who are not exclusively breastfeed. The research shows that toddlers who are exclusively breastfeed have better nutrition status compared to those consuming formula milk or supplementary food during their 0-6 month age, thus their motor development is also supported by exclusive breastfeeding. In line with another research, the duration of exclusive breastfeeding has positively affected the motor development in toddlers (Grace, Oddy, Bulsara, & Hands, 2017).

The fact shows that there are parents, especially mothers, who really pay attention to their infants' nutrition status, in this case, breastfeed them exclusively so that there is a 62.18 per cent accomplishment of developmental tasks in motor development in toddlers. Breast milk is the most suitable diet for infants because of its nutritional values compared to baby diet made by human or animal milk, like cow milk, buffalo milk or goat milk (Atika *et al.*, 2014).

From Tables 22.1 and 22.2, the data presents frequency distribution of finc and gross motor skills in toddlers, where the mean of gross motor skills (71.14) is greater than fine motor skills (52.22) in group of toddlers who were breastfed exclusively. The fact is in line with toddler developmental tasks which define that motor development in toddler is initiated by gross motor skill like walking (Hurlock, 2004). Table 22.1 also presents the difference between toddlers who were exclusively breastfed and those who were not, which can be observed from gross motor skill like riding a bicycle, catching a ball, tipping and jumping on one dominating leg. Fine motor skills develop in line with those toddlers' growth (Papalia & Olds, 2008). Fine motor skills related to independent action like taking a bath or eating, usually can be accomplished faster, according to the result of this research which presents higher percentage in Table 22.2.

Gross motor skill is a good sign of nerve development at the early infancy and related to micronutrient status. However, it is difficult to evaluate psychomotor in early infancy. There is no clear agreement between parents and pediatrician on reasonable delay to be evaluated and intervented. Pregnancy, breastfeeding, and infancy are a period characterized by fast development, resulting in the risk of lacking micronutrient for both mother and baby. Exclusive breastfeeding for the first 6 months provide more data for micronutrient status for both mother and baby (Lise & Monsen, 2014).

The difference in motor development in toddlers, who were breastfed and those who were not, is clearly observed in some research areas. From Table 22.4, it can be seen that the area in Semarang and Solo provide higher frequency distribution of motor skill achievement compared to two other areas, Kendal and Jepara which are assumed that the residents of those area are in different level of understanding on exclusive breastfeeding. In line with the face, it was observed that mother's level of education and socio-economic status has a negative correlation to exclusive breastfeeding (Silva *et al.,* 2016; Thet *et al.,* 2016). The virtue of exclusive breastfeeding is well acknowledged and is believed to support development in children, while for toddlers who were exclusively breastfed, yet experiencing malnutrition, it is generally caused by factors related to mothers like psychological factors or food consumed by mothers and the consumed food is closely related to their socio-economic condition (Prasetyono, 2009).

Based on Table 22.5, there is a result of Mann-Whitney Test which was used to define the differences of motor skills in toddlers aged 3-4 years old which were both breastfed and not, in Central Java, and shows the value of calculated Z = –2.694 with p-value =.02, since the p-value (.02) <(0.05), it can be concluded that there is a significant difference in exclusive breastfeeding and without exclusive breastfeeding to motor skills in toddlers aged 3-4 years old in Central Java, Indonesia, especially in Semarang, Kendal, Jepara and Solo since the calculated Z > the value of Z in the table (–1.96). It presents that exclusive breastfeeding in infants affects their growth and development, including motor skill accomplishment according to developmental skills in toddlers.

According to WHO (2012), breast milk is the only ideal diet for infants until they are 6 month old because breast milk has the most ideal composition for the growth and development of infants and breast milk is able to support infants' need for nutrition for their first 6 months and supports infants' development in the following years. The recommendation to breastfeed exclusively during the first 6 months of infants was based on scientific evidence of adequate nutrition for infants and better infant growth as well as lower morbidity. Correlation between brain and food is important since adequate oral intake is essential to prevent morbidity related to food and death (Hallowell, & Spatz, 2012). Besides that, longer duration of exclusive breastfeeding reduces the risk of toddlers suffering illness like asthma, during their first 12 years in life (Verduci, Banderali, Peroni, Lassandro & Radaelli, 2016).

There are reasons why mothers refuse to breastfeed their infants, obtained from data analysis to a group consists of 135 mothers who are not breastfeeding exclusively, which presents that 25 mothers stated that their career and health are the main obstacles. One of the factor influencing mothers' decision on breastfeeding is that their decision to pursue their career so a support from office environment is important (Gu *et al.*, 2016; Thet *et al.*, 2016). Modern culture and community decision to imitate Western culture, has influenced mothers to wean their infants earlier and provide formula milk for their 0-6 month old infants (Atika *et al.*, 2014).

Conclusion

Toddlers who were exclusively breastfed shows better motor development supported by the Mean=62.18 with SD=1.408, compared to those who were not exclusively breastfed. The data also presents that frequency distribution of fine and gross motor skills in toddlers, where the mean of gross motor skills (71.14%) is greater than fine motor skills (52.22%) in group of toddlers who were breastfed exclusively. The areas in Semarang and Solo provide higher frequency distribution of motor skill achievement compared to two other areas, Kendal and Jepara. The result of Mann-Whitney Test which was used to define the differences of motor skills in toddlers aged 3-4 years old which were both breastfeed and not, in Central Java, and shows the value of calculated Z =–2.694 with p-value =.02, since the p-value (.02) <(0.05), it can be concluded that there is a significant difference in exclusive breastfeeding and without exclusive breastfeeding to motor skills in toddlers aged 3-4 years old in Central Java, Indonesia, especially in Semarang, Kendal, Jepara and Solo. The next finding is that gross motor skill can be observed in toddlers who were breastfed exclusively like riding a bicycle, catching a ball, tipping and jumping on one dominating leg. While, fine motor skills related to independent action like taking a bath or eating.

References

American Academy of Pediatrics (2012). Breastfeeding and the use of human milk. *Pediatrics*, *129*(3), 827-41.

Arya, P.K. (2008). *Rahasia mengasah talenta anak*. Jogjakarta: Think.

Atika, N., Susanti, R. and Setyowati, H. (2014). Perbedaan pemberian ASI eksklusif dan susu formula terhadap status gizi bayi umur 7-12 bulan di desa Reksosari kec. Suruh Kab. Semarang. *Thesis*. Akademi Kebidanan Ngudi Waluyo.

Berk, L.E. (2005). *Child Development*. United States of America: Pearson Education Inc.

Bernard, J.Y., Agostini, M.D., Forhan, A., Alfaiate, T., Bonet, M., Champion, V., and Kaminski, M. (2012). Breastfeeding duration and cognitive development at 2 and 3 years of age in the EDEN mother-child cohort.*The Journal of Pediatrics*. *163*(1), 36-42.

Broderick, C.R., Doorn, N.V., Ward, R.E., and Parmenter, B.J. (2017). Interventions to improve fundamental motor skills in pre-school aged children: A systematic review and meta-analysis. *Journal of Science and Medicine in Sport*. Available online 23 January 2017.http://dx.doi.org/10.1016/j.jsams.2016.11.008.

Charlick, S.J., Fielder, A., Pincombe, J., and McKellar, L. (2017). Determined to breastfeed: A case study of exclusive breastfeeding using interpretative phenomenological analysis.*Women and Birth*. Available online 16 February. 2016.http://dx.doi.org/10.1016/j.wombi.2017.01.002.

Clark, P., and McDowel, G. (2008). *The Developing Child Observation Guidebook*. Woodland Hills: The McGraw-Hill Companies, Inc.

Deoni, S.C.L, Dean. D.C., Piryatinsky, I., O'Muircheartaigh, J., Waskiewicz, N., Lehman, K., Han, M. and Dirks, H. (2013). Breastfeeding and early white matter development: A cross-sectional study. *Neuro-Image*, *82*, 77-86.

Desiningrum, D.R. (2012). *Developmental Psychology I. The Overview of Child Developmental Psychology*. Semarang: Diponegoro University Press.

Dordić, V, Tubić, T., and Jakšić, D., (2016). The relationship between physical, motor, and intellectual development of preschool children.*Procedia-Social and Behavioural Sciences, 233*, 3-7.

Early detection of child's development, http://www.pkpu.or.id/berita, diunduh 10 April, 2012.

Gaul, D., and Issartel, J. (2016). Fine motor skill proficiency in typically developing children: On or off the maturation track? *Human Movement Science, 46*, 78-85.

Grace, T., Oddy, W., Bulsara, M., and Hands, B. (2017). Breastfeeding and motor development: A longitudinal cohort study. *Human Movement Science, 51*, 9-16.

Gu, Y., Zhu, Y., Zhang, Z., and Wan, H. (2016). Effectiveness of a theory-based breastfeeding promotion intervention on exclusive breastfeeding in China: A randomized controlled trial. *Midwifery, 42*, 93-99.

Habicht, J.P. and WHO Expert Consultation (2004). Expert consultation on the optimal duration of exclusive breastfeeding: The process, recommendations, and challenge the future. Conclusions and recommendations. *Advances in Experimental Medicine and Biology, 554*, 79-87.

Hallowell, S.G., and Spatz. D.L. (2012). The relationship of brain development and breastfeeding in the late-preterm infant. *Journal of Pediatric Nursing. 27* (2), 154-162.

Hidayat (2007). *Metode penelitian kebidanan dan teknik analisa data*. Jakarta:. Salemba Medika.

Hurlock, E. (2004). *Developmental Psychology*. Jakarta: Erlangga Press.

Jager, E., and Broadbent, J. (2015). A longitudinal study of the effect of psychosocial factors on exclusive breastfeeding duration. *Midwifery. 31* (1), 103-111.

Julius, M.S., Rivka Meir, Nissim, Z.S., and Japha, E.A. (2016). Children's ability to learn a motor skill is related to handwriting and reading proficiency. *Learning and Individual Differences. 51*, 265-272. http://dx.doi.org/10.1016/j.lindif.2016.08.034

Kitano, N., Nomura, K., Kido, M., Murakami, K., Ohkubo, T., Ueno, M. and Sugimoto, M. (2016). Combined effects of maternal age and parity on successful initiation of exclusive breastfeeding. *Preventive Medicine Reports, 3*, 121-126.

Lise, A., and Monsen, B. (2014). Is exclusive breastfeeding ensuring an optimal micronutrient status and psychomotor development in infants? *Clinical Biochemistry, 47* (9), 7-14.

Lucas, R., and Judge, M. (2015). Effect of maternal body mass index on infant breastfeeding behaviours and exclusive direct breastfeeding. *Journal of Obstetric, Gynecologic and Neonatal Nursing, 44*, (6), 772-783.

Maslihah, S. (2005). *Deteksi dini perkembangan kognitif anak.* Paper presented on Optimalization Early Childhood Development on Kecamatan Cisarua,

August 18, 2005. Papalia, D.E., and Olds, S.W. 2008. *Human Development* (9th ed). New York: Mc Graw Hill Companies.

Peleg, M.K., Dardikman, M.S., Hermoni, D., and Ginzburg, K. (2015). Breastfeeding motivation and Self-Determination Theory. *Social Science and Medicine, 144*, 9-27.

Pinto, E., Chaves, C., Duarte, J., Nelas, P., and Coutinho, E. (2016). Maternal Affection and Motivation for Breastfeeding. *Procedia—Social and Behavioural Sciences, 217*, 1028-1035.

Prasetyono (2010). *ASI eksklusif.* Jakarta: Diva Press.

Pusponegoro, H.D. (2006). *Stimulasi penting untuk perkembangan anak.* Accessed on April 12, 2012. http://www.sahabatnestle.co.id/HOMEV2/main/TKSK/TKSK_ndnp.asp?id=955.

Qur'an (2010). *Tafsir dan terjemahan per-kata.* Semarang: Sunnah Press.

Santrock, J.W. (2011). *Life Span Development.* Updated Seventh Edition. New York: McGraw Hill.

Silva, C.S., Lima, M.C., Andrade, L.A.S.S., Oliveira, J.S., Monteiro, J.S., Lima, N.M.S., Santos, R.M.A.B., and Lira, P.I.C. (2016). Association between postpartum depression and the practice of exclusive breastfeeding in the first three months of life. *Jornal de Pediatria.* Available online 26 December, 2016. http://dx.doi.org/10.1016/j.jped.2016.08.005.

Soetjinngsih (2001). *Pertumbuhan dan perkembangan manusia.* Gde Ranuh: EGC.

Stewart, J., Benford, P., Wynn, P., Watson, M.C., Coupland, C., Deave, T., Hindmarch, P., Newman, G.M., and Kendrick, D. (2016). Modifiable risk factors for scald injury in children under 5 years of age: A Multi-centre Case-Control Study. *Burns, 42*(8), 1831-1843.

Thet, M.M., Khaing, E.E., Smith· N.D., Sudhinaraset, M., Oo, S., and Aung, T. (2016). Barriers to exclusive breastfeeding in the Ayeyarwaddy Region in Myanmar: Qualitative findings from mothers, grandmothers, and husbands. *Appetite, 96*, 62-69.

United States Department of Health and Human Services Centres for Disease Control and Prevention (2014). Breastfeeding. Online: http://www.cdc.gov/breastfeeding (retrieved 29.3.2016)

Verduci, E., Banderali, G., Peroni, D., Lassandro, C., and Radaelli, G. (2016). Duration of exclusive breastfeeding and wheezing in the first year of life: A longitudinal study. *Allergologia et Immunopathologia.* Available online 8 November, 2016. http://dx.doi.org/10.1016/j.aller.2016.08.013.

World Health Organization (2012).Breastfeeding. Online: http://www.who.int/topics/breastfeeding/en/ (retrieved 29.3.2016).

SECTION VII
Work Life Balance

23

Some Representations from Work Life

A Narrative based Study of Indian Immigrants in Paris

Jyoti Verma

Introduction

For the Indians, the history of migration is an old one. Today migration to economically advanced countries has become an acceptable option and answer to the questions of finding livelihood and better quality of life. Though some feel disillusioned by their experiences and some decide to return to their country of origin after a stint, the phenomenon of migration has come to stay and remain attractive for the Indians. There is a migration motive. "Economic inequality within and between regions, expanding mobility of capital, desire to pursue opportunities that might improve life chances, political strife, wars, and famine are some of the factors that remain at the heart of the impetus behind migrations" (Brah, 1996 : 178). Those who move include labour migrants (documented and undocumented both), qualified specialists, entrepreneurs, students, refugees and asylum seekers and people who are household members of previous migrants. The migration motive of Indian immigrants in Paris, France too, fall under one or the other of the above mentioned categories.

Richmond (1993) contends that migrants could be ranged on a continuum between *reactive* and *proactive*. *Reactive* migrants are motivated by factors that are constraining or exclusionary and generally negative in character. On the other hand, *proactive* migrants are motivated by factors that are facilitating or enabling and generally positive in character. These contrasting factors have also been referred as push/pull factors in the earlier literature on migration motivation. On the other hand, immigrants are the group of people who come together with other groups *voluntarily* or because they have migrated to a new location due to *mobility* and some of them are *permanently settled* in their new society (Berry, 1997). At this point it would be useful to briefly examine what is meant by acculturation and acculturation strategies.

Acculturation

"Acculturation comprehends those phenomena which results when groups of individuals having different cultures come into continuous first hand contact with subsequent changes in the original cultural patterns of either or both groups" (Redfield, Linton & Herkovits, 1936). Similarly, Berry (1990a) contends that acculturation is all about how individuals and groups may change as a result of continuous intercultural contact. Apparently, acculturation occurs within the societal network of inter-group relations and the nature and evolution of these inter-group relations are essential part of the acculturation process. It may be said that acculturation as a 'culture level' phenomenon refers to culture change resulting from the contact between two autonomous cultural groups (Redfield *et al.*, 1936) while as an 'individual level' phenomenon, acculturation requires individual members of both the larger society and the various acculturating groups, to engage in new behaviours and work out new forms of relationships in their daily lives (Graves, 1967).

The earlier researches conceived acculturation as a *cultural change process* that occurred along a single dimension meaning thereby that the immigrants would move along a continuum ranging from 'maintenance' of their original culture to 'adoption' of the host society's culture (Gordon, 1964). It appeared that the uni-dimensional models consider 'assimilation' and 'acculturation' as equivalent because assimilation (i.e., giving up one's original cultural identity and obtaining a new identity in the host society) was considered the ultimate goal for the acculturating individuals and therefore, acculturation as a uni-directional process expected only the immigrants to change.

The reality, however, is that for many plural societies, the majority culture group also has to undergo certain amount of changes when the culturally distinctive ethnic groups become accepted as members of the host society, and the expectation that they would eventually assimilate into the mainstream culture doesn not hold true. The bi-directional model defines acculturation by two independent dimensions: (a) maintenance of the values, norms/customs and identity aspects coming from the heritage culture; and (b) participation and involvement in the host society. The bi-directional models are nowadays generally considered as being more comprehensive and useful (Snauwaert, 2002). They suggest that the immigrants who take over elements from the dominant society do not necessarily have to give up their original culture and also talk about the changes in the host acculturation orientation discernible through the two independent dimensions of *maintenance* and *adaptation* and by putting similar but not identical questions to the host group.

Acculturation Orientation/Strategies

Groups' and individuals' orientation towards the acculturation process may be examined on the basis of a combination of their attitude towards the two already mentioned confronting issues or independent dimensions namely, *maintenance* and *adaptation*. The relevant questions put forth in this regards to the ethnic minority group members would be: "to what extent they want to maintain their original culture" and second, their "desire to develop intercultural relations with the host group." Berry's (1980) bi-directional model distinguishes between attitudes towards maintenance of the minority culture, and attitudes towards contact with the dominant culture in the host society. The latter dimension may be referred as *adaptation* rather than *contact* since it is about the immigrants' interest primarily in the cultural adaptation of the values, norms and customs of the dominant society. It may be noted further that these questions do not measure as to what the ethnic minority members 'actually do' in terms of acculturation but instead they rather assess "what these people prefer and want to do." Therefore, the term 'acculturation orientation' seems to be more suitable than calling those as actual behavioural patterns.

It is contended that across cultures, most immigrants combine positive attitudes towards *maintenance* and *adaptation* in so-called 'integration' orientation and compared to the alternative 'assimilation' (i.e., adaptation without maintenance), 'separation' (i.e., maintenance without adaptation) and 'marginalisation' (i.e., neither maintenance nor adaptation), the 'integration' orientation is not only the most popular one but also the most adaptive in terms of psychological adjustment and competence (Berry & Sam, 1996; Ward, Bochner & Furnham,

2001). Further, integration has been found to be the most successful; marginalization the least while assimilation and separation as the intermediate level successful strategies for positive adaptation. A simple explanation for this widely noted observation could be that "integration involves two positive orientations; marginalization involves two negative one, while assimilation and separation involve one positive and one negative relationship" (Berry, 1997 : 31). Individual differences are noticed in the *acculturation strategies* of people or in the manner in which they attempt to deal with the acculturative changes which may often be reflected in:

1. Acculturation attitudes or peoples' preferences (Berry *et al.*, 1989).
2. Behavioural shifts or how much change they actually undergo (Berry, 1980a), and
3. Acculturative stress or how problematic these changes are for them (Berry *et al.*, 1987).

The Present Chapter

This chaptre is part of a study (which was completed in the year 2000) and the researcher's first one on the acculturative experiences of Indian immigrants in Paris, France. The said study aimed at arriving at a worldview of the host culture as represented in the perception, beliefs, experiences and observations of the Indian immigrants in Paris. It was contended that the immigrants' worldview of the host culture takes shape as they interface critical issues of everyday life and meet the expectations and challenges offered by the country of settlement in the personal and professional domains of day to day life. Both quantitative and qualitative methods were used for collecting the data for meeting the objectives of the study. However, the present chaptre shall deal only with a few related concerns namely, why the respondents chose to leave India, what were their experiences from their job, and what happened to be their preferred adaptive strategy/strategies in the work domain. Since, acculturative strategies are meant to make the immigrants functional and effective in general including in their work life (which belongs to the public domain), studying the acculturative strategies of the public domain was of interest for the present chaptre. More specifically the objectives for the presentation are as follows:

Objectives

1. To look into the reasons and aspirations behind leaving the country of origin.
2. To study the Indian immigrants' experiences from work life with the help of observations based on qualitative data (i.e., narratives) collected through a fairly long interview.
3. To arrive at the respondents' adaptive strategies pertaining to some public domains of life.

Method

Sample: The sample comprised of 28 adults of Indian origin both males (16) and females (12) between the age range of 25 to 58 years. Fifty per cent of the women out of the total number of 12, were not working at the moment. All the respondents were at least Graduates with the exception of two (cases # 2, 8) who had only completed high school. The respondents came from a number of Indian states namely, Gujarat, Punjab, Bengal, Pondicherry, Maharashtra, Kerala, Karnataka, Uttar Pradesh, Andhra, Pradah, Delhi, Kashmir, Orissa and Rajasthan. The sample was a heterogeneous one as regards to the occupations of the respondents and included students, personals in jobs and businesspersons. There were at least two performing artists, one textile designer and a psychiatrist besides, two Indian Embassy staff and a highly qualified aeronautical engineer. A break-up of the time spent in terms of number of years in France by the respondents is as follows:

Years spent in the host country	1 to 5	6-10	11-15	16-20	21-25	26-30	31-35	Total
Number of respondents	7	9	3	5	1	1	2	28

Instruments

1. The Guiding Questions (Interview Schedule): A list comprising of eighteen guiding questions was used to interview the respondents. The respondents where requested to tell about their major aspirations and how far they have been realized, how they perceived the French culture and its people, what were the major hurdles faced during the adaptation process and what was good and nice in the host country. Further, how did they find the job environment and in what ways the country of origin

(India) still mattered to them. It may be noted that the present chapter includes observations only against some selected questions (i.e., question 2 and from questions 12 to 16). Given blow are the guiding questions for the interview.

1. When did you come to France?
2. What was the main reason/s for you to come and stay here?
3. How long do you want to stay, and what did you expect when you came here?
4. To what extent (you may indicate in terms of percentage if you wish) have your dreams and aspirations been realized?
5. Which is (what are) the greatest hurdle/s in adjusting to this culture?
6. What was the easiest thing to do as regards to adapting with the French society?
7. Do you repent being here?
8. Given a fair chance will you go back home?
9. Would you always choose to be in France if you have to. If "yes", why if, "no", why?
10. Do you find French people friendly, unfriendly or indifferent towards immigrants?
11. What is that you like very much in this society?
12. Do you feel satisfied with your job/business?
13. What is more that you expect from your job?
14. Do you find your French co-workers/seniors/juniors helpful and cordial?
15. Do you think that the French co-workers/seniors/juniors keep a distance from you because you are not French?
16. Do you think that there is not much scope of becoming economically prosperous by doing petty businesses in France?
17. Are you able to earn enough for your self and your family with a small business?
18. Where do you like to spend your retired life? Is it in France or you prefer to go back to India when you are not able to work and are retired?

2. Assessment of the Preferred Adaptive Strategies in Public Domains: The public domains include work place and public places like college, school, Government offices, market, business places, railway stations, airports and post office while some relevant behaviours of the workplace would be meeting appointments, being punctual, seeking appointments for rendezvous etc. For the measurement of the preferred public domain adaptive strategy of the respondents, five questions related to the workplace, were asked along with the four possible answers to choose from. The four alternative options presented in the form of a statement, were formulated to operationalize one of the four adaptive strategies each namely, assimilation, integration, separation and marginalization. The respondents were requested to select the option which they found closest to their own adaptive strategy against each respective question. The following 5 questions were asked and are presented below with the alternative answers to choose from.

(1) While meeting your appointments, what is your stand?

I am very careful not to miss my appointment (A).

If something unexpected comes up, I would still try my best to meet my appointment. However, if I must cancel it for some unavoidable reason, I will seek apology and explain the situation (I).

I would expect the other person to understand and sympathies with my problem if I am not able to meet an appointment (S).

I understand that it is very important to meet one's appointments. However, this does not guarantee that the other party will hold you in high esteem for this forever (M).

(2) Do you appear in time for your meetings, engagements or work?

Absolutely (A).

Always unless something quite unexpected and important comes up in the family. In this case I would inform and explain things and seek leave for absence (I).

Well, I give my family matters top priority over anything else and such matters decide whether I am likely to reach in time for meetings, engagements or work (S).

I try to be as punctual as a French person but I am not sure whether French people will believe that Indians are punctual (M).

(3) Do you behave the way French behave at their workplace?

(e.g., producing reports in time, meeting deadlines, being prepared for internal conference with senior persons, dressing according to the occasion, being polite to colleagues and working honestly etc.)

Absolutely (A).

If it does not clash with my personal interest (S).

Always, but with the rare exception of meeting some extremely important and unavoidable family demands (I).

I try to be as perfect as a French person would be in his/her official work, but I am not sure that this is sufficient to give you a lot of respect as a professional/worker (M).

(4) Do you seek appointment before meeting someone?

Undoubtedly and always (A).

Not always. I decide this in the light of the demands of the situation`(S).

Yes, however, I could take a chance with a few very close friends (I).

I think it is impossible to meet someone without taking an appointment (M).

(5) How do you behave at public places like railway station, post office, school etc. (standing in a queue, not littering the premise, not being impatient, talking only when asked to, not interrupting others, going to your reserved seat not disturbing others)?

I would behave exactly like how my French counterpart would behave (A).

I think there is no scope for behaving in the unexpected way (M).

I feel very uncomfortable at times but I guess there is no way out (S).

I behave like my French counterpart and find the system very convenient (I).

(*Note:* A =Assimilation, M = Marginalization, S = Separation and I =`Integration)

Observations

The observations from the narrative cases shall be presented under the following headings:

The migration motive: Reasons and aspirations behind coming to France.

The acculturation strategies in the public domain.
Representations from work.

Reasons and Aspirations behind coming to France

The sample basically comprised of the proactive migrants (Richmond, 1993). Barring the exception of a petty businessman (#8) who left India seeking asylum, no one else qualified for the reactive migrant category. In fact, this man too sneaked into France in search of economic prosperity more than anything else. The other Punjabi respondent (#2) who looked for refugee status but did not come from a poor family, migrated for the reason that he wanted to earn his livelihood and settle down his family in Europe after his father died. Initially, he was invited by a relative in Germany to help him in his business and perhaps, he belonged to the category of Diaspora more than of an immigrant because, it was important for him to "have an opportunity" and it did not matter so much as to where he went. Similarly, the sample had at least two male young professionals (#5, 21) and spouses of two young men for whom the opportunities decided where to migrate and the place carried little meaning (#25, 26).

At least four respondents came through their Pondicherry link (#4, 7, 17 and 20) and one from The Reunion Island (#19). Generally speaking, all the respondents came here looking for an economically secure future and a prosperous life. However, a number of educated and professionally qualified females came to join their working husbands (#7, 11, 13, 19, 23 and 26). Five young people arrived either as Master of Business Administration students or language students (#1, 3, 5, 18 and 21). One of them wanted to study French classical music besides popularizing the South Indian classical music in France (#6) while the other, a female came to avail a scholarship on fashion management (#9).

Interestingly, a few respondents arrived in Paris by chance. True, they wanted to leave India for higher studies and to acquire professional degrees but not that they wanted to be in France in particular. For example, Abhijeet Dave (#1) came to Paris because he could not get a visa for Australia. Suneet (#5), wanted to go to the USA or Canada, came across an advertisement announcing a scholarship for MBA programme to be taught in English in Paris and got selected. Similarly, if Nishant (#27) had not been in a cultural troupe, he would not have met his future French wife and been here or had Yesudas (#6) not taught Carantic music to a French student in his village in Kerala, he would perhaps not have been here. Chiman Shah (#8) wanted to immigrate to the USA but could manage to cross the Swiss border and came to France with the help of agents.

Mr. Diwakar Saxena (#10) came to Europe in his youth for higher studies, was lucky to find a successful career as an aeronautical engineer and decided to settle down in France. Dr. Preetpal (#25) had a similar reason to come to Europe but his take off to a materially successful life was delayed for some reasons. Two young men (#5, 21) working for the UNESCO, found their jobs during their MBA internship while Mr. Sharma (#14), a highly enterprising engineer, was presently placed in Paris working for a multi-national company. Finally, the accountant Mr. Krishnavenu (#12) arrived in France after his marriage to a French national (a native of Andhra Pradesh, India) and was employee of the electricity board in Paris.

The young people gave some interesting reasons behind their decision to leave their country. For example, they came looking for challenges and new experiences, widening their horizon, meeting people, and being out of the "small well" (*kupmanduk*) they were in. Majority of the young students after completing their education wanted to get a good job and earn money in France or in the USA. At least one performing artist (#6) said that he did not come here with the sole purpose of improving his economic well being but also wished to improve his talent and work upon his spiritual life. For all those who were now well settled, the purpose indeed was to assure a financially secure future and a good quality of life.

None of the total of 28 respondents felt that their aspirations were frustrated. It was true however, that at least three persons were not very happy with their present job situation and expected more recognition and respect from their jobs (#4, 12, 20). The young men in jobs looked forward to more salary, and those in business, towards expansion of business and more money. Women who came to join their employed husbands, did not have individual aspirations to pursue however, some of them took-up part time jobs (#7, 13, 19). At least one middle age woman became a full time baby sitter to support herself after her Indian husband left her (#23).

Engineer Mr. Sharma (#14) aspired to head the company that employed him and the distinguished aeronautical engineer Mr. Diwakar Saxena (#10) while enjoying his high position and social contacts believed that his aspirations were more or less fulfilled. The two performing artists aspired for name, fame and economic well-being in a city known to be kind to the performing artists and the lone female textile designer wanted to present "the real spirit of India" to the French through her creative work plus earn money and popularity.

Acculturative Strategies in Public Domain

Generally speaking the most preferred adaptive strategies in the public domains of the immigrants' life were either integration or assimilation. This pattern was observed quite consistently across all the five questions. Accordingly, 71.42 per cent, of the respondent preferred meeting appointments in time, 67.85 per cent, tried their best to meet their scheduled appointments and 53.57 per cent preferred to behave in accordance with the French normative standards in the public places (integration). On the other hand, a fairly large percentage of respondents (64.28%) showed willingness to go by the French normative standard and always sought an appointment before meeting some one. Further, around 39.28 per cent and 35.71 per cent of the respondents chose to behave exactly like their French counterparts in their workplace, and at the public places (assimilation).

In sum, (a) it was either integration or assimilation which were selected quite frequently as the most helpful adaptive strategies in the public domain, and (b) out of the 5 public events, integration was the most preferred adaptive strategy for meeting appointments in time, trying one's best to meet the appointments, and behaviour in the public places. On the other hand, in the remaining two instances that is, seeking appointments and behaviour at the workplace, assimilation was the most often selected strategy followed by integration. It may be concluded, that for functional reasons the Indian immigrants of the present study preferred to choose integration and assimilation more often in the public domains of day to day life where integration showed an edge over assimilation.

Representations from Work

As already mentioned all the respondents were not employed. However, those who were had the general feeling that work facilities were good in France. Nevertheless, the respondents expected more salary, recognition, more personally fixed target realization, and opportunity to grow from their respective jobs. What follow is the respondents' perceptions and experiences from their respective work life presented under the six headings of:

- Job satisfaction and perceived discrimination at work
- Importance of French degrees and diplomas
- Relationship with colleagues/employers

- Work culture in France
- Work culture in Indian concerns in Paris
- The petty worker

Job Satisfaction and Perceived Discrimination at Work

Apparently at least a couple of immigrants (# 4, 12) were not particularly happy in their jobs. For example, the 45 years old accountant of a British company Krishnavenu (#12) had to say, "Before you come to a foreign land you have dreams but after you are there you are struck by the reality and the only possibility is compromise." Krishnavenu's personal opinion was that a decent guy with marginal intelligence should not choose a life like this. This man experienced little job satisfaction followed by a nagging feeling that by working hard one could have made it here or even in India so why come here? Unfortunately, he could come to this conclusion only after having walked the bumpy path to 'economic independence' in a foreign country. Moreover, the desired economic independence for this man did not come without a price. The cost included coming to join his wife's family in France contrary to what usually happened in India, leaving behind his near and dear ones and not being able to find a lot of job satisfaction. Further in his opinion, non-French could be paid a little less than the French (as this was sometimes decided at the concerned company's policy level) but this was also one of the reasons for feeling exploited.

Krishnavenu believed that French society was not really non-hierarchical. People maintained differences in their status and this seemed to be true in medium size companies. People preferred to do their own jobs and did not interfere with others' businesses. There was a "sense of compartmentalization" people kept to themselves and there was less of human interaction unlike what we find in India. He added, "We can live as Indians but cannot perhaps be treated like French and if you have a French visa that was not enough reason for a rapport. In the office there is nothing to relate at the personal level". With his present feelings, Krishnavenu could not say that his aspirations were realized. He was somewhat bitter about all this and said that there were no alternatives but to accept what you have. However, he realized that India could have been bad too and for sure the physical working environment was good in France.

The Indian Embassy staff Hariharan Iyer (#20) when asked whether he experienced job satisfaction, quipped "not really." He explained that job satisfaction was affected because of the change in the highest position in the Embassy. He added "every 3 years the system changes at the Embassy and each new management has different expectations and different ways of functioning." Similarly, Aparna Mahadevan (#17) another office staff of the Indian Embassy who had a fairly long work experience and received a good pay packet, did not experience much job satisfaction either. She admitted however, that job facilities were good in France and some companies offered a lot of fringe benefits to its employees.

Suneet Siddharth (#5), the 31 years old male MBA who worked for UNESCO considered UNESCO's job as nice because it was open for all the nationals. Though Suneet had some good experiences he did not find his present job 100 per cent satisfying or "stimulating" enough. At best he considered it to be "ok". Further, he had to say that jobs were not easily available to the non-French persons and it was difficult for non-French to rise to the top. He observed that if you were perceived as "threatening" somehow by the people of the dominant group (especially at the higher levels) then you could have difficulty.

The only psychiatrist in the present sample Dr. Preetpal Rajhans (#24) was earning enough but was worried about his future. Since he started late as a practitioner, his security benefits were not going to be the best ones. He explained that to get the maximum benefit of the social security system in France one has to begin working as early as 18 years of age.

Discrimination at Work

Aniket Pundit a company employee (#21) pointed out that foreigners normally cannot reach the highest positions in offices and jobs in European countries. Moreover, those who do not belong to the European Union member countries were not likely to get employment easily in France. Airing almost similar feelings Suneet (#5) had observed, "In all over Europe it is difficult for people from other cultures to rise and be in high or very responsible positions. At higher levels in France for example, one cannot get ahead of the French nationals. There might be very few exceptional cases in Europe when the non-dominant group's persons were placed at higher positions." On the contrary, mechanical engineer Mr. Sharma (#14) working in a multinational company observed that French were open to "racial integration" while racial intermixing was not popular in the United Kingdom or for that matter in Italy or in Germany.

Pradeep (#4) a 45 years old male came to France in the year 1975 and worked in the French Government's job. He was a special case in the sense that he felt particularly unhappy in his present job situation. His suggested adaptive strategy was 'marginalisation' and it appeared to be linked to his job experiences, feeling of dispersion grounded in the observation that foreigners cannot reach the top, and his failure to be in the profession of his choice. Pradeep said, "One must know the French language for positive adaptation, that is the very basic requirement and then you might have to make adjustments at cultural level here and there." He added "... you may be required to give up your values and become French. If you can ask questions, if you do not feel inferior than this may not be acceptable." There was something about Pradeep's general elusiveness and unwillingness to elaborate what he said and perhaps, one could see that there was fear of being punished (as a non-French person) for being honest and vocal about one's grievances against the people, against one's work or against the system of the dominant group.

Pradeep observed that at the lower levels in the office you could get along well with the other colleagues and there was no problem. At the higher levels however, there could be discrimination. He believed that being a person from another culture created hurdles for reaching the top positions in a job and perceived this as a form of discrimination against the outsiders. He nursed some hard feelings and observed, "French want to be in the dominating position, and even if you have the qualification and competence they would like to put you down."

The experiences of a small businessman Chiman Shah (#8) gave some vivid account of the discrimination experienced by a self-employed petty businessman due to the colour of his skin. However, this was the lone case which suggested racial discrimination and perhaps cannot be generalised. Chiman Shah was a 50 years old male who earned his living by raising a stall at the local 'marche' for selling small plastic articles and goods, toys and items used by women. He generally dealt with Chinese traders for buying his goods in whole sale and his relationship with them was more of contractual kind but nevertheless, they gave him due respect as a customer.

Chiman Shah had very limited contact with the French people, but he had his opinion about them. According to him French people would first buy things from the white skinned (French) businessman. He observed, "Sometimes they would not like to acknowledge your presence, respond to you or talk to you." The white customers and shopkeepers would push his cart with their foot which he found very disrespectful. Occasionally, Chiman Shah got very angry with the French and told them that they were "inhuman devils." His bitterness was expressed in the following words: "French are not helpful to the outsiders and reserved their human touch for their own people. They do not like coloured skin people and in general maintained distance."

Nevertheless, for practical reasons Chiman Shah wanted to choose France if he had to select a country to come back to and was happy that his financial condition had improved.

A middle aged businessman Mr. Pankaj Patel (#15) believed that if people perceived racism in France it was perhaps, at the higher levels. That is, you or your children may not be able to get the highest positions in the jobs and only the French would enjoy this privilege. At the higher administrative levels you might be discriminated, but not openly or in general. Mr. Patel wanted to say that if there was racism in France it was not obvious, but quite "subtle."

Vasundhara (#7) a 39 years old non-working female volunteered to share something from her husband's experience at his job. Her husband worked with French people and she tried to give vent to his feelings by saying that "French people always kept a distance. They could make you feel like a stranger. They are not racist people but could make you feel small. They are subtle in their ways to suggest their racist attitude". She observed that at times her husband was in conflict with his co-workers or seniors. On the other hand, there was belief in equality in this society in the sense that one could reach one's seniors or boss and discuss things with him/her. However, people will not go out of way to help you.

Mr. Rituraj Sharma (#14) a well placed mechanical engineer employed in a multinational company had to say a few positive things. He observed that French were open to "racial integration". Racial intermixing was not popular in United Kingdom or for that matter in Italy. In France however, there was evidence for marriages between blacks and whites. There was racism in Germany too, however, one cannot deny a subtle undercurrent of racism in France but there was some mixing as well. Language student Rani (#3) felt that French do keep a distance from people of other cultures or groups.

Importance of French Degree and Diploma for Job Seekers

According to middle aged successful aeronautical engineer Mr. Diwakar Saxena (#10), the prospective job seeker's original degree was not treated at par with the French degree. He observed, "The French degree gets more respect. It was not like in England or in the USA where qualifications from Anglo-Saxon countries may be treated as equal." Mr. Saxena also sensed some competition between different educational institutions and alumni groups who helped their own members to study and speak exactly like them. Krishnavenu (#12) had aired similar feelings and argued, "Knowing French language was not enough and one had to be an expert in the language. To be recognized as competent, you have to have French degree and diploma. You may be very capable but that does not help without having French degree and qualifications. Here Anglo-Saxon people could have difficulty. Integration was faster in UK or in the USA than what we find in France."

Another case in point was Dr Rajhans (#24) who had the MBBS degree, but his basic degree was not recognised and he had to get the necessary qualifications again in England and France respectively. This was the greatest hurdle faced by him and due to this he started off late in his profession. He believed that this made his integration more difficult and also delayed his professional success in France.

Relationship with Colleagues/Employers

It would not be fair to conclude that all the respondents experienced discrimination or felt absence of cordial relationship at their workplace. In fact, it was frequently mentioned that the French colleagues, seniors and juniors did not maintain distance from their non-French colleagues (#5, 9 and 10). Dr. Preetpal (#24) worked all by himself but occasionally met colleagues from the same profession in conferences and seminars and found them nice. The two members of the Indian Embassy Hariharan Iyer (#20) and Aparna Mahadevan (#17) felt that their French counterparts at the Embassy liked Indian colleagues and were friendly and helpful. Roshni (#16) a research assistant shared similar feelings and Aditi (# 13) a school teacher, found her colleagues nice, friendly and cordial.

Udayan Yesudas (#6) a young male Carnatic music singer found his French colleagues and team-mates emotionally very supportive. He had to say, "At times I was broken, depressed, but they were my strength. They were curious and wanted to know how I felt." He came across important persons at the concerts from the fields of judiciary, labour, films, literature and painting etc., and did not find them "keeping a distance" from him. For 30 years old, part-time school teacher Parveen Sultana (#19), her two male colleagues were good, helpful and treated her well. Parveen could communicate with them and they did not mind sharing information with her. Sanyukta Panda (#23), a 56 years old, female baby sitter had many good words to say for her French employers with whom she shared very cordial relationship. She had arrived in France in the year 1980 and the French couple who employed her trusted her well. Her employer's were working as Air-France crew and therefore, at times they had to leave their children with her for a day or two. In that case, Sanyukta stayed at their home. Sanyukta at times even cooked simple Indian food (*khichari*) for the kids and tried to speak in Bangla with them. On the other hand, the kids loved her too. Sanyukta's relationship with her employer's family had grown into an intimate one over time and she felt close to her employer's family. Businessman Mr. Pankaj Patel (#15) employed French people for running his shop and found them helpful, cordial and nice.

Mr. Diwakar (#10) however, wanted to point out that since hierarchy was prominent in France therefore, "French expected homogeneity with little apprehension." Suneet (#5) was in UNESCO's job and the nature of his job did not give much scope for maintaining distance from each other. Nevertheless, Suneet felt that one came across some "strong personalities." In company employee Aniket Pundit's (#21) opinion, "You cannot put pressure on them (i.e., colleagues). You have to be careful about what you say and labour laws were strict in France." Responding to the question "whether co-workers and seniors maintained distance" (because you are a foreigner), Aniket had to say that "distance depends and it is up to you. I can go out to them. It could be different from person to person. If I want to talk to somebody I can." Similarly, Vineet a young job trainee found his French colleagues helpful and in fact more helpful and cordial than his Indian co-workers. He had to say that good co-worker relationship also depended on the person concerned and could differ from person to person.

Jasvinder Singh (#2) a 39 years old male chef of an Indian restaurant had arrived in Paris in 1983. Having moved little among the French group his observations were limited. Nevertheless, he had to say, "French people are not sacrificing, and they keep work relationship this however, is good in the sense that you do not feel the pressure on you from their side (*bojh nahi parta*). Jasvinder Singh felt that "French are not involved in you."

The French Work Culture

The commonly shared feeling of the respondents was that France had a good working environment. The infrastructural facilities were excellent and the system was functional. Moreover, there was certain accountability in the work done and dealings were straight and rather irreversible (Mr. Saxena, #10). Mechnical engineer Mr. Rituraj Sharma (#14) believed that his multi-national company's co-workers were conscientious and did their work properly. He interpreted this as an expression of the employees' nationalist feelings at the individual level. His other observations suggested that people did their jobs well individually and no one was unnecessarily inquisitive. However, unlike Japan, people did not interact a lot among themselves at the workplace. In the same vain, one of the respondents (#12) felt that in the office "there was nothing to relate at the personal level."

It appeared from the narratives that the different organizations imparted their duties with sincerity and seriousness. Roshani (#16) a research assistant admired that the universities made effort to provide conceptual clarity about the concepts being taught and the teaching method was from "thesis to antithesis and synthesis". Even children in school were taught through this method. According to Adithi (#13) a part-time school teacher, schools imparted practical education and children were taken to other countries on educational trips. They were given personal attention and the classrooms were not crowded.

The sample had a few students and their experiences gave some idea about France as a place for professional education. Abhijeet Dave (#1) was a 25 years old MBA student and had only recently arrived in Paris (March, 1999). Abhijeet found the facilities for work and business good in France and personally speaking he could meet his expectations in his studies. In his opinion, the educational system in India was flawed. He argued, "Here you have more chance, more choices to move in the direction of your liking and taste and I have the freedom of using my talent."

Rani Mukherjee (#3), a thirty three years old female language student was a recent arrive in Paris. Generally speaking, Rani felt satisfied as a student but did experience one problem at the university. She noticed that her teacher's rating for her performance was inconsistent and therefore, she did not know where she stood. She did not find her teachers "organized" in that sense. Further, they maintained a professional attitude and one missed the "personal touch and attention" in the teacher student relationship. Rani felt that "the teachers were cordial but not the helping kind" and though she could speak French language, she found it difficult to associate with the French and said "they would not do more than necessary." Having said this, Rani wanted to say, "It was still better to be here than in India in many respects. Because, even those who were not very well educated, could find some job such as that of a baby sitter."

Another student in his early twenties namely, Vineet (#18) worked as a job trainee in a computer company. He had arrived in Paris in the year 1998 and liked his internship job where he could work at his own pace and use his time the way he wanted to. The only expectation was that he was expected to complete his projects in time and submit his reports.

The sample had a couple of performing artists and it was interesting to go through their experiences in this context. Nishant (#27) was a 26 years old male Indian Kathak dancer who arrived in Paris in 1993. He happened to meet musicians, people from the world of cinema, painters and performing artists, his feeling was that “meeting such persons and being in an art group was like having exchange of cultures.” In Nishant’s opinion, the Indian scene in the field of art was “egoist.” He believed that, in this country “people get respect as human beings.” Perhaps, he was referring to the respect that creative people and performing artists of all stature received in France. According to him there was competition in the field of art but perhaps, a healthy one and in that sense Nishant perceived “equality” among the artists. He had to say further, “Artists wished to become stars and liked to be recognised but for this they had to make tremendous effort at the personal level. This was a different situation and people were not trying to beat others. It was however, true that special people received a lot more respect and recognition.”

According to this young performing artist, the facilities for performing Indian artists in France were good, but the real scope for their art was in India. He elaborated his point by saying, “Here one has to market one-self well through agents which was an expensive affair. To become commercially successful you have to let yourself be known and advertised. Paris is the cultural centre of the world so to make a place here as an Indian artist you have to make effort from different angles. Though you can expect respect as a creative person it was not a guarantee for a successful career.”

Another performing artist Udayan Yesudas (#6) found India “very competitive” for the artists and perhaps he meant young artists. In that sense there was less competition for a person like him in France. He found respect for performing artists and art in general in this culturally sensitive society. For example, he was able to go to a few workshops at different places which might not have been possible in India. Yesudas was able to earn just enough for him but was aware that if an artist wanted to commercialize himself/herself then he/she had to market himself/herself with effort and by spending money.

Finally, the researcher came across some amusing observations regarding the French peoples' work attitude. It was pointed out by a job trainee (#18) that French people did not work very hard and were "lazy". He wondered as to how France is so developed. He meant to say that French do not slog themselves for work while Indians worked real hard here. He made another amusing observation, "France runs through the labour of the foreigners."

The MBA student Abhijeet Dave (#1) observed that French people worked at their own pace, seemed to enjoy their work and cared more for prestige than for money. Another one wondered, "When do the French work, if they spent so much time in the restaurants"? The answer to this question was available, and it was argued that French discussed important issues while eating out and met their appointments in a cafe. The aeronautical engineer Mr. Saxena (#10) made an interesting observation, "French do not prefer to do small jobs more so, the menial work so there were small jobs available for those who can do them."

New Job Prospects

According to the accountant Krishnvenu (#12), it was not easy to get collaborations or start a business in France and it was too expensive to do so. He observed "For starting a business you are asked for enormous amount of security money and may be required to deposit two millions of French Francs. It was hard to take risk here. Further, if you wished to make an effort for setting-up some business, the forces that held you back came-up very strong". On the contrary, the small businessman Chiman Shah (#2) felt that "Business prospects were good in this country. One could sell anything here as people have money and they wanted to spend money and buy things." Despite some experiences of discrimination Chiman Shah believed that France was still a better place for earning money and observed, "This was a country where I began my business from 500 Francs but could earn 5000 Francs. It would have been impossible for me to earn this much with so little seed money in India." He also felt that one could live fairly comfortably in France with limited resources. Obviously, the situation was better for those who had the work permit.

According to the tour operator Surjeet Minocha (#22), it was difficult to co-ordinate with travel agencies who could act as future liaison offices for getting business for his Indian travel agency. There were at least 26-27 such tour operators in Paris whom one could tap for developing a business network, but it was not an easy job and there was competition. Some agencies were here for the last 25 years and offered very tough competition to those who wished to acquire new business for their respective organizations.

The Work Culture in the Indian Concerns

Surjeet Minocha (# 22) regretted that his Indian senior carried the mentality of an Indian boss and therefore, he had to be careful about not hurting his "ego". He observed that the French work culture was different. Here people took full responsibility of their work and cared for the quality of the work. However, this was not necessarily the main worry for the Indian concerns. Both Hariharn and Aparna the two Indian Embassy staff members believed that the work culture in the Indian Embassy was close to what we see in India and whether it is going to become better or worse depended upon the expectations of the Ministry of External Affairs. Personally speaking, Hariharan preferred to have a more "modernised" job environment and wished that the Embassy worked more swiftly. He also wished for much more effort for improving public relations. At the same time, Hariharan felt that working with the Indian colleagues was like being in a family. Roshni (#16) who served in an oriental resource centre observed that occasionally she came across difficult colleagues and in that sense; the work environment was not drastically different from that of India.

Petty Workers

Majority of the respondents believed that petty businesses did not offer scope for economic prosperity. It was argued that people who were desperate and did not see a future in their own country, wanted to try their luck in a rich foreign country. Normally, they were not well educated or skilled persons and did not have proper documents to travel and therefore, were forced to live an unpredictable life in constant fear of being punished. Mechanical engineer Rituraj Sharma (#14) believed that petty jobs could perhaps assure just a little better future to a few but not to all. In general, there was not much future in practices like selling things on the pavements and remaining illegal entrants in France trying for a prosperous future. France was not like USA and these practices did not assure a bright future.

The lady at the Indian Embassy (Aparna, #17) knew much about petty worker and told that those who came without proper papers were exploited by the agents and the employers both. She explained why it was hard to motivate the illegal immigrants and refugees to go back. In fact, often such persons wanted to organize or manage their papers. Some could manage to marry a French citizen by making a deal while some left for another country like Spain and remained in Europe. Often they saved money with great difficulty for meeting the demands of the marriage deal and lived in perpetual hardships. Those who could manage to live here for 10 years, applied for the stay permit. Since, it was important to be around, they tried to hang on and it was very difficult to motivate them to go back.

In the present sample, Jasvinder Singh and Chiman Shah (#2, 8) perhaps, belonged to the group of petty workers but they were the ones who survived. Two female respondents (# 9, 16) personally knew at least one case each where the person concerned could make a fairly decent livelihood through petty jobs despite all the hardships. It was however true that the petty workers could not reach or live up to the French standards no matter what they did. In Mr. and Mrs. Patel's (#15) opinion, though people involved in petty jobs were managing life with great hardship, they were still able to earn more than what they did in India and could save a little money too. They did not have quality of life but with hard work they could make money which was not always assured in India.

According to Krishnavenu (#12) petty jobs cannot lead to a secure future and life was full of threat and fear in this situation. Often people in the small jobs did not have the right papers and therefore, lived in uncertainty. France was liberal in the sense that even when the illegal petty workers got held by the police the police often let them go after a fine without being very harsh to them. Interestingly, those who did not have proper papers could not submit the fine as the processing of the fine had to be done through the proper documents which the petty workers did not have.

A number of respondents (#1, 5, 7, 21, and 22) shared the feeling that petty jobs can perhaps help one survive in France, but cannot bring prosperity. It may be recalled that French did not prefer doing menial work therefore, if someone was prepared to do hard physical labour it was possible for him/her to earn money. Dr. Rajhans (#24) observed that petty workers needed help and struggled for five to ten years. In fact, nine out of ten such persons were in difficult situations. A little variation in opinion in this context could also be seen. For example, a non-working woman Meenakshi Lele (# 25) believed that if some people chose to work and live in such great hardships, they must be having some hope and perhaps, they had a reason to look forward to a better life through such means of livelihood. There were also some people who wanted to be here because they had talent and believed that they could make a future out of their talent for music, dance and painting, etc. in the world's cultural capital. Parveen Sultana (#19) believed that the petty workers do not know the French language and they cannot prosper without knowing the language or without having proper work permit.

Conclusion

Reasons and Aspirations behind coming to France

Generally speaking, all the respondents came to France looking for an economically secure future and a prosperous life and were therefore, proactive migrants. Those who came through their Pondicherry link had more or less the same objective to pursue. Young students came to learn the French language or to acquire a professional degree, but each one of them ultimately wanted to find a good job and earn money. The two young performing artists managed to come with the help of others but they chose Paris because it was the appropriate place for young aspiring performing artists to try their luck and earn name, fame and money. Around 80 per cent of the respondents were well settled in their respective jobs or professions and only a small percentage (10-11%) felt that their aspirations were not fully realized.

The Acculturation Scene in the Public Domain

Generally speaking, the most preferred adaptive strategies in the public domain were either integration or assimilation. Furthermore, out of the 5 public domain questions, integration was chosen most frequently followed by assimilation.

Representations from the Work

The general feeling was that work facilities were good in France. On the other hand, jobs were not seen as easily available to the non-French persons or to those who did not have French degree or diploma. It was frequently mentioned that French colleagues, seniors or juniors did not keep a distance from their non-French colleagues. In a number of cases however, the concerned employees experienced 'discrimination' and were forced to believe that foreigner normally cannot reach the highest positions in jobs.

A few missed the "personal touch and attention" at the workplace and found nothing to relate at the personal level. Those working in the Indian Embassy or with Indian concerns found the work culture more or less similar to India and hoped for improvement. A small number of respondents found it difficult to co-ordinate with others due to highly competitive environment and observed that much risk and money were involved in starting a business in Paris. However, teaching in schools and universities was found quite satisfactory.

One came across some interesting observations regarding the work attitude of the French. It was pointed out that French did not work very hard, worked at their own pace, seemed to enjoy their work and cared more for prestige than for money. It was argued that French who loved to go to restaurants discussed important issues while eating out, and met their appointments in a cafe. It was also suggested that French do not like to do menial jobs. Majority of the respondents believed that petty businesses did not offer scope for economic prosperity. Nevertheless, since, it was important to be around for organizing one's stay and documents some how, the petty workers kept hanging on.

Author's Note: The present research was fully supported by the fellowship of the French Ministry of Higher Education and Research and coordinated by the Maison Des Sciencs de L'Homme, Paris, June 2000. The author wishes to thankfully acknowledge the helpful comments and observations provided by Prof. J.B.P. Sinha and the team of faculty members at ASSERT, Patna during the development of instruments, analysis of data and discussion of the observations. Please address correspondence to Jyoti Verma at her e-mail: *jyotiverma _us@yahoo.com.*

References

Berry, J.W. (1980). Social and Cultural change. In H.C. Triandis and R. Brislin (Eds.), *Handbook of Cross-cultural Psychology* (Volume 5, Social Psychology). Boston: Allyn & Bacon.

Berry, J.W. (1990a). Psychology of Acculturation. In R. Brislin (Ed.), *Applied Cross-cultural Psychology.* London: Sage Publications.

Berry, J.W. (1997). *Culture in Contact: Acculturation and Change.* G.B. Pant Memorial Lecture, delivered at the G.B. Pant Social Sciences Institute, Allahabad, India on February, 21-22, 1997.

Berry, J.W., Kim, U., Minde, T. and Mok, D. (1987). Comparative studies of acculturative stress. *International Migration Review, 21*, 491-511.

Berry, J.W., Kim, U., Pawar, S. and Bujaki, M. (1989). Acculturation attitudes in plural societies. *Applied Psychology, 38*, 185-206.

Berry, J.W., and Sam, D.L. (1996). Acculturation and adaptation. In J.W. Berry, M.H. Segall & C. Kagitcibasi (eds.), *Handbook of Cross-cultural Psychology*, Vol.3, Social Behaviour and Applications. Boston: Allyn & Bacon.

Brah, A. (1996). *Diaspora, Border and Transnational Identities: Cartographies of Diaspora: Contesting identities*. London & New York : Routledge.

Gordon, M. (1964). *Assimilation in American Life*. London: Oxford University Press.

Graves, T. (1967). Psychological acculturation in tri-ethnic community. *South-western Journal of Anthropology, 23*, 337-350.

Redfield, R., Linton, R., Herkovits, M.J. (1936). Memorandum on the study of acculturation. *American Anthropologist, 38*, 149-152.

Richmond, A. (1993). Reactive migration: Sociological perspectives on refugee movements. *Journal of Refugee Studies, 6*, 7-24.

Snauwaert, B. (2002). A Social Psychological study on acculturation orientations of ethnic minority members and autochthons. Doctoral dissertation, K.U. Lueuven.

Ward, C., Bochner, S. and Furham, A.F. (2001). *The Psychology of Culture Shock*. London: Routledge & Keagan Paul.

24

Justice towards Women' Empowerment

Some Reality based Issues

Purnima Awasthi

Introduction

"We not only want a piece of the pie, we also want to choose the flavour, and to know how to make it ourselves" quoated by Ella Bhatt, Formal President of Self-Employed Women Association. This statement provides a clear picture about existing poor status of women in the society. Women who comprise approximately half population of this world generally receive ill treatments that are embarrassing, disgusting, intolerable and barbarous. They are deprived of even vital support for leading and commending their lives that are fully human. This lack of support is frequently caused by them being women. The Constitution of India clearly states that women must be given the freedom exactly the same as men are enjoying. Law of country evidently guarantees that women are sanctioned the rights and respect as men's equal in all areas of existence. A woman may have the highest office in India, she can go into several professions and even the ground of politics is not a forbidden part to them. Indian women living in urban areas have come forward to compete with men and demand their share of places or jobs in legislatures, government offices and other institutions, including business concerns. In spite of all these facts, they live under the control of their parents or their husbands, or their sons in different phases of life and enjoy less of autonomy and participation (Chatterjee, 1990; Desai, 1994; The World Bank, 1996).

These factors tend to have unenthusiastic impacts on the survival, empowerment and development of Indian women.

Study (Srinivasan, 1997) indicates that women in rural areas are perhaps condemned to live forever in the state of permanent slavery, and whatever the authorities may do to uplift them; they can never be brought on a par with urban women, who enjoy many facilities and some comforts of life up to some extent. In urban areas women have no idea managed to secure a position of equality with men. They work as administrators in offices, banks and insurance companies, they occupy positions of authority in hospitals, law courts and institutions of business, and being as capable as are men, they have learnt to accomplish the tasks required for specific job conditions, including different strategies. Some women may thoroughly enjoy their new found freedom of urban life, but still striving for getting equality. Although on the basis of certain kinds of freedom enjoyed by urban women it cannot be said that they have managed to win equality, and are no longer subservient to men.

There still exists gender discrimination, which hinders development of women from various perspectives (Riebschleger & Fila, 2009). So while denial of basic rights (e.g., education, employment, health care for women etc.) is detrimental to women, this denial, ultimately also harms the society, the nations at large too, by hampering women' growth and development.

Women's Empowerment with special reference to status of Women in Ancient Asia

During ancient times, among Asian countries like China, there were mainly three aspects of obedience for women such as to obey their father prior to marriage, to obey their husband after marriage and to obey their sons in widowhood. The Ancient Chinese did not give any importance to educating the women in their society. As a result they never went to school. Girls, whose fathers were scholars could learn from them but female scholars, were very rare. The work of women was limited to four boundaries of the wall. Women were expected to have many children and felt the pressure to bear a son instead of a daughter. Throughout the thousands of years, Chinese history reveals the fact for those wealthy Chinese men having a wife and numerous concubines. Women were treated like slaves and prostitutes during 1900s (Lunes, 2010).

The women in Japan during those days led a very simple and basic life. They normally made clothing and prepared meals. They even had to perform minor additional chores like tending to garden and protecting their home and land. Women did not marry for love and their marriages were arranged. The upper class women were rendered the privilege to learn martial arts and even took part in fighting. The women of the Samurai class had to fight in times of need, till their last breath with weapons in their hand (Isobelle, Dalena, Anthony & Michael, 2013).

While In India, the Rig Vedic women enjoyed high intellectual and spiritual status. There were many women *Rishis. Sati* system did not prevail during this period. Women in India during the Vedic period enjoyed a free and esteemed position. With the advent of post Vedic period, the condition of women started being deteriorated. They were discriminated against in fields of education and other rights and privileges. Child marriage, *purdah* system, widow burning and polygamy worsened the status of women in the society. The role of women in ancient Indian literature is quite immense. There were two types of women, one who never married for culturing the *Vedas* throughout their entire life and were known as *Brahmavadinis* and the other were the *Sadyodvahas*, who studied the *Vedas* till they married. Women in ancient India did excel in fine arts, music, painting and even wrote Sanskrit plays and verses. Women also enjoyed the prominent roles in politics. Prabhavati, the daughter of Chandragupta II, ran the administration on behalf of her prince Vakataka. Following the Gupta period, queens used to rule in Kashmir, Orissa and Andhra. Women were also the provincial and village administrators in the Kannada region. Hence during the ancient days, the women who belonged to the aristocratic classes enjoyed the freedom of education and other privileges while the normal women still had to undergo through various hurdles and face deprivation (Basu, 2014).

Deterioration in the Condition of Women Empowerment with the passage of Time

Mason (1995) reported that the situation of women in any country is highly effected by the socio-cultural traditions that are prevalent in the particular region or country. Thus, the socio-cultural factors seem to overpower the economic or political conditions that affect the situation of women. Economic development in any country may improve the condition of women in certain aspects but the other spheres of their lives remain totally unapproached. There are broadly two groups of opinions regarding the condition of women in present scenario. One group says that the economic development of women has of course increased the access to resources, rendered autonomy, freedom and power and benefited the general well-being of women. The other group argues that the economic advancement of women in Asian countries have set an offset by a deterioration in other aspects of women's status.

As a result, we see women's lack of political power, legal barriers to full economic and social participation. Not only this, there is difference between the occupational status and pay levels of men and women in Asian countries. There is lack of control of women over the agricultural resources and hiking rates of violence against women is reported in economically advanced countries of Asia (Mason, 1995).

Women's Empowerment and Health with special reference to their status in Asia

Though understanding women's health and empowerment status is a complex mission, numerous efforts have been undertaken to observe the real picture of women's empowerment and health status in Asia. Reports state that India is one of the developing countries in the Asia, where females and males have nearly the same life expectancy at birth. The fact about the typical female advantage in life expectancy is not apparent in India indicates that there are systematic problems with women's empowerment and health status. Indian women have high mortality rates, particularly during childhood and reproductive years. They have low level of education and low participation in labour force (Chatterjee, 1990; Desai, 1994; The World Bank, 1996). These reasons tend to have negative consequences for the empowerment and health of Indian women.

Facts also reveal that women experience discrimination in the allocation of household resources including food, access to health services and breast-feeding (International Institute of Population Sciences, 1995). During illness boys are more likely to be taken for medical care than girls (Bhalla, 1995; Jejeebhoy & Rao, 1998). Studies also indicate that between 1-4 years more girls than boys die due to factors related to living conditions and negligence such as accidents, injuries, fever, and digestive disorders (Government of India, 1995). It is anticipated that in the first half of the 21st century, upholding of the women's health would be a one of the giant challenges in developing countries.

A repeatedly reported cause for poor health of Indian women is the discriminatory practices against girls and women. The main alarming evidence for this is provided by the large number of "missing women" (the females who apparently died in the past). About a decade ago the

World Bank (1996) estimated a deficit of 35 million females, who should be part of the population, but are not there mainly due to higher female than male mortality rate for every age group up to the age 30 (Registrar General, 1996). The most extreme manifestation of this problem is the sex-selective abortion. Use of medical technology to determine the sex of a foetus is on rise in India, and over 90 per cent of the foetuses that are aborted are female (The World Bank, 1996).

Women in much of the humankind lack social support for vital function of a human life in sufferings even in the collectivistic country like India. Awasthi and Mishra (2008) assessed the nature of expected and obtained social support by women suffering from cervix cancer and diabetes. With respect to the delivery of support, the findings showed that diabetic women received greater amount of emotional, informational, social and practical supports than women suffering from cervix cancer. While educated women received greater emotional, informational, and social support than uneducated women, urban women received practical support more than rural women. The findings indicated that both cancer and diabetic patients had almost similar level of expectations for emotional, informational, social companionship and practical supports, however, some differences in the expectation of supports were evident due to educational and residential background of women.

A remarkable feature of these findings was the discrepancy between the amount of expected and actually received supports. The level of expectation was always higher than the level of support actually received by women. Both the cancer and diabetic women showed greater discrepancy on emotional and practical supports than on informational and social-companionship supports. This is understandable in view of the fact that the majority of women, who participated in the present study, were married and hailed from a traditional middle class background. In this group, women play a central role in managing household and caring for other family members. Their emotional bonding with family members and friends develops greater expectation for emotional and practical supports from them during the course of illness. It may also be noted that in many Indian families the family income (e.g., through agriculture or family business) is shared, and the husbands are not free to use it the way they want. This situation may lead to greater expectation for both emotional and practical supports (Awasthi, *et al.*, 2008, 2015).

In another study Awasthi and Mishra (2015) also made comparative analysis between women patients and normal healthy women and examined the nature and the extent of social support women suffering from cancer receive from their social network and compared them with those of healthy women The findings showed that the control group perceived greater support than the patient group in terms of social companionship. Perception of social support was greatly influenced by educational and residential background of women. Educated women believed more strongly in self-control of illness than uneducated women. Uneducated patients believed more strongly in doctors' control of illness than educated non-patient women. Belief in supernatural control was strongly placed among uneducated rural women than among educated urban women; however, some differences in the perception of control were evident due to educational and residential background of women. Women generally believed strongly in psychological and interpersonal consequences than physiological consequences but non-patient women felt more severe consequences for cancer. Educated women felt more severe consequences than the uneducated women and rural and urban women have approximately similar experience of severity of illness.

The findings of above mentioned studies clearly indicate that educated women, irrespective of residential background, perceived greater amount of emotional, informational, social-companionship and practical support than uneducated women and cancer patients. This clearly indicates a significant link of education with the perception of social supports availability. Much of the work on the effect of education has been focused on health education intervention programme (Samarel, Tulman, & Fawcett, 2002). Findings generally reveal a positive effect of such programmes to the extent that women's health education has been considered as an effective means of management of their health problems. Educated people can provide useful information about health problems and also suggest practical ways for handling them. The findings of these studies suggest that educated women can also provide greater emotional support and effective companionship to women in their sufferings. Beneficial role of education in these studies provides with evidence that it increases the possibility that people will apply their existing cognitive abilities to a variety of situations. School education makes people feel more at ease so that educated people can control and manage the affairs of their life more effectively than those who have not been to school (Mishra & Dasen, 2004).

Mishra (2009) carried out a study with women of the Kharwar tribal group residing in villages of the Naugarh region and attempted to assess their major health problems, attribution of causes, control and responsibility for health problems, factors in maintenance of good health and prevention of health problems. Findings revealed that diarrhoea, fever, conjunctivitis, arthritis, skin diseases, unwanted pregnancy, and child mortality were the major problems related to the health of Kharwar women. Attribution analysis revealed the existence of physical, behavioural and supernatural causes of health problems in their cognitive system. Local *vaidya*, healers and family were reported as the most dominant support systems for dealing with health problems. The efficacy of government health system was almost denied.

Chaudhuri (2010) made a comparative analysis for women's Empowerment in South Asia and South-east Asia. The countries surveyed were Cambodia, Vietnam, the Philippines, Indonesia, Pakistan, and Bangladesh. This survey was only partially done, and by no means asserts to have covered all cultural, economic, and political elucidations for women's status and empowerment of the mentioned Asian Nations. The findings revealed that whatsoever improvement in the women's status has been made is through inadequate access to resources. In Vietnam, women have achieved high levels of education and labour force participation relative to comparable countries, and yet Vietnam is one of the poorer nations. Likewise, high ratio of living women to men and high female labour force participation in Cambodia is hardly the result of any resources provided to women and is certainly not the result of any changes in their position in society.

In Pakistan and Bangladesh estimated education was indicated to be only around 2.4 years, economic participation of only twenty three per cent in 2007, Pakistan has some of the lowest estimates of most empowerment variables [(Toor (2007) and Fatima & Ambreen (2009)]. Mumtaz (2007) reported the pronounced gender bias in Pakistan, including exclusion of women from property rights, restrictions on physical mobility, domestic violence, low political rights, low educational attainment, and low rates of economic participation. The author revealed "religion" as the main medium through which gender bias operates in Pakistan. Due to attempts taken by non-governmental organizations, a sharp decline in fertility in Bangladesh was realized, but was not escorted by major increases in women' education or economic participation.

Women of the Philippines benefit from higher self-sufficiency than rest of the developing world, particularly in household decision making (Chaudhuri, 2010). Women of Philippines enjoyed equal rights in the pre Spanish colonization period (pre-1521.) While the Spanish clergy preached male dominance, nevertheless, even during this period, the treatment of Filipino women was much more egalitarian than in other countries. Filipino women have owned land and inherited property for centuries. Husbands often hand over their income to their wives and financial and other decisions are jointly made by husband and wife. Feminist movement of the Philippines has advocated equal rights for women for several decades (Sobritchea, 2004).

Despite of higher levels of development that has been taken place in Indonesia, Indonesian women enjoy lower empowerment. Indonesian society conventionally favours sons over daughters, although this gender bias is not as striking as in South Asia. Kinship norms in Indonesia are different. It can be either patrilineal (i.e. less empowerment for women) or matrilineal (more empowerment for women). The authors argue that due to ethnic diversity of Indonesia, women's ethnic background has an impact on empowerment. Indonesian families by tradition have strong male bias and prefer having sons over daughters as their first child, evidenced by the traditional norms and rules of Indonesia that dictates gender behaviour and roles (Rammohan & Johar, 2009).

After having reviewed the glimpse of studies regarding the status of women in Asia it seems that future efforts in improving women's empowerment should focus on improving the organizations and resources scope. Deep seated traditions, social, and religious norms hamper women's agency. Enhancement of resources such as improved admittance to quality education and health care services, economic participation, favourable labour laws, inheritance and property rights are essential for continued advancement in women's status empowerment.

Gender Gaps in Various Organizations

Women are unequal to men in many ways in India. Their level of education is less as compared to men. The literacy of men was 79.3 per cent and female was 57.9 per cent in 2011. The mortality rates of mothers at the birth of child are extremely high, at over 200 per lakh. Same trends are found in the cases of anaemia and malnutrition rates. Merely 10.9 per cent was the percentage of women found in the Parliament in 2012 and 29 per cent in labour force. In India, approximately 2.40 lakh incidents of crimes alongside women were stated in India. Offenses are related to rapes, kidnapping, acid-throwing, abductions, torture, trafficking, child marriages, prostitution, dowry deaths etc. Women' participation in employment is much lower as compared to their proportion in the population. They cannot raise their voice, if they do so they have to undergo abuse (e.g., physical, mental), face elimination and have deprived from admittance to redressal. They are inadequately authorized (Dhar, 2014). Thus gender inequality is abundant in many grounds such as population, education, health, employment, social stereotyping, domestic violence and their safety and security.

A non-governmental organization which stands to demand justice for people, whose rights have been violated (Amnesty International) has pointed out that the women residing in Pakistan are discriminated in various ways as they are not able to occupy their rightful place in various government offices and also are devoid of being a member of various professions and are hence denied equality with men in the society as a whole. Although unlike Afghanistan, the girls in Pakistan are allowed to attend schools and colleges, a lot needs to be done to render them with the status of equality with men. It has also been pointed out that in some parts of Africa certain young tribal girls still have to undergo through the process of circumcision just to conform to a strange social custom of superstition (Kakkar, 1998).

Human Development Reports revealed that over the past two decades, the female labour force participation rates have dropped down globally from 57 to 55 per cent. Women and men are not seen to be working together in the same sectors, occupations and firms because the women are seen working more in low paid activities where they have lesser access to productive inputs. The reason behind all this is the mental set of men "Men have their occupations, women have theirs. It is like that since childhood, it is our heritage". The report also states that it totally depends on one's ability to sort whether to go for a paid job and also what type of job to pursue which is intrinsically linked to human development (Klugman, 2015).

The comparative focus of women in respect to men still finds a great deal of difference and there still exists underrepresentation of women in fields like healthcare, nurturance and professional occupations. There has been remarkable improvement in US as women comprised more than 90 per cent of pre-school children and kindergarten teachers, dental hygienists and hair dressers in 1972 but now they are more than 90 per cent. In the field of nursing, share of men has quadrupled since 1972 but nine in ten nurses are still found to be women (Klugman, 2015). Women are not able to escape from legal discrimination in various fields as there still exists barriers which restrict them to access property, get job, build credit or even in some cases obtain an ID card. In 2013, out of 153 economies, 128 were found to be having at least one legal difference in the way women and men are treated, 56 countries have more than five such legal barriers and 28, more than ten. Also to add to the misfortune, in 15 countries, husbands can yet avert their wives from working (Human Development Reports, 2015).

Women are treated as mere instruments of the ends of others. They have a certain role set to perform like caregivers, reproducers, sexual outlets and agents of a family's prosperity. In their natal family, the girl children are treated as a burden because one fine day they have to leave the house and they cannot support their parents in their days of need. Also the family will have to bear up with the big fat expenses of her wedding and dowry. This is the sole reason why the birth of a girl child is often an occasion of sorrow rather than joy (Nussbaum, 2000). Thus, they are neither given proper education nor are they taken care of, the way a boy child is treated and brought-up. Despite of the fact about India, which claims to be a constitutional democracy but in reality women are still treated as second class citizens.

According to Barbara Matera (2015) in developing nations, the gender gap in education is very problematic as over two-thirds of the illiterate people in the world are women. Although in many developed nations a large number of educated women across all levels have risen but still in underdeveloped nations there still persists lack of women in the field of education which results into being less productive in comparison to what they could be. In many nations, the government is fully aware of the fact that education is power and to devoid women of the power they suppress the right of women to be educated. This clearly indicates that education can help women to feel more empowered, to stand up for themselves and also elevate their confidence in their own bodies, health and minds. It helps women to realize their potential to the fullest and cope up with the various adversities that they face in day to day life.

It has been estimated that on an average, a girl who completes seven years of education will have 2.2 fewer children and a woman who completes even just basic education can reduce her chances of contracting HIV threefold. Also children who are born to mothers who have at least completed secondary education are twice as likely to live past the age of five. Barbara Matera (2015) opines that "education for women is on the go, but a lot of work remains. By giving women proper education on par with that of their male counterparts, we can empower them to change the world for the better by living longer, healthier lives and contributing to the great social human capital. We celebrate the great progress that has been made over the last century, and look forward to working towards equality across the board. By not educating women and suppressing their skills and talents, it is not just them we are robbing of what they could be—it is the world."

Gender violence and Psycho-physical Health of Women

The rate of violence against women has also risen considerably during the last decades. At least one in three women experience some form of gender-based abuse during her lifetime worldwide (Heise, Ellsberg, & Gottemoeller, 1999). Report reveals that violence against girls and women can begin before birth and continue throughout their lives into old age (Watts & Simmerman, 2002). Generally, women are hesitant to discuss abuse and may accept it as part of their role. The most common forms of violence against women are physical, sexual, and emotional abuse by a woman's husband or intimate partner. Surveys indicate that 10 to 58 per cent of women have experienced physical abuse by an intimate partner in their lifetimes. Multi-Country Study on Women's Health and Domestic Violence indicate that in some parts of the world as many as one half of women have experienced domestic violence (Garcia-Moreno & Heise, 2002).

Evidence indicates that male perpetrated violence not only has physical after-effects but also has enduring psychological aftermath. The symptoms vary considerably among individuals, across social contexts, and across different types of violent encounters. Nonetheless, a remarkably consistent picture of the psychological sequelae of violence, particularly sexual and physical assault emerges from the empirical and clinical literature (Goodman, Koss, & Russo, 1992). Domestic violence has a significant impact on the health and well-being of women both in the direct and longer period. This continues even after the relationship has ended. The psychological consequences of violence can be as severe as the physical effects. Disclosure to violence leads to poorer physical health overall compared with women who have not experienced violence, and it increases the risk of women developing a range of health problems. Some immediate health impacts of violence against women may include: physical injuries—such as cuts, scrapes and bruises, fractures, dislocated bones, hearing loss, vision loss, miscarriage or early delivery, sexually transmitted diseases, knife wounds and gunshot wounds (Goodman *et al.*, 1992).

Numerous long term negative health consequences may include gastro-intestinal disorders associated with stress, headaches, back pain, fainting, seizures, gynaecological problems, anxiety, depression, eating disorders, post-traumatic stress disorder, sleep disturbances, alcohol and substance misuse, smoking throughout pregnancy, homelessness and suicide (World Health Organisation, 2000). One Australian study has also founded that intimate partner violence was the leading contributor to death, disability and illness in Victorian women aged 15 to 44 (VicHealth, 2004).

A great deal of linkage has been found between the violence practiced against women and their insurmountable negative effects like chronic pain, acute injuries, gastrointestinal illness and gynaecological problems. Also the mental health of women does not remain devoid of its harmful consequences as the risk of experiencing depression increases two to three folds as a result of intimate partner violence. It also reduces their economic opportunities as the women who are exposed to violence have lower productivity, higher lower earnings than women who are not exposed to violence or are not beaten. Thus, there is an urgent need to address and modify social norms and work upon the widespread breaches of human rights (Klugman, 2015).

If we switch on to area of health and nutrition, women in developing nations are discriminated here also. There is a standard belief that where equal nutrition and health care are present a sex-ratio of something like 102.2 women to 100 men is expected. But in India this ratio is 92.7 women to 100 men which is the lowest sex-ratio since the census began (Nussbaum, 2000).

Another area of life which is a major contributor of injustice to women is the area of care and women have to perform this crucial task without expecting any rewards or recognition in return. They spend long hours to cater to the physical need of others which makes it more difficult for them to participate in other important areas of life like self-expression, play, citizenship and employment. As they are the sole caregiver in most of the cases like caring and nurturing the young child, the elderly and those with physical and mental handicaps, they do all this at the expense of their independence which characterizes a so-called 'normal' human life. In some cultures, a male baby is preferable to a female baby. This applies specially in the case of India and China. In India, it is practiced because of the fear of dowry that the girl childs parents would have to give and in China because of the one child policy. Not to forget that numerous cases of infanticide and sex selective abortions have taken a toll due to these reasons only (Omari & Creighton, 2000).

In the fields of income, job and profession, women still have a long way to go to cope up with the gender gap as it contributes to a great deal to the various impediments to development. The only solution to this lies in the core of development policics where the issue of social justice to women should be the issue that needs to be given prime importance. Thus ensuring social justice to women will strengthen a nation's ability to reduce poverty, to prosper and provide its people with a satisfactory life.

The general issues of poverty, education and development of women cannot be well addressed until and unless an international and economic thought is build up to cater the grievances of women that they face as a result of gender differences in almost every nation of the world. Until nations are able to resolve this issue of social injustice to women in various spheres of life, one cannot expect that the circle of vicious cycle would come to a haul because poverty leads to discrimination and discrimination in turn again leads to poverty.

The international development of a nation should be assessed for its capacity to meet the demand of the suppressed section of the society, i.e., the women of the country. We must not forget that women just like men have the inborn right and freedom to become capable to certain human functions, given proper guidance, social support, sufficient nutrition and education. We will know that we have succeeded in our efforts when:

All women have equal rights, equal work opportunities and equal access to government offices, resources, justice and power.

All women have equal access to decent work and are given a fair share of reward for their work.

All women have equal participation in the decision-making process at all the levels and can raise their voice in times of need and as per situations.

All women and girls live their life free from all forms of discrimination and violence.

Unpaid care work no longer hinders the development and progress of women in various spheres and is also equally divided between men and women.

Women can make decisions about their health, their body and sexuality without any coercion.

Discriminatory norms, beliefs and attitudes no longer limit the opportunities of women.

Conclusion

To conclude this brief overview of justice towards women's empowerment and some reality based issues, mention must be made on the prompt need that the participation of women in the field of power and decision-making should be increased and greater flexibility and choice is rendered in the field of workplace else they would be pushed to lower status and menial jobs than their male counterparts and hence would be more susceptible to poverty. The various barriers need to be addressed in a strategic manner through the joint action and collaboration of various departments for women's upliftment and empowerment. For this, the economic policies should focus on the objective-subjective divide and should adopt a pragmatic approach during the policy formulation so that the policies are guided by objective conditions of deprivation and also by the subjective conditions, i.e., people's sentiments. The issue of female labour deprivation should be focused upon and also the gender norms which sometimes affect the perception of deprivation can be worked upon. Not to forget that deprivation if handled properly can pave the way for prosperity and development, especially if the role of women is utilized to her fullest and actual potential.

It is truly said that if you teach a man you only teach him and if you teach a woman, you educate an entire household. The role of women should be expected and welcomed beyond, than only the hands at work and there should be due acknowledgement to the role of women in her different expressions of wife, mother, home-maker, career women and entrepreneur. Thus, the nation should be willing and able to implement various policies for women empowerment.

Women are still made victim of the biased and adverse norms which denies them the equal access to credit, bank accounts or land especially as farmers and entrepreneurs. This is due to the existence of certain man made gender roles that dictate a women's life throughout her life span. As a result despite of the fact that gender gaps are overcome in one area such as school enrolment but due the gender biased regulations they are still devoid of economic opportunities.

In a nutshell it can be said that despite of various schemes and acts of government to empower the women, they are still discriminated and marginalized at various levels of the society. There is a need to formulate goals in order to reduce the feminized poverty, prevention and elimination of violence against women and promote education. Despite of the fact that India has made progress in various economic and social fields, there is still an urgent need to bring about a sea change in the mindset of the people because the implementation of various policies, schemes and goals cannot be achieved until and unless the minds of the people is ready to accept the change and be the change. As Ban Ki Moon, Former Secretary-General, UNO, has rightly opined, "Break the silence, where you witness violence against women and girls. Do not sit back. Act". Michelle Obama stated "as women, we must stand up for ourselves. As women, we must stand up for each other. As women, we must stand up for justice for all".

References

Awasthi, P. and Mishra, R.C. (2008). Expectation and availability of Social Support in Cancer and Diabetic Women Patients. *Indian Journal of Clinical Psychology*, vol. 35, *2*, 127-137.

Awasthi, P. and Mishra, R.C. (2015). Social support and illness beliefs in women cancer patients. *United Journal of Awadh Scholars, 1 and 2*, 43-52.

Barbara Matera (2015). https://www.theparliamentmagazine.eu/articles/opinion/lack-education-making-women-powerless

Basu, A. (2014). Retrieved from Role and status of Women in ancient India. http://www.importantindia.com/ 11058/role-and-status-of-women-in-ancient-india/

Bhalla, A.S. (1995). *Uneven development in the Third World: A Study of China and India* (2nd ed.). New York: St Martin's Press.

Chatterjee, M. (1990). *Indian Women: Their Health and Economic Productivity.* World Bank Discussion Papers 109. Washington DC.

Chaudhuri, S. (2010). Women's Empowerment in South Asia and South-east Asia: A Comparative Analysis. *Munich Personal RePEc Archive*, pp. 1-46.

Desai, S. (1994). *Gender Inequalities and Demographic Behaviour: India.* New York: Population Council.

Dhar, T.N. (2014). Women's Empowerment and Social Justice in India. *Indian Journal of Public Administration, 3,* 637-648.

Fatima, Ambreen and Humera Sultana (2009). Tracing out the U-Shape Relationship between Female Labour Force Participation Rate and Economic Development for Pakistan. *International Journal of Social Economics*, 36(1/2), pp. 182-98.

Goodman, L.A., Koss, M.P., and Ruso, N.F. (1993). Violence against women: Mental health effects. Part II. Conceptualizations of post-traumatic stress. *Applied and Preventive Psychology, 2*(3), 123-130.

Government of India (1995). *Country Report, Fourth UN World Conference on Women at Beijing.* New Delhi: Department of Women and Child Development, Ministry of Human Resource Development.

Heise, L., Ellsberg, M. and. Gottemoeller, M. (1999). *Ending violence against*

Women. Population Reports, Series L, No. 11. Baltimore: Johns Hopkins University School of Public Health, Population Information Programme.

International Institute for Population Sciences (1995). *National Family Health Survey, 1992-93*. Bombay: India.

Isobelle, Dalena, Anthony and Michael (2013). *The role of Women during Ancient Japan*. Retrieved from https://prezi.com/qjyjy25qm6no/the-role-of-women-during-ancient-japan/

Jejeebhoy, S.J., and Rama R.S. (1998). Unsafe Motherhood: A Review of Reproductive Health. In M. Das Gupta, L.C. Chen, and T.N. Krishnan (Eds.), *Women's Health in India: Risk and Vulnerability*, pp. 122-52. New Delhi: Oxford India Paperbacks.

Kakkar, B.N. (1998). *The Sterling Book of Essays* (1st revised edition). New Delhi: Sterling Publishers Private Limited.

Klugman, J. (2015). *Women: Still Lacking Justice at Work, Still Lacking Safety At Home*. United Nations Development Programme: Human Development Report. 16 March 2015, http://hdr.undp.org/

Lunes. (2010). *Chinese women's life*. Retrieved from http://chinesewomenslife.blogspot.in/2010/10/traditional-role-of-women-in-china.html

Mishra, R.C. (2009). Health cognition and practices. In A. Shukla (Ed.), *Culture, Cognition and Behaviour*, pp. 264-276. New Delhi: Concept Publishing Co. (P) Ltd.

Mishra, R.C., and Dasen, P. (2004). The influence of schooling on cognitive development: A review of research in India. In B.N Setiadi, A. Supratiknya, W.J. Lonner, Y.H. Poortinga (Eds.), *Ongoing Themes in Psychology and Culture*, pp. 207-222. Yogjakarta, Indonesia: Kanisius.

Mason, K.O. (1995). Is the situation of women in India improving or deteriorating? *Asia Pacific Population Research Reports*, No. 6.

Mumtaz, Khawar (2007). Gender and Poverty in Pakistan. *Development, 50* (2), 149-53.

Nussbaum, C. Martha (2000). *Women and Human Development: The Capabilities Approach*. Cambridge: Cambridge University Press.

Nassbaum, M. (2000). Women's Capabilities and Social Justice. *Journal of Human Development, 2,* 219-242.

Omari Cuthbert K. and Creighton Colin (2000). *Gender Family and Work in Tanzania*. Brookfield, Vermont, and Aldershot, England: Ashgate Publishing.

Registrar General (1996). *Fertility and Mortality Indicators 1993*. New Delhi: GoI.

Riebschleger Joanne and Fila Brittany (2009). Voices of women in rural India: Empowerment, entrepreneurship, and education. *Journal of Contemporary Rural Social Work, 1*, 1-16.

Samarel, N., Tulman, L, and Fawcett, J. (2002). Effects of two types of social support and education on adaptation to early-stage breast cancer. *Research in Nursing and Health, 6,* 459-470.

Sobritchea, Carolyn I. (2004). Women's Movement in the Philippines and the Politics of Critical Collaboration with the State. In *Civil Society in South-east*

Asia, (Ed. L.H. Guan, pp. 101-21). Singapore: Institute of Southeast Asian Studies.

Srinivasan, S. (1997). Breaking rural bonds through migration: The failure of development for women in India. *Journal of Comparative Family Studies, 28,* 89-102.

Toor, Imran A. (2007). Returns to Education the Case of Fertility. *Pakistan Economic and Social Review*, *45*(1), 107-23.

Watts, C. and Zimmerman, C. (2002). Violence against women: global scope and magnitude. *The Lancet, 359* (9313), 1232-1237.

World Bank (1996). *Improving Women's Health in India: Development in Practice*. Washington, DC: World Bank.

World Health Organization (2000), Women and Mental Health: An Evidence Based Review, World Health Organisation, Geneva. Retrieved from http://www.who.int/mental_health/publications/women_mh_evidence_review/en/

Vic Health (2004), *Violence Against Women in Australia as a Determinant of Mental Health and Well-being*. Retrieved from http://www.vichealth.vic.gov.au/Publications/Freedom-from-violence/Violence-against-women-in-Australia-research-summary.aspx

Index